AMERICAN EXPLORATION AND TRAVEL

DIARY & LETTERS OF

Josiah Gregg

Excursions in Mexico & California
1847–1850

Edited by
MAURICE GARLAND FULTON

With an Introduction by
PAUL HORGAN

Norman
UNIVERSITY OF OKLAHOMA PRESS
1944

Copyright 1944 by the University of Oklahoma
Press, Publishing Division of the University. All
rights reserved. Set up and printed at Norman,
Oklahoma, U.S.A., by the University of Oklahoma
Press. First edition.

To the Memory of John Gregg
1800–1887

"Place my effects and memoranda . . . at the
disposition of my brother John."
        JOSIAH GREGG, *in his letter,*
                November 1, 1849.

This volume witnesser
of a trust well held.

Editor's Introduction

THIS volume completes the publication of the diary and letters of Josiah Gregg. It comprises a narrative of his movements and activities for the three years, 1847 to 1850, spent mainly in Mexico. In order to have an adequate perspective, we must return to the previous volume at least as far as the spring of 1846, when, after an absence of six years spent in the States, Gregg yielded to the lure of his old stamping ground, Santa Fé, and made himself and baggage a part of the caravan of Samuel Owens. Hardly had Gregg started on this journey, undertaken, as he explains, for the joint purpose "of recruiting my health and to endeavor to promote my pecuniary interest," than he changed his plans at the solicitation of Arkansas friends and joined "the division of our army destined for Chihuahua, or some other point in Northern Mexico." Getting to the rendezvous at San Antonio involved a horseback tour of some 1,200 miles, which Gregg gladly undertook upon the possibility of serving his country. Though he soon discovered that neglect and disesteem were to be his lot, at least so far as General Wool was concerned, he continued his quasi connection and accompanied the column into Mexico until it reached the vicinity of Monterrey and Saltillo. There he found some surcease of disappointment under the appreciation gained from General Taylor and the resumption of his old occupation, "looking at the country."

With this linkage, we pass into the contents of the present volume. Gregg found himself in February, 1847, an eyewitness to the battle of Buena Vista. The experience moved him to try to embody the occurrence in a brief but full-length account. While he was engaged upon this self-imposed assignment, there arrived at General Wool's headquarters the courier party from Colonel Doniphan, whose regiment of Missourians was marooned at Chihuahua City after capturing it and finding General Wool's division belated in joining them. The situation was precarious; therefore, Colonel Doniphan had sent messengers to inquire for instructions. Gregg eagerly embraced the chance to cross over to Chihuahua with the returning party, and so to reach what was really a second base for him in his days of Santa Fé tradership. Setting thither had been one of the inducements to joining the army, for he knew that General Wool was supposed to proceed if possible to Chihuahua, and much of Gregg's restlessness had arisen from the fact that the expedition had failed in this purpose. It would have been only human if Gregg had not secretly entertained the feeling that had the commander consulted with him he might have received advice that would have prevented some noticeable ineptitudes and mistakes. Thus, with elation Gregg obtained permission to accompany the returning party. He had but a few days in Chihuahua, for Colonel Doniphan was ready and waiting for the order to march towards Saltillo; but there was time enough to foregather with old acquaintances among the First Missouri and the traders' caravan and to come into possession of the books, scientific instruments, and other equipment he had abruptly deserted when he left Owens' caravan for San Antonio. All this baggage had remained with the caravan, reaching Santa Fé and then being carried along to Chihuahua.

While in company with Doniphan's regiment, Gregg learned more than he had before concerning the indecorum and misbehavior of the American volunteers towards the Mexicans, and found himself shocked and outraged. Towards the end of the trip, he was flattered by an offer from no less a person than the important "proprietor," Samuel Magoffin himself, of a trading partnership, and Gregg at once hurried out of Mexico with the Missourians in order to buy goods. Then, while in New York, he heard from Magoffin that he was withdrawing from the venture; Gregg swallowed his disappointment and returned to Mexico, not in a commercial capacity, but in a professional one. When he stopped among his friends and admirers in Louisville and St. Louis, he must have received the incentive to begin the practice of medicine in Mexico, with scientific pursuits as avocations. His year of practice in Saltillo proved lucrative beyond expectations. By the autumn of 1849 Gregg found that his purse had regained its heaviness, and with that provocation, the desire for travel re-asserted itself. He took advantage of an opportunity to go with a party of prominent residents of Saltillo to the capital city, Mexico, which he had never before visited. He was again in his element, going about and seeing the country and making notes thereon. In a letter to his St. Louis friend, Dr. Engelmann, he confided that such had been his hope "ever since entering Mexico the last time," although when he left Saltillo his future route was undefined. During his stay in Mexico City he formulated his itinerary, describing it to Dr. Engelmann as "a tour upon the Pacific Coast as far north as California and perhaps Oregon." As partial justification, he added, "Now that so much is said about the mines of California, I have added inducement to go that way." If this passage smacks of the *comerciante*, perhaps the truer motive may be discovered in the exclamatory remark in the same communication to the effect, "an untrodden field for a scientist."

By early summer of 1849, Gregg was under way for the coast town of Mazatlan at the head of what was virtually a private sci-entific and exploring party, with himself in the role of "angel." His plan was to reach the Pacific coast at Mazatlan; then to pro-ceed overland to Guaymos, where he proposed to cross the Gulf of California and continue along the coast via San Diego, Mon-terey, and San Francisco. The program, however, was too am-bitious for the hot summer and his own increasing debility, and became modified into Gregg's going on alone to San Francisco as a passenger on the *Olga*.

During the stay in Mexico City, Gregg had found time for correspondence, and from one of these letters we learn definitely of his intention to make a reappearance in "the capacity of a book-maker," as he expressed himself in the preface of *Commerce of the Prairies*. While he was shaping the accumulations of his three-year stay in Mexico into a book, he wrote to Dr. Engelmann that the book was nearing completion and asked the more famous botanist for assistance in the shape of an essay relating to the collections which Gregg had been sending him from time to time. Appended to this letter of April 14, 1849, is the disclosure, "I hope to be able to publish within a twelvemonth as I shall probably make my way home pretty direct from California." How futile that hope was we know too well now. The journal ceases with Gregg's arrival at San Francisco. All that happened in the few months, all that ought indeed to compose the last chapter of his career, comes not through his personal narrative, but from putting together piecings of biographical details from first one and then another source. Fortunate was it that before starting for "the mines of California," he left his materials for this second book in safe hands, and wrote back to his friend and former business associate Jesse Sutton, dating from "Trinity River below 3rd Canon Nov. 1st 1849," directions regarding placing "effects and memoranda at the disposition of my brother John." Jesse Sutton faithfully executed the commission; John Gregg, the devoted brother, hoped for long years to memorialize his brother by publication of the material. When, however, he found it impossible to accomplish that purpose, he put the material into the hands of Samuel Hardwicke, as the nephew whose means and abilities made him a logical selection. He, too, was unable to execute the commission, and in due course the materials passed into the custodianship of his son, Claude Hardwicke. This grandnephew in turn was handicapped by invalidism, and his widow, Mrs. Antoinette Hardwicke, has finally brought about the editing and publishing of Gregg's "memoranda," making deputies out of the undersigned and his associate, Paul Horgan, and the University of Oklahoma Press.

What is offered nearly a century later than Gregg intended to have it appear is of course not the transmuting of journals and notebooks into a finished book. We do none the less gather from it the outlines of a figure, or rather a personage, whose qualities of courage and serviceability were so conjoined as to make him a remarkable instance of human gallantry. Gregg would have gained certainly a niche among the "people who went west in 1846," to use a phrase from Bernard De Voto's recent *The Year of Decision: 1846*. Gregg is highly informing in his particular way about the Mexican War, although it would never per se have been the central feature of the proposed book. He was a shrewd student of human motives and temperament, as well as a note-maker of scientific fact. Gregg's unassuming handiwork in *Commerce of the Prairies* bore the imprint of his habitual carefulness and authoritativeness, and his second book would have presented the same credentials to a public eager for anything concerning the vast territory then on our hands and requiring momentous decisions on our part. The last half of the 1840's witnessed the nation's becoming genuinely expansive. The air was quick with promise and expectation, and Gregg might have conferred a benefit by a book about a region which he knew thoroughly and sympathetically. He would have become to us an intelligent eye-witness of matters connected with what we realize as a critical period in American development. Nearly a century later, the land is again agog on a larger scale with enlargement of the national horizon and kindred matters. It may be that Gregg's contribution will fall not on stony ground, but on fertile soil.

The editing of the material in this volume has tried to accent, even more than was the case with the earlier installment, the biographical, rather than the historical, value. Gregg's writing has so much of the quality of personal experience that it is impossible to treat it monographically. With his change of locale to Mexico, the shift to the personal and autobiographic is decidedly marked; hence the editing has been done with the notion that the volume ought to find shelf-room in that division of books known as "Travel and Topography" rather than the strictly historical. In order to afford insight into Gregg's methods and type of mind, it has seemed best to present the material without abridgement. Should portions be boresome (and no one would claim that the "courses" and other data were intended for reading matter), all a reader has to do is to lift his eyes over the obstruction and let them rest on something more palatable in the way of experience, observation, or comment. Gregg's addiction to "marginal and interlineal annotations" has renewed the problems that arose in connection with the first volume, but without resorting to facsimile reproduction, we have tried to reveal the besetting carefulness and desire for accuracy that was in Gregg. Occasionally there has been a small job of correcting or adjusting, where Gregg had by inadvertence made a slip or error. Always, however, the purpose has been to preserve the color and flavor of the original. Much the same principles have governed the annotating. Footnotes have not been made for themselves, but for clarifying and enhancing the presentation of Gregg's experience and personality. A catalogue of acknowledgments and a statement about bibliography have been placed at the end.

M. G. F.

Roswell, New Mexico
March 23, 1944

Table of Contents

****

List of Illustrations

Josiah Gregg Himself

✳✳✳✳✳✳✳✳✳✳✳✳✳✳✳✳✳✳✳✳✳✳✳✳✳✳✳✳✳

Josiah Gregg Himself

An Introduction[1]

Prelude to Battle

JOSIAH GREGG—Santa Fé trader, author of *Commerce of the Prairies,* and medical doctor—interrupted his plans for a trip across the western plains in 1846 to answer the appeals of friends and government officials to serve in the Mexican War. But he was wasted upon a job neither wholly civilian nor wholly military, and he fretted for months about both his situation and the slow progress of the war.

"This is a singular warfare we are waging, is it not?" he asked in one of his letters to the editors of the *Louisville Journal* in 1846. From his point of view the whole thing was a cumulus of irritations, inefficiencies, and humiliations.

Gregg was rarely the man to temper his judgments, either of himself or of others. He had survived the hardships of the plains, during that decade when the Santa Fé trade was the prosaic instrument of our national design. He was forty years old, and felt, and looked, much older, in the robust and thoughtless company of the United States Army in Mexico, whom he was accompanying as what: guide? translator? interpreter? The point of his status was never cleared up, although he was supposed to receive "the pay and perquisites of a Major." If he felt like an outsider, he certainly talked and wrote like one. His ex-

---

[1] Continued from the essay in *Diary & Letters of Josiah Gregg:* Southwestern Enterprises, 1840–1847 (Norman, University of Oklahoma Press, 1941).

3

periences with the army invading Mexico left a bitter taste. He
was genuinely eager to be of service. He was ready, like a patri-
otic American, to march with a well-disciplined force under brilliant officers to a rapid and humane and, above all, efficient conclusion of the Mexican adventure. What he met with was altogether different. Everywhere he turned, someone or something
served to bring out his most acidulous opinions. The war was to
be fought, here, on this map? Then why was it not done exactly
so, on the ground itself—? that baked and reptilian desert, where
few men have subdued the natural world according to their orderly designs. General Wool, first of all, the commanding officer, was unpopular with "at least ninety-nine hundredths of the
troops he commanded. Ergo: could all have been right" with
the state of affairs? Wool may have been "an amiable gentlemanly man; yet I fear rather crabid and petulant, and perhaps
. . . old-womanish—more efficient in minutiae and details than
in grand and extensive operations."

That was what was wanted: "grand and extensive operations,"
and the war would simply not live up to them. Endless sky, the
grit of hot sand, an amateur army, the growing pains of the
Nation, the vanity of men contending with sense. General Wool
moved about the town with staff and guard of twenty mounted
dragoons with drawn sabres, a spectacle which Gregg did not
like. The other officers, too, were "petulant," "out of their element." They quarreled, they resigned, they wrote lengthy "reports" and justified themselves, they bore themselves haughtily,
even Captain Albert Pike, though he deserved "to stand decidedly 'number one' in point of talent and acquirements;" even
Pike, on the way to Chihuahua, later, was very remiss of his
men's comfort, and was sternly caught at it and duly noted in
the evening's session with the bound notebooks.

A certain Colonel Hamtramck was even worse than General
Wool at pomposity, a quality which was just a disguise: "The
fact is, any man with a fair degree of cunning and management,

who is abjectly subservient, and will use a sufficiency of flattery, will hardly fail to gain a great influence over the general's weak mind." As for General Shields and General Butler, the one "is a military monomaniac—crazy—his head addled by his elevation . . . one of the veriest *military* simpletons" and the other, "as a military man, though brave as need be, no doubt, he is rather imbecile." Josiah had occasion to smart under "the rudeness of Gen. Lane and more especially his aide . . . who, to make up for his ignorance and want of talent, put on an air of insupportable presumption—at the same time inclining to treat me as his 'orderly' while I was gratuitously interpreting for them. The low grade in which interpreters are held, and the low class of people, in fact, generally engaged as such, is one reason why I have refused to accept this office, even though at a high salary."

He said that he, himself, would never solicit an army commission from the President, it being beneath his dignity. However, he added, with the offhand sort of hint so binding to relative or friend, that his brother John might take steps, if he liked. As to rank, it was now too late to satisfy him with the rank, as well as the perquisites, of a major; "but *Lieut.-Colonel* I should be very well pleased with." He underlined it to make it perfectly sure, and saw himself suitably uniformed; but nothing came of this delicate intrigue, even after he left General Wool to join the staff of General W. P. Butler; and when he left Butler, eventually, Josiah refused the pay accrued and due to him, for the very Greggian reason that although yes, he had earned it, he disdained to accept it because he had never been given a definite appointment. A propriety so fierce, so baffling to the very spirits it intended to educate with an austere rebuke, must have appeared merely cranky to them.

He was tempted many times to give up his association with the army, and set out as a free-lance reporter of the fantastic campaign. During the previous spring he had started for Santa

Fé across the plains from Missouri, and had turned back to join the southern-bound army. His effects—books, instruments, records—had gone on to Santa Fé with Colonel Owens and from there had been taken down to Chihuahua, where they now awaited him. He was spoiling to get to Chihuahua; to be free of this military society in which he was so uneasy; to recover his possessions; to know again the consuming duty of observing the country, accountable to no one. But there were delays. One of them, as it turned out, was worth the bother.

✿ BATTLE PIECE

At last, for a time, all was forgiven to that infinitely puzzling army. For when the long time of preparation was somehow done with, and the foes met by the hacienda of Buena Vista at the foot of that mountain which looked so beautiful at times, Gregg was full of fellow-feeling and ardent sympathy with the very soldiers whom he had judged with a sniff, and who had hazed him back, in their cruder way. The battle, he wrote to John, was "that glorious but awful affair." It had been coming for days—a Mexican spy in the town kept reporting to Gregg, and there is an innocent sense that the town evidently knew of the battle plans from day to day.

When the day came and the troops were moving to their stations, the wagons rattled so that the Mexicans thought the noise came from artillery fire.

Josiah was there, riding a horse all in and around the battle, maintaining himself "on high and commanding points . . . so as to have a view of all the operations." He was in great danger from musket fire throughout, with his calm, orderly, recording eye in the midst of the confused action. As usual, his factual net took in details which were the prosaic seedlings of poetry, of feeling. He heard the United States soldiers greet a Mexican cannonade with "hearty yells," and the words suddenly resume their original meanings, and in the smoky blue battle air we see

6

again the toiling little figures by the batteries, and we feel the thudding valor of their hearts, which saved a day and swayed a century.

Josiah wrote several accounts of the battle, the most vivid and detailed of which appears in the notebook of this volume. He described it to John by letter, and he wrote more formal accounts which appeared in the newspapers back home. Even now, his description reads with excitement and awe, ennobled with the emotion which a less embarrassed and cynical age than that between our two World Wars felt free to associate with patriotism. In the hand-to-hand warfare of Gregg's time, pity was still a right of the victor; and he described not only the suffering of the defeated Mexican troops, but also the mercies of the United States soldiers to the wounded enemy after the battle was over. He saw his compatriots tending the wounds of the Mexicans on the battlefield, and giving them water, for which they cried. He found and helped to bury his old friend Colonel Yell, of Arkansas, who had persuaded him in the first place to turn back from an expedition out on the plains and join the Arkansas Volunteer Regiment. From the smoke and loss of the battle, a new continent was struggling to arise. Gregg had intimations of it. The active war, in effect, was over, though much yet remained to be concluded with the withdrawal of troops. Patience? Patience was never one of Josiah's virtues. Possibly the analytical intelligence cannot wait, once it has the answer in mind. But when the answer took form and was paid for dearly in flesh and blood, then the long argumentative months, the uncouth maneuvers, the rude manners of campaigning soldiers were forgiven; and at the Battle of Buena Vista, Gregg admired as heroes the officers and men whose other values and purposes had not reached any sympathy in him.

❁ THE MISSOURI INDEPENDENT

After the battle came an opportunity to make the trip to Chihuahua. A Santa Fé trader named Collins, now interpreter to

Doniphan's regiment, had come from that city bringing dispatches from Colonel Doniphan, who had marched down from Santa Fé and was now in control of north central Mexico. Collins was about to return to Doniphan after Buena Vista, and Gregg was eager to attach himself to the party and reclaim his effects in Chihuahua. It would be a suitable arrangement. Collins' party was to be escorted by troops under the command of Captain Pike, "decidedly 'number one.'" There was only one obstacle, and it had to do with vanity: to go with Collins and Pike, Gregg had first to obtain official permission through petition to General Wool. To ask a favor of this miniature Napoleon! This indeed posed a struggle between pride and utility. Pride lost, but haughtily.

He made his request in a personal interview. The General had been reading the papers, all along. He was smarting under the published criticisms of his irritable guest, and, worse, he even had heard that Gregg "was going to write a book." It was a chilling rumor. The General received Gregg with a sense of injury. Doctor Gregg bore himself with the mein of justice incorruptible. They conversed. Immediately afterward, Gregg wrote down a report of the meeting, which may be read on page 79 of this volume. It is plain that, for whatever reason—an eye on posterity in the presence of book-writers, or whatever—the General tried to make friends. But Gregg was suspicious, declaring that the General was only angling for admiration and approval. In Gregg's report, Wool does most of the talking, borne on by a torrent of words—"that state of irritability in which a man has to talk, talk, talk, merely to convince himself that he is in the right," as Tolstoy said of the original Napoleon. In any case, the interview ended with permission for Gregg to set out with Collins and Pike.

Free of his doubtful army connections at last, he started off on the five-hundred-mile trip through enemy territory to recover his belongings at Chihuahua. He was fully aware of the dangers involved, but he was as lofty toward peril as he was toward ignorance.

Even the Mexicans themselves were in danger from Indians, and the United States troops sometimes had to help. "This is certainly a novel warfare," wrote Gregg, "fighting and defending the same people at the same time, and killing those who would be our allies if we would permit them. True, although at war with the Mexican *nation*, we have never pretended to hostilize the unarmed citizens, and, under no circumstances, could we permit the savages to butcher them before our eyes. This display of a spirit to defend the people against their worst enemies, the Indians, will, I hope, be attended with good effect."

Gregg had some just and sensible remarks to make on the subject of military reprisals against enemy nationals. General Taylor had issued some particularly sharp orders, and Gregg could see, at the time, how cruel and unjust they were. He took justice and reason with him wherever he went, or tried to, despite the unreliability of his health and his resultant capacity for indignation, which was at times boundless. But if he became indignant on his own account more often than was quite dignified, he also spared no wrath upon those who persecuted others. In his accounts of the army in Mexico, and of people on the move generally, we get his ethical flavor at its best. He never felt that the laws of home should be left behind by the traveller, or that character was a *local* matter.

At Chihuahua he gathered together his belongings, and eyed Colonel Doniphan's column, which had marched down from Santa Fé, won the battle of Chihuahua, and was now prepared to march east to join General Taylor.

Gregg joined the column, but of course in his own fashion. One day, under the blazing sun, the soldiers beheld an apparition, which they hailed with incredulity and finally with roars of laughter. It was Doctor Gregg, bolt upright in his mule's saddle, with various outlandish accoutrements strapped about him, wearing his habitual expression of disdainful interest, and holding over his head a red silk parasol. Rejuvenating their tired spirits at his expense, the soldiers began to release their wit. Catcalls and remarks, at which he was "a little annoyed as well as amused." He was irked, too, at the "impertinence of the volunteers in other regards. Being constantly employed in collecting botanical specimens, etc.," as he said of himself, the soldiers "must needs know every particular about them . . . often accompanied by taunting and insulting expressions; so that the naturalist has to pass an ordeal in laboring among ignorant people, who are wholly unable to comprehend the utility of his collection."

For Gregg never ceased his scientific labors, and kept making bundles of specimens of Mexican flora to send, fully catalogued, to his friend Doctor George Engelmann, of St. Louis. His work was of genuine value; but everywhere his experience in performing it was the same. Among the cheerful, the lusty, the rascally, occasionally criminal, characters of our frontier century, with its necessarily muscular values, he was often regarded as a crank. The one quality which might have saved such a judgment he did not have. It was humor. Now and then a pleasantry gleamed wanly through his careful writing; but nowhere was there a healing gust of laughter, which would have blown away the clouds of irritation he so often knew among people. If we imagine him, severe, correct, careful, at his scientific observations, with a solemnity which ruder men might take for disdainful superiority, it is not hard for us to understand, though we would not justify, their view of him. After all, he gravely recorded that at Castañuela, he not only saw a dwarf, but measured him.

At Monterrey, he found old General Taylor, and measured him, too, though in words. The General was all dressed up in uniform ("pants, with stripes") for the first time—he always used to wear an old, civilian coat, and to dispense with the striking insignia of his rank. Now he wore epaulettes and had sentries, for the presidency was a genuine possibility, and he made these grand gestures, said Gregg, as marks of respect for Doniphan's Missourians, whom he had previously reprimanded, and whose arrival must now be an agreeable occasion for them to recall at the polls in the autumn.

Through with the army, and far removed from his old life on the plains, Gregg was readily receptive when Samuel Magoffin, veteran Santa Fé trader, proposed a partnership in an "enterprise," the word that Gregg used to mean a trading venture. Gregg was to go, now, to Philadelphia, where Magoffin had established large credits, and buy merchandise, which would be shipped to Mexico. It was a familiar return to the pioneer trade, and he went East in the late spring of 1847. He had barely arrived in New York when word came that Magoffin considered the "enterprise" too great a risk financially and that the deal was off.

"He has done me great injustice," wrote Josiah with restraint, "and caused me immense inconvenience; for I had left most of my baggage at Saltillo, upon the faith of the engagement to return." It meant that he would have to go back after this useless journey, to get all his possessions, books, instruments, data.

In New York he tried to see his old friend Bigelow, who was never in; nor did Bigelow respond to any of the notes and cards which Gregg left upon him. The venture was altogether a nuisance, and it was in an attempt to snatch something from the long and expensive journey that Gregg went (by way of Brandywine Springs) to Washington "with the idea I might obtain some government employ in Mexico." But he was appalled, as a proper citizen, at the state of government affairs. He had a visit with the President, and was "astonished at the evident weakness of Mr. Polk." Making a hard judgment upon the man, at first contact, as he usually did, Gregg withdrew from Washington with almost an air of ceremonial disdain for Polk, feeling that he "would not accept anything at his hands." It was "remarkable that a man so short of intellect should have been placed in the executive chair." And yet, to a democrat, with a small "d," it was not so surprising when it is remembered that Polk had not been elected by the people, who would never have done it, "but by a caucus at Baltimore who rather desire a 'creature' than talent to leave designing politicians a tool."

Gregg started west again, writing several letters on the way to his friend Doctor George Engelmann, on botanical matters.

☼ THE "UNACCOMMODATING"

Always cursed by steamboats and their "unaccommodating" officers—it was his eternal word of censure—he started down the Mississippi. He noted "the great self-importance and commanding tone of the 'mate.' Really, these petty steamboat officers exercise their authority with more 'zest' than a general over thousands!" and "Captains and clerks are unfortunately too often . . . perfect despots within their little floating realm." They were aboard the *Martha Washington,* and she went aground several times. A day later (August 27, 1847) he was on board the "small steamer 'Ellen'—a wretchedly mean clerk again." Four days later, "in little stern wheel steamer 'Jim Gilmer.' Another mean clerk!" As for the captain of the S. S. *Telegraph,* "being pretty tipsy, he flew into a great passion."

He had meant to go straight to New Orleans on the great river, and thence direct to Monterrey, but the yellow fever was raging in New Orleans, and he turned aside again to visit the John Greggs at Shreveport. He improved his stay by exploratory wanderings on the Red River and by listening to accounts of the Great Raft which natives had seen, a frontier marvel too extraordinary to omit. Intermittently for some two hundred miles, and continuously for sixty miles, the Red River was once covered with a solid, water-level roofing of logs and vegetation so dense and "so overgrown with timber for many miles, that the traveler might pass over across the river without knowing it."

The phenomenon was mentioned by other frontier recorders, including Farnham and Edwin James, though Gregg had "never seen the person who has witnessed such a state of the river." But he declared that Farnham's account was exaggerated. James noted that the water-borne jungle had been blasted out with powder by government agency.

Presently he moved on again, and in New Orleans on September 24 was obliged to glare at "a hotel clerk—Fallon—most surly, unaccomodating and I fear ill-faithed fellow." It was a description, too, of Captain Dubbs of the steamer *Ashland*, on which Gregg sailed for Brazos from New Orleans in November, 1847. It was a preposterous voyage. "This wretched vessel is short and round-bottomed, without keel or cut-water, and therefore would slide over the water sidewise" before the wind. The master was drunk day and night. Unseaworthy, the *Ashland* was almost disabled in the Gulf of Mexico, when the schooner *Miranda*, of New York, was sighted. The miserable passengers of the *Ashland* were joyful at the chance to be taken off; any change would be, they felt, an improvement. The *Miranda* at first refused to take them aboard and sailed away. But before long, she came about and returned, signalling that she would take the passengers, but that the *Ashland's* boat would have to bring them. This the drunken Captain Dubbs refused to agree to, and the *Miranda*, of New York, resumed her course. Gregg and his fellow victims were in "despair."

It was a really intolerable adventure, taking seventeen days to cover a voyage ordinarily done in four. When at last they dropped anchor off the Brazos, their drunken captain could not make up his mind. First he would, then he wouldn't, put them ashore, pending repairs on the boiler. He finally let them go, and they drew up and signed a bill of complaints against master and vessel, and through its almost spinsterish genius for converting irritation into logical complaint, who wrote it is unmistakable.

Gregg's next embarkation was on the steamer *General Jesup*, with his luggage and a dearborn carriage, up the Rio Grande; and at last, on board the light draft steamer *Oreline* he found a steamboat captain who passed muster, "a son of the celebrated divine, Rev. Mr. Moffitt," with whom there was no occasion for "a tart repartee," as Josiah sometimes described his own weapon in his endless quarrel with the "unaccommodating" wretches of frontier travel.

At last he was back in Saltillo, after a wearing journey. The United States armies were still in occupation, but everybody was hoping for a signing of the peace treaty before long. When the troops went home, new heroes would go along; and politics would be enlivened by battle cries. He wrote to Bigelow . . . who had written a "very gratifying letter" so that his apparent indifference in New York was magnanimously forgotten . . . giving him a cool and balanced view of General Taylor, from whose readiness the home sentiment was roughing out a piece of presidential timber. Far from the excitements of national politics, Gregg was able to resist the political contagion of the warrior's legend: "—a very clever sort of old fellow, but as to his being a very *great* man—even as a warrior, and much less in every other regard—it is all nonsense to talk about it." However, politics aside, and the enthusiasm of backers discounted, "if the people would let him stand at what he merits, there is no man, whom, in his way, I would esteem higher than Gen. Taylor."

☼ "WAYS AND DOINGS"

In the winter and spring of 1847–48, he stayed in Saltillo as a medical practitioner, the only time in which his studies at Louisville were formally applied. His services were enormously popular. He wrote to John about it, and said that his fees had grown steadily month by month, and that his high of over $400 for the month of April could actually have been worth over $5,000 if he had wanted to charge as unfairly as his competitors in the town.

There is a sense that he was happy in Mexico: it was a new

14

*From a daguerreotype in the possession of
Mrs. Antoinette Hardwicke, presumably
taken in New York about 1844 and
believed to be a likeness
of Josiah Gregg*

country to be looked at, and recorded about, and when he was doing that, he was really alive. He seemed fond of the people. Was there a possibility that here he might find a society in which he would be at home? Here is what might have been an arch hint:

"Tell Eliza and Kitty that I got pretty 'high in the paper' at Saltillo among the *señoritas*. At least I became 'De biggest boy in all de town' with the belle of the city. I was even invited on visits with her and gallivanted through the streets, with her trailing on my arm. 'That's some,' you'll say, *pero no habia mas.*[2]"

The accent of dead slang and the flurry of quotation marks, and his embarrassed complacency all give us the bachelor unaccustomed to romance. Aside from the gifted widow who painted miniatures and who was not averse to a life on the prairies, this was the only reference to relations with women in all his known writings.

He collected the little grains of interest which go to make up any local scene. Gossip of the time does more for its history than solemn tablets. The mountains near Saltillo he called "decidedly romantic and beautiful," and we get a flavor of his period from that usage. There was a horse-thief who escaped by joining in the hue and cry of "stop thief!" and we note how unbroken a lineage sustains rascals in their ingenuity. As for politics, or intrigue, there was a project (October 1848) to form a new and separate republic out of four Mexican frontier states, Tamaulipas, Nuevo León, Coahuila, and Chihuahua, to be called *La Republica de la Sierra Madre*. But since there were private adventurers behind it, Josiah objected and would have none of it.

Gregg's medical partner in Saltillo was a Doctor G. M. Prevost, and in Josiah's cool, scolding account of him, we can still feel the poor human warmth of folly nearly a hundred years old: "He unfortunately became in love—desperately so—and what was more remarkable for a man of his intellect, with a little girl

---

[2] "But there will be no more."

15

(13 years old) without any special beauty or merit—and still less talent and intelligence." The young man was "of rather unusually handsome person." He was swept away from his medical responsibilities by "his high empassioned temperament," and when reproached gave himself "airs of haughtiness and self-importance." Nothing was more distressing to his senior partner than "his utter want of system and order . . . everything in the way of medicines topsy-turvy and in perfect confusion. . . ."

To the self-disciplinarian, such an affair could only be exasperating. What a waste of time and attention! He had a better scheme for improving evenings. He got up Spanish classes in Saltillo, to meet in the evenings, to

1) have "social collections"
2) educate the officers
3) "break up . . . card parties."

He organized his venture ardently; but only a few came, and it perished. In February, 1848, at Saltillo, he was turned out of his house by the army, and a Major Howard and "a family of prostitutes" moved in. But he was busy as a doctor, he was happy, and he seemed satisfied. "If I could make myself as easy in American society," he wrote John, "I would be willing to live in the United States."

He was evidently liked by the people, and it seems clear that at last he liked them, although he was always more or less in hot water with the official world, even in Mexico. On one occasion he was held in Guadalajara by the local governor, and was proceeded against by troops, but he felt outlandishly confident of being able "to defeat them with only his servants." But good sense dissuaded him from amateur warfare, and the affair ended with an apology from the proper quarter.

Again and again we run up against a quality in him which in the cool medium of his own words sounds priggish, and which in the more vital medium of his living presence must have obscured his great virtues and services from less thoughtful men than he. (We must not allow the infirmity and impatience of this period of his life to disguise his great achievement as historian of the prairies, and we must remember that the dignity and courage of his last days were yet to come.) If he served science, it must often have seemed that he served it with indignation that others—all others—did not see the responsibility, and the priority, of the act. Often he betrayed that he could not grant the satisfaction of Catholicism to its believers. To observe the "ways and doings" of the people, as he said—this was his object, but sometimes we feel that he disdained any attempt to understand them. In watching the Mexican observances of Holy Week, he was again the literalist.

He rarely felt the human climate so sharply as he did meteorology. And yet—such was the honesty of the man—he reported the wise "lecture" which General Almonte gave him (April 12, 1849) on Mexico's comparative infancy in the modern world, and the impatience of the United States. Still, a masquerade which he described, and which, by his own details, we find charming, he called "brutally absurd."

It must be remembered that he was not feeling too well during this period. His irascibility was that of the invalid, the man who found his resources of body unequal to the wants of his interests and imagination. In visiting the mines of Real del Monte, he was "too weak" to go down ladders to the bottom of deep ravines. "As usually happens to me, the ride out in the stage so disordered my stomach, that I was greatly debilitated for a day or two after." Had he become clumsy and uncertain in his movements? He lost his keys by dropping them somewhere. Bending over a pool, he lost his Colt's revolver out of its holster, and saw it vanish in the water. It happened again, and the party he was with impatiently went on without him while he tarried behind trying to recover the pistol.

But he had plans for examining new lands and finding new

specimens. He wrote to his friends about these ideas. One project was to go from Mexico City down to South America, passing over the Isthmus, to explore the outlines of the great continent, going first down the Atlantic side, around Cape Horn, a fabulous land-voyage, and then back on the Pacific side up into California, and across to Santa Fé, (which was by now a territorial capital) and thence home to the United States. He was forty-three years old. There seemed much time yet. The California coast alone would repay an attentive traveler with many new specimens of plant and earth. Abandoning the great coastal survey of the southern continent, he finally decided to cross Mexico to the Pacific and travel north overland along the west coast. There were inconveniences . . . a robbery of $100 from one Richardson, who was his house guest, by two young men whom he had befriended and trusted and who escaped on his mules which they stole. The thieves were caught and jailed, but the money and the mules had been "made away with."

There was a scandal at Chapultepec, too, where Josiah had gone to inspect the historic castle. Questioned by a guard, he answered with asperity. There followed insults, he was jailed, reviled, released, and he made a protest to the United States minister demanding punishment of the offending officers. Would anything be done? "Nous verrons," he wrote in gloomy sarcasm. He tried, and failed, to meet President Herrera of Mexico. "Mere curiosity," he shrugged. The toll agents on the road in Mexico, of course, betrayed "ill breeding and rascality." Discovered in a cornfield with his animals and party, Gregg was attacked with excited words by the owner, and only the arrival of the local *alcalde* prevented serious trouble. But Josiah was "unable to believe that the judge was really in good earnest— or it were only a *ruse* to get out of what he considered a bad scrape—Nevertheless, I felt charitable enough to believe the former." Here was Gregg's lack of grace at its worst, or sickest, for his health was gradually leaving him.

On the other hand, his ingenuity and the plains craft taught him so long ago by his frontiersman father were triumphant when his wagon was upset in a wild hinterland, and with nothing but the rude materials at hand, he managed to replace a broken axle, so that the wagon was in even better repair than before. He rolled on toward the west coast of Mexico, full of the idea of Manifest Destiny in which he "foresaw" Pacific Mexico all occupied by United States citizens down to Mazatlan and even farther south. In this he echoed the popular idea of his time, which seems so foreign to our view of the sacredness of the independence of the other republics of the hemisphere.

❀ TO CALIFORNIA

But it was a time of extraordinary energies and rumors and news.

What had everyone heard? Gold? In California? First there were exaggerated reports of bonanzas, and then stories of their having given out.—"The placers are said to be failing very much, yet I think it is chiefly owing to the overflowing of the Sacramento river," Gregg decided from Mexico before ever having seen California.

Not feeling really up to a long land journey and knowing what heat and fatigue could do to a toiler on the overland march, he took ship at Mazatlan on July 16, 1849, on the barque *Olga*, for San Francisco. Just before sailing north, it was no surprise to him to discover that Captain Pearson of the S. S. *Oregon*, bound south for Panama, was "unaccommodating;" but how consoling it was to find that Captain Bull of the *Olga* was an admirable ship's master and citizen. As much could not, however, be said for the supercargo of the *Olga*, Mr. Hammersley. But it was a generally pleasant voyage, highlighted by such events as "an agreeable sermon" (July 22) "from a Quaker Universalist on board, the Rev. Mr. Bull" (who was no relation to the captain). At Monterey, where the *Olga* put in briefly, on August 26, there was a delightful, almost reassuring, surprise. He met a United States paymaster who also botanized. "It is very agreeable to meet with one in thousands who will not permit their ample opportunities to escape, for improving our knowledge of Natural history." At this port, thirty passengers left the ship to proceed to San Francisco on foot, presumably in a great hurry to reach the gold fields.

Aside from the "agreeable and interesting" sermons of the Quaker Universalist who was a man "of sterling honesty, no doubt, and the best intentions, but of no brilliancy of talent," there were the added diversions of "a company of German minstrels—three lone females, who had wandered from their native land; first to England—then to the U.S.—afterward into Mexico—and now finally on their way to the 'land of golden promise.' They seemed not wholly destitute, as they sustained a character of virtue and unceasing industry." Between the Universalist's unalarming sermons and the conspicuous virtue of the wandering actresses and the appetizing novelty of canned boiled meats from New York, passage on the *Olga* was pleasant; and at last they reached journey's end, and the Golden Gate, which Josiah noted as "decidedly romantic."

❂ CHALLENGE

After that, there was no direct news of him for several months. But in October, he was at Rich Bar, where a little community of forty people had gathered on the Trinity River. The rainy season had started, and it snowed as often as it rained. Cloudy mountain barriers lay between this inland settlement and the seacoast. It was wild and remote country, inhabited by scattered Indians on *rancherias*. Yet the Trinity River with its gold placers would one day before long have to have its trade route. Travel overland was not easy or quick, and the mountains forced the route to the south, by inland courses. If a seaport could be found that might serve as the supply center for northwestern California, the country would open up, as they said, ever so much more quickly. What would happen if travelers from here went westward until they reached the ocean? Was there a bay? Would the site support a town? Nobody knew anything but the Indians, and they said there was a bay; but they also said it was almost impossible to reach from here, far up the Trinity, with rain and snow falling every day, and the mountains towering there, and food hard to find.

If they had conceived a challenge for Gregg, they could hardly have made it better.

According to tradition in the Gregg family, Josiah was under government commission to help find the northwestern bay. Twenty-four men at Rich Bar made up the exploring party and elected Gregg captain. But the weather disheartened more of them every day until only eight in all were left. The Indians tried to discourage the party, saying that the continuous rain here in the valley was snow up in the mountains. But Gregg never abandoned a course of action once decided upon; and on November 5, 1849, he led his seven followers up the rainy mountainside. Among them was a young man named L. K. Wood, from Mason County, Kentucky. What happened to them all he never forgot, and many years later wrote an account of the ordeal which contains our only picture of Josiah Gregg in California.

Halfway up the mountain they met the snow. Gregg led them up the steepest slope in order to reach the top more quickly. At nightfall they were there, but to the west lay another wilderness of mountains separating them from the coast they were headed for. In silence they put their blankets on the snow and went to sleep. This first day was the pattern of many that followed. Crossing mountain ridges became almost a hopeless obsession. One night they thought they heard the ocean, and their hopes rose; but the next day they found the swollen waters of the south fork of the Trinity River. Now and then they encountered astonished Indians who traded them bits of food. Weeks were passing in this search. There came one night when they had no food at all amidst the rock and the needles of the mountains. They spoke of going back. But reason—we may guess whose reason—prevailed, and they went on again in the morning. In the next evening they came hungry to a small high mountain meadow, and during the next few days they found venison. But when it was gone, they toiled through ten days without sight of any game or growth for food. They went through the trees, "this world-wide forest," and now and then found little meadows where they would rest and hunt, without reward, until one day three of them shot a bear and some deer.

They rarely made over seven miles a day.

But at last the land was changing. The peaks were not so high, although the trees were denser. Any change must presage the country they sought, and their spirits quickened. They calculated that they must be only twelve miles from the sea. The ground was leveling off. They kept some semblance of discipline, which had been worn thin several times before now. They needed it, for now they came into the redwood forests, a prehistoric landscape where nothing but those vegetable giants could be seen. The refuse of centuries lay across their paths and they had to cut their way through it. Their going was slower than ever.

Yet here were matters of interest. "Dr. Gregg frequently expressed a desire to measure the circumference of some of these giants of the forest and occasionally called upon some of us to assist him. . . we not infrequently answered his calls with shameful abuse." Here again is that calm belief in knowledge which was his central concern, even in "this forest prison" where "there was not the least sign indicative of the presence of any of the animal creation," said Wood. Their own pack animals were dying of starvation. Two men went ahead with axes and chopped a system of crude steps up one side of the fallen trees and down the other so the animals could be coaxed onward.

The sounds of the air traveled high in those ancient aisles; and one night, they heard ... once again they thought they heard ... the "sound of surf rolling and beating upon the shore." They were sure this time; their hearts rose, and the next day three of them went to see, and came back, and sure enough they had seen the Pacific, not over six miles off. At last they reached it, the open coast. Once more starving, they separated to hunt. All they could find were an eagle, a raven, and a dead fish upon which the raven had been feeding. All three were put into the pot for supper. It had taken them over a month to make the journey, though the Indians at Rich Bar had said it would have taken eight days in good traveling weather.

And now that they knew more or less where they were, something seemed to happen among them which released the fears they had not dared give up to before. They had all become increasingly contemptuous of Gregg's scientific attentions to the route. "During our journey over the mountains, the old Doctor took several observations." They derided him for it. Here on the Pacific shore he took observations on a certain plateau, and engraved the latitude and longitude on a nearby tree, "for the benefit," he said, "of those who might hereafter visit the spot, if perchance such an occurrence should ever happen." (A town stands there today.)

It was not long before a collapse of character overtook the whole party. One day "in crossing a deep gulch the Doctor had the misfortune to have two of his mules mire down. He called lustily for assistance, but no one of the company would aid him to recue them." They had been "annoyed so much," confessed Wood, "and detained so long, in lifting fallen mules ... that one and all declared they would no longer lend assistance to man or beast, and that from this day forward, each would constitute a company to himself, under obligations to no one and free to act as best suited his notions."

Again, they came to another river, much swollen by recent

rains. They made ready to cross it, but Doctor Gregg prepared to take observations. The inevitable happened. The others refused to wait for him. They had arranged for canoes with near-by Indians, crossed their possessions, and then made ready to push off themselves. Only then, Gregg "as if convinced that we would carry our determination into effect and he be left behind, hastily caught up his instruments and ran for the canoe. He had to wade through the water to catch it." He kept silent while they crossed, but when they reached the opposite bank, his rage escaped him, and he "opened on us a perfect battery of the most withering and violent abuse." He heaped such devastating insults upon the men that some of them moved to pick him up, instruments and all, and throw him to drown in the river. He was sick; these companions constantly spoke of him as an "old man," and "the aged doctor." Yet he was only forty-four. His tenacity must have burned in him with an enabling power to have brought him this far against such obstacles of man and earth. At last, "fortunately for the old gentleman, pacific councils prevailed, and we were soon ready and off again. This stream in commemoration of the difficulty I have just related, we called Mad River," and so it appears on the California map today.

❁ ALLEGORY

This affair (to try and see it from Gregg's view, which is our job) was more than a lot of roughnecks running out on a crank. It was ignorance defying knowledge, and it illustrates how a crisis in relations assumes the shapes of allegory. It was a faith trying to maintain itself amidst fear. The scene is ridiculous. The "old man" probably seemed half crazy, a freak, going through cabalistics with astronomical instruments, offending the body's merit of those strong, younger men. But his qualifying genius kept him at it, and he suffered them, which for a sensitive man was probably torture. He had more to endure than the others; it was their contempt, the sense they gave toward him, of being an

24

old fool, taking all that trouble. He was once again and always the theorist, encountering psychological hardship in the practical world—the essential pattern of Gregg's experience everywhere on the rugged frontier.

Ironically enough, on this day, with its crisis in relations which had made the party forget the object of their search and concentrate their hopes on simply getting away from the wilderness of seacoast where they felt themselves trapped by time and distance, they found a hint of what they had started out to find: one of the men out scouting brought back a sample from "a bay of smooth water." It was dusk, on December 20, 1849, "and was undoubtedly the first discovery of this bay by Americans." They called it Trinity Bay the next morning when they went to see it, and when they left it to go inland, they thought their name secure. But before they could return to civilization to report their find, a party came by sea, headed by "a Captain Douglas Ottinger," who claimed to have discovered it, and he gave it the name of Humboldt Bay, which it bears today. Four considerable towns are on its shores.

And now to get back to the settlements was all they wanted, although they had dreamed of staking claims on the bay and of laying out a city. The eight of them decided to divide into two parties of four men each. The ammunition was nearly gone. They were sick of each other. It was bleak wintertime on the foggy coast. Every scrap they could find to eat meant hours of laborious search. One party of four voted to go eastward, inland. Gregg and his three planned to go down the mountain ridges parallel to the coast until they reached San Francisco. But the mountains defeated them, and at last they, too, turned inland, hoping to come eastward to the Sacramento Valley.

But for one of them, almost any decision would have been all the same. They had no meat; they were living on acorns and herbs; and Gregg, according to one of his last three companions, grew weaker and weaker, though he struggled to go on. But one day—it was in February, 1850—"he fell from his horse and died without speaking—died of starvation."

His three companions did what offices were possible. He was buried right there, under rocks, somewhere near Clear Lake, California.

He had left in San Francisco a cache of his "memoranda," together with "a work in manuscript, nearly ready for publication," which was the book of his Mexican observations, regarded as lost for nearly a century, but now at last, and for the first time, published in this volume. These effects, with the news of his death, came back to his home slowly.

❁ THE GRAND COMMUNITY

About a year after Josiah Gregg died, a certain Dr. George W. Bayless, to oblige a friend of his who wanted to know the story of Gregg's life, paid a visit to Susannah Gregg, Josiah's mother, and her daughter. What a family! He found the old lady, at seventy-seven, reading "a History of the Reformation in ordinary print." Dr. Bayless saw evidence of superior stock in the whole family. The sister and the mother were both "persons of clear good *(strong)* sense." The sister was much like Doctor Gregg both physically and mentally, and the old lady's conversation was "marked by clearness and strength." There were nieces and nephews of Josiah visible, and they partook "of the same character." The visitor and Mrs. Gregg spoke of the death of her son, and she remarked:

"He overtaxed his energies that time."

How often had she seen him come and go! Every time he came back, he could hardly wait to get going again. What had he written John? "I could never live under my oppression of spirits anywhere in the U.S. where I would be liable to continued annoyance."

The refrain was so frequent that we cannot help asking why. Why wasn't he comfortable in "civilized society"? He was literate and well acquainted with polite observances—indeed, he was sometimes very stiff about them. To judge from his photograph[3] he was personable, with a look of vitality and keenness about the eyes, which were dark and deeply porched by fine brows. His face was rather pointed, clean-shaven, revealing its bony formation frankly. He had a well-shaped mouth, at rest in a reserved expression. His clothes were of rich material. In his whole bearing, there was dignity; and there is also latent even in the photograph here described a sense of quick feeling, however controlled it might often be. It is a thoughtful countenance; and like many such, it has evidence of sadness, such as the man himself might not consciously want to show.

"I have no desire to be considered an odd fish," he used to say, according to John. He never drank, didn't like it, was temperate in both food and drink; but he "sometimes would take a glass of spirits with a friend, as it would appear, merely not to be considered *odd*." It is a wistful gesture, the complete solitary reaching out to become one with his fellows. In the curious laws of personality, he was made to *feel* eccentric, and so increasingly, protectively, he *acted* eccentrically, and thus became a "type," a sort of wandering intellectual cartoon among the venturesome men of the westward period. We may smile at the circumstance, but what remains is admiration for the steadfastness of his essential self, which created his satisfactions out of the hardest materials.

What always moved him, anyway, was not so much the things that *people* did; the human, or psychological view, was not his concern so much as the life of the land, the rhythm of the wilds, and its creatures. It is hard to blame anyone for misunderstanding him, when we reflect upon his vision of propriety and its inflexibility. He had a curious anesthesis toward human preoccupations and frailties. Perhaps it is fair to excuse him for such lack

[3] A fine one has recently been revealed by Mrs. Antoinette Hardwicke, and is used in this volume.

of sympathy by saying that he was equally harsh in self-judgment, and disciplined a poor body and an unsocial spirit until he felt their human claims reduced to unimportance. His severity to others was matched by his severity toward himself.

He was neither wholly a trader, nor a scientist, nor an artist, nor a physical man, but a thoughtful combination of all these, and on the frontier, where judgments were simple and likenesses were apt to be crudely reckoned, he was a puzzling creature. He was not even an out-and-out fraud, a pretentious "professor" whose intellectual claims could be howled down in hazing. No, much though he may have puzzled his comrades during his enormous travels—he ranged the whole West, and Mexico, and was frequently in the Atlantic East on business—they had to respect him for his talents, even though he often used them loftily in critical judgment of his fellows, and seemed to enjoy the bleak satisfactions of lonesome superiority. Does this explain why he should be so eternally insulted by steamboatmen, soldiers, lady hotel keepers, frontier travelers on the trail, the thousand and one thoughtless opportunists who were doing their share in the frontier life he was describing so truly and coolly?

He was, among them, alien.

They were doing jobs of butting against obstacles and lending their bodies and their shrewdnesses to the task of conquest, and of surviving it. All this time he was acting in one further dimension of effectuality. He was analyzing, reasoning, recording; he was observing the conditions of natural life through which other men passed with shorter sight. To him the highest act of man was to understand. He would have been at home in New England; he could have talked with Emerson. But he was torn between the freedom of the prairies, where he was accountable only to his thoughts, where, indeed, they had no audience; and the need for sharing these thoughts.

Gregg, in his anomalous position among the arch-typical men of his time, may be taken as an illustration of the man of mind, or vision, in a society of movement; but, as such, he may be also a harbinger of our ideal maturity, in which, within our corporate character, as we find individually in his, we may hope to see the freedom of educated men combined with the sense of democratic responsibility. He is among those of our national autobiographers who, simply because they were articulate and honest men, tried with the labors of their lives to make cultural awareness the simple norm of American life. Such early prophets may have been personally lonely men; but there is no loneliness in their work; there is instead a grand community of conviction and enlightenment about the terms of the lives we inherit from them as literature.

Gregg was of the order of men who create literature out of their most daily preoccupations, that is, without a transfiguring act of the imagination. Romantic inaccuracy may produce masterpieces, of course, but so may the sublime magpies, the gossips of fact, they who sense the marvel in the trivial, the whole from the part, and so translate acts of life for us that we come to know ourselves better for knowing them, since their bustling literary acts imply much of larger life itself.

For Gregg said, by implications and acts, that freedom was as desirable as growth—indeed, possibly that they were the same thing; that the prairies were natural domains for America to grow into; that the life of the prairies was beautiful and instructive; that wisdom can be brought to bear upon new experience if conscious observation is an ally; that intelligence is a better mate for courage than simple enthusiasm; and that if a man is alive to the best opinion of his present and aware of his inheritance from the past, then he may perform work valuable to later times.

When Gregg was born in 1806, there was no organized civil life west of the Mississippi. When he died in 1850, four great paths had reached the Pacific. In his short lifetime, forty-four years, the United States achieved its continental design; and he was among the men who helped this to happen.

He might be called the intellectual frontiersman of the natural world. There is high poetry in the quality of his achievement, though its terms at the time never looked so. His story is part of a great conquest, in which his weapons were curiosity and a batch of little bound books with blank pages, waiting to be written upon. No writer who loved the truth ever needed more.

PAUL HORGAN

Roswell, New Mexico
March 23, 1944

PART I

Observing the Battle of Buena Vista

****

Observing the Battle of Buena Vista

FEBRUARY TO MARCH, 1847

Diary, February, 1847[1]

MON. 11—Left Monterey this morning, at 10 o'clock, for Saltillo, with my servant Diego, and incidentally with Capt. Sherman[2] and Lieut. Benham and others. On parting with Gen. Butler,[3] he urged me very much to accept a salary, protesting that he had understood me to be on wages, having told his nephew to inform me that he would give me $100 per month. This he did not do (I mean his nephew made me no such proposition); yet if he had I should not have acceded to it: in fact, having declared both to his Adj. Gen. and nephew that I would not serve as interpreter on hire, he might very

[1] This opening section of the second volume of Gregg material is taken from the earlier portions of what Gregg designated as Manuscript No. 3. He remained under the shadow of the army in spite of misunderstanding and rebuff, and found himself in a short time an onlooker at the battle of Buena Vista, an event that seems to have been the most impressive episode of his Mexican War experience. "A glorious but awful affair" is his verdict a month later in a letter to his brother, John; the truth of such an epitome is evident from the details recorded in the diary. The recital of the train of events culminating in this decisive battle has evidently received the writer's careful attention, and seems to have crystallized his determination to write a book about his experiences. As he had severed official connection with General Wool's army, he felt barred from an active role in the battle. At one point in the narrative, he indulges in an exposition of reasons for not becoming a participant, even as a volunteer *pro tem*, and shows a tinge of regret that he had not taken a greater part in the battle. He took upon himself, however, the part of observer, and watched the fighting from a point well within the danger zone itself. This fact gives eyewitness value to the bare and laconic narrative.

[2] Thomas W. Sherman, brevet major.

[3] Although Gregg was friendly toward General William Orlando Butler, he was willing to say that Butler was more politician than military man and to disapprove of his electioneering ability.

33

well have dispensed with offering me a salary, knowing, as he must, that I could not consistently accept it.

On parting with Gen. Butler (who, by the way was also to leave for the U.S. the following Saturday, on account of his wounds growing worse—for he received a wound in the leg at the battle of Monterey), I may be allowed to record here some brief and hastily formed opinions. He is I consider a very kind-hearted clever fellow, but without that brilliancy of talent that I had expected, from his character. The truth is, as a military man, though as brave as need be, no doubt, he is rather imbecile. His *forte* is most probably politics. Indeed, his manner seems very well suited to popular electioneering,—which is now-a-days the all-important talent as politician. It was painful to see, in fact, indications of his propensity to bring "politics into the field." When outrages were committed on Mexican property, by volunteers under his command, instead of holding subordinate officers responsible, who permitted (and whose influence at home, he seemed to fear), he looked to, and proposed only to punish the insignificant privates, who, he knew, could not injure him. This electioneering propensity, in fact, seemed to pervade the whole volunteer corps, unfortunately, which is doubtless the cause of the very bad order which is maintained among them. In reality, this propensity descends from the president himself; for he (like many volunteer officers) in every appointment and every act seems to calculate to what extent it will serve him in a political way. Gen. B.'s Adj. Gen., Maj. Lorenzo Thomas,[4] tho also a man of no brilliancy of talent, is a very efficient adjutant, and certainly one of the most amiable and truly *clever* men, that I have had to do with during this campaign.

Frid. *12*—Stayed last night at Rinconada, and arrived at Saltillo this afternoon.[5] [NOTE: Observed the following courses as

---

[4] Lorenzo Thomas, major, chief of staff to General Butler.

[5] With Gregg's slackening interest in the army, came a return to studies of towns and cities. The part of Mexico in which he found himself afforded opportunities for gathering his beloved "observations." Parras, Monterrey, Saltillo, made a cluster

I came up: From Alto to Monterey, East—To Pesquería Grande, N.E.—Rinconada, W. 5° S.—Muertos, W. 20° S.—From Palomas Cr. to San José, E. 5° S.—San Lucas, S. 40° E.—Jaral, S. 12° W.—Ojo Caliente, E. 32° N.—Santa Maria, N. 18° E.— GREGG.] Gen. Taylor[6] had moved his principal camp out to Agua-Nueva, nearly 20 miles from Saltillo, on San Luis Potosí road. Maj. Warren[7] with 4 companies of Illinois Infantry and Capt. Webster's[8] battery of two 24 lb. Howitzers were left to garrison the town. These maintain much better order than the Indiana volunteers—in fact, the Illinois volunteers have been remarkably orderly, and committed very few outrages on the property of the people.

Sat. 13—Went out to Gen. Taylor's camp, at Agua Nueva. He has about 5,000 troops, all of whom are volunteers, except 2 squadrons, (May's[9] and Steen's[10]) of dragoons, and three batteries (2 of four pieces each—Bragg's[11] and Sherman's) and one of eight—Washington's[12]—besides Capt. Webster's. His volunteers are 2 regiments of Cavalry (Kentucky and Arkansas) and — regiments of Infantry—one Kentucky, two Indiana and two Illinois.

[I should have remarked that the 11th was remarkably cold; and during the night, it snowed lightly at Rinconada. The next day (12th) was still colder—thermometer in the morning, below freezing point. When I came in sight of mountains west of

that evoked his interest. To Saltillo, however, went the distinction of becoming his base for the remainder of the war as well as afterwards. Saltillo ranks with Santa Fé and Chihuahua City as being Gregg residence-places.

[6] In the first stages of the battle General Taylor happened to be absent. In the hands of General Wool matters had gone badly for the Americans, but all was changed when General Taylor arrived and displayed himself conspicuously on his famous horse, "Old Whitey." The inspiration of personal appearance rather than ability in strategy was the General's contribution toward victory.

[7] W. M. Warren, major.

[8] Lucien B. Webster, captain of the First Regiment of Artillery, a brevet major at this time.

[9] Charles A. May, brevet lieutenant colonel, Second Regiment of Dragoons.

[10] Enoch Steen, captain, of the "regulars."

[11] Braxton Bragg, brevet lieutenant colonel, Third Regiment of Artillery.

[12] John M. Washington, brevet lieutenant, Third Regiment of Artillery.

Saltillo, they were partially white with snow—the first snow I have seen this year was today.][13]

Before going out to Gen. Taylor's camp, I had heard of an unfortunate affair which had transpired a few days before. At camp I heard most of the particulars. An Ark[s] volunteer (named Colquitt[14]) was out in the adjoining palm grove, when some Mexicans came upon him, lazoed him, and dragged him a considerable distance, leaving him dead, and tied up to a palm-tree by the neck. His friends soon found him; and repairing to a neighboring rancho, in the border of the mountain, they found a fusil or two, a sabre, and some articles of clothing belonging to an Illinois volunteer, as was said, who was missing and supposed to be killed: but, nothing, I believe that pertained to Colquitt; for I understood they did not take his clothing, and he was without arms. This rancho was but a recently established [one] by people who had evacuated Agua Nueva, and San Juan de la Vaqueria—they living only in camps. Our volunteers were greatly exasperated (as they had reason to believe that the murderers were of these people: therefore vowing revenge, a secret party was got up the following day, from different corps—Ark[s] Cavalry—2[d] regiment Illinois Infantry and Kentuckians, but, it was said mostly of the first,—that is of two companies, Danley's & Porter's,[15] Hunter's,[16] I think, for the balance of the regiment was absent on detached duty)—therefore most of the blame attached to the result of the affair was fixed upon this corps:—this secret party proceeded to the rancho, fired upon the unarmed inhabitants, killing, as the alcalde of the rancho afterward reported, 12 of their number. The matter was afterward investigated; but as no one was willing to inform on the perpetrators, they were left undiscovered; yet I understand Gen. Taylor has threatened to send to Camargo, the two Arkansas companies that

[13] The brackets are Gregg's in this case.
[14] Samuel A. Colquitt, a private in Company B, Arkansas Mounted Volunteers.
[15] Andrew R. Porter, captain, Company D, Arkansas Mounted Volunteers.
[16] Edward Hunter, captain, Company B, Arkansas Mounted Volunteers.

were then in camp: still this would be decidedly unjust, not only on the innocent in the same companies, but because many Illinois men as well as Kentuckians were as guilty as they. This was the first serious outrage laid to the charge of the Ark. Vols.; for though some heavy complaints were laid in against them at Patos, these turned out to be virtually false.

While at camp, I regretted to observe some indications of partiality of Gen. Taylor for Gen. Wool,[17] and to learn, as would necessarily be the case, that it did not fail to have a prejudicial effect with regard to Gen. T. among the troops generally; destroying to a degree their preconceived very great confidence in and partiality for him. But how could it be otherwise, when, I think I may say with safety, that no officer could ever have been much more unpopular in an army than was Gen. Wool with at least ninety-nine hundredths of the troops he commanded? *Ergo:* could all have been right?

Sun. 14—This evening a spy formerly occupied by Gen. Worth (and in whom he had great confidence) and afterward by Gen. Butler—but subsequently unceremoneously dismissed by Gen. Wool, after Gen. B's departure for Monterey—called on me this evening, and informed me that he was just from a peddling tour out south, and on Friday (on which morning he had left) he saw at an hacienda called Potosí, 50 or 60 miles from Saltillo & perhaps 20 east of the direct San Luis road, Gen. Miñon[18] with what was called 5,000 cavalry, and at another place, about halfway between this and San Luis Potosí, called the Hacienda del Prado, 2000 more (said to be); hearing at same time that Santa Anna,[19] with all his army was on the way

[17] For General Wool, see I, 217 ff.

[18] J. V. Miñon, general in charge of a brigade of choice cavalry numbering 2,000. See page 230 for Gregg's account of a visit to this Mexican officer after the war.

[19] Antonio López de Santa Anna (1795–1876) was the noted Mexican general and politician who for several decades was an outstanding figure. In 1836 he led the army against the Texas insurgents, but was defeated at San Jacinto, April 21, 1836. In the war with the United States he again commanded the army, and was the head of the Mexican forces at Buena Vista.

from San Luis to Saltillo, and a portion already arrived at En-carnacion, some 30 m. south of Gen. Taylor's camp. This I com-municated at once to Maj. Warren, who sent an express with it to Gen. Taylor. This report was soon corroborated by General report obtained through foreign residents from the citizens. However, the number of cavalry with Gen. Miñon was doubt-less greatly exaggerated, being the same officer that captured the party of Majs. Borland & Gaines,[20] he doubtless had the same force, which, we hear, was then estimated at *seven regi-ments*, with but about 3000 men.

❂ LETTER TO JOHN GREGG

Saltillo, Mexico, Feb. 15/47

DEAR JOHN:[21]

Although I wrote you from "camp," but a day or two ago, I will drop you another line by mail—not only because the other letter may fail to reach you, as it was by private conveyance, but on account of some additional news.

I mentioned that the alarms of the approach of Santa Anna's legions were still kept up. Yesterday evening a Mexican for-merly employed as a spy, by Genls Worth & Butler, called to see me, and informed me that he was just from a tour about 60 miles south, to an Hacienda called Potosí, which is to the left of the road to San Luis Potosí. He asserts that he saw there 5,000 Mexican cavalry, under Gen. Miñon, the same who captured

---

[20] Gregg's account of the capture of the party of Majors Borland and Gaines, as given earlier in the diary, is as follows: "We have just received the unfortunate intelligence (which is believed authentic) of the capture of Maj. Borland of the Arkansas Volunteers, with a reconnoitering party of some 80 men. He had vol-unteered several days ago to search for the enemy, and proceeded about 50 miles on the San Luis road to a place called Encarnación. Though expected to return at once he, I suppose, imprudently, remained several days at that exposed point—until on Friday night last, he was surrounded by a superior Mexican force, (we didn't learn how many) and taken with his 80 men, prisoners, without firing a gun."—I, 346. The whole party was taken as prisoners of war to Mexico City.

[21] John Gregg was an older brother, with whom Josiah was on particularly inti-mate terms. (For further identification, see I, 16ff.) The letter to him is more de-tailed upon some points than the diary; it is also more sequential.

Maj. Borland and party. At the Hacienda del Prado (nearly half way on this side) he also saw 2,000 cavalry. From these he says he learned that Santa Anna's Army was rendezvousing in the north to attack Gen. Taylor. They also told him that most of the Mexican army was at Mateguala and Salado, nearly half way between here and San Luis, and a considerable number besides those already mentioned, were at Encarnación, the point at which Maj. Borland's party was taken. Here he says, the "General Review" was to take place on the 19th inst. and the attack to be made about the 25th.

I give the above particulars as related to me; and though Gen. Worth, and afterward Gen. Butler, seemed to have great confidence in this spy, I place but little reliance in his stories—any further than that he saw Gen. Miñon's cavalry when he states. These we had learned from other quarters, were seven regiments (but little over 3,000), which have been magnified into the 7,000. I have little doubt that these have been in that neighborhood ever since the capture of Majs. Gaines & Borland's parties. The rest, our spy only gives as reports, and I think he is either deceived, as he has before been, or misrepresents; for, in truth, if he could gain by it, I would as soon suspect him of serving the Mexican army as us. If Santa Anna is really dispatching his army toward Vera Cruz, as I still believe he is, it is precisely in accordance with his strategy and rise, to endeavor to keep up an excitement here, with a detachment of cavalry, hoping to draw away part of Gen. Scott's forces—or at least to prevent Gen. Taylor from pushing south—while he (Santa Anna) gets his army to Vera Cruz. But, *nous verrons*—a few days must unravel his plans to us. [NOTE: Still our army should be on the alert, as appraised by our weakness, Santa Anna might be encouraged to attack us, believing, as he has some right to do that the black vomit will prove a sufficiently formidable enemy to Gen. Scott, at Vera Cruz].

There was a very unfortunate occurrence took place, with regard to our army—and especially the Arkansas regiment—a few days ago. One of the Little Rock Volunteers, named Colquitt, was out in an adjoining palm grove, to Gen. Taylor's camp, after a horse, when he was *lazoed* and murdered by some Mexicans. His comrades soon found his body, where it had been dragged a considerable distance, and then lashed by the neck to a palm-tree. At a neighboring *rancho*, they found a gun, a sabre and some articles of clothing, which were recognized as belonging to an Illinois Volunteer who was missing, and doubtless also murdered. The following day, a party of volunteers was secretly made up out of different corps (but mostly Arkansas, it was said), who proceeded to the rancho, fired upon the inhabitants, killing 20 or 30 as some say! (though only five or six as stated by others.) All the rest of the men that they could catch, they paraded in a line, and were about shooting them, when another party of volunteers, under an officer, approached fortunately, and stopped further destruction. The Mexicans were taken to Gen. Taylor's camp, but discharged again.—Though there is but little doubt that there were numerous villains in the rancho, who had been robbing and murdering the volunteers, yet, of course, the shooting them down indiscriminately was a most savage atrocity. To the credit of the volunteers, there seemed to be no officer concerned in it. The matter has been investigated, yet, owing to the difficulty of identifying the men engaged, nothing has been done with them. I learn, however, that Gen. Taylor talks of discharging the only two Arkansas companies that were there at the time—Danley's and Hunter's. Yet, I suppose it will not be done.

Of the Arkansas men taken with Borland, I presume you know none. They were made up from different companies. Capt. Danley of one of the Little Rock Companies, was taken, but no other Arkansas officer, The report that they had been shot seems wholly disbelieved.

If I see any prospect of getting to Chihuahua, I shall endeavor to go in that direction within the next month or so.[22] If I only had Pickett's store here (or any good assortment)! I should like to remain; as, at present, merchandising in the wake of the army is the best business that is doing here. And I am heartily sick of the army—at least in the way I have been connected with it.[23] It is true, if I had a creditable appointment, and one that would entitle me to be respected, I would be willing to continue in service. From our latest accounts, I suppose the bill to increase the regular army has passed Congress. The officers I suppose are all to be appointed by the President. I will not solicit an officership myself, yet did I think there was any chance, I should suggest for you to make some move in my behalf. Still, knowing as I do, that political demagogary only stand a chance, I cannot suppose there to be the least prospect. Moreover, I would not accept anything short of that of a "field officer": even *Major*, I have no desire for; but *Lieut. Colonel* I should be very well pleased with.

I have not heard a word from you later than October. Write me duplicates—one to this place via Matamoros, Camargo and Monterey—the other to Chihuahua, via Missouri and Santa Fe. My love to Eliza and all.

Your affectionate Brother

JOSIAH GREGG

P.S. Frank Ross[24] is doing well—his present office that of Sergeant Major. He was appointed Quartermaster but Gen. Wool wouldn't confirm the appointment, as he was not a commissioned officer. Diego doing well—also my horse.—Capt. Dillard[25] is sick, but getting better.

[22] At the outset, General Wool's orders were to reach Chihuahua City, but circumstances had altered the program. Gregg, however, wanted to reach Chihuahua City, not only because it was former trading ground but because his important baggage and equipment had gone there. See I, 197–98.

[23] Gregg had become decidedly disgusted with life both within the army and under its shadow. His nondescript connection was a disappointment.

[24] Frank Ross was a young man who before going to the army had been a clerk in the Pickett & Gregg store at Van Buren, Arkansas.

[25] John J. Dillard, captain, Company F, Arkansas Mounted Volunteers.

P.S. As I mentioned in my last, Gen. Taylor's camp (with about 5,000 troops, and say 15 pieces of artillery) is at Agua Nueva, about 20 miles south of here. Garrison of some 200 men is left to guard the city—and two pieces of artillery.[26]

☀ DIARY, FEBRUARY, 1847

Frid. 19—Gen. Taylor having become pretty well satisfied that Santa Anna's army is really approaching, he sent an express to-day to Monterey, for Gen. Marshall[27] with a regiment or two of infantry and Capt. Prentiss[28] with two long 18 pounders. They are expected up Sunday night: Capt. Field is also ordered in from Rinconada.

Gen. Taylor is having a quantity of supplies moved out from town; yet having far the greater portion in the city, I am very much surprised that he does not take his position on the heights above the city, not only to protect the supplies in town, and to keep his already too small force united, but because it looks to me a much stronger point, any how than the one he occupies, at Agua Nueva. In fact, being in a broad plain I see no particular strength in the Agua Nueva position. True he has some show of fortification—a ditch or two with levees, yet it will be perfectly easy for the enemy to get in his rear, where his fortifications would be useless.

Sun. 21—There being so many indications of an approaching battle, I rode out to the camp at Agua Nueva, yesterday evening. Just before starting, our spy called on me again (in fact, he had given me reports almost every day) to inform me that it was understood and devoutly believed, that Gen. Taylor's camp and the town were to be attacked simultaneously on Monday morning at daylight. This was also corroborated by other reports through town. It was also asserted, as, in fact, was to be expected,

---

[26] A garrison of some 200 men had been left at Saltillo, that is.

[27] Presumably Colonel Humphrey Marshall, one of the important commanding officers.

[28] James H. Prentiss, captain of the First Regiment of Artillery.

that several hundred or perhaps thousand, rogues were to be set loose upon the Americans, with the object of plunder. Even the prison doors were to be thrown open—where about a hundred of the vilest robbers were encarcelated. In fact, Saltillo has always been famous for rogues, and now they have flocked to this point from every quarter, with the prospects of a battle and opportunities to plunder. Walking the streets of an evening, I could count virtually hundreds of loungers about the corners and squares, who had the very villainous thief and cutthroat stamped upon their countenances.

I learned that Col. May with two squadrons dragoons (about 180 men) and Col. Roane[29] with 120 Ark. Vols.—also two pieces of artillery—had gone out yesterday morning to Hedionda, to see if any of the enemy were there. They returned this morning at 4 o'clock. They saw none of the enemy but had every reason to believe there were a considerable number in the vicinity. A piquet, Lieut. Wood, with 11 dragoons, was sent out after their arrival at Hedionda, with instructions to return before sundown; yet at half after ten they had not returned, and they supposed them lost. Another piquet, Lieut. Sturgiss[30] and one man went out to return also before night, yet did not appear. [MARGINAL NOTE: Lieut. Sturgiss was taken prisoner, and exchanged for after the battle of 23ᵈ.] In fact, five guns were heard in the direction he went, which induced the corps to believe them killed. In addition to these things, they learned that from a Mexican or two there, that Santa Anna was at Encarnacion with 10,000 men, and Miñon in direction of Potosí. They therefore left for Gen. T's camp at half past ten, P.M. and arrived as before stated.

Capt. McCulloch[31] also went to Encarnacion yesterday morn-

<hr>

[29] John S. Roane, lieutenant colonel, Arkansas Mounted Volunteers.

[30] Samuel D. Sturgis, lieutenant of the First Dragoons. Gregg's spelling is slightly awry.

[31] Benjamin McCulloch, captain, who commanded a small company of Texas scouts that was very useful to General Taylor.

ing, with half a dozen Texan rangers, and did not return till to-day. He reports having approached very near a large Mexican force—supposed 8 or 10 thousand—perhaps Infantry and artillery.—The most current report among Mexicans is that Santa Anna (whom all now say is with them) has about 18,000 regular troops (i.e. all those he brought from San Luis, though most of them recently pressed into service)—of these 3 to 8,000 cav-. alry, and 36 pieces of artillery—some very large. The report of Capt. M.Culloch was to a degree corroborated by a Mexican (styling himself a discharged soldier), caught yesterday, and two Mexicans brought from Hedionda by Col. May.

To-day Lieut. Wood and party also got in (but not Sturgiss) reporting, as I learn, that he went yesterday evening 15 or 20 miles, southward, till he saw fires of the enemy (perhaps Miñon's), and then returned.

Gen. Taylor concluded to move in toward Saltillo, to take a position, as it seems almost evident that Santa [Anna] intends to attack him. I feel every confidence in the success of our arms, particularly now that a position more to my liking is to be taken. —Col. Yell's cavalry,[32] with 2 companies Kentucky Cavalry, being ordered to remain at Agua Nueva to-night, to protect supplies, until they can be removed, I concluded to remain with them.

Mon. 22—Last night, about 11 o'clock, while a number of wagons were being loaded with corn, etc. at Agua Nueva, a number of guns were heard, fired at our piquets, in the gap of the mountain, 2 or 3 miles on the road toward San Luis. In a few moments, the piquets made their appearance, and reported a consider[able] body of Mexican troops, which were doubtless the advance guard of Santa Anna's army. The Ark. Cavalry with a squadron of Kentucky cavalry under Col. Field (one squadron Ark. vols.—Pike's[33]—was at Saltillo), formed in the rear of

[32] Belonging to the Arkansas Mounted Volunteers. For further details regarding Colonel Yell, see I, 198n.
[33] Albert Pike, captain, Company E, Arkansas Mounted Volunteers.

the Rancho—to receive the Mexicans, while the wagons were moved rapidly toward Buenavista. [MARGINAL NOTE: The wagons moved off rapidly, and with such a thundering rattle that the enemy mistook them, perhaps, for artillery, which may have prevented them from advancing at the time. The wagoners were so frightened that they left several wagons on the way—which doubtless afterward encouraged the enemy considerably.] At the same time a large stack of wheat was set on fire, that it might [not] fall into the hands of the enemy—also the thatched roofs of the huts of the rancho were fired, to give light to see the enemy on their approach. This last was not only useless, but I think improper and even detrimental; for the light would have been of more advantage to the enemy than to us: it enabled them to see our position; and, had they attempted to approach, they would evidently have passed around the light, and attacked us in the rear or on one flank. Then burning of ranchos serves to exasperate the *rancheros* (even though they were not present), and will cause the[m] to seek revenge on one way or other: therefore such devastations should be avoided, except some for some evident advantage to ourselves.—

Just at this moment, Col. Marshall, with rest of Kentucky Cavalry, arrived at Agua Nueva, an anticipatory report of an attack on us there have reached the main camp, two hours before. Having waited some three hours, and no enemy appearing, our Cavalry moved on toward Buenavista, and arrived at the principal camp about between 4 and 5 o'clock, A.M.—which was pitched near Buenavista. However, Gen. Taylor, with two batteries of artillery, Bragg's and Sherman's—and the regiment of Mississippi Infantry, with Col May's squadron of dragoons.

I came into Saltillo, early—not suspecting—nor did any one else, I believe,—that the Mexican army would advance any further than Agua Nueva, to-day. Having slept but little the night before, I went to sleep, and was wakened, toward 11 o'clock, by a report that the Mexican army had already attacked our forces

45

at Buenavista. I rode out immediately toward the camp; yet before reaching there, I learned that the Mexicans were only approaching, but had not yet commenced the attack. When I came upon the ground, I found our forces had advanced over a mile from Buenavista, and were formed for battle. The Mexicans were also forming about a mile in advance of our front;—but a considerable portion of their rear had not yet got up.—Our right flank rested on a narrow pass, between a deep ravine (to the right) and some precipitous hills, under which the road passed, which was fortified by a breastwork and ditch, and defended by artillery, and infantry upon the hills, as well as behind the works: [MARGINAL NOTE: Just in front of our right wing there was a fine spring, and an old abandoned rancho of two or three dilapidated huts, called *Chupadero*.] our left extended to the mountain, over a mile distant. The Mexican centre consisted of large hollow-square, the wings spreading out on their right, to the mountain, and on their left, some distance across the ravine already manned. A detachment of our dragoons were also stationed beyond the ravine.

Santa Anna[34] was in command of the Mexican forces—Gen. Taylor, the Americans. After the Mexican chief had arrayed his army before us, he sent a white flag to Gen. Taylor, demanding a surrender within one hour. The old hero responded that he would give an answer after the battle.[35] A few "big guns" were now fired—thinking to frighten our volunteers, I suppose (the first about 1 o'clock, I believe), [MARGINAL NOTE: This gun was responded to by our troops, with hearty yells: but no cannon were fired, this evening from our side.] when Santa Anna sent another message to Gen. T. telling him that he was surrounded by more than 20,000 of the best troops Mexico could produce, while he understood that the Americans were but 5,000 strong: this last was near the truth—in fact, Maj. Bliss[36] (Gen.

[34] Although Gregg asterisked the word and placed the companion asterisk at the foot of the page, he prepared no note.

46

(North) Map of the Vicinity of Saltillo.
The Position of the Armies at the
Commencement of the
Battle of Buenavista.

Explanations
A. ....
B. ....
C. Front of American line
D. Squadron of Dragoons
E. Mexican Line
F. Santa Anna's Camp
G. Mountain Gorge
H. Hill occupied by Americans
K. M'Roy's Demonstration
T. Gen. Taylor's Camp
W. Webster's Redoubt

Anajardo

x Small Ranches
o Larger do. or villages
⊙ Still larger Haciendas or towns

101?

Santa Maria

S. Diego

Capellania Road to Monterey

Ojuelo

S. José

Jaral

S. Lucas

Bosques de Abajo
Bosques de Arriba

R. de Cardenas

Caja Pinta x   Rodriguez

Saltillo
Valdeses
Gonzalez

Palomas

o Ramon
La Fabrica (Cotton Factory)
o Torrecillos

Road to S. Antonio del Jaral,

Saltillo

Florida, & to Parras, &c.

Cerritos

25

Pueblo   Pareira
W
Rancho de Sanchez   R. de Buena ...
R. de los Narros   Molino, or Mill
        R. de los Leonas
R. de Moreno

West   (East

Alamo

San Juan Bautista   Guerregdero
Chupadera Spring   Buenavista
P.
20

Guachichil x (?)

Encantada

Road to S. Juan de la Vaquecia   (?) Jaguey
to Parras &c.

Hedionda

Road to
S. Juan

Agua Nueva

Road to S. Luis Potosi

Note — Double lines indicate Wagon Roads —
Dotted lines — — Horse Paths.

T.'s Adj. Gen.) told me that our force, including sick, was but 4,800; however, I think he meant those on the field: Maj. Warren's command, in the City, (with Webster's in the Redoubt) would make up, perhaps, nearly 5,000 efficient men.—Santa Anna therefore advised our general to accept grace before it was too late. Old "Rough-and-Ready" thanked him for his good advice, but informed him he could advance as soon as he pleased. Cannonading was kept up by the enemy until late in the evening, firing about 10 guns, with shells and single balls. Nothing more occurred this evening of importance—except two or three hours skirmishing, on the mountainside, between a party of our riflemen and another of Mexican infantry. This was kept up until dark, but with little effect, except two or three wounded on our part: some Mexicans were supposed to have been killed.

Tues. 23—I came into town last night, and returned to camp again this morning about 8 o'clock. Yesterday we learned that a body of cavalry, then said to be 4 or 5,000 had made its appearance in the plains (or valley) northeastward from Saltillo. I saw them this morning, from Capt. Webster's redoubt; but I did not think they could exceed 2,000. They were moving

[35] The correspondence was highly typical of the two commanders. Santa Anna showed his characteristic arrogance and bombast:

"You are surrounded by twenty thousand men, and cannot in any human probability avoid suffering a rout, and being cut in pieces with your troops; but as you deserve consideration and particular esteem, I wish to save you from a catastrophe, and for that purpose give you this notice, in order that you may surrender at discretion, under the assurance you will be treated with the consideration belonging to the Mexican character; to which end you will be granted an hour's time to make up your mind, to commence from the moment when my flag of truce arrives in your camp.

"With this view I assure you of my particular consideration. God and liberty!
ANTONIO LOPEZ DE SANTA ANNA"

General Taylor's reply was as follows:

"SIR: In reply to your note of this date summoning me to surrender my forces at discretion, I beg leave to say that I decline acceding to your request.

"With high respect, I am, sir,
"Your obedient servant,
"Z. TAYLOR
"MAJOR GENERAL, U. S. ARMY, COMMANDING"

[36] William W. S. Bliss, by brevet a lieutenant colonel in the Adjutant General's Department. He was General Taylor's right-hand man.

southeastwardly, as though to gain the plain, between the camp and the city. This is said to have been Gen. Miñon's Division of Cavalry.

Before I reached camp, I learned that the Mexican army was moving up in solid column, against both our flanks. That against our right was perhaps only intended as a demonstration, to call the attention of our troops in that quarter, while a powerful effort was made on our left. I had barely reached the rear when I heard a most vigorous musketry fire open on the left. Soon after, both the artillery and musketry opened upon the enemy from our right, and drove back their advance. But our left was less successful. This wing consisted of the 2ᵈ Kentucky infantry, and 2ᵈ and 3ᵈ Indiana In. supported by the regiments of Kentucky and Arkansas Cavalry—less Capt. Pike's Squadron, who had been attached to Col. May's command, at his request, as was said.—But the force of the enemy was overwhelming—at least 3 or 4 to one—both of infantry and Cavalry. The fire was incessant for several minutes—platoon after platoon, from both sides, kept up a most terrible roar. I did not expect raw volunteers to stand so severe a fire, and less did I expect the Mexicans to endure it. But they finally gave way, and the 2ᵈ regiment of Indianians, I am informed, retreated in considerable disorder; many, in fact, fled from the field. The cavalry met the enemy, but were too weak to sustain a charge: They therefore fell back, a portion of them in a good deal of disorder. In the truth, the 4 companies of Ark. riflemen (commanded by Col. Roane), were, I believe, almost entirely dispersed.

A large body of the enemy now succeeded in turning our left flank, and marched down along the mountain border, occasionally skirmishing with detachments of our cavalry.—Our prospects no[w] seemed decidedly gloomy—indeed, it looked much like the day would be lost. At this time, our train of wagons— some 200 in number, I suppose—was started toward Saltillo, so as to disembarrass the retreat of the army, should it prove necessary. Very soon after, however—and after they had strung out half a mile from the rancho of Buenavista toward the city— they were compelled to return precipitately to the Rancho, by a charge of Mexican Cavalry. Some 2,000 (perhaps) of *lanceros* and *fusileros* had already advanced opposite the rancho, and were but little over half a mile distant, when they turned down to the charge. I was on a high point near Chupadero, when I saw them start. At the same time I saw an officer in that direction, which I took to be Gen. Wool, motion to Col. May, who was half way between me and the rancho, with his squadron of dragoons and Pike's Squadron of Ark. vols.—to move in the direction of the rancho; but this they did not do until it was too late. [MAR-GINAL NOTE: Some have since endeavored (and especially Capt. Pike himself) to give much credit to the *charge* of Col. May's command in this case. For my own part, I saw nothing praise-worthy, in the affair, and, if justice could be meted out with impartiality, I fear the reverse would be the result.] I descended the hill as soon as possible, and moved in that direction, but when I reached the rancho, the skirmish was over, and the Mexicans retreating.

I learned that the portion of Kentucky and Ark. Volunteers that had fallen back before the Mexicans to the rancho (in all not 500) were formed to resist the charge. A portion of them met the *lanceros* with much bravery, but others fled in disorder. Our force was so greatly inferior to that of the enemy, that they could not successfully resist the charge; and a detachment of lanceros charged entirely through the rancho, and passed across the creek, to the westward. [MARGINAL NOTE: See Note (1) at end of this Ms.[37]] As I rode up toward the rancho, I met with the wreck of our two regiments of cavalry:[38] they were little over 200 in number, and seemed to think (at least many of them) that these were all that remained of them. But the balance had

[37] Page 70, below.
[38] That is, the Arkansas Mounted Volunteers.

made their escape—except 15 or 20 that were killed—many not stopping till they reached Saltillo. There were perhaps a dozen of the lanceros killed in their charge through the rancho. They passed out through a gap in a low ridge of mountains west of the creek—a battery of our artillery firing several shots at them, with some apparent effect, before they disappeared behind the hill.

Not observing Col. Yell with his regiment, I inquired about him: the adjutant told me he feared he was killed. I rode to the place where the charge was met, and there lay his body, somewhat disfigured, by a cut which cleft the upper lip. He had been killed by lance-wound in the breast. Col. Yell, I had for some time been convinced (whatever doubts I may previously have had) was brave, even to temerity, but lacked a sufficient degree of prudence. The truth is, he mistook his talent, when he entered the army—he was much better suited to politics. But as a warm hearted friend and social companion, he stood pre-eminent. Near by him lay Capt. Porter of the same regiment, and Adjutant Vaughn[39] of Kentucky Cavalry, who were killed at same time.

I should have mentioned that Col. McKee[40] and Lieut. Col. Clay[41] (*Henry Clay's* son) were also killed during the first warm attack on our left wing, already mentioned. [MARGINAL NOTE: This is an error; they were killed near the close of the dreadful engagement, in which Col. Hardin perished. I had been erroneously informed: the 2d Kentucky was not on the left at all, until ordered there to aid the retreating Indianians.] In fact, Col. Clay, as I learn, was on the border of the mountain with the rifle skirmishers, and having been wounded, he was started in, but overtaken and slain by the lanceros. I should have said also, that the mountain-side skirmishing recommenced early this morning, and

[39] Edward M. Vaughan, first lieutenant and adjutant of the Kentucky Cavalry.
[40] William R. McKee, colonel, Second Kentucky Foot Regiment.
[41] Henry Clay, Jr., lieutenant colonel, Second Kentucky Foot Regiment. To the bereaved father, Henry Clay, Sr., General Taylor wrote, "To your son I felt bound by the strongest ties of private regard; and when I miss his familiar face, and those of McKee and Hardin, I can say with truth that I feel no exultation in our success."

continued until the principal attack was made. Capt. Lincoln,[42] (Gen. Wool's Adjutant) was also killed in this first attack.

The Mexican lancers still continued to retreat, but they were somewhat hastened by a battery of artillery which was now brought to bear upon them, and fired very rapidly with a good deal of effect. A heavy body of infantry which were also passing down the border of the mountain, began to retreat likewise. At this time our cavalry and dragoons began to move up upon the enemy, whom the effective cannon-shots began to throw in a good deal of confusion. A large b[od]y of Mexican infantry, with a heavy support of cavalry had advanced down the deep valley of a ravine which descended from the mountain, and had been already warmly engaged, for some time with the Mississippi regiment, and others. A battery of artillery was now brought to bear upon them, and began to throw them in confusion, about the time that the retreating advance met them. Two additional batteries were at this moment planted on a commanding point, so as to rake the valley. I was close by the nearest, and really [thought] that our troops [were] about to gain a complete victory; for, besides the execution which it seemed evident the batteries must do, our forces, as well cavalry as infantry, began to move upon the disordered masses of the enemy from every direction. They had already began, indeed, to steer into the gorge of the mountain, whence the ravine descended.

The cunning Mexican general, seeing the peril of his army, sent a messenger (as I was since informed) to Gen. Taylor, inquiring what he wanted—who answered that he wanted the whole Mexican army. This mse [message] induced Gen. Taylor to suppose that the Mexicans might surrender, and immediately sent a white flag to those in the valley. This unfortunate flag passed in before the batteries, near which I was, just as their aim was taken, and this forced them to suspend their fire for some

[42] Captain George Lincoln, acting adjutant general on the staff of General Wool. He was a distant relation of Abraham Lincoln.

ten minutes—in fact, until the enemy had time to extricate themselves from their unfortunate position. Had it not been for this, this entire section of the enemy—about half their army—would have been driven, I doubt not, into the gorge in the mountain, and thus been cut off from support. A complete victory would have been the result. It seems singular that as judicious an officer as Gen. Taylor should have been entrapped in such an error. How he could suppose they would surrender, when a few minutes placed them out of danger, it is difficult to imagine!

I now passed down further to the right and in advance (near our center) where a battery of our artillery were exchanging shots with one of the enemy. I found Col. Hardin,[43] with a portion of his regiment. Minor's infantry, under cover of the hill to protect the battery. The Col. inquired the news below—I told him of the death of our friend Col. Yell and others. "They will not give me a chance," exclaimed Col. H.: "here I am out of musket range, only dodging cannon shot." And pointing to the battery of the enemy—"If I had permission I would take that!" He had previously been stationed on the hills which commanded the pass on our right, but all attempt on that side having been abandoned by the enemy, he was moved up to the point where I found him. The battery being now ordered to move up a little, he advanced also: and, in a few minutes his corps, with the artillery, were most warmly engaged with a large body of the enemy had been under cover of a hill beyond. I had started toward a commanding point to the right, and in advance, and was some 200 paces in the rear of our combatants when the attack was commenced. A more incessant fire of volley after volley, of musketry, accompanied by a rapid fire of artillery, could not well be conceived. As the Mexicans shoot too high, almost universally, I was perhaps in more danger than if I had been in the

[43] John J. Hardin, colonel, of the First Illinois Regiment. He was a prominent man in the state; after his death Lincoln said, "We lost our best Whig man."

52

line of battle.[44] Such a whizzing of balls, on either side—before
—behind—above—then striking the ground under my horse's
feet—could only be compared to a hail-stone in a hurricane!
How myself and horse escaped was difficult to conceive; in fact,
I heard one strike upon the blanket of my saddle, but it was
too far spent to penetrate. Many of our troops fell by the fire, not
half nor quarter as many as would have been expected. They
made, in return, great slaughter in the ranks of the enemy. But
the great superiority of the numbers of the latter enabled them
to force our troops over the hill, yet the enemy soon retreated
in turn, and finally fell back under cover of the hills. During
this excessively warm engagement, the valiant Col. Hardin was
slain. In a charge, he had advanced ahead of his corps, and it
becoming necessary to retreat again he was overtaken and killed
by a *lancero*. Col. Hardin was one of our very best and skilled
volunteer officers, and a braver man could hardly have been
found on the field. His loss will be severely felt by his corps,
the army, and the country, and mourned by a large circle of
friends, whom his gentlemanly qualities had endeared him to.

This was the last warm engagement—especially with musketry—that took place. Both the cavalry and infantry of the
enemy, soon disappeared from the field, or remained under cover
of the hills. But a battery or two exchanged shots with ours until
nearly night.

I now said—and repeated to many—that the Mexicans were
whipped—and prepared to retreat; though it was generally believed they would return to the attack the following morning.
—I came into town again, this evening.—The distance of the
Battle-field (I mean of our front) is full seven miles southward
of the city, being over a mile from Buenavista.

Before coming to town I heard of an attempt upon the city,
by Gen. Miñon: here I learned some of the particulars. While
the battle was raging on the field, toward midday Miñon's di-

[44] Gregg could rightfully say that his position was a dangerous one.

vision of *lanceros* and *fusileros* made their appearance southeast-ward of the city; but the gallant Capt. Webster opening upon them with bombs, etc. as soon as they came in reach of his re-doubt on the hill, the[y] soon retreated toward the mountains, giving the worthy Captain but little opportunity to direct his formidable instruments of destruction upon them. No further attempt was made on the city. This was defended by Maj. War-ren, with four companies (I believe) of Illinois infantry, in the church, etc. to defend the plaza, where there was a large lot of supplies—and Capt. Webster with two 24 lb. howitzers, in a strong redoubt, upon a high point commanding the city—a few Mississippi infantry left to guard Gen. Taylor's camp.

Wed. 24—Just as I was preparing to start out to camp this morning, the joyous news was spread of the retiring of Santa Anna's army, during the night. It appears from information received of prisoners (and I saw 50 or 60 in one party, brought in this morning, besides many more), as well as from the best our piquets could judge—that the Mexican infantry and ar-tillery retired early in the night, the cavalry, as a rear guard, leav-ing about an hour before day. They had left all their dead upon the field, besides many wounded, and a hospital with a surgeon, an assistant and a hospital steward, and 56 wounded in camp— the whole number of wounded left being nearly 200, which were afterward brought into Saltillo, for hospital attendance.

The retreat of Santa Anna last night seemed not very intelli-gible, [MARGINAL NOTE: See Note (2) at end of this manu-script. Also see Note (6).[45]] and therefore some *ruse*—for which he is conspicuous—was feared. He might certainly, just as well have waited, so far as our army was concerned, till open day, and made at least a less dishonorable retreat. But I believed then, and still continue to believe, that his army commenced deserting (after night—in fact, a great many had deserted into the moun-tains during battle, in the day), at such a rate, that he found him-

[45] Pages 70 and 74, respectively, below.

self obliged to fall back to Agua Nueva (to use the mildest term) to save the wreck of his army. This is since corroborated by reports of Mexicans, who have told me that they left "by droves" during the night, after battle—and there is a current report that there were 7,000 missing at Agua Nueva!—Among the prisoners of today, there was an aide of Gen. Torrejon's taken.

Gen. Taylor having learned that Santa Anna's army was encamped at Agua Nueva, he sent his Adjutant Gen¹ Maj. Bliss, with a white flag, to propose an exchange of prisoners, bury the dead, and the like. I met the Major on his return. He informed me that a good deal of disorder seemed to reign in Santa Anna's camp—had no piquets out, so that he was virtually upon the camp before they knew it. In addition to the above business, the Maj. informed me that he repeated what Gen. Taylor had before communicated to the Mexican General in writing—the great desire of our government to conclude peace. Upon this Santa Anna flew [into] a great passion—passing the bounds of courtesy—and said it was idle to talk of peace under existing circumstances: the Americans had raped their women, devastated the country, burned their haciendas, etc.! If our armies would retire beyond the Nueces river, he might then begin to think of talking about peace, and concluded by giving the "wholesome advice" that we had better do so!

I made a tour today over the battle-field, and dreadful was the view! Large numbers of our own dead yet lay upon the field! But still greater quantities of Mexicans were scattered there. I did not count, but in riding through, thought I saw from two to 300, yet I suppose I did not see the fourth-part. Their killed must have amounted to more than 1000—some say, from 2 to 3,000! Our killed (on the field), according to official reports, were 264 (I believe) yet there were doubtless many wagoners and stragglers not pertaining to the army, killed, making up perhaps a total of some 280? Our wounded were between 3 and 400 —some of whom soon after died, and others will yet die.

With regard to the destruction of Mexicans on the field, I observed that our artillery had made great havoc among them. In one row I saw seven that had been mowed down by a single cannonball! in another five, and in many places, three and four! I also saw a great number of wounded on the field. They all protested, with one accord, that they had been brought to battle by force: this I think probable enough. One poor fellow showed me a little bag containing hardly a hint of unsifted flour: "This is all they give us, for a day's rations," said he; "and it is more bran than flour." "And why do you fight for such a government?" "How can I help it? They seize us and force us on at the point of the bayonet." My attention was attracted in another quarter by three poor fellows with a white rag stuck up on the point of a stick. "Oh! how unfortunate[,"] said one! ["]we were arrieros[46] on our way to Saltillo. They took our mules, packs and all, and made soldiers of us!" "Then how happens it that you are dressed in uniform?" ["]O, they had plenty of that along, and dressed us in it at once." [MARGINAL NOTE: See note (3) at the end of this Ms.[47]]

Thurs. 25—We had a blustering alarm this morning that Santa Anna was returning with his army upon the Americans: but it turned [out] only a party with white flag, for exchange of prisoners, burial of dead, etc.

Frid. 26—This morning we had another false report of the approach of Santa Anna's army. But it had its origin I believe, from our scouts having discovered that the Mexican army was preparing to move; yet it turned out in the contrary direction: for it was reported this evening—and

Sat. 27—It was confirmed this morning, that Santa Anna had moved southward with all his army—or rather its wreck. The report is that the army "broke up in a *row*"—desertion being so great, and confusion such, that they had "scattered to the four

[46] Muleteers.
[47] Page 71, below.

winds," leaving scarcely over 3,000 together, chiefly cavalry, to retreat in a body.—Gen. Taylor moved to-day, his camp to Agua Nueva, leaving only a few Mississippi infantry on the hill at his old camp and Capt. Prentiss with two 18 pounders—Capt. Webster, with his two howitzers, etc. in the redoubt, and Maj. (now Colonel—elected to fill the vacancy of Col. Hardin) Warren, with 4 companies of Minor's[48] infantry. I am not sure but Gen. Taylor's advance to Agua Nueva is a little rash and premature. Although the chances are decidedly in favor of the Mexican army's being broken up, and its wreck retreated southward, with little or no prospect of their being brought against us again; still, the general ought to have some more proofs than the mere fact of the enemy's having abandoned their camp, before he advances too far. Santa Anna, we know, is a crafty fox, whose *forte* is in *ruse*. He might play some trick on old Rough-and-Ready yet.

But we will now rest upon the supposition that Santa Anna and his army have retreated and "gone to the devil," as the expression is. The victory, though not finished on the day of battle, is now complete. And such a victory is scarcely on record in modern history. That less than 5,000 efficient men should whip— beat so signally between 4 and 5 times their number, will scarcely be credited abroad. The precise number of the Mexican Army was not known; though we have Santa Anna's own signature for it that he had over 20,000 of the best troops of Mexico. This has been corroborated, on the one part, by an order book of the Mexican army that has been found:—in an order on leaving San Luis, Santa Anna directs that all weak, inefficient and untrained troops be left there; so that it seems he had a picked army. Some of his officers have said that the number on the field was but 12,000, while others have stated that they were 24,000 in number. If we would split the difference, it would perhaps be nearer the truth: in truth, I had supposed from appearance, that the num-

[48] Captain Minor commanded Company K, Second Kentucky Foot Regiment.

ber on the field could hardly pass 15,000; yet I might have been mistaken.

Our troops certainly fought bravely—very bravely, for raw soldiers—untrained volunteers—who had never sustained a fire before. Indeed but a portion of the regulars (who were but 7 companies—4 of dragoons and 3 of artillery—hardly over 400) had ever been in a battle before. The volunteer infantry, especially, fought with all the bravery and firmness of veterans—with only a few exceptions. The unusual resolution of the Kentucky, the Missouri, the Mississippi, and third regiment of Indiana, infantry, has been highly lauded. Gen. Lane of Indiana was wounded early in the day, by a musket-ball through the arm; yet he remained on the field the whole day, demonstrating great bravery and gallantry. Col. Davis[49] of Mississippi was also shot through the foot, yet continued on the field, as valiantly as his regiment.

Col. May and his command including Capt. Pike's squadron; though composed, perhaps, of as brave men as any, seemed to be held in reserve, and therefore did virtually nothing during the whole day of battle. Therefore the Col. will hardly get another brevet for this battle. In fact, I hope it may not appear that there was nothing but negative operations on his part: I observed several occasions w[h]ere I thought he might have used his command to good advantage, yet did not do so.

I should have stated that Gen. Marshall arrived at Saltillo on the morning of the 24th, with two or 300 infantry, and Capt. Prentiss with his two 18 pounders, and two small pieces (4's, I believe) as I have understood. He had lain at the Rinconada for two or three days, in obedience to Gen. T.'s orders. It is very unfortunate that he had not been ordered up a day sooner, as the two large guns would have been of great service. But it was perhaps most prudent for him to guard the pass between Rinconada and Muertos, in case a retreat had become indispensable.

[49] Jefferson Davis, colonel commanding a regiment of volunteers known as "Mississippi Rifles." The stand made by these soldiers at the critical juncture largely saved the day for General Taylor.

About this time (i.e. 26 and 27th) our wounded were removed from the Church, which had been occupied, since the night after the battle, as a hospital. The necessity of this was unfortunate, as nothing tends to incense the people so much as any desecration of their churches.

In procuring other hospitals, I noted that want of prudence, judgment and knowledge of the country and people, which is so frequently demonstrated in our army operations: especially among some of our young upstart officers, of whom a young surgeon, on this occasion, seemed the very essence. He selected the house which pleased him, (which happened to be the Vice-governor's house) and the Medical director, Dr. Harris, to all appearance a very amiable man, but inexperienced in the affairs of this country,—ordered it to be given him, and the quarter-master had ordered the family out of it, when I found it out, and succeeded in having the decree changed. I had expected nothing better of the quartermaster, however (Capt. Chilton[50]), who is one of those morose, abrupt, unaccommodating, (and I fear uncharitable) officers, so many of whom are in the staff of the army). I can only account for this upon the supposition, that the repugnance which their own corps had for them, induced their fellow-officers to recommend them to staff appointments. Nevertheless, I am happy to say that by no means all the staff-officers are of this character: I have had the pleasure of making the acquaintance of many amiable exceptions.

But to return to houses taken for quarters: I must report that many families were forced out of their dwellings to accommodate our officers; and I report equally that nothing is expected to be paid for the rent of houses. How our commanding officers can reconcile to themselves this measure, I am unable to understand. Why they make a distinction in private property, I should like to have explained. In my own humble opinion houses are as much private property as anything else, and civilized nations

[50] Robert H. Chilton, captain, First Regiment of Dragoons.

have acknowledged the use of them to have a real value. It would therefore be no more unjust to take a man's corn and beef without pay, than his houses: in fact, the latter has the worst effect; for any gentleman would prefer giving up his movable property without pay, to being turned out of doors. I regret that Gen. Butler countenanced this procedure, and still more, that a citizen was forced to abandon his house to furnish the general quarters in this city. While we are paying for private property at all, we should certainly pay all equally.

Sun. 28—Today I learned that near 200 wounded Mexicans were brought in from Agua Nueva, left there by Santa Anna, on his retreat: and it is said he took near 400 with him. This, if true, would make up their number of wounded, 8 or 900! (See Note 5,[51] at end of M.S.)

❀ DIARY, MARCH, 1847

Wed. 3—Nothing of interest has occurred since my last date. Gen. Taylor still at Agua Nueva, with the body of his army. Col. Belknap had been sent out as far as Encarnacion to reconnoiter. This evening I heard he had returned, bringing information that, as far as he could learn, Santa Anna's army was moving toward San Luis Potosí, by forced marches. He had left sick and wounded Mexicans scattered all along the road—and 2 or 300 in Encarnacion—apparently to perish! What inhumanity and cruelty!

I should have mentioned that our army lost, during the battle, our three smallest pieces of artillery, on account of the horses being killed or disabled. Of this no doubt a great boast will be made: in fact I already understand that Santa Anna informed the dignitaries of this country, that he took three pieces of artillery and two or three colours from us; but was compelled to retire for want of subsistence: other reports are that he said he was ordered to retire and return to the seat of government, by a com-

[51] Page 74, below.

munication which he received on the field of battle from the Mexican Congress. All subterfuge to excuse him in the eyes of the people here, for his dishonorable retreat! I predict that he will not again be able to raise an army against us—in fact, that he will most probably be hurled from his present pinnacle of power.

Before closing the subject of the battle of the 23^d I will add, with regard to myself, that prior to the battle, I had thought of taking an active part in it; yet, upon maturer reflection, I declined joining in any engagement for several reasons, as I thought, sufficiently good: First, I had no position—no office—and I should have had to enter the ranks as private: even worse, in fact, for had I been killed, I ran the chance of its not being known how, nor where, nor when: Secondly, I had no desire to fight for the mere sake of *killing* or *being killed:* nobody but a savage in principle, could enter battle except for the love of fame (which is perhaps the most powerful of all stimulants), or to serve one's country; and as a mere private, I could have hoped to do very little in either of these regards: Thirdly, I had offered my service to our Government; [MARGINAL NOTE: In addition, I had offered my services, but lately, to Gen. Taylor, "whether a volunteer aide, or in any other creditable capacity:" The general slighted the offer; it would therefore have been more than simple in me to join in the battle, "on my own hook," when all might be lost, and nothing could possibly have been gained to me.] but, instead of placing me in a respectable position, it occasioned me great sacrifices without bestowing anything upon me —therefore, I would have had little to do, after such notable neglect, to have risked my life in fighting for it gratuitously, and without hope of reward or honor: Fourthly, I wished to witness, as much as possible, the operations in every part of the field; and if I had joined any particular Corps, I found my observations would have been chiefly confined to that corps, and its vicinity— instead of maintaining myself on high and commanding points, as I did, so as to have a view of all the operations. Nevertheless, I was frequently in about as much danger from both musket and cannon shot, as if I had been actually engaged in battle.—I make these remarks, because I had previously observed, unreflectingly, that I thought of joining in battle.

Mon. 8—On Saturday, Gen. Taylor came in from Agua Nueva, and encamped on the hill, above the city, with a battery of artillery, Col. May's dragoons, and some other troops. To-day he left for Monterey—taking also the Kentucky regiment of Cavalry with him. I regret to have witnessed, on this occasion, a degree of neglect and injustice, in Gen. Taylor, which I was not prepared to expect. The spy who had given some important information (already alluded to), and had been dismissed by Gen. Wool, had not received a cent from our Government for more than a month past. I therefore made a statement of his services and merits to the general, but was mortified to perceive that he paid little or no attention to the subject. Thus the poor fellow, who was paid and held in high confidence by Gen^s Worth and Butler, is left by Gen. Taylor without remuneration or protection, after evidently faithful efforts to furnish us important information with regard to the Mexican Army! How can we expect to get the services of spies, under such treatment! I have given him some trifles myself, and shall give him more, individually. [MARGINAL NOTE: *March 31$^{st.}$* Today he made his appearance for the first time after my interview with Gen. T., and I gave him $10, which he said was all he needed for the time— to release himself from bondage.] Besides furnishing us the first information of the approach of Santa Anna, as already related, he gave an account of the contemplated day and manner of attack—all of which was virtually corroborated, by subsequent events.

Thurs. 11—About this time Gen. Wool paid a visit to the city; and one could not but note the parade and pomposity of his "suite," etc. especially when compared with the very unostentatious style of Gen. Taylor (as also of Gen. Butler, when here). We could see Gen. Taylor riding about the city and elsewhere, frequently with no escort but his adjutant, and an aide perhaps, while Gen. Wool was not only everywhere followed by a portion of his staff, but a guard of some 20 dragoons, with drawn sabres! In this style he not only entered the city, but his guard, with sabres drawn, thus followed him from house to house, and from hospital to hospital, in his visits through the city!

A day or two after the departure of Gen. Taylor, Gen. Wool moved the main camp in to Buenavista again.

Mon. 15—Died to-day, Lieut. Ribera, one of the Mexican officers wounded in the battle of the 23ᵈ ult. Lieut. Ribera had been shot through the leg with a cannon shot, and his leg was amputated here by Dr. Hitchcock.[52] He was doing very well, until seized with fever, three or four days ago; and, as the army surgeons ceased to attend, I volunteered my services to do what I could for him: but his disease concentrating in the bowels, resulting in a peritonitis, which could not be checked, he died to-day.—I regret to feel bound to record a considerable degree of neglect on the part of our army-surgeons, not only with regard to Ribera, but some other wounded Mexican officers brought here. True they attended occasionally upon them for a while, though under no *positive* obligation to attend them at all; yet it would certainly not only have been handed down in history as a deed of noble generosity, reflecting much credit not only upon the individuals concerned, by the army surgeons generally, and the American name. But, instead of this, I regret to have witnessed a disposition, even in Dr. Hitchcock, to withhold attention, until the poor officers should be forced to offer pay for medical service. Capt. Zuñiga (shot through the leg) has also been wholly neglected by all, except myself for the last week.—Also Capt. Roana had his leg amput[at]ed by Dr. Hitchcock. His case soon assumed a very critical character, and seemed to be left

52 Charles M. Hitchcock, assistant surgeon.

wholly to me. I protested against it, as I did not consider my experience sufficient to warrant my taking the responsibility. True, I could have done like others, and withdrawn also; yet I could not have the conscience to abandon him wholly, while in such danger: their own surgeons might have attended them (as there were two or three in the city), yet the poor wounded men had placed their hopes on us. Happily, however, Capt. Roana took a favorable turn, and is now doing well. [MARGINAL NOTE: But he afterward took an unfavorable turn in the hands of Gama, and died.] Since the death of Ribera, I have thought it advisable to transfer the care of both Zuñiga and Roana upon the principal Mexican surgeon, Gama: for, finding it exceedingly difficult to get even the counsel of our army surgeons, I do not consider my experience sufficient for me to take further responsibility; should another Mexican officer die upon my hands, I should feel much mortified; for though I had executed every power, I am not only aware of my want of practical knowledge, but many ill-faithed Mexicans would hardly fail to accuse me of ill-faith!

❂ LETTER TO THE *ARKANSAS INTELLIGENCER*[53]

Saltillo, Mar. 22, 1847

Since the battle and retiring of the Mexicans, there had been almost a continual report that Santa Anna would return again; lately, however, he seems to have given up, but another report is out that General Paredes is on his way here, with a still larger force than Santa Anna originally had. Nevertheless I place very little, if any faith in this, though the Mexican army might be upon us again when we least expect it, for to say the truth, I did not believe the report before, until about four or five days before the battle. Yet if they do come again, and our army is

[53] Gregg's letters were never sent directly to the newspapers. His practice was to address the editor, usually a friend, and leave the question of publication to him. By a similar route went Gregg's accounts of the battle of Buena Vista to the *Louisville Journal*.

fairly prepared for them, I think they will get another sound drubbing.

You will ere you receive this have heard who were elected colonel and lieutenant colonel of the Arkansas regiment. You are now informed that B. Franklin Ross of Crawford county was elected adjutant vice Mears promoted. Huzza for Frank—most meritorious promotion of any, I believe. His wounded arm is nearly well.

We have a report that General Kearny[54] has taken Chihuahua and is on his way here to join General Taylor, but it is not yet sufficiently confirmed for me to start in that direction.

I informed you in my other letter of the death of Colonel Yell. Supposing his family might hereafter wish to remove his remains, we had a tin coffin prepared, which was placed in a strong wooden one. The burial I superintended myself.[55] I had him interred above the southern border of the city, at the foot of the hill, under Captain Webster's fort, so that his grave remains protected; otherwise, there would have been much danger that Mexican rogues might have disinterred him for his burial clothes. I set a cross at his head with his name cut upon it, so that his friends may know his grave. By him, I had buried John Pelman,[56] with his grave marked in the same way. Near by were also buried Col. Hardin, Captain Lincoln, Captain Porter, and others.

JOSIAH GREGG

---

[54] It seems strange that Gregg knew so little of what had happened in New Mexico. General Kearny, after taking New Mexico, had proceeded with the larger part of his army towards California. He had, however, sent troops under command of Colonel Alexander W. Doniphan southward into Mexico, via El Paso, with orders to effect a juncture with General Wool's column. Colonel Doniphan's force reached Chihuahua in the early part of 1847, after winning brilliant victories over Mexican forces at Brazito (December 25, 1846) and Sacramento (February 28, 1847).

[55] The body was later transferred to Fayetteville, Arkansas.

[56] John B. Pelman, Jr., a private in Captain Danley's company—Company B, Arkansas Mounted Volunteers.

❊ LETTER TO JOHN GREGG

Saltillo, Mexico, March 23, 1847

MY DEAR BROTHER:

I wrote you two or three letters, soon after the battle of Buena
Vista, giving you some account of that glorious but awful affair;
yet as communication has since been rather uncertain, I have
neglected to write again, for the last two or three weeks. Nothing,
however, of any very important interest has since occurred; Gen.
Taylor, as I told you, moved his camp out to Agua Nueva immediately upon the retreat of the Mexican forces; and sent a detachment 30 or 40 miles, southward, to Encarnación, under Col.
Belknap. The Col. gave an appalling picture of the route of the
retreating enemy: Mexican soldiers dead and dying, scattered
all along the road, having been abandoned destitute, by Santa
Anna! And, at Encarnacion, there were between 3 and 4000
sick and wounded, in the most wretched condition—virtually
perishing for want of sustenance and attentions. I suppose they
would have been taken care of by the Col. had he been provided
with the means of transportation: as it was, but a few were
brought in. A wounded Captain Zuñiga (a man of intelligence)
upon whom I have been attending—and who was brought from
Encarnacion,—tells me that the number of wounded could not
have been less than 1000—perhaps more; while that of the killed
was perhaps fully as many!

Speaking of the wounded—I believe I already told you that
between 200 and 300 were left by Santa Anna, upon the field of
battle, and at Agua Nueva—abandoned to their fate—and to
American hospitality. They were hauled in here, by our wagons,
in the course of the first and second day after the battle; for
many of the poor wretches were not found immediately, as they
had hidden themselves in the ravines, supposing they would be
murdered by our troops. But, I am happy to say, that I have
heard of no such atrocities having sullied the fame, so justly

gained by our troops on the day of battle. The day after the battle, I rode over the field myself, and saw great numbers of Mexican wounded, while at the same time several hundred of our soldiers were scattered about—some in search of their slain comrades, while others were prompted by mere curiosity; and yet, instead of perceiving any disposition to maltreat their fallen enemies, it was most gratifying to witness many of them, administering them bread, water, or any other refreshment they chanced to have with them! I hope such noble conduct will at least serve to eclipse some of those outrages of which I have before told you, as having been committed, some time before, by a few wanton, dastardly fellows, which are generally to be found in every corps, and who bring disgrace even upon their worthy comrades!

But the mortality among the poor wounded Mexicans has since been great:—whether on account of their long suffering upon the field, or want of attentions and skill in their surgeons (for they are attended by three or four Mexican surgeons), nearly half the number brought here have died. I have no doubt both causes have had their influence. Of our wounded, but a small proportion have died—they are generally doing well.

On the 8th inst. Gen. Taylor left here for Monterey: it is not understood when he is expected to return. Gen. Wool remains in command of the forces here. The general camp has been moved in to the vicinity of Buena Vista again: though the Arkansas regiment is encamped 6 or 7 miles beyond, at Encantada, as an advance post.—In a former letter I mentioned the elections in this regiment to fill vacancies: Roane, elected Colonel, to fill the vacancy occasioned by the death of Col. Yell, —Mears, Lieut. Col., in place of Roane, and B. Frank Ross, Adjutant, in place of Mears. I have not witnessed a more just reward of unpretending merit and efficiency than this last promotion. Ross himself was absent at the time—in town here laid up with his wound; therefore he knew nothing of the vacancy he was called to fill, and so was not an aspirant: but I feel very sure that he would have been just as easily elected Lieut. Col. had his friends bethought themselves to present him as a candidate! I saw him the other day: his wound has healed remarkably fast, and he was actively engaged in the discharge of his duties.

For some time after the battle, we had continual reports that Santa Anna intended returning upon us; yet it seems now fully understood that he has gone, "post-haste," to the city of Mexico, with the select portion of his troops, to quell an insurrection against his government there.

[Your brother,]

[JOSIAH]

❀ LETTER TO DR. GEORGE ENGELMANN

Saltillo, Mexico, March 25, 1847

MY DEAR DOCTOR:

From Monterey, I sent you by the party of Gen. Butler, a "batch" of plants—as also one to Prof. Short. I hope they may have been duly received. I now send you another lot by Dr. Zabriskie, who goes directly to St. Louis. I fear this will be more confused and uninteresting than even the other. I have had to put them up in the greatest haste; for not being advised in time of the departure of the party, I worked at them, and the lot I accompany to Prof. Short, the whole of last night, without having gone to bed at all: and now I find I have to mount my horse and overtake the party, for I could not get everything ready in time. Therefore I am compelled to cut short. The remarks accompanying the former package will serve to explain this. I hope to be able to send you another package before leaving here, when I will write you more fully. I intended sending you some mineral specimens, but had not time to put them up. I will send them hereafter. I send you a few specimens of wood and seeds, as you will perceive. I fear they will be of no interest.

Please have the kindness to forward to Prof. Short the package directed to him: the two go bound up together.

I remain,

Yours truly,

JOSIAH GREGG

☼ DIARY, MARCH, 1847

Mon. 29—This afternoon, Gonzalez, the Gefe Politico of Saltillo & vice gov^r handed me the following document from Col. Warren, requesting me to translate it:

Saltillo, March 29, 1847

To EDWARD GONZALES, VICE–GOV^R

I demand that the city authorities return to me, this day, the following property, stolen since I have had command of this city, to wit:

7 mules, the property of Capt. Naper
7   "   "   "   "   "   Prentiss
7   "   "   "   "   "   Steen
2   "   "   "   " Lieut. Franklin
2 Horses from Q.master Department
1   "   "   "   "
1   "   " Mr. Underhill
1 Anvil and Hammer from Qr. Mr. Department.

In the default of returning the property, I demand of the authorities, in money, as follows:

17 mules	$850.00
4 Horses	330.00
1 Anvil & hammer	100.00
	$1280.00

If the money be not paid by tomorrow, 10 o'clock, I will take property to twice the amount.

(Signed) W. B. WARREN,

GOVERNOR OF SALTILLO

I went to Warren, at the solicit[at]ion of Gonzales, to get him to prolong the time, as it was utterly impossible to hunt up the animals in a few hours. But the Col. peremptorily refused, saying

69

they must come (or their value) immediately, and that such was the order of Gen. Wool: and that it had already been nearly a month since the animals had been demanded in a similar manner. This, not only from the protestations of Gonzales, but from circumstances, I knew to be at least partially false. It had yet been but 15 or 20 days since Gonzales returned to the town after the battle, and then a portion of the animals had been lost but a short time. Gonzales asserts (and I suppose nearly the truth) that only seven animals (of Capt. Prentiss) had been demanded —that he knew nothing of the others—and these had not been demanded in such a formal and peremptory a manner.

Now, whether it was proper to require pay for stolen property or not, there would be a difference of opinion: as for my own part, I think not, unless it could be made appear that the authorities were abetting, etc. and more especially as our troops had destroyed and stolen immense amounts of property from the Mexicans which had not been compensated for. True, Warren said that he was determined to make Americans responsible for what they had stolen, and Mexicans also. This I knew to be erroneous, for I had heard Gen. Butler declare he would respond for no stolen property—except it or the rogue be found; and Gen. Taylor refused to listen to complaints of the kind.—As Gonzales justly remarked, many persons would thus suffer three times: first what Mexican rogues stole from them: 2dly what our troops stole and destroyed: and 3dly what they have to pay for property stolen from Americans. I repeat, unless we could come at the guilty, I can see no justice (while we profess the principle of respecting private property) in this indiscriminate retaliation; for such it is in principle. Could we come at the guilty, I should say "Go ahead;" but the burden is likely to fall on the most innocent.

OBSERVING THE BATTLE OF BUENA VISTA

[Notes Accompanying Manuscript No. 3]

[NOTE 1,[57] from page 49]—I was informed that our cavalry being drawn up in a line, in single-file—the Mexican cavalry *(Lanceros)* after approaching within about 70 yds. halted; at which our cavalry *all* fired their carbines, but without killing a man—which emboldened the enemy to make the charge: otherwise they would probably have approached no nearer. This demonstrated what I had already thought—that volunteer cavalry should not be left to fight on horseback. Their horses are useful for scouting, pursuits, etc. but when brought into regular battle, they should be dismounted. Neither their horses nor themselves are trained—they are "out of their elements"—can neither shoot nor use their sabres; but put them on foot, the way they have been in the habit of shooting, and they are very efficient soldiers.

With regard to troops intended to fight on horseback—such as our Dragoons—I differ with many as to how they should be armed. I should discard the carbine altogether: these embarrass them, not only in the use of the sabre, but in riding. In its stead, I should give them two pistols instead of one—the U.S. horse-pistol being almost as efficient as the carbine, and so much less in the way—else, still greatly better, a pair of Colt's large patent revolvers. But, really even with the carbine, I have been wholly unable to comprehend the expediency of giving a dragoon a pair of holsters with but one pistol—two would even be more conveniently carried, as they would balance each other. Certainly, the insignificance of an additional pistol was not a desideratum to cause them to be restricted to one!

[NOTE 2, from page 53]—Santa Anna has since stated in his reports and letters, that the cause of his falling back upon Aguanueva, was a want of provisions: he even urged also a lack of water. This last is utterly false, as his camp was within a few

[57] These brackets, and those in a similar position in the following notes, are Gregg's.

71

yards of the border of a small creek, affording water enough for 5 times as many troops as he had. There may have been some more truth in his scarcity of provisions; for, though I have heard that he had about 100 beeves (a large portion of which were killed on the spot—as signs indicated), which ought to have furnished beef rations for at least two or three days,—yet I doubt if he had much if anything else—neither breadstuffs, beans nor vegetables. True this would seem remarkable, as he then commanded the country—and appeared able to command it, *ad libitum*—which was supplying us in bread-stuffs, etc. and has since continued to supply us, in abundance; yet as he paid nothing—and there is no such thing as disinterested patriotism among the Mexicans—the country people would conceal from them while they would bring freely and abundantly to us for pay. Were there no other reasons, this ought to afford sufficient proof of the policy of *buying* supplies from the natives, instead of *taking* them by force, as many have recommended—"foraging upon the country," as their favorite expression is. In that event, the consequence might, and most probably would be, that like Santa Anna's army, we would be driven out of the country for want of supplies. My opinion is, that, by keeping up the system of purchasing everything we want, we could live in abundance, where the *Mexican* armies would perish with hunger. And yet there is another—a philanthropic—reason against foraging upon the country: the burden, instead of falling upon the Mexican government and rulers—our true enemies—would light upon the poorer classes—the laborers and farmers,—the best people of the country, and the most disposed to be our friends.

[NOTE 3, from page 71]—Our volunteers deserve great credit for their treatment to the Mexican wounded, the day after the battle. I saw large numbers of volunteers strolling over the battle-field, on the 24th—some in search of slain friends and relatives—others, no doubt, executed by curiosity. With feelings of grief, and inclined to seek revenge, it was to be apprehended that [they] would treat roughly, and probably kill some of the Mexican wounded found upon the field. Yet, on the contrary, I not only saw no violence offered, but much kindness shown to those unfortunate wretches. A great many of them I found with cups of water and a little bread by their sides, supplied them by our volunteers!

[NOTE 4,[58] from page 134]—Copy of a Table of Barometrical observations, etc. which Dr. A. Wislizenus did me the favor to send me—having had the pleasure of traveling from Chihuahua to Matamoros with him.—Names, etc. corrected—

The mean of about 90 Barometrical Observations made by me in the city of Chihuahua, at different times, from 25th Aug. 1846 to 1st April, 1847, is . . . . 25.506 inches

Highest stand of Barometer on 23d Dec. '46   25.765
Lowest   "   "   "   on 30th " '/46   25.215

Date 1847	Hour		Barometer in Eng. inches	Thermometer Attached	Detached	Remarks
April						
27	5½	A.M.	26.250	60.0	59.5	Camp in Bachimba
28	9	A.M.	26.240	74.0	73.5	About 1 m. south of Santa Cruz
"	12¼		26.195	89.0	86.5	" " " "
"	3	P.M.	26.190	95.0	90.0	" " " "
29	3½	"	26.180	90.0	88.5	Camp in Sancillo
May						
1	9	A.M.	26.125	89.5	87.0	Camp near Santa Rosalia
"	1	P.M.	26.115	95.0	90.0	" " " "
2	3	"	25.790	86.0	85.0	" near La Ramada
3	4	"	25.615	81.0	82.0	" Guapiquilla
4	Sunr.		25.680	56.0	56.0	" "
"	12		25.595	89.0	85.0	" 3 m. S. of Guapiquilla (Hac. de Dolores)
5	9	A.M.	25.470	75.0	75.0	(During march on dividing ridge between waters of Rio Anchez & slope of Rio Grande (say 25 m. S.W. of Guapiquilla)

[58] For context for Note 4, which has no direct connection with Gregg's account of Buena Vista, see page 134.

73

6	Sunr.		25.615	63.0	65.0	Camp at San Bernardo
"	4	P.M.	25.585	97.5	98.5	" " Andabazo Creek
7	4 -	P.M.	25.500	90.5	94.5	" " Pelayo
8	4	"	25.220	95.5	94.0	" " Cadena
9	3	"	25.725	96.5	98.0	" " Mapimi
10	6¼	"	26.325	87.5	81.0	" " San Sebastian
11	5	"	26.310	91.5	93.0	" " San Lorenzo
12	3	"	26.365	100.0	99.0	" " San Juan
13	5	"	26.150	92.0	93.0	" " El Pozo
15	12	"	25.220	83.0	84.0	Camp at Parras
"	3	P.M.	25.275	83.5	83.0	" " "
16	12	"	25.275	82.0	83.0	" " "
"	3	"	25.210	84.5	85.0	" " "
17	6½	"	25.910	72.0	71.0	" " Ciénega Grande
18	3½	"	25.485	84.0	84.5	" " Rancho Nuevo
20	5½	A.M.	25.285	63.0	62.0	" " La Vaquería
"	3½	P.M.	24.435	81.0	82.5	" " San Juan de la Vaquería
21	12		24.260	77.5	75.5	" " Encantada
22	9	A.M.	24.270	70.5	72.5	" " "
"	12		24.255	77.0	75.0	" " "
23	8	A.M.	25.010	79.0	79.0	Saltillo, near Plaza
23	6	P.M.	25.215	75.0	76.5	Camp about 6 m. N.E. from Saltillo
24	5½	A.M.	25.265	67.0	66.5	" " " "
25	5½	"	26.665	68.5	68.0	" at Rinconada
26	9½	"	28.425	74.5	74.5	Monterey, near Plaza
27	5½	A.M.	28.450	62.0	62.0	Gen. Taylor's camp
26	4	P.M.	28.440	77.0	77.0	" " "
28	5½	A.M.	28.795	63.0		Camp at Marin
29	5¾	A.M.	29.015	72.0		" " Rancho Viejo
"	1½	P.M.	29.205	94.0		" " Cerralbo
30	6	A.M.	29.365	73.0		" " Puntiagudo
31	4½	"	29.695	77.5		" " Mier
"	5¾	P.M.	29.740	90.0		" " Camargo

June

1	8¼	A.M.	30.000	86.5		" " Reynosa (June 2?)
6	6	"	30.110	87.0		Mouth Rio Grande about ½ mile from sea

8	9	"	30.075	86.0	"	"	"	"
"	3	P.M.	30.070	88.5	"	"	"	"
18	1½	"	30.280	91.5	New Orleans			
19	6	"	30.165	85.0	"	"		

[Note 5, from page 60]—Gen. Santa Anna, in a letter dated "Angostura, Feb. 23, 1847"—says, "—El egército de los Estados Unidos, al mando del Gen. Taylor, compuesto de 8 á 9,000 hombres"—& further on,—"Mas de 2000 cadáveres de los enemigos, tendidos in [sic] el Campo de batalla"—& still in the same—"entre generales, gefes, oficiales y tropa, hemos perdido, entre muertos y heridos, segun se calcula, cosa de mil hombres."[59] —This is one of those one-sided exaggerated reports for which Gen. Santa Anna is so very famous. The killed alone of the Mex. army was generally a[c]knowledged even by the Mexicans, to have been about 1000—the wounded, perhaps double.

[Note 6, from page 74]—Although in Note 2, I have said that Santa Anna had stated that a principal cause of his retreat was want of food and water, I have since been able to find no communication of his to this effect; although I had grounded it upon a positive assertion that there was: all I meet with is an extract from a private letter (of some officer, I suppose) in which is the following: "Nuestra tropa se muere de hambre: no bebe agua de dos dias acá, y no come nada desde el dia que salimos de la Encarnacion, y una tajada de asada en la Paca."[60]

[59] The army of the United States, under command of General Taylor, composed of 8 to 9,000 men—More than 2000 of the enemy dead, stretched out on the field of battle—including generals, chiefs, officers and troops, we have lost, dead and wounded, according to our estimate, something like a thousand men.

[60] Our troop is starving: for the past two days they have not had water, and they have had nothing to eat since we left la Encarnación, only a bit of roast meat at la Paca.

PART II

With Doniphan's Missourians

With Doniphan's Missourians

APRIL TO MAY, 1847

Diary, April, 1847[1]

FRID. 2—Late this evening, James Collins,[2] with 13 Missouri volunteers, arrived with an express from Chihuahua, giving account of the capture of that city by Col. Donophan[3] and regiment of Mo. Vols.[4] and the attendant battles, of which I will speak more definitely here after. As I have been very desirous to get to Chihuahua, I will go with the return express—starting in a few days.

[1] The material for this section is drawn from the extended Manuscript No. 3. The account continues Gregg's movements in the month or two following Buena Vista. By April he seems to have needed a freshened interest, which came in the form of an opportunity to journey out to Chihuahua City. Ever since his zeal for serving with the army had become damped, he had fallen back upon the hope of again getting into that section of Mexico which he delighted to speak of as his "old stamping ground." Probably he hoped to connect with the baggage, books, and equipment ("all my preparations of outfit and conveniences for the tour") that had gone forward when he abandoned his projected return to the Santa Fé region in the spring of 1846 for the unfortunate connection with the army. When the small group sent by Colonel Doniphan under the leadership of Collins arrived at General Wool's camp, Gregg saw an opportunity to return to Chihuahua City with them. Before this could be done decorously, he felt he should have General Wool's permission. Hence a visit, during which General Wool aired his grievances, Gregg exculpating himself with characteristic dignity and independence. To insure his cause's being reported aright, Gregg recorded the interview, using, for him, the unusual device of dialogue. The diary record of the trip to Chihuahua and back is not in Gregg's best vein. He was too much preoccupied with mere topographic matters, the raw material out of which a map might be made, and not concerned with incidents and personalities, such as give the accounts of Edwards and Wislizenus greater interest and attractiveness.

[2] James L. Collins was a Santa Fé trader from Missouri whose first trip was as early as 1827. He continued active in the trade until the Mexican War, when he became Colonel Doniphan's interpreter, scout, and dispatch-bearer. He was an intrepid fellow, and had many thrilling adventures while in the Mexican War. After-

DIARY & LETTERS OF JOSIAH GREGG

Sat. 3—Going out today, with Mr. Collins, to Gen. Wool's camp, and being called by the business of the former to the General's tent, I was called back after leaving, by the latter, for an explanation of the causes of my dislike for him,—when the following colloquy, in substance, came off:[5]

"GEN WOOL—Sir! I understand you are a very violent enemy of mine! May I ask the cause?

GREGG—General, I have not considered myself as a *very violent* enemy of yours; otherwise I should not have visited your tent.

GEN. W.—It seemed so; therefore I thought proper to ask the explanation.

G.—You are aware, however, that things did not go very smoothly between us, while I was with your command.

GEN. W.—I deny it: I had no difficulty with you.

G.—I so understood it, and endeavored to make you understand it so, likewise; at least from the time we crossed the Rio Grande. A not[e] I wrote you from the camp on this side, con-

---

wards he settled in Santa Fé, owned and edited the *Santa Fé Gazette*, and served as a government official. While in charge of the government depository, he was murdered. His body was found one morning in the office, with bullet wounds; the safe was open and the money gone.

[3] With all allowance for Gregg's failure in spelling proper names, it is singular that he should have mutilated that of so well-known a man as Colonel Alexander W. Doniphan. Doniphan was from Liberty, Missouri, but probably he and Gregg had never met, even when the latter visited Independence upon his visits back from Santa Fé.

[4] Doniphan's forces embraced the eight companies of the First Regiment of Missouri Mounted Volunteers, numbering some 700 men recruited from Jackson, Lafayette, Clay, Saline, Franklin, Cole, Howard, and Calloway counties. On the march south from Santa Fé about 100 men comprising a battalion of light artillery were added, and about 100 others belonging to the "Chihuahua Rangers," a group made up at Santa Fé. After getting into Mexico, Doniphan decided to muster in as soldiers the traders and their teamsters, thus increasing his force of effectives by some 300. Some idea of the equipment may be had from the following account, that of Frank S. Edwards, who had enlisted in the battery of St. Louisans which Captain Weightman commanded:

"The service was to be for one year or for a less period if found expedient. Each soldier was to furnish himself with a good horse, saddle and clothing—in short everything except arms. Although we were not absolutely required to uniform ourselves, it was recommended that a suitable uniform would be desirable, so we pro-

80

veyed, very clearly, I think such an intimation: I thought I had reason to be dissatisfied; and, in frankness have to confess, I have formed an unfavorable opinion of you.

GEN. W.—And pray what may have been the cause of your dissatisfaction and unfavorable opinion.

G.—These have been numerous: one of the most important causes of my *dissatisfaction,* has been an apparent fixed determination, on your part, to show very little confidence in me or my opinions,—which my sensibilities could not very well brook.

GEN. W.—I have had great confidence in you, and have at no time aimed to deport myself otherwise: On the contrary, I have striven to treat you with particular regard and attention; and made you a major at San Antonio. [This was entirely new to me: Gen. Wool positively denied all power to confer *rank* (this was most probably true, though he seems to have exercised it in other cases), and therefore could only agree to *hire* me, giving me for salary, the pay and allowances of a major.][6] Gen. Shields, with whom you were familiar, was, as I have since

---

vided a neat dress, somewhat similar to the fatigue dress of the regulars. We also got our Spanish saddles all made of one pattern. The common but good article we procured could hardly, strictly, be called a saddle, as it consisted of nothing but the skeleton or tree of one, with the girth and stirrups attached. The object of this simplicity was to render it as light and cool as possible to the horse; and by putting a good Mackinaw blanket above as well as beneath, it made a comfortable seat— the blankets forming our beds at night. Our horses were good, being principally Illinois grass-fed animals, just suited to the service for which they were now wanted. Mine carried me more than two thousand miles in the Mexican country, and he was, at last stolen from me at Saucillo, about eighty miles below Chihuahua, and I almost felt I could have cried when, after long search, "Old Tom" could not be found. An important part of our equipment was a stout leathern waist belt, supporting a good butcher-knife, to which many of us added a revolving pistol—a weapon we found very useful. And knowing that we should be obliged to go over long distances without finding water, we all provided ourselves with tin canteens holding half a gallon:—these covered with a piece of blanket, kept wet to cool the water, are a very necessary article."—*A Campaign in New Mexico with Colonel Doniphan* (Philadelphia, 1847), 21–22.

[5]This colloquy sheds light on the characters of the two men concerned. The trouble was mainly a clash of personalities. The experienced traveler who knew much about Mexico and its people and the military commander who was master organizer and disciplinarian were unable to appreciate each other's excellencies.

[6]These and the remaining brackets in the colloquy are Gregg's.

learned, also very inimical to me, although, while with me, he flattered me more than any other man. Hear what I wrote by him to Gen. Taylor, when he left me, and you will perceive how much I was deceived. [Here he read copy of a letter to Gen. Taylor, commending Gen. Shields to him in high terms. I was much surprised at this, I must confess; for I myself had heard Gen. S. speak very severely of Gen. W. on many occasions.]

G.—Well, general, I detest everything in the shape of double-dealing; and if you think I have ever professed more friendship than I really possessed, I now, once for all, disavow it.

W.—No, I had not supposed so: but what made me think you so hostile, was, that I heard that you said, the other day, that you wished my name was to a certain document: that I was the man you wished to hold responsible for it. [He referred to Col. Warren's order to Gov. Gonzalez, on a previous page.[7]]

G.—I did say so: I considered the document a very improper one—decidedly tyran[n]ical,—and I preferred holding the commanding officer responsible, who, as I was informed had so ordered it.

W.—But, when I heard of that, I directed the Col. to allow more time.—Besides I have heard that you have had letters published against me.

G.—I deny having written any letters—not a single one since I started on this expedition—*expressly* for publication. My letters have all been private; although I have heard that some of them have been published. In these private letters, I have frequently expressed my opinion of you to my friends, which I confess was unfavorable: I know not whether any of these opinions have been published or not.

W.—Moreover, I hear you are writing a book, in which you are assailing me.

G.—Has any one told you that *I said* I was writing against you?

7 See above, page 69.

W.—No, but I hear that you are.

G.—This is all gratuitous! I have before heard that you had said so; and my reply was, that I had not yet written that book; and if I should write one, Gen. Wool might find himself mistaken. Though, as I have said, I acknowledge an unfavorable opinion of you, which I have often expressed verbally as well as in letters. It is difficult however, to give all the causes; if you inquire what has made you unpopular with so many of the officers of your command, you will know many of the causes which have combined to impress me unfavorably.

W.—But your opinions on that score have been formed from one-sided stories: you ought to have asked me about them before forming an opinion.

G.—This was a liberty I did not feel that my position warranted me in doing: I could only form an opinion upon the best testimony before me.

W.—Then you might have inquired of my staff. [I might have responded that his staff—with but one or two exceptions—entertained full as bad an opinion of him as myself.] I am aware that many of my officers were displeased because they thought me too strict; but they have changed their opinions: since the battle, most of them have confessed to me their error—declaring that they can now see how much better their corps fared than if I had been more remiss. Is this not so, Col. Bissell?[8] [who, in the meanwhile, had entered his tent.]

Col. B.—It is about as you state, General.

Gen. W.—You were intimate with Col. Hardin: You are aware he was inimical to me: I learn that, before his death, he regretted ever having been opposed to me. [This, I am constrained to think, very doubtful.] I have labored incessantly to keep good order in my division: and Capt. Washington remarked to me, the other day—"General, that book [laying his hand on one which was upon the table—his order book, I suppose. His orders

_____
[8] W. H. Bissell, colonel of the Second Illinois Foot Regiment.

have been so very numerous, that his army has acquired the cog-
nomen of "the Column of Orders," among some] will be a guide
to future armies.

G.—General, my company is waiting—I must leave you.

GEN. W.—I give you my hand: I buried all my disputes in
the battle. All I ask is that you do me justice."—G.—I would
not knowingly do anything else, for the world.

Some other unimport[ant] remarks intervened which I omit
—or even may not remember.—I do not pretend to quote, word
for word, yet I feel sure the general would acknowledge the substance correct. He was so incessant in his remarks, that I often
omitted saying what I wished, for want of opportunity.—Some
time during the conference Gen. Wool observed that he had
not written a word against any officer in his command: "that
you may insert in your book," continued he, "that Gen. Wool
says he has never written a word against you."

Besides Col. Bissell (Colonel 2[d] regiment Illinois volunteers) who was present but a few minutes at the close, Maj.
Roman, U.S. Commissary was there all the while—retained purposely by Gen. Wool as witness, I believe: for the general's
object was evidently to make me do as he had doubtless made
many others—confess their errors and pronounce him a great
man—by thus plumping the question to them before witnesses;
for it is well known that there are only a few endowed with sufficient firmness and resolution, to frankly speak their minds, to
a general—when unfavorable.

Before leaving Saltillo, [MARGINAL NOTE: Or Leona Vicaria, as it was some years [a]go officially christened: yet the
people prefer the old name of *Saltillo* (Santiago del Saltillo),
as they say that Leona Vicaria though a sort of Jeanne d'Arc in
the revolution was not of unexceptionable habits, and consequently they think it no credit to have their city named for her.
Saltillo doubtless originated from some beautiful little cascades
(Saltos de Agua) on the spring branch.] I will insert a few gen-

eral notes of the city, and surrounding country. The latitude of the public square (principal), according to a mean of 8 observations of sun, Sirius and Polaris, is 25° 25′ 15″. Longitude, west from Greenwich, according to the mean of 7 lunar distances, in time 6 h. 44ᵐ 12ˢ—in degrees, 101° 3′ [MARGINAL NOTE: According to an eclipse of Jupiter's satellite No. 1—Dec. 12—13/48—Longitude resulted 101° 0′ 0″.]

The climate is mild, pleasant & healthy—intermittent, or bilious disease of any kind, being almost wholly unknown. The winters are mild, as it but seldom freezes or snows—though sometimes lightly—and the heat of the summers is moderated by the great elevation; so that the mean temperature must be between 70° & 80° Fahr. The temperatures of various springs at Saltillo, and vicinity, were as follows: Principal spring, which waters the city, 65½°, with atmosphere about 70°.

Spring of Capellanía	65½°	with atmosphere about	45°
(Small) Spring of Encantada	60°	" " "	75°
" Chupadero	67½°	" " "	60°
" Buenavista	67½°	" " "	75°
" Guencadero	66°	" " "	"

The valley of Saltillo contains almost innumerable springs—some fine and flush, while others are small. It is said a bishop, a few years ago, had the curiosity to count the springs of this valley, and made out the number equal to those of the days of the year, 365. And much of the valley being of very fertile alluvial soil, the agricultural productions are very abundant. The staple of these are Indian corn, wheat, barley, beans, etc. Fine & abundant crops of wheat are grown here; and it is carried even to the market of San Luis Potosí. Sweet potatoes or rather yams *(Camotes)*, though not cultivated to any extent, are said to grow wild near Monterey. Irish potatoes *(papas)* not cultivated to any extent, but found wild in some plains.

Although we do not find the profusion of fruits (especially tropical) here that we do at Monterey (for it should be noted that though 15' further south, Saltillo has much the coldest climate of the two) there are many excellent orchards—especially of apples, pears, peaches, figs, apricots, quinces, cherries, and some others.[9]

The climate is perhaps too cold for *sugar*—at least it is not planted: yet I can see no reason why *cotton* should not do well, although it is no where found in the valley; though cultivated in the surrounding country. There is a demand for this article, created by an excellent cotton factory, in the vicinity of Saltillo, belonging to an English (or rather Irish) company, Dr. Huitson[10] and others. Water-power is employed, working, I think, near 100 looms (the whole machinery being excellent, having been made at Boston) and worked by Mexican girls, who have become quite expert at the business.

I am told by Vice-Govr Eduardo Gonzalez, who favored me with much statistical and other information, that the City of *Santiago del Saltillo* is said to have been founded on 25th July, 1575. It is said to have take[n] its name from a *Salto de agua* (*leap* or fall of water) of which there are many *diminutive* ones, as the name expresses, along the course of the spring-branch.

After the first settlement, a number of families of the Flascalteca Indians were brought from near the city of Mexico, and settled in a Pueblo (Pueblo de San Estéban), on west side of the city, for the purpose of protecting the Spanish population against the wild Indians, and to aid in civilizing them.

I see by a detailed census, furnished me by Gonzalez, that the population of the city proper is set down at 7,596, and the Pueblo at 572—making a total population of 8,168 souls. Yet I believe this erroneous—too small—and did Gov. Gonzalez; for it seemed out of the question for the total population of the entire city to be less than 10 or 12,000.—I mean when the inhabitants are all there. The same statistical paper makes the

[9] See below, page 88.
[10] Dr. James Hewiston.

population of the entire jurisdiction, from Patos on the west to the boundary of the state on the east & south & Capellanía on the north, 24,068—it is believed to be more. [NOTE: According to the census of 1832, the population of the state of Coahuila is set down at— males, 42,143— females, 42,154—total 84,297; but this also includes Texas, or at least Texas set down at 1403: too small, no doubt.—Here the whole jurisdiction of Saltillo is put at—Males 11,613—females, 12,474—total, 24,087: Jurisdiction of Parras, we find at— males, 4,027— females, 5,944— total, 11,971: Co. of Monclova— males, 2,408— females 2,613 —total, 5,021: Do. of Capellania, 3,576— Do. Candela, 2,491: Abasolo, 1,298— Santa Rosa, 2,334: Guerrero (or Revilla) 1,015: S. Fernando de Rosas, 2,122: Nava, 569: Gigedo, 863: Morelos, 608: Allende (S. Juan de), 678.]

Speaking of indigenous plants, I should have mentioned that flax, though cultivated to no extent (or rather not at all, except in gardens) is said to grow wild in some places. A sort of Punche or wild tobacco is found almost everywhere.

Salt is brought from the lake of Alamo de Parras, chiefly, for the supply of this region. Some lead-mines exist—besides one not far from Salinas, in N. Leon, a good lead-mine is said to exist near Ojo Caliente, on the road to Monterey.

Courses and distances from hill above town to villages in the vicinity of Saltillo: To Plaza Pública of Saltillo N. 30° E. ½ m.

To Capellanía	(pop. say 1000)	10 m.	N.	23°	E.
Bosques de Abajo	(100)	7 "	"	25°	"
Guanapiato	(pop. 100)	9 "	"	28°	"
Santa María	(" 1000)	16 "	"	29°	"
Rodriguez	(" 100)	5 "	"	30°	"
San Gregorio	(10)	18 "	"	38°	"
Los Valdeses	(pop. 150)	5½ "	"	40°	"
Los Gonzalez	(" 100)	5 "	"	42°	"
Saucillo	(" 80)	6½ "	"	44°	"

La Fábrica (cot. factory)	(100)	4	"	E.	40°	N.
Ramon	(pop. 100)	5	m.	E.	33°	N.
Torrecilla	(" 60)	4½	"	"	28°	"
Cerritos	(" 200)	4	"	"	20°	"
				(on Palomas Road)		
Palomas	(" 2000)	12	"	E.	13°	N.
Rancho on Palomas road	(20)	1	"	"	29°	"
" " " "	(pop. 30)	2	"	"	24°	"
" of Pareira	(pop. 30)	1½	"	"	12°	"
Molino de Arizpe	(" 50)	2	"	S.	30°	E.
Guerrca Icro	(" ")	5	"	"	22°	W.
Buenavista	(" 60)	6	"	"	25°	"
Guajasdo	(pop. 50?)	8	*leguas*,	N.	40°	W.
Mesillas	(" "?)	13½	"	"	10°	E.
Encantada	(" 50)	12	m.	S.	30°	W.

The populations designated are those supposed to exist before the war: many are now abandoned.

Speaking of the productions of Saltillo, I should not forget the *Maguey,* which is cultivated to great extent, particularly in the Pueblo. Here, whose fields are filled with it, furnishing abundance of *pulque* for the daily market. Also, *agua miel,* which is the *pulque* or juice of the maguey unfermented.—Also *mezcal* distilled from it, as well as from the *lechuguilla.* The maguey is transplanted from young scions of sprouts, around the roots of the older ones, and is said to be fit to cut at the expiration of 5 or 6 years—that is, the period that the *quiote* or seed-stalk begins to shoot up. If let pass this period,—the plant is good for nothing except for the quiote, which is a useful pole for building purposes, as house rafters, etc.

Of the wild plants, among the most useful is the *lechuguilla,* which abounds upon the dry hills & plains, round about—of whose strong fibres abundance of excellent ropes, bags, etc. are made. We find also in aboundance, a species of palm, producing an edible date, two or three species of palmetto or palmilla, the sotol, various species of cactus—Pine and oak in the mountains, piñon around their borders—mezquite, guizache & Uña-degato, (gatuna, or *gatun*) the first two in great abundance— Agrito, Frijolillo, governadora, etc., etc.

Frid. 9—Having determined on a tour to Chihuahua, in company with the returning Express,[11] etc. I set out to-day, about 9 o'clock, with Mr. Collins and 13 Missourians, and an escort of Arkansas Volunteers, under Capt. Albert Pike, of 26 men— making up the entire number of 42 men, including Pike, Collins and myself.

This expedition, in any other country than Mexico, would have been one of almost unpardonable temerity. For 42 men to set out openly to traverse an enemy's country, for 500 miles, is what has seldom been undertaken. True, Mr. Collins and his party, had just passed the same road in safety—only 14 of them! Yet they were unexpected, and travelling very fast, as well as passing around the principal towns,—(the largest, Mapimí in the night) the news—of their advance seldom got ahead of them: therefore they were almost out of reach before preparation could be made to pursue them. But we passed in open day —publicly along the highway, and through the towns on the way: we were, in fact, expected, and the people of the country had full time to make arrangements to intercept us—to send to Cerro Gordo, Cuencamé, and other neighboring posts for succor, where it was known that considerable numbers of troops were stationed—or even to the city of Durango itself. And, moreover, their not undertaking to oppose us, could not be for want of will (as the hostility of the country was well known), but for cowardice.

We had not proceeded very far, before we had ample reason to know that our men were not Mexicans, in more ways than fighting: they could neither *lazo* a mule, nor lay a pack upon

[11] The Collins party sent out by Colonel Doniphan to General Wool.

one, so as that would remain much longer than they were about it. After several bungling efforts at the former, they permitted a mule to escape in the *chaparral;* and they tied on the packs so badly that we were detained nearly half our time in readjusting them. We therefore learned, when too late, that we would have made much better speed, had we taken a light wheeled-vehicle, instead of packmules, for our baggage.

33 m.   The following were the approximate courses and distances of today's travel. W. 15° N. 10 m.—West 10 m. to Sulphur Spring. W. 15° S. 5 m. West, 5 m.—W. 20° S. 3 m. to Hacienda de la Florida, containing 3 or 400 souls—and pertaining to Patos.—I. Jacobo Sanchez.—Aguachiquita, 10 m. back—other rancho 3 m. back.

Sat. 10—W. 10° S. 6 or 8 m. to Rancho of Narigua, (of 30 or 40 souls) in gap in small ridge of mountain to left. Yesterday evening my excellent riding horse took sick (colic principally, I believe), and died to-day, at this rancho,—leaving me to mount the first mule I could procure. I had to take to-day, a most shabby little "Shave-tail" mule, which had been hired by the express party as they passed down. But like "the singed cats," it performed much better than it looked. But I finally bought a good little mule of the express, sufficiently strong to carry me to Chihuahua.

21 m.   From Narigua, W. 10 N. 5 m. to point of ridge—thence W.S.W. 8 or 10 m. to Castañuela, where we stopped for the mountain.—We stopped with a Mexican married to an Irish woman, whose father had immigrated to Parras when she was but 12 years old. She spoke the language perfectly—in fact, better than English, and seemed to have adopted all the manners and habits of the Mexicans: however, we were treated with much kindness and attention by her and her husband.

The people of the village of Castañuela were in a state of considerable alarm, as they had received information that a party of Indians (thought to be Comanches), 40 on foot and 1 on horseback, as the account stated, had just killed six arrieros and a gentleman of some standing, at Venadito, and were making their way into the interior. Our landlord, a man of some intelligence, made the humiliating confession, that even 10 Indians could enter that village (of over 200 inhabitants) and do what they pleased with impunity: that the people would shut themselves up in their houses, and not dare resistance for fear of punishment. [MARGINAL NOTE: I observed a somewhat remarkable *lusus natura*[sic], at Castañuela. Filimeno Mendez (brother of the principal man of the place) measured 4 ft. 2 in. high—to knee-cap one foot—crotch or fork 20½ in. Hip 2 feet—heavy built.— Has wife and children, age being about 35 years.]

Sun. 11—W. 10 S. 10 or 12 m. to San José. We came a near route, up the creek of Castañuela, a very rugged road barely passable for horses, the same I had travelled going down. Some 2 m. above the village there is a remarkable dam across the creek —built of massive hewn stone, with the abutments cornered with brick—a work of excellent finish and great cost—which it was difficult to conjecture the intention of: it would have seemed probably intended for manufactures. But ex-Gov. Viesca informed me that it was built some 70 years ago, by the Marqués de Aguayo, at a cost of over $100,000, to dam up the creek for the purpose of collecting water, to irrigate the valley below; but the first freshet filled up the pool with mud (for even in dry weather the stream is muddy), and rendered the dam useless. The dimensions of the dam are as follows: Length 170 to 180 yards, Height about 50 feet—Thickness or width, 16 or 17 feet —8 principal abutments.

From S. José, same course, 5 m. & W. 10° N. 7 m. to Ojuelo —& W. 12° N. 6 m. to Parras.—Thence N. 50° W. 5 m. to S. Lorenzo or Hac. de Abajo. [MARGINAL NOTE: Lat. as taken tonight, 25° 30′ 29″.] This estate belongs to Don Manuel Ivarra[12] and his brother, both of whom were educated at Bards-

[12] Owner of a large hacienda, and friendly towards the American army. See I, 364.

town, Kentucky, and speak very fair English, especially the brother: and possessed of enlightened, liberal, *American* principles, they were anything but popular with Santa Anna and his party. Don Manuel to[ld] me that, as the Indians committed constant depredations upon his property, he had armed his work-hands, etc. yet these were again disarmed by the Mexican government—a noble government, indeed, which would neither protect, nor allow others to protect themselves against the savages. Upon representation afterward, however, to Santa Anna, he had his arms restored again.

This estate contains something like a thousand souls who are all virtually the slaves of the proprietors, for being indebted and bound consequently, they have no alternative left but to labor for them. I was not a little interested, next morning, at observing about 100 of them carrying wheat to the "tread-yard,"—for all the world resembling the operations of ants—a line in continual motion either way, the one empty, the other laden with bundles of wheat.

The principal dwelling of this hacienda is one of the best, largest and most commodious I have seen; besides which there are just being finished, a couple of very neat looking buildings, covered with shingles, in American style—the only ones I have seen thus covered in the interior.

Mon. 12—W. 12° or 15 N. 7 or 8 m. to top of ridge—Back to Parras about E. 35° or 40° S.—From ridge W. 20° N. 18 m. to Pozo [NOTE: Here after I will leave courses and distances for the return, except where travelled different routes.]—Country somewhat hilly: no timber except a little mezquite underbrush, etc. Soil barren—no water. The only water at Pozo a well; but sufficient perhaps to water several thousand men and horses.—Pop. of Pozo 40 or 50 souls. It belongs to Ivarra.

Tues. 13—W. 20° N. 3m. then W. 30° N. say 17 m. to three miles to left of Rancho of San Nicolas. [MARGINAL NOTE: Population of S. Nicolas but about 50.] Six miles from Pozo we came to the border of the dried up lake of Muerto [MARGINAL NOTE: Laguna del Muerto.] (as called here) now nearly all dry. This is one branch of the famous lake Cayman which has figured on maps for the last half century, but a name unknown here. The principal branch of this lake is over 50 miles to the northwestward, and is called Tahualilo. Our camp on southern bank of the southern branch of Rio Nazas—here but an insignificant, now apparently not running.—Though, it is disputed by some Mexicans here, I have been assured by others, that in great freshets, Lago del Muerto has been known to discharge itself by the valley of la Pastora & Alamo Macho, to San Antonio or Anelo river. It seems certain that this is the only natural outlet for the Nazas and Rio Grande (or *Guanaval*, or *Buenavá*, as more currently called by the people): at least from here to the Anelo or Salinas river, there is a continuous valley, into which the streams of Parras, Castañuela, etc. flow. What is very strange, however, is, that, according to all concurrent accounts of the natives of the country, water frequently runs from Nazas into the Guanaval, and Alamo lake, but never in the other direction, i.e., from Guanaval, & Alamo into Nazas river, and lakes Tahualilo and Muerto. But I suppose this must be a mistake: I take it that those who gave me the information, had only never happened to see it running in the other direction.—It rained a slight shower tonight, the first we have had for a great while.

Wed. 14—S.W. nearly 2 m. to deserted rancho of Maigran (belongs to D. Jacobo Sanchez,[13] as also San Sebastian on Nazas.) This is nearly 5 m. S.W. from San Nicolas. [MARGINAL NOTE: I should have noted that we were led this route, 5 to 10 m. out of our way, by a Scotchman named Charley Clark, who took us thus astray with the sole motive, apparently, of selling us some corn, etc. Really, I find a large number of the foreigners settled in the country, of as little faith as Mexicans.] Direction

[13] Owner of large estates, notable ones among which were Hacienda de las Hermanas and Agua Nueva. See I, 270–71.

from here to Tahualilo lake, (according to a ranchero) W. 35°
W.—to Parras E. 15° S. To Pozo same course: to town of Alamo
south; San Lorenzo (on Nazas) W. 10° N.—8 m. to San Juan
(Bautista) south of course to S. Lorenzo. Thence 15 m. to S.
Lorenzo. Stopped to noon. In my hurry in getting off from here
after noon, my writing instruments were stolen by some Mexican. Not recollecting precisely what was in the case (perhaps
memoranda, etc. of importance) I was very much vexed at first.
Capt. Pike was just starting with his escort: I solicited him to
stop while I made some search, well knowing that the presence
of the escort would be of a good deal of importance: but this
he neglected to do—which of course vexed me still more.[14] Now,
on our arrival, Pike & Collins went into the town, and stopped
at the *Administradores* for a good dinner, without taking any
account of the men. When I came up in the rear, I had to attend
to pitching camp, as well in part to provide for dinner. But as
soon as Pike got his "good dinner," he came down in a great
bustle and pushed off the company before they had fairly time
to finish their dinner. So, I found it was nothing to him, to delay
hours, if necessary to gratify his own appetite, but would not stop
a moment for the men, or for me. At Parras, I should also have
noted, Pike left his men in the square, most of them to get drunk,
as they did, while he himself went to the house of one of the
magnates to partake of wines and a "good dinner." It is not
strange then, that, though one of the best tacticians, he should
have become one of the most unpopular officers in his regiment:
too aristocratical to attend to the comfort of his men, while he
thought of little but his own.

From S. Lorenzo, a little north of east to Alamito, 10 or 12 m.
[MARGINAL NOTE: Lat. of Alamito 25° 44′ 5″ from observa-

---

[14] It is not likely that Pike's refusing to give him time enough to find his writing
implements would tend to make Gregg alter the frank comments made earlier in
the diary about Pike. He noted that Pike was "the best disciplinarian and drill officer
of the corps—and stands decidedly 'number one' in point of talent and acquirements.
But Pike is too stiff and aristocratic in his manner to be popular . . ."—I, 219.

tion of Polaris.] Crossed Rio de San Lorenzo four or five miles back from Alamito. This is the southern outlet of Nazas. Pop. of San Lorenzo near 1,000 souls—that of Alamito but little less, at least over 500—Course from Alamo to Tahualilo lake about N. 25 W. distance at least 30 miles. Course of Mapimí, W. 15° N. called 18 *leguas*.

Thurs. 15—Six miles (a little north of course) to crossing of northern branch of Nazas (running to lake Tahualilo), here called Rio de las Víboras. Thence 16 or 18 m. (still a little North of course) to deserted rancho of San Rafael. Thence 10 m. to Vinargríos (or Vinagrillos?) a village of say 200 souls. It was nearly 8 at night before we reached Vinagrillos. On the plain, several miles back, a rain storm (with hail) came upon us, of a pretty copious character. This is the first *real rain* I have witnessed since last August!

After we stopped tonight, we were unexpectedly visited by a committee of three of the citizens of Mapimí, who brought from the *Gefe Politico* (in character of mayor, somewhat) a series of resolutions of the city council, or *ayuntamiento*, of a rather extraordinary character, reading as follows:

"En el Mineral de Mapimí, á las dos de la tarde de dia quince de Abril de mil ocho cientos cuarenta y siete, el Gefe Político de este partido de Norte-Americanos que se encontraba en el punto del Alamito, a diez-y-ocho leguas de esta villa, se dirigia á este lugar; y deseando estorbarle un funesto golpe, ó cuando no, tocar los remedios que la prudencia prescribe pa evitarlo, [se] mandó y suplicó á los vecinos de alguna representacion, tuviesen á bien reunirse en las Casas consistoriales, con el fin indicado; y habiendo ejecutadolo, y hecholes ver las noticias que se tenían, acordaron con unanimidad de votos, las siguientes bases:— 1a Ponerse en la posible defensa todos los vecinos que tuviesen armas, reuniendo al efecto las companías de la Guardia Nacional que hay en la Cabezera:—2a Nombrar una Comision con el objeto de saber del Gefe Norte-Americano, si han de ser respetados las vidas é intereses de los vecinos en general de esta villa: —[3a] En caso que el Gefe Norte-Americano no accede á la base segunda, se obliga todos los habitantes, sin distincion, á tomar las armas para defenderse, tratando al que no lo hiciere, como un enemigo de los Mejicanos:—4ª La Comision será nombrado de tres ciudadanos por la gefetura del partido.—Las que, habiendo sido aprobados generalmente por todos los vecinos, las suscribieron por ante mí, el espresado gefe."[15]

JOAQUIN GONZALEZ,
& 16 OTHERS

This communication could scarcely be viewed in any other light than as an offer to capitulate the town, a place of no little importance, in the state of Durango, containing some 3,000 inhabitants. Only think! a city capitulating to 42 Americans! At the request of the Captain, I wrote a note to the *Gefe Politico*, promising, as had always been our policy and practice entire security of lives and private property.[16]

[15] At the Springs of Mapimí, at two o'clock in the afternoon of the fifteenth day of April, eighteen hundred and forty-seven, the leader of this party of North Americans which was at the place called Alamito, eighteen leagues from this city, started towards this place; and desiring to prevent him from delivering a serious blow, or if that were not possible, to find the means which prudence prescribes to avoid it, the citizens of any importance were ordered and requested to have the kindness to assemble in the Consistorial Buildings, with the aforesaid purpose; having done so, and being made acquainted with the news received, they agreed by unanimous vote on the following measures:—1. All the citizens who might have arms to prepare for defense in every way possible, as a matter of fact mustering the companies of the National Guard which are at la Cabezera:—2. To appoint a Commission with the object of finding out from the North American chief whether or not the lives and property of the generality of citizens of the city are to be respected:—[3.] In case the North American chief does not agree to this second measure, all the inhabitants, without distinction, are required to take arms to defend themselves, any who do not do so to be treated as enemies of the Mexicans:—4. The Commission will consist of three citizens appointed by the officials of the district.—These, having been generally approved by all the inhabitants, were sworn in before me, the aforesaid mayor.

[16] Pike's account of the surrender of Mapimí exists in the unpublished notes toward an autobiographic sketch preserved among the Pike materials in the Library of the Supreme Council, Scottish Rite of Freemasonry, at Washington, D.C. The party was camped some three miles from Mapimí. Collins, Gregg, and Pike were occupying the same room of a house. "All at once about 8 or 9 o'clock," writes Pike, "while we were sitting there, the woman of the house came and told us there were two men from the city, one of whom was the comandante, who wanted to see me. I knew there were troops at Mapimí because 150 had followed Collins when he came down. I told her to show the gentlemen in. Old man Collins, who was as brave as a lion, was sitting on a pack; and Gregg was busy with a whole pack of papers, which he was putting leaves into for pressing and preservation. The gentlemen came in—and they were gentlemen, too, nice looking fellows, and they asked who was the comandante, and were directed to me. They told us they had been

Frid. 16—About three miles to Mapimí. Before reaching the town, we were met by our "Committee of Three," of the night before, and some of the *magnates* of the place. When we had approached in less than half a mile, one of the "magnates" inquired first of a committeeman if information of our approach had been sent to the Gefe Politico, that he might determine whether to receive us in a friendly manner or not. Finding that this did not intimidate us to turn our course from the town, he inquired of me what route we intended going—if by La Cadena or Jaralito: and upon my answering, by the latter, he said we should take a right hand, just ahead of us, as it would save us half a league's distance. I inquired of Capt. Pike what he thought about it: and finally, upon their promising to send us out corn and other provisions, we concluded to take the right hand. We were surprised, however, after skirting the border of the town, to find no road in that direction, and that we had to continue around the border till we intersected the road which passed through the town. It is therefore evident that the only object of the Mexicans was to induce us to pass around the town: perhaps to save themselves the disgrace of so small a party of "the enemy" passing, without opposition, through the public square, or may be, that they might boast that we fled around the town, and the[y] could not catch us! Another cause, however, seemed about as likely. They had showed much severity to American citizens (and even had one in prison at the time), and perhaps

---

deputed to come over to our camp, and they handed me a paper. I handed it to Gregg, and he read it. It was in substance a statement that the people of Mapimí understanding that the advance of the army of Gen. Wool was approaching the town had held a meeting and resolved to surrender the city on the condition that the property and persons in the city be respected. So with a great deal of dignity—all I could muster—I told Gregg to write out a guarantee that the persons and property of all citizens of Mapimí should be duly respected by the advance of Gen. Wool's forces. (I had told all along the route that General Wool's army was coming after us). I kept the papers of the 'surrender' and intended to keep them permanently. I never did know how I lost them. It was a regular formal surrender to 42 men. On our way back we found out that the error had been discovered. The alcalde was arrested and taken to Durango."

feared revenge. In fact, they had been active here, in their demonstrations to take Collins and party: some Americans told us they sent 400 men—this was doubtless exaggeration; yet I suppose they really did send one to two hundred men, in the pursuit: however, *no les pudieron alcanzar*,[17] and returned. Still, a party of about 100 from Rio Nazas did overtake Collin's party; and surrounding them, travelled along on either side for several miles: but would not venture an attack, and so finally left them and returned.—Provisions, etc. having been sent out to us, and a crowd of several hundred citizens, women, children, etc. having visited us, Capt. Pike's command moved on. But Mr. Collins and another of the party desiring to get their horses shod, sent them into town for that purpose, and I stopped with another (four in all) to wait for them. The rascally blacksmith (an American) detained us until between 12 and one o'clock, though Pike's command had left before nine. Being on a hill but a quarter of a mile from the main square, I had a fine view of the place, with its cinder heaps, etc. for it is a mining town of some importance. The animals having finally been returned, we proceeded on, and overtook the command at an abandoned rancho, called Jarolito, [MARGINAL NOTE: Lat. 26° 8′ 17″] encamped,: Courses, etc. W. 40 N. [MARGINAL NOTE: or, according to subsequent observation N. 20° W.] 25 m. thence west 5 m. to Jarolito.

Sat. 17—West (or W. 10° N.) bending to north, 10 m. to Ojo or San José (a tequerquite spring), where stopped to breakfast. Fine bold spring, but unpleasant water: in a flat country.—Temperature of this spring, 69°—Thence W. 20° N. 7 or 8 m. & N.W. 5 mi. Then N. 35° W. 6 m. to Zarca Cr. (dry) & N. 30° W. 7 or 8 m. to Cerro Gordo Cr. or Arroyo de Andabazo—old abandoned rancho of Andabazo (or Andavaso?) on north bank.

Sun. 18—8 or 10 m. to Ojo de San Bernardo, or "Green Spring," as called by our party. Beautiful small spring, breaking out at the point of a romantic hill—altogether a wild pleasant picturesque spot. Temperature of spring 82°. Thence 8 or 10 m. to San Blas or Cottonwood Spring. Old abandoned rancho—house still standing; as also at San Bernardo. Thence 20 to 22 m. & camped without water.

Mon. 19—About 30 m. to Guajuquilla—having had no water for animals from yesterday at noon, till three or 4 miles before reaching Guajuquilla.

Guajuquilla or Jimenes is a clever town of 2 to 3,000 inhabitants (say 2500), on the S.W. bank of Rio Florido. On approaching the town (within half a mile) we met an officer or two (Mexicans) and as many soldiers, and when we arrived in town we were informed by foreigners that there were a considerable number of both Mexican officers and soldiers about the place, remnants of the army of Chihuahua—this is the first settlement we came to in this state. Nevertheless we rode directly to the Prefect's, and demanded quarters, and a supply of provisions and forage for selves and horses—all which was promptly furnished. And though an Englishman who happened here (David Workman) seemed to think we would be attacked before morning, the night passed away altogether quietly.

Tues. 20—Some 28 or 30 m. to Ramada: encamped 10 m. ahead (without water, halfway between Ramada and Santa Rosalía.) Lat. of camp, 27° 35′ 8″.

Wed. 21—Ten miles to Santa Rosalía.

Thurs. 22—20 to 22 m. to San Pablo: thence about 20 m. to Bachimba. Here Capt. Pike gave us another demonstration of his *prudence* and *economy*. At San Pablo, he neglected to procure any provender for men and animals, though we stopped there to noon long enough to provide it, and they had both been on "half rations" or less, the night before. At Bachimba, however, he bought more corn than was needed, and two calves, when one was sufficient, so that both corn and meat remained on the ground, when we left next morning: verifying the old proverb of "Either a feast or a famine.["]

Frid. 23—Started before day this morning, and made the distance to Chihuahua—say 27 m.—by about 3 o'clock, P.M.

By the time we had approached within five miles of the city, we were met by a considerable number of volunteers, friends of those who were with the express—some with horses and mules which they were bringing out to help their friends in, as they had learned that we were nearly all afoot—and all demonstrating the greatest joy (as well they might), at the safe return of their friends.

But this was but a foretaste of what was yet "behind the scene." We were scarcely in the city, and I safely lodged in the Hotel of Messers. Riddells & Stevenson (the principal American house in the place), when a general uproar was heard through the city; and a tavern was crowded "to overflowing"—drinking and carousing "with a perfect vengeance."[18] Such an uproarious hurly-burly — talking, yellolling, screaming — quarreling — fighting—I certainly had never before witnessed. I was in the room of my worthy friend Capt. (Dr.) Waldo;[19] but foreseeing the "up-shot on't" the Dr. requested us to leave the room that he might close, else everything would run a risk of being torn "to the four winds." I retreated with my old friend Dr. Connelly[20] to his store where we shut ourselves up snugly in his backroom, remote from the scene of confusion, and thus secured

[17] They could not catch them.

[18] Gregg's impression of the behavior of Doniphan's Missourians during their sojourn in Chihuahua is corroborated by other accounts. Bored by their inactive life, they were getting dissatisfied and unruly. With the object of finding something for them to do, Colonel Doniphan sent a letter to General Wool by the Collins party, asking instructions. "I am anxious and willing," so Doniphan put it, "to protect the merchants as far as practicable; but I protest against remaining here as a mere wagon-guard, to garrison a city with troops wholly unfitted for it, and who will soon be wholly ruined by improper indulgences."—Letter to General Wool, March 20, 1847.

[19] Dr. David Waldo, a friend of many years' standing. He had become a captain in the battalion which Colonel Doniphan had formed out of three hundred traders and their teamsters with the expedition into Mexico.

[20] Dr. Henry Connelly was a Missourian who engaged in the Santa Fé trade as early as 1824. For some twenty years thereafter he was a merchant in Chihuahua, but after the Mexican War he removed to New Mexico, making his home at a

a quiet evening. Fortunately nobody was killed, or even seriously injured; for even the fighting seemed "in fun."

These Missourians are certainly a brave and gallant, but nevertheless rather ungovernable and disorderly set of fellows. The battles they have fought prove the former, if not the latter. As fuller accounts may be obtained from official reports, and the letters of persons present, I shall not enter at this time into any detailed history of the conquest of Chihuahua. Nevertheless I will insert a few notes which occur to me.[21]

The battle of Brazito was fought on Christmas day (I think), 1846, about 40 miles above Paso del Norte (on east side of Rio del Norte) between the advance of Col. Donophan's Command —about 500—and some 1100 Mexicans. The latter, though they were the attackers, retreated in disorder, after a few fires, with a loss, I believe of 8 or 10, while the Americans lost none. The command then proceeded forward, and took possession of Paso del Norte without further opposition—where it remained until early in February, when the march toward Chihuahua was undertaken.

The Mexicans, for two or three weeks previous to the arrival of the Americans (if not longer), had been fortifying a rough and difficult pass at the crossing of a creek, near an old abandoned village called *El Sacramento*. The Mexicans were said to be near four thousand strong [MARGINAL NOTE: See note 7 at close of this M.S.[22]], over half of whom were regulars, while the American force was less than 1000 efficient men, and all volunteers. Nevertheless this great disparity of force had the almost unheard of bravery—if not temerity—to attack the enemy in their en-

ranch near Peralta and engaging in business activities in Santa Fé, Las Vegas, Albuquerque, and Peralta. In 1861, President Lincoln appointed him governor of the territory of New Mexico, an office he filled with distinction until his death in July, 1866.

[21] Gregg's notes on Doniphan's campaign are regrettably brief and matter-of-fact. To offset this quality a few parallels from other writers are included in the footnotes.

[22] Page 130.

trenchments (which were decidedly strong, being on a series of commanding hills. In addition, they had 10 cannon, fours, sixes and eights, besides four *esmeriles* or musquetoons, while ours had but four (I believe), fours and sixes, and perhaps, in addition a very small howitzer. The defence was opened in a sharp and active manner, by the enemy, which seemed to render the result doubtful; but our artillery had played upon them but a few minutes—which it did with extraordinary effect—when began to abandon their entrenchments. It was nearly an hour, however, before the rout became general; and the pursuit was kept up by our cavalry until night,—say some five hours; for the attack commenced, I think about one, P.M. The number of killed, on the part of the enemy was said to be about 150, with about an equal number of wounded. On the part of the Americans, there was but one man killed on the ground, Maj. (late Col.) S. C. Owens,[23] of Independence, Mo. He had been elected Major of Corps of temporarily organized troops of the wagoners. The act which occasioned his death was certainly desperate if not willful temerity—some have even denominated it suicide. He started to charge a redoubt with Capt. Reid's Cavalry,[24] but the latter being recalled, he proceeded with but one or two others,— and charged up to the very border of the Redoubt (within 30 feet or such matter, as I am assured) where he stopped and fired his pistols, etc. at the enemy, until he was shot first through the knee, which brought both him and horse down (as the same ball passed through the latter), and afterward in the head. Besides Col. Owens, there was a soldier mortally wounded who died soon after, and another that died at the expiration of near a month—from carelessness of surgeons as some assert. The rest of the wounded, hardly a dozen, recovered.

[23] Samuel Combs Owens, merchant and Santa Fé trader, was another who was with Doniphan's organization. He had become major of the traders' battalion and had been killed in the battle of Sacramanto. When Gregg left for Santa Fé in spring of 1846, he had shipped his equipment in the wagon train of Owens.

[24] John W. Reid, captain, Company D, First Regiment, Missouri Mounted Volunteers.

Although fortune accords to Col. Donophan the principal credit, on account of his being the chief in command, there were many subordinate officers, who certainly merited much more.[25] Those who deserve most credit appear to have been Capt. Weightman[26] of the artillery, Lieut. Chouteau[27] of same and Capt. Reid of cavalry. The conduct of Capts. Hudson,[28] Waldo, and many others, was meritorious. As to Col. Donophan, he was doubtless brave and valiant, but as he enforced no subordination, and attended very little to the duties of a Commander, but little more agency could he have had in the sweep of the attack, than any other individual. The truth is, the battle seems to have been fought in Indian style of every man "on his own hook"—an impetuous, helter-skelter charge, which bore down everything before it. Had they met with a reverse, occasioning a necessity to fall back, the fate of the day would have been critical.

The Battleground, Sacramento, is some 20 miles northward from Chihuahua. The battle was fought on 28th Feb. and, on the 2d of March (I think) they took possession of the city. The routed forces of the enemy continued on southward immediately, though the larger portion was wholly dispersed. It was under command of Gen. Heredia, Gen. Garcia Conde, Gov. Trias[29] (Don Angel), and several colonels. Gov. Trias rallied a few men at Parral about 150 m. southward from Chihuahua, where he established his government for awhile; but upon Col.[30] Dono-

[25] Gregg's frankness about giving credit to subordinate officers for the success of the expedition comes probably too late to stem the acclaim that has been bestowed upon Colonel Doniphan.

[26] Richard Hanson Weightman, captain of Company A, Light Artillery Battalion, Missouri Volunteers.

[27] Edmond F. Chouteau, a first lieutenant in Captain Weightman's company.

[28] Thomas B. Hudson, captain of the "Laclede Rangers"; i.e., Company E, First Regiment, Missouri Mounted Volunteers.

[29] Don Angel Trias, governor of Chihuahua, who, as brigadier general commanding the Chihuahua volunteers, had taken part in the battle of Sacramento.

[30] Following the word "Col." Gregg wrote the topic, "Ragged and savage appearance of the Missouri Volunteers." Evidently he intended to enlarge upon the matter, but never did.

phan's starting in that direction about the first of April, Trias fled southward, and did not stop, I believe, short of the city of Mexico. On this occasion Donophan, with one batallion proceeded no further than San Pablo, whence he returned to Chihuahua, on account of a report that a large Mexican force was on its way up from Durango, etc.

Col. Donophan seemed in a "great sweat" at being ordered southward—desirous, as I understood it, to proceed directly across the plains to the U.S. [MARGINAL NOTE: I have since been greatly surprised to see from his official communication to Gen. Wool, that he solicited to be ordered south to Saltillo, etc. or at least to join Gen. W.] Therefore, on account of his chagrin, he determined to set out immediately; and so, the morning after our arrival, he issued his order for his command to march on the next day, the 25th. The advance—first batallion under Lieut. Col. Jackson,[31] did march on the 26th, but, Col. Donophan was finally prevailed upon to suspend the march of the other batallion (under Maj. Gilpin[32]) to the morning of the 28th, to afford a little more time to the merchants, to prepare for this precipitate breaking up.[33]

Col. Donophan's dispositions, in this regard were certainly hasty and ill-advised, if not altogether culpable. One of the motives of Gen. Wool as well as Gen. Taylor, in ordering his command to Saltillo, was to afford protection to the merchants—an escort into safety—should they desire to bring their effects southward. But the Colonel's precipitate move prevented them, almost absolutely from profiting by it. Some were without wagons and trains, and all unprepared to move with such short notice; but

[31] Congreve Jackson, at first captain of Company H, Howard County recruits in the First Regiment, Missouri Mounted Volunteers; later lieutenant colonel.

[32] William Gilpin was highly prominent in the development of the West. He was a graduate of West Point, but after serving in the Florida Indian War he resigned from the army, mainly because he was not allowed to lead an exploring expedition to the Columbia River. When the Mexican War came on, he was located at Independence, Missouri, and at once became an active participant. He was defeated by Doniphan for the colonelcy of the Missouri Volunteers, but contented himself with the office of major.

within a week or 10 days most of them might have been ready. As it was, many were compelled to remain, and ran the risk of losing their effects as well as their lives, while others made great sacrifices to leave and to dispose of their goods.

In the first place, it appears superlatively strange, that this command should have been ordered home by this route, thus doubling the distance and the expense: the extra expense etc. of getting them home via Saltillo & Matamoros, would doubtless have been sufficient to have paid for all the property saved by it —that is, artillery, outfit of wagons, etc. which were turned [out] of the Q.M. department at Saltillo & elsewhere. Then it cost much fatigue and many lives, for doubtless over a dozen men more died on this route, than would have died direct across the plains. Again, if they had been left to go home by the Prairies, they might still have remained another month in Chihuahua, which would have been of great importance to our merchants: but verily, it seems very much as though our government thought less of protecting our commerce than anything else.

While at Chihuahua I made an observation for latitude, by North Star, [MARGINAL NOTE: It being most convenient—not requiring to wait for meridian passage—I took everyone of my latitudes during my trip to Chihuahua, and thence to Mata-

[33] Gregg never forgot that he was a Santa Fé trader; he was therefore naturally critical of Colonel Doniphan for abruptly ordering this group to leave Chihuahua. The circumstances provoked comment from Dr. Wislizenus:

"But in due time Mr. Collins made his appearance. In about 30 days he had travelled with a mere handful of men, about 1,000 miles through a hostile country, with no other passports but their rifle. In going out, his party consisted of but 12 men; on his return it was increased to about 40. The gallant Squire was received in Chihuahua with enthusiastic joy. He brought us definite orders from General Wool to march at once, and on the most direct road to to Saltillo. Within two days our troops were on the march. Colonel Doniphan, before he left, called the Mexican authorities of the place and made them promise to treat the American residents of Chihuahua in a decent manner, and threatened them, in case of disorder, with a return of the American troops and a severe chastisement. The Mexicans promised everything. Many Americans and other foreign residents, however, had so little confidence in Mexican faith, that they preferred to accompany the army."—*Memoir of a Tour to Northern Mexico, Connected with Col. Doniphan's Expedition in 1846 and 1847* (U. S. 30 Cong., 1 sess., Senate Misc. Doc. No. 26), 61.

moros, by observations of *Polaris*.] and was surprised to find it some two miles further north, than I had before made it. In fact, I fear, the disadjustment of my sextant from carrying it on a mule, may have occasioned too great an angle; though at most I would suppose of half minute to one minute; which would, of course, have made but a quarter to half minute in latitude, so that the latitude must be at least 28° 30′, instead of 28° 36′ as I had formerly made it. My observation on April 24, 1847, resulted in 28° 38′ 30″ N. latitude.—I also made three observations by lunar distances—sun, Venus & Jupiter—the most reliable of which, Jupiter, made the longitude about 7 h. 6 m. in time (west from Greenwich), which is 106° 30′: the others, made it 15′ or 20′ greater. This (even the first) is about a degree greater than I had before *supposed* it. But, if it be true that my sextant gave a minute too great an angle this would account for ½° too great longitude, as every minute in angle is about 30′ of longitude.

I also made two observations with the barometer, [MARGINAL NOTE: I had sent my Barometer direct from Missouri to Chihuahua, with other baggage.] in Chihuahua, which stood as follows:

April 25, 1847—2½ o'clock, P.M.—½ cloudy—light shower night previous—

Barometer, mercury stood at	25.48 inches
Thermometer (Fahr.) in Atmosphere	74°
Thermometer " in Mercury	74¼°

April 27, 1847—9½ o'clock, A.M.—Half cloudy:

Barometer stood at	25.5 inches
Thermometer, in atmosphere	72°
" in Mercury	73½°

The principal object of my trip to Chihuahua, was to get my baggage, books, instruments, etc. which I had sent across from Missouri to Chihuahua, by Col. S. C. Owens and James Aull, Esqr. These I found all safe and in good condition.[34]

[34] The baggage Gregg refers to is catalogued in I, 199–200.

Wed. 28—On the morning of the 26th inst. Col. (Lieut.) Jackson, with first batallion of Missouri volunteers, and all the artillery, marched in the direction of Saltillo, with orders to wait for the rear on the way. This morning Col. Donophan, with 2^d batallion, under Maj. Gilpin took up the line of march, leaving a number of American merchants, with much the larger portion of the merchandise that had been taken to Chihuahua this year, subject to being seized by the Mexicans; to say nothing of the danger to the lives of the remaining merchants, viz. Messers. Aull, Connelly, Glasgow, McMannus, and others.[35] It will certainly be a remarkable circumstance if these goods be not seized, as they are a lawful prize, having been taken in, in contravention to their laws—and it is well known that Mexicans are not scrupulous about seizing even unlawfully. Nothing but fear of future retribution could prevent them for taking them.

To-day Col. Donophan marched about 35 miles (to Bachimba), which, to say the least of it, indicated but little prudence, or knowledge of travelling; for he thus at the very start gave his unaccustomed animals a backset from which they never fully recovered. Though, from the unaccommodating spirit which he displayed, then, and at all times afterward, toward the merchants, I am disposed to believe that he did it more to distress them than anything else. And it did distress them, so that nearly all— Magoffin, Messervy, East, etc. had to encamp at Ojito 8 m. back, at which place they arrived even after night. I had joined with East, Anderson and Fristoe[36] to the last of whom the wagon

[35] These men were all noted Santa Fé traders. James Aull was a partner of Samuel C. Owens. After the latter's death he was in charge of their goods, and elected to remain in Chihuahua when Doniphan departed. A few weeks afterward he was murdered in his store and the place looted. Dr. Henry Connelly, long a merchant in Chihuahua, and Edward J. Glasgow were in partnership at this time. Little is known of McMannus beyond the fact that he was of the trader group.

[36] The only one in this group about whom there is information available is Alfonso C. Anderson. He was a Santa Fé trader who, in 1847, was merely a merchant in Chihuahua, so well thought of that he was permitted to remain in the city when the American merchants were deported to Casuhuiriachi. When he returned after the exodus with Doniphan's regiment, Anderson became vice-commercial agent for the United States. The others of these associates were Santa Fé traders

belonged which hauled my baggage, etc. Our mess consisted of Dr. George East, Alphonso C. Anderson[,] John Fristoe and myself.

From Chihuahua S. 40° E. 3 m. to hills—thence E. 40° S. near 10 m. to hills west of Mápula Cr. thence turning more south about a mile to Arroyo de Majuila. Thence to entrance to Cañon of Ojito say 11 or 12 m. whence back to Chihuahua, W. 43° N.—thence two or three miles, nearly east or E. 10° N. to Ojito—whole distance from Chihuahua, about 27 m.—

Ojito is a small rancho of but one family (I believe) who certainly run much risk in residing here, as the Indians (Comanches & Apaches) make many inroads in this quarter. But a short time previous they waylaid the road and killed five or six Mexicans not a mile east of this rancho.—Army encamped at Bachimba—i.e. Col. Donophan & 2d Batallion. [MARGINAL NOTE: Lat. of Bachimba, 28° 26′.]

Thurs. 29—Nearly east 2 or 3 m. or E. 5° S. thence to Bachimba E. 30 S—whole distance say 8 m.—Thence to San Pablo S. 30° or 35° E. 20 m. Bachimba an hacienda containing a few families—say 20 to 50 souls. Lat. according to observation on night of April 22, 1847, of Polaris, 28° 25′ 58″—San Pablo, situated on northern bank of San Pedro river (a branch of Rio Conchos) contains a population, I suppose of nearly 2000 souls. Old abandoned *rancho* about 5 m. back from San Pablo.

Course down Conchos from San Pablo (or rather, the mouth of San Pedro) is about N. 25° W. up Rio San Pedro, about S. 40° W. Santa Cruz 2 *leguas*, up, on same side of river—a little smaller than San Pablo. Julimer is situated on east or opposite side of Conchos, just below mouth of S. Pedro. Pop. said to be 500 to 1000—Army came by Santa Cruz, where encamped.

Frid. 30—S. 25° E. 4 m. (Rancho del Ojo 2 m. from San Pablo)—S. 40° E. 14 or 15 m. and E. 30° S. 2 to 4 m. to Saucillo.

---

and presumably of prominence. Gregg was on terms of acquaintance, and even intimacy, with some of the outstanding and reputable men among the trader group.

General course S. 40° E. & whole distance about 22 m. or 23 m. [MARGINAL NOTE: Lat. of Saucillo 28° 2'. Long. 105° 38¼'.]

Latitude of Saucillo, as taken on night of Apr. 21/47 is 28° 2' 3"—Longitude by moon and Jupiter, 7 h. 2 m. 33 s. in time— and in arc, 105° 38' 15".—This was formerly a rancho and wholly depopulated, on account of Indian depredations, about the year 1835; but since I last passed there in 1838,[37] a mine has been discovered in its vicinity, and it has now grown to be a village of 2 or 300 souls. The mine is in the mountains some 10 or 12 miles to the westward. It produces a mixed metal of lead and silver—each mule load of the ores, say 300 to 400 pounds, produces 40 to 50 pounds of the mixt metal, and this about one per cent. of silver.—From Saucillo, there is a pathway leading across through the wilderness eastward, to Laguna de Jaco, [MARGINAL NOTE: This road passes along the southern border of Laguna de Jaco.] the watering place of San Antonio de los Alamos, and thence to the town of Santa Catarina and Cieñegas (or Cuatro Cieñegas) to Monclova; but it is almost impassable during the dry season, for want of water. Collins and his party started that way, but not finding the water (spring in the mountain) near Laguna de Jaco, they returned to Saucillo and proceeded thence via Mapimí, etc.—The Army camped to-night near the old abandoned rancho of Conchos, three or four miles above Saucillo.

❁ DIARY, MAY, 1847

Sat. 1.—S. 40° E. say 14 or 15 m. to La Cruz del Refugio,— Pop. 500 to 1000.—Road leaves river two or 3 m. also above La Cruz.—Thence 4 m. S. 10° E. to Las Garzas—pop. say 100 to 200—where crosses Rio Conchos. Thence to Rancho of Corra-

[37] The reference is to a visit made during the years when Gregg was active as a Santa Fé trader, although no mention of Saucillo appears in *Commerce of the Prairies*. Very likely the visit was made when he went into the interior as far as Aguascalientes.

109

leño ½ m.—Thence S. 15° E. 10 m. to Santa Rosalía [Margin-
al Note: Here we overtook the advance under Col. Jackson.
And hence Lieut. Col. Mitchell and Capts. Reid & Pike were
sent in advance with about 100 men.]—whence up Conchos, S.
35° W. Rancho de los Flores over half way down to Garzas.

The population of Santa Rosalia, is said to be over or about
2000 souls. Here Gov. Trias determined, as seems, to prepare
to meet Gen. Wool, when he was expected to proceed to Chihuahua, last year. He therefore built a fort and otherwise fortified the place by ditching around it, etc. Yet, it seemed evidently
intended rather to shut up and defend the lives of the troops,
than to defend the pass; for artillery and even heavy wagons
might have passed around at the distance of some two miles on
either side and proceeded to Chihuahua, without the necessity
of taking the fort. The doughty governor had about as well shut
his troops up in Durango, as to all the good they would have
done here toward defending the pass.

Santa Rosalia is located on south bank of Rio Florido about
a mile from Rio Conchos. On the west side of latter river there
is a warm sulphur spring[38] (& village called Ojo Caliente) said
to possess important sanative virtues by bathing in it. In fact,
there are three springs near together (with about 100 yds.)
Temperature of upper and principal spring 103½° (Fahr.)—
Lower spring 108°—middle spr. about same as upper. Course
of spring from Santa Rosalía about W. 30° S. 2 m. [Marginal
Note: 27° 35'.]

Sun. 2—S.E. 2 or 3 m. to Rio del Parral—thence same course
to La Ramada—whole distance 20 to 21 m. Took lat. as we passed

---

[38] In connection with the sulphur spring, the remarks of Dr. Adolph Wislizenus
may be quoted: "Near the river [the Conchos] in this direction some sulphur springs
are found, which are resorted to by the Mexicans for cutaneous and other diseases.
I was not at leisure to visit them, but Dr. Gregg, who made an excursion there, informed me that the temperature of the different springs had been from 105 to 108°
Fah., while the atmosphere was 85° Fah. Sediments of pure precipitated sulphur
are found at the bottom of the springs."—*Memoir of a Tour to Northern Mexico*
(U.S. 30 Cong., 1 sess., Senate Misc. Doc. No. 26).

Josiah Gregg's Medicines

mentioned in I, 200 n.

and II, 106 n.

Josiah Gregg's medicines opened at Chihuahua

1304	100	1	Mat Cinnamon		
252	38	1	Gro. Print Corks	150	
2	18	2	H Starch	150	
60	15	1 "	Uva Ursi	4	
75	20	1 "	Grd. Bayberry		
50	30	1/2 "	Turpeth Root	4	
	20	2 "	Sal Nitre	1	
40	32	2 "	Sup. Carb. Soda	141.91	✓
120	150	1 "	Red Bark		
110	110	2 "	Tart. Acid	141.91	
25	30	2 "	Arsenic	2	
	33	1 "	Windsor Soap	150	
220	125	1 "	Ipecac		
125	31	4 oz	Granulated Jinpo		
100			For Glove		
25	6	1/4 lb	Ext. Loguana	2	
25		1 "	Precip Chalk	2	
200	44	1/4 "	Red Precip	4	
25	5	1/4 "	" Chalk	2	
25	8	1 "	" Lead		
250	25	1/4 "	Prus Blue		
100	25	1/4 "	Ergot		
100	10	1/4 "	Spermaceti		
Soda 10		1/4 "	Tart. Emetic		1.
200	19	1/4 "	Kino	8	
400	44	1/4 "	Gamboge		
40 Dol 13		1/2 "	Sugar lead	103.25 7 031 81	1.25
80 Duty		1/2 "	Pulv. Galls	4	2
Soda		1 "	Manna		4.
75	6	1/2 "	Nux Vomica		
80	6	1/4 "	Valerian	3	
4 oz 100		2 "	Gum Arabic		6.
280	35	1/4 "	Cantharides	5	

4 | 31

odaz	3 tt W. Castile Soap				
117	11¼ " Zinc	.50			
19	2 oz. Flor Zinc	1.			
6	¼ ℔. Calamine	4.			
4	¼ " Flor Emery	2.			
6	2 Pots Ext. Cology ℔ Camp.	2			
160	1 doz Lees Pills	½ doz $1⁰⁰			
Ocean	1–16 oz. Syringe			5	–
Sved 30	½ ℔. Pat. Lint			1	50
Fred 30	1 " Hops			2	–
21	5 " Saleratus	1.00			
old 31	1 " Flex. Senna			4	–
7	3 " Arrow Root	3 –			
21	2 oz Cochineal	.75			
6	¼ ℔ Blue Vitriol	2.			
old 63	½ " Dovers Powders			3	–
90	3 " Sal Rochelle	2. 1½.#2.			
300	5 " White Wax	3.			
10	¼ " Guaiacum	4			
27	¼ " Cor. Sub.	6			
120	2 oz. Saffron	6.50			
300	1 doz Saratoga Powders				
200	1 " Seidlitz	"			
	1 " Yeast	" 50			
Ocean	1 " Ginger Beer	"		5	–
	3 ℔. Ber. Mustard Seed			.	
Dozy	3 Gro Vial Corks	1.		2	21
	1 doz. Soda Cordials				
oda	2 ℔ Sarsaparilla			6	–
30	1 " Pink Root	4			
120	11 " Blk Pepper				
75	4 " Alspice	1			
27	4 " Am. Vermillion	4			

J Gregg Continued

Dra	70	2 lb Cloves	2	
90	140 140	2 " Rhubarb Root	4	
7	40	5 " Flor. Sulphur	1 lb $1. 1st $75	
75	35	1 " Rad. Senica	4	
75	30	1 " Vir. Snake Root	4	
25	20	1 " Rad. Gentian	2	
Dra	124	1 Bot. Spts. Lavender 3.12/13	8	08
Dra	81	1 " aq. Ammonia fort 3. 4/13		8.
Dra	26	2 " Chloride Lime		8
Dra	98	1 " Sweet Spts. Nitre 6.12/2 6		13.
Dra	244	1 " Laudanum 6/2 6		18
Dra	30	1 lb Cam. Flowers		2
Dra	251	1 Bottle Paragoric 6.13/2 3		18.
Dra	47	1 " Spts. Turpentine		4.
80 Dra	147	1 " Sul. Ether 5.13/2 3		6
	47	1 " Linseed Oil Spts. 4—		4
Dra	194	1 " Cal. Magnesia 3.15/1 11		9

Boy	150	11 Bottles Castor Oil	56	
246 Dra 50		2 " Sweet Oil		4.
Dra	400	10 " Sy. Sarsaparilla		20.
225	540	3 " Hydrarg Sub. Vire, Eng 4—		
	484	1 " " Destillat (4 lb 1st 70)		
Dra	44	1 " Wine of Colchicum		4.—
Dra	42	1 " Hive Syrup		5:
Dra	224	2 " Pil. Hydrarg		10.
Dra	175	4 " Lemon Syrup		9.—
Dra	70	1 " Powd Cubebs 2 3/12		. 5.
	57	1 " Carb. Ammonia 2. 2/1 4 4.		
75	25	1 " Rose Water 2—3.		
100 lb	70	1 " Lobelia 4 lb 4.		
Dra	89	1 " Ant. Wine 3/3		6
Dra	42	1 " Barb. Tar 3 0/1. 10		4.

	74	1 Bottl Tinct Digitalis	3.1/2 4.		
	80	1 " Soap Liniment	3.1/2 3		6
Doce	101	1 Jar Broz. Ointmut	3.3/4		
	87	1 " Tamers Cuate	2. 2/4 4.		
	40	1 " Tamarinds (Broken)			4 -
Doce	81	1 " Wine of Iron			4
Dol"	109	1 " Tempte Cuate	3		
	25	1 doz Eye water	4.30		
48	48	3 lb Aloes	2. 1lb/2		
	30	2 " Squills	4.		
	165	1 " Nutmegs	5.		
	45	1 " Myrrh	4. 1/8 50		
	10	1 " Red Columbia	4.		
Doce	70	2 " Pulv. Rhubarb			8. -
	34	2 " Madder	2.		
	4	2 " Rosen	1.		
Doce	24	2 " Pix Burgundy			6. -
10	10	2 " Alum	1. 1/2lb 50		
	70	2 " Carb. Magnesia	4.		
	243	1/2 " Chi Vermillion	4.		
	11	2 " Camphor	2		
	130	3/2 " Asafoetida	1.30		
Doce	63	1/2 " fine Sponge			1. 50
	88	1/4 " Scammony	16.		
	13	1/2 " Verdigris	2.		
Doce	4	1 " Opium			.16
	35	1 " Gum Tragacanth	4.		
Doce	34	2 " Crem Tartar			4. -
Doce		1 " Skice Coparia			6
	14	1 " Best Glue	2.		
	2	1 " Chalk	1.		
	16	2 " Precip. Chalk			
	45	5 " White Lead	100		

50

J. Gregg   continued

25	20	2 ℔ Rad. Ginger	1.		
Sold 25	2	" Grd. Ginger			2
" Bread 80	1	" Jalap			4
100	40	2 doz. Court Plaster	2.		
21	30	1 " Lamp Black	3.00		
	25	½ " Oil Spike	3.00		
150	8	1 " Oppodeldoc	3.00		
75	38	1 " British Oil	3.00		
100	125	1 " Liquid Oppodeldoc	3.00		
40	38	1 " Batemans Drops	3-		
	50	1 " Esp. Cinnamon	3-		
100	75	2 " " Peppermint	2		
Sold 100		1 " Pure Lemon Acid			6 -
	150	½ " Rouspells Shaving Cream			
300	63	½ " Fem. Syringes	500		
Sold 25		1 — Sin Spatula			1
	100	1 Set Weights			
	175	1 pr Scales			
250	80	1 Mortar & Pestle	5		
50 Dols 50		1 Gro. Bottle corks	2		
	25	2 Nests Crucibles	100		
	150	Platina Wire	3-		
75	38	½ oz. Ext. Hyosciamus	2		
75	38	½ " " Blk. Hellebore	2		
75	38	½ " " Aconite	2		
75	23	½ " " Strammonium	2		
75	58	½ " " Belladonna			
75	156	4 " " Quassiae	4		
Sold 250		1 Case Cupping Instruments			25
		1 can carp. Compound Fluid Ext. Sarsaparilla	3		
Sold 175		Jar Balsam Coparia 4 ℔ 8 oz			12
150 ℔ 297		1 " Merc. Ointment	5		

Box 112	1	Stomach Pump	5		
	102	1 Set Scales Apothecaries	4		
veal	1				
	11	1 Vial Croton Oil	2		
	15	1 " Oil Anisi	1.50		
	12	1 " Bergles	1.50		
	12	1 " Oil Juniper	1.50		
Dole 19		1 " Lunar Caustic		1	
Dole 12		1 " Fowlers Solution		2	
	43	1 " Oil Wormwood	2		
	15	1 " " Amber	1.50		
	13	1 " Acetate Zinc	1.50		
	50	1 " Pure Tannin 1oz	2		
	15	1 " Oil Savin 2	2		
Dole 13.25		5 oz. Sulph. Quinine		50	
solu		11 Bottles Cologne			
		1 " Carb. Soda	1		
	25	1 " Nitric Acid	4		
		1 " Oin Turpentine	3		
solu		1 " Mur. Acid		5	
		1 " Chlor. Potassa	3		
veal		1 Jar Merc. Ointment	5.5 2.5		
		1 " Ungt. Rose	5		
	20	1 " Sulph. Ferri			
	54	1 " 2oz. Cyanuret Potassa	2		
	11	14 Bt. Hypo. Sulph. Soda	3		
Dole 23		1 " Liquorice		2	
	14	1/2 " Sulph. Zinc	2		2
	50	1/2 " Isinglass	4		
	56	1 " Solable Tartar	4		
	62	6 Male Catheter	80¢		
	62	6 Set Catheters Bougie			
	19	1 " Bladders			

J. Gregg Continued

20	34	3 paper Pill Boxes	50¢
25	48	3 " "	50
	100	1 doz. Tooth Brushes	
	40	1 Lot Vaccine Matter	58
75¢	15	15 Paper Tea	
144	{ 1 Large Jar	100
	5 Smaller Jars	75
88	4 Small "	50
	1 Vial Phosphorus	
80	3/4 doz. Cologne (4 Bott.)	
25	1 Pill Tile	1 —
75	1 Flex. Male Catheter	3 —
124	1 Bot. Oly. Vitriol 2 N 2 oz	4.
145	1 Keg Ep. Salts	30
40	1 Bottle Oil Vitriol	4. —
90 442	1 Keg Alchohol S p Salts	
	1 Gro. Meal	12 —
350	1 " "	12.
25	1 doz Cayenne Pepper	3 4-50
50	1/2 " Oil Cloves	450
50	1/2 " Cinnamon	450
35	1 Vial Kreosote	
225	2 " Hydro Potass	250
44	3 " Indelible Ink	
250	2 " Solide Iron	250
125	1 " " Merc	250
375	3 " Iodine	250
140	2 " Morphine	
140	2 " Sulph Morphine	
100	1 " Strychnine	
125	1 " Varatrine	
40	1 doz. Male Syringes	
75	1 Spirit Lamp	

up half way from Ramada to Santa Rosalia and resulted 27°35′ 8″. Army camped (mostly) a mile above Rancho of Villela still, say 2 m. above. Ramada near west bank of Rio Florido (½ m. from river) contains some 3 to 5,00 souls—Hacienda.—Here the proprietor, gave a dinner to Col. Donophan, and staff; and I much regretted even without such friendly treatment, to learn that he permitted the horses to be turned on the wheat fields, doing much damage; the men tore down (as I was told) a batting machine and other parts of a mill near their camp, for fuel! —It rained a heavy shower, this evening.

Mon. 3—S. 10° E. 15 or 16 m. to Rancho of Saucillo (perhaps 2 m. west of Rio Florido. (Passed rancho of Villela 2 or 3 m. above Ramada off of road near west bank of river).—From Saucillo, south 10 m. thence S. 20° W. 3 or 4 m. to Guajuquilla. —General course from Ramada to Guajuquilla, about N. 5° ″. —But two or three days before our arrival, the Comanches paid "a flying visit" to Saucillo—drove all the stock (horses, etc.) which could be found, and continued their campaigns into the interior of the country, there to commit with impunity, further depredations. At Saucillo, the rancheros, to save their own lives, turned the stock out to the Indians, with which they were satisfied and went their way.

Guajuquilla (or Jimenez) [MARGINAL NOTE: About the year 1835 (I think it was) the state of Chihuahua, as well as some others, got into a great fever of changing names of places— thus, Parral was christened *Hidalgo,*—Valle, *Allende,*—Saltillo, *Leona Vicaria*, etc.] is on S. W. bank of Rio Florido—pop. said to be about 2500. [MARGINAL NOTE: Lat. of Guajuquilla 27° 7-¾′. Longitude 105° 15-¾′.]

As we passed up, I took the latitude of this place, April 19, 1847, and found it, 27° 7′ 43″. I also made an observation for longitude—moon & Venus,—& made it, in time 7 h. 1 m. 3 s. or in arc, 105° 15′ 45″—but doubtless a few miles too far west.

From Guajuquilla it is called 14 *leguas* to Ramada—to Hac.

of Rio Florido 12 *leguas*—To Valle de San Bartolomé, 14 l. To Parral 21 or 22 l.—From Chihuahua to Guajuquilla and Parral, said to be same, 72 leguas, *measured.*

Tues. 4—S. 25° W. 4 m. to Hac. de Dolores: Rancho of Presidio Viejo half way from Guajuquilla. Course up river from Dolores, S. 40° W.—Thence S. 30° E. 1 m. to *Acequia*[39] of water. Thence, say, 17 m. and camped without water.

Wed. 5—6 m. this morning to dividing ridge—whence course to Guajuquilla N. 30° W.—Thence S. 35° E. 10 m. & S. 30 E. 12 m. to a filthy watering place called San Antonio. Water being insupportably bad, continued on to Green Spring, or Ojo de San Bernardo.—From S. Antonio—S. 15° W. 3 m. to small spring of San Blas—thence S. 15° E. 6 or 7 m. thence S. 10° W. 2 m. to San Bernardo. [MARGINAL NOTE: Barometer at San Bernardo, May 6/47—11 o'clock, A.M.—Nearly clear—wind south:

Barometer	25.5 in.
Thermr in atmosphere	85°
" in mercury	84°
Temperature of springs (in Apr.)	82°]

Thurs. 6—S. 12° or 15° E. 9 or 10 m. to Andavazo or Cerro Gordo Cr. [MARGINAL NOTE: Lat. of Andavazo 26° 22'.] Old abandoned *rancho* of Andabazo on N. side. Course down creek east—up, west. Latitude as taken on 17th April, 1847, is 26° 22' 3"[.]

Frid. 7—S. 35° E. 7 or 8 m. to Zarca Cr. (dry)—course up W. 25° S.—Down E. 35° N.—whole distance to Pelayo, S. 35" E. 25 to 28 m. Col. Mitchell having learned that there were Mexican troops at Pelayo, took it on his way (leaving Jarolito to east) and took the few that were there; though it is said there were but about 15 soldiers at the fort at the time. I believe these were released upon parole. The few citizens who lived there, mostly took fright and fled to Mapimí; so that we found the place nearly depopulated.

[39] Irrigation ditch.

Made observation for latitude of Pelayo, [MARGINAL NOTE: Lat. of Pelayo, 26° 4–¾′] which is the first I took since I left Chihuahua, having been hindered by cloudy weather, except at S. Bernardo & the night before that, when, besides being much fatigued, I did not consider it of importance. Lat. 26° 4′ 42″.— Temperature of principal spring at Pelayo, 94° with atmosphere 80°.

San José de Pelayo is an old frontier military post;[40] but I am told that most of the fort (particularly under the hill) was built but last year, as a defense against Gen. Wool's army. But an isolated hill (of hardly an acre surface) commands the place, being at its immediate border, upon which a sort of fortification (of many years standing) has been erected—though but a simple stone wall enclosure, high as a man's head or shoulders. Were this hill well fortified and manned, it would be almost impregnable, as it rises over 100 feet above the plain, and the ascent on every side very steep—most places, too steep to be ascended, even by footmen. But, as at Santa Rosalía, this could only have been intended to defend the troops, and not the pass, as a rather nearer and better road passes several miles to the eastward.

Course from Pelayo to Palomas lake (into which Andabazo Cr. empties) N. 10° E. 50 to 80 m. (Lag. de Jaco as much further beyond Palomas.)—To San José spring, N. 35° E. 4 or 5 m. (on same ravine with Pelayo)—To Tahualilo lake E. 10° N. 30 to 50 m. Both Palomas & Jaco lakes are salt, and crystalized [salt] is collected from them for use, but that of Jaco is best, the Palomas salt being *Salitrosa*[41][.]

In making inquiries here, as well as at Cadena, concerning the

40 "Our men this night gave loose to their foraging propensities, by slaughtering almost all the pigs, fowls, and young calves in the village below the fort. I never saw our soldiers act so before—they had invariably treated the people with great forbearance—always paying for what they took. But, to-night, the spirit of destruction seemed to seize on all, while no effort was made to suppress the outbreak. From remarks made, all the fowls were supposed to have been cleared off, but a companion told me, he positively, in the morning, heard the crowing of one solitary cock!"—*A Campaign in New Mexico with Colonel Doniphan*, 136.
41 Nitrous.

country roundabout, I was reimpressed with (what, it is true I had before observed) the singular topographical notions of the generality of Mexicans. Inquiring about the courses and outlets of streams, I found that they could not very well conceive how a river or a creek continued any further than there was water running. Therefore, if you asked if a certain stream disembogued into a certain lake or into Rio del Norte, etc. they were certain to answer, in the negative, if water did not actually run the whole distance, though the dry bed of the stream should continue to the point. In fact, as the water in these sandy streams, frequently sinks, and rises again below, they generally appear to consider each fresh breaking out of the water, the source of a distinct creek or river. Again, they seem to know no other names for the larger number of the streams, than the names of the villages on their banks; so that you hear a new name for a creek, etc. (upon inquiry) at every town you pass, situated upon its border. For instance a creek passing by the town of Cerro Gordo, is known there as Arroyo de Cerro Gordo—lower down as Arroyo de Andabazo, from the rancho of Andabazo; etc. Again, between Saltillo and Monterey, etc. we have a creek, rising near the Hac. of Santa María, which bears that name for some distance—then Arroyo de *Ojo Caliente*—then, of *Muertos*—then, of *Rinconada* —then, of *Pesquería Grande*—then (where the road from Monterey to Marin passes it), of *Agua Fria*—and, I don't know how many more names.

From all that I could collect, I became convinced that Andabazo Cr. ran N.E. in the direction of Lag. de Palomas—some said, into it, while others asserted that Lag. de Palomas was to the left of the channel of the cr. and that a ravine made from the lake to the stream—then, that Andabazo cr. (though without water, except during great freshets) continued on to Lag. de Jaco—and thence possibly to Rio del Norte, via the Aguaverde river. San Antonio de los Alamos would seem east of this valley (though but a short distance—discharging itself into it. Others asserted, however, (among them, a man of a good deal of intelligence at Mapimí, by name of Oyarzu) that, during very high water, Palomas & Tahualilo lakes connected with each other: the most probable information, however, was, that there is a dividing ridge (of high lands, though not of mountains) between them, which prevented them from ever connecting with each other.—I was assured by some Mexicans that Lag. de Tahualilo discharged itself by way of Cuatro Ciénegas; but, I afterward became convinced that there exists a ridge of highlands, if not mountains, between them; and that the reason my ignorant informants represented it so, was because they supposed the springs of Cuatro Cienegas to be fed by Tahualilo lake! the water passing under the mountains.

On the right bank of Andabazo cr. 10 or 15 m. below this *rancho* (abandoned since 1835) called *Jaral Grande*. Water seldom runs in this creek lower than Jaral Grande.

Sat. 8—From Pelayo, S. 5° E. 4 m.—thence S. 40° E. 9 m. to valley of cr.—thence S. 15° W. 3 m. to Hac. de Cadena. Lat. of Cadena, 25° 53′ 0″. [MARGINAL NOTE: For Barometer at Cadena, see page 163. (See page 118 this volume.)]

I was a little annoyed as well as amused, to-day, at the ill-breeding of some of the volunteers. As the sun shone hot, and I was in rather weak health, I stretched my umbrella over me. This was insup[p]ortable to them—that I should be shaded while they were compelled to take the sun—and therefore they commenced taunting me with insulting expressions.[42] This amused me at first, [and] I paid no attention to it; but as it was

---

[42] By the side of Gregg's version of the red umbrella incident may be placed that of Meredith T. Moore (as related to William Elsey Connelley), who was a private in Company F, First Regiment, Missouri Volunteers:

"The weather was extremely warm the day the army marched out of Chihuahua, and when the sand-wastes were reached, it was scorching. Gregg was never physically a strong man, and at that time his health was poor. He raised a red-silk umbrella to protect himself from the intense heat. At that time he was near the rear of the line. The soldiers were always on the lookout for something to furnish them diversion and amusement. They all knew Dr. Gregg, and upon sight of his red umbrella they began to cheer and make such remarks as men in their station will. It

continued I became weary of it, and their officers paying no attention to their disorderly conduct, I remarked to Maj. Gilpin that his men were certainly very disorderly. I was much surprised to find that he fully justified them, in every regard,—said he wouldn't have them otherwise! And, when I alluded to previous disorders (such as their taking a great number of pigs, chickens, etc. at Pelayo [MARGINAL NOTE: I was pleased to learn that Col. Donophan took somewhat active measures of restitution, in this case.]) he would either deny or justify, *in toto*. In fact, when I would prove an act to be unjustifiable, he would resort to denial; and when I would prove it to be true, he would again *justify*—thus leaping most clumsily from one horn of the dilemma to another. Yet, he who knew Maj. Gilpin's character —a most consumate demagogue—would not be surprised, when he knows that the conversation was in hearing of several of his officers and men, and therefore intended to have its effect.

I was also frequently annoyed at the impertinence of the volunteers in other regards. Being constantly engaged in collecting botanical specimens, etc. they must needs know every particular about them—what the plant was good for—if for "greens"—for medicine, etc. often accompanied by taunting and insulting expressions: so that the naturalist has to pass an ordeal in laboring among ignorant people, who are wholly unable to comprehend the utility of his collections.

From Cadena, it is called 9 leagues (*leguas*) to Mapimí—18 do. to La Zarca—7 do. to Jarolito, on same Cr.—Cadena cr. comes from Gallo (on road from Durango to Chihuahua) and country thence to a little south of Palo Chino, which last con-

---

was all good-naturedly meant, but he rode hurriedly down the line to escape it, which caused the efforts of the men to be redoubled. Gregg reached the position of Colonel Doniphan in no good-humor, believing that the men knew him well enough to realize that in even fair health he would rough it with any of them. He complained to Doniphan, but a few words from the Colonel restored his equanimity."— John T. Hughes, *Doniphan's Expedition and the Conquest of New Mexico and California* (Edited by William Elsey Connelley, Topeka, 1907), 172n.

nects with Zarca cr.—Course up cr. S. 30° W.—There are the remains of an old mining village, Hornillos, half way back to Pelayo, producing copper, but being of inferior quality, it has been abandoned.

Sun. 9—E. 15° S. 3 m. to gap in mountain—Thence east 2 or 3—& E. 13° S. 15 or 16 m. to Mapimí. [MARGINAL NOTE: Lat. of Mapimí, 25° 50¼′] Course from Mapimí to Tahualilo about N.E. [MARGINAL NOTE: From Mapimí, it is called 40 *leguas* to Cuencame and thence 40 *leguas* to Durango—whole distance, say 200 m.]

Although we had already heard a "flying["] report of the victory at Cerro Gordo, it was here that we received the first authentic information. I was here shown Mexican newspapers, in which their letterwriters, and even Santa Anna himself, acknowledged a complete defeat, and the loss of everything, particularly all their artillery. This and that of Sacramento were the only complete defeats they had ever acknowledged—at Palo Alto & Resaca de la Palma, they boasted of advantages—at Monterey of an honorable and advantageous capitulation—at Buenavista (or Angostura, as christened by Santa Anna) of a victory! but here all confessed a thorough route. On the occasion of the joyful news, a salute was fired by our artillery—a gun for every state in the Union, I believe.

At Mapimí Lieut. Caleb Jackson[43] died, after having been ill for a week or two of typhus fever. I regretted to observe, in his case, as well as in many other cases, of great, and I fear quite culpable, neglect on the part of the surgeon, Dr. Morton. Col. Jackson (the patient being his brother) had informed me, that, in the most critical period of the disease, the surgeon had left him for four or five days without attention or medicine. An anecdote, in which this surgeon Morton was concerned, which I might have related, would have explained his character, and

---

[43] Possibly a correction in the name should be made. John Taylor Hughes says it was Stephen, brother of Lieutenant Colonel Congreve Jackson.

the reasons of his neglect to patients: his attentions were all absorbed by a Mexican mistress! The night after his departure from Chihuahua, two Mexicans, girls, as I have been informed on good authority, who had been "in keeping" before, dressed themselves in men's clothing, shouldered muskets, and mounting horses, astride, they followed their paramours. One of these "beloved" men had sense of propriety and decency enough, to dispatch his Dulcinea back to Chihuahua, but the other continued with Dr. Morton to Saltillo, in whose tent I frequently saw her, living with him in the most public manner! With so little sense of decency, it is not to be wondered at that his mistress should divert his attention from his patients!

And at Mapimí my barometrical observations resulted as follows—

May 9/47—4½ P.M.—¼ cloudy—wind southward

Barometer, height of mercury	25.63 inches
Thermometer, in atmosphere	90 °
" in mercury	86 °

Barometer at Cadena, May 8/47—5 o'clock, P.M.—¼ cloudy—brisk south wind—stood,

Barometer, height mercury,	25.05 in.
Thermometer, in atmosphere	90 °
" in mercury	88 °

Latitude of Mapimí, 25° 50' 10".

Mon. 10—E. 17° N. 3 m.—thence E. 5° S. 1 m. to Vinagrillos—thence E. 32° S. 5 m. whence back to gap in mt. W. 25° N.—Thence E. 25° S. 10 m.—Thence E. 40° S. 2 m. to *rancho* of El Renoval. Water from well—only one family living there, I think.—Thence E. 40° S. 6 m. to Palo Blanco—rancho of three or four families.—water from well.—Thence E. 35° S. 8 or 9 m. to San Sebastian. This an *hacienda* of 100 souls or such a matter, on N.W. bank of Rio Nazas. From Mapimí south (and some say still further north, we are in the famous Bolson de Mapimí—Cove of Mapimí.

Lat. of San Sebastian, 25° 37′ 37″. Barometer stood as follows,—
May 10/47—6 o'clock P.M.—calm.—¼ cloudy—

Barometer, height mercury	26.17 in.
Thermometer, in atmosphere,	82½°
" in mercury,	85½°

From the natives, I collected the following data with regard
to the surrounding country: Rancho del Merto say 5 m. below
S. Sebastian, S.E. side of river—abandoned.—Concepcion, 100
to 200 souls, 1 m. up river, S.E. side—Aviléz, 12 m. above S.E.
side—Thence up to San Juan de Castro, [MARGINAL NOTE:
Rio de Nazas is sometimes called *Rio de San Juan de Castro,*
here & below.] say 5 m. N.W. side—La Loma, 3 to 5 m. further, S.E. side—Goma, 2 m. further up on N.W. side.— Village
of Cinco Señores, above Durango & Chihuahua road, is sometimes called Nazas, whence name of river.—Los Huertos, small
village, 2 or 3 m. above S. Sebastian, N.W. side river.—Course
up the river to gap in mountain, S.W.—Do. to San Lorenzo. W.
20° N.—Nazas (like Mississippi) forks as it descends. Upper
branch which runs into Rio de Guanaval (generally called Buenavá, by the people) forks off between San Sebastian and Muertos
—lower fork (and principal) running to lake Tahualilo, separates opposite Alamito. Middle fork runs by San Lorenzo, and
into lower lake, which has three names, viz. Lag. de las Avas,
de S. Nicolas & del Muerto—from three ranchos in its vicinity,
located as below:

> The latter (del Muerto) seems most used by the people
> there abouts. The branch of Nazas on south, joins the
> Guanaval or Buenava) about 10 m. below the rancho of
> Matamoros, which is some distance, N.W. or branch ac-
> cording to Hughes,[44] one of Collins' party.

[44] John T. Hughes gave up teaching at Liberty, Missouri, when the first Mexican
War began, and enlisted as a private in Company C, First Missouri Mounted Volunteers. As he had a bent for newspaper writing, he conceived the idea of becoming
the historian of Colonel Doniphan's regiment, the Colonel himself giving his en-
couragement and aid to the project. The result was the volume *Doniphan's Expedition,* published in 1848. The preface, however, is dated "Liberty, Mo., September
25, 1847." The book has been accepted as the classic account of this remarkable

Tues. 11—South, 1 m. & crossed Nazas, at Concepcion—then 2 m. a little east of south—E. 20° S. 2 m.—thence E. 38° N. 12 m. to point of mountain—whence back to San Sebastian, W. 30° S. (?)—.To Mapimí, W. 15° N. (?). To Alamito, W. 20° N.— To San Lorenzo, E. 20° N. 6 m. [MARGINAL NOTE: Course from San Lorenzo to Alamo de Parras, S. 30° E. 16 leguas— Tahualilo, N. 20° W.—To San Sebastian, W. 35° S. (?)]— Rio de Nazas is the line here between Durango and Coahuila to Lake Tahualilo, and, probably on to Jaco, via Palomas.

The valley of Nazas is of unusually rich soil, in almost every part—from San Sebastian to San Lorenzo—Alamito— & where we crossed it to the westward of latter—until we get lower down, when it becomes too sandy. The vegetation is more luxuriant than I have seen it in any part of Mexico—the mesquite timber, especially, is unusually large—40 or 50 feet high, and of proportionate dimensions. Besides this, we find uña-de-gato (but no güizacho) and some other underbrush. The annual vegetation is quite diversified. And, although there is a lack of water for irrigation, as the river goes nearly dry during the dry season, yet, the natural moisture of the soil is such that it produces very good Indian corn, wheat and cotton, without watering; and it appears to me it ought to produce sugar. The cotton is planted around only every few (three or four) years, as it springs up from the old roots. This valley forms a large portion (and nearly the only tillable portion) of the Bolson de Mapimí. Here there are many hundreds of thousands acres of superior soil still lying waste. The Bolson de Mapimí, is nearly 100 miles in length, and 30 to 50 in width, being pent in, in every direction, by ridges of mountains, except the inlets of the streams which enter it, and the valley leading toward the San Antonio Cr.

Soon after we reached (in fact, before a portion reached) San

military exploit. William Elsey Connelley edited the book under the title *Doniphan's Expedition and the Conquest of New Mexico and California,* the voluminous notes making this volume a compendium of the part taken by Doniphan's Missourians in the Mexican War.

Lorenzo, an old Mexican arrived from Mapimí (whom I had seen in fact, at Pelayo, and said he was a sergeant there), with information that a force of some 2000 Mexican troops under Gen. Filisola, were marching from the direction of Durango against, being by that time, at Alamo de Parras. This occasioned some alarm; and as Saml. Magoffin,[45] with about 30 wagons which he had brought from Chihuahua, was considerably in the rear, much uneasiness was felt for his safety. Indeed, an express arrived from Magoffin, with similar annunciations. A corps of some 60 volunteers were immediately dispatched back for his protection—and all arrived, though after night, in perfect safety. The fact is, the alarm was doubtless false; yet we could not learn whether our Mexican informant, acted in ill faith or not. However, lest he might have come as a spy, Col. Donophan had him taken into custody, and brought him along.

Lat. of San Lorenzo, [MARGINAL NOTE: Pop. 1000, or more.] 25° 42′ 27″—Course to Alamo de Parras, S. 30° E. 16 leguas.

Wed. 12—Nearly S.E. 2 m. to forks of road—right hand to Alamo—left to San Juan. [MARGINAL NOTE: Lat. of S. Juan, 25° 39¼′.] Then 3 m. to bend of river & 10 m. to San Juan Bautista—general course E. 23° S.—From San Juan to Alamo S. 28° E. 25 to 27 m.—to Parras, say, W. 20° S. (?)—To upper end of lake about N.E. to Maigran E. 5° W.—To S. Nicolas E. 8° W.—Tahualilo lake N. 40° W.—Punto del Rio de Guanaval, S. 35° or 40° W.—San Juan is a rancho of but two or three fam-

---

[45] Regarding this concern for the safety of Samuel Magoffin, John Taylor Hughes states: "After our arrival in San Lorenzo, a Mexican courier came to the colonel [i.e., Doniphan] with the news that Canales had made an attack upon Magoffin's train of wagons and that Magoffin and his lady were likely to fall into his hands. A detachment of sixty men under Lieut. Gordon was quickly sent to his relief." (*Doniphan's Expedition*, 474-75). Samuel Magoffin, of the famous Kentucky family, had with him his bride, Susan Shelby Magoffin, whose diary, published under the title *Down the Santa Fé Trail and into Mexico* (Edited by Stella Drum, Yale University Press, 1926), affords interesting sidelights upon the trip. Unfortunately however, her zeal for recording failed after leaving Chihuahua, and was not revived until her arrival at Saltillo. Hence there is no reference to this episode.

ilies. Lat. 25° 39′ 12″—Barometer stood at San Juan, May 12/47—5½ o'clock P.M.—½ cloudy—calm—

Barometer, height mercury	26.26 in.
Thermometer in atmosphere	80 °
" in mercury	84½°

Thurs. 13—E. 20° S. (?) 15 m. to abandoned rancho of Refugio.—well of saline water.—Thence to hill, 1 m.—whence, to S. Nicolas, N. 15° W. (?)—To middle of lake (water) N. 25° E.—San José del Pozo, E. 5° to 10° S. 10 m.—course from Pozo to Hac. de Abajo, about E. 20° S.—Lat. of Pozo, 25° 33′ 36″. At Pozo, May 13/47—4 o'clock, P.M.—wind, S. W.—⅛ cloudy—

Barometer stood at	26.07 inches
Thermometer in mercury & atmosphere	95°

This forenoon, a Mexican came up to where Col. Donophan, myself & others were riding in from, and solicited the liberation of two or three prisoners that had been taken the day before,[46] who, he protested were perfectly innocent of any hostile or treacherous intention against the Americans. This appeared probable enough, and the colonel promised to release them as soon as we reached Pozo. [MARGINAL NOTE: At the same time, the Col. released the old sergeant (as he called himself) who had given us the information at S. Lorenzo which occasioned the alarm. I could see little necessity in keeping him even so long; for, first, it was difficult to conceive what could have been his motive even for good or evil; and, as his intentions toward us might possibility have been good, it was certainly more charitable to run the risk of letting his (possible) guilt go unpunished than to stand a chance of punishing innocence, and that after an effort

[46] A slight amplification of Gregg's mention of the prisoners is to be had from the parallel chronicles of Wislizenus and Hughes. Hughes gives it as follows: "On the 12th, early in the morning, the front guards charged upon and took three Mexicans prisoners; they were armed and lurking in the mezquite chaparrel near the road, and were doubtless spies sent out by Canales to obtain information of our movements, but no positive proof appearing against them, they were released." (*Doniphan's Expedition*, 475).

to serve us: especially, as no evil could possibly (as seemed) have resulted from his liberation.] The circumstances were about these: Not long after leaving San Lorenzo, yesterday morning, our front guard saw two or three Mexicans at a distance coming meeting them. The frightened rancheros (as they appeared to be), as soon as they espied our troops commenced a precipitate flight—throwing away their arms, before the volunteers could catch them. This conduct and their being armed seemed to render them suspicious and they were kept in custody. But the fact of their carrying arms was nothing, as they necessarily ought to travel, prepared to defend themselves against the Indians, who were ravaging the country everywhere, at the time. And their precipitate flight was doubtless only the result of fear.

When we reached the rancho of San José del Pozo (a place of perhaps 50 souls), I was surprised to see stretched on the ground near it, half a dozen dead Indians.[47] I soon learned that they had been killed by Capt. Reid and a party of our troops. It seems that a party of some 50 or 60 either *Comanches* or *Lipanes* (it could not be positively determined which), had, for several days

[47] The Indian fight at San José del Pozo excited a good deal of interest and afforded each of the chroniclers a version. Perhaps that of Frank S. Edwards is worthy of quotation in comparison with Gregg's:

"Two days afterwards, on reaching large rancho called El Poso, we found, lying just outside the walls, some dozen naked bodies Indians, badly cut up by rifle balls. The mystery was soon explained:—a band of about sixty Lipans (a branch of the Comanches [sic]) had been observed coming up the valley from San Luis Potosi, with many stolen horses and captive Mexicans. A guard that had preceded us, with Colonel Mitchell, was then at Parras, twenty-five miles off; and the owner of El Poso, knowing that the savages would attack his rancho, went to the men composing Mitchell's guard, and offered each one the use of a good pony to go up and repel them. About a dozen agreed to do so, and having ridden nearly all night, arrived just before daylight at the estate. Soon afterwards, a small party from our troops, principally officers, who had left the main body early that morning to push on to Parras by the evening, came up, thus increasing the force to twenty, who, as soon as it was daylight, perceived the Indians advancing up the valley. As they came in front of the buildings, the Americans sallied out, and took up a position in front of them; and, after receiving a heavy flight of arrows, fired a volley at the Indians, which apparently, did no harm, as they kept waving their bodies about in their saddles, thus disturbing the aim. A sturdy fight began and lasted about an hour— sometimes one party retreating, and then the other. But the savages soon found out they had not Mexican carbines to deal with, but Yankee rifles; and they fled the field, leaving all their animals and about a dozen prisoners, together with over

been committing depredations—first, in the ranchos not very remote from Saltillo—then in the neighborhood of Mazapil—and of Parras: among others, upon the property of Don Manuel Ibarra, proprietor of San Lorenzo, or Hac. de Abajo. Col. Mitchell, with his advance command being in the vicinity at the time, dispatched Capt. Reid, with (I think) 13 Missouri volunteers (accompanied by Ibarra himself and two or three servants) in their pursuit. As it was known that the Indians were proceeding toward Pozo, and would most probably resort there for water (as there was none other near), Capt. Reid went directly to this rancho, to await their arrival. He had not been there very long when the Indians made their appearance in the distance—perhaps between 10 and 11 o'clock. Meanwhile some 20 or more of Col. Donophan's command had arrived at Pozo in advance of the main body, which made the American force at Pozo about 35 men. Capt. Reid first sallied out to reconnoitre alone, when the Indians chased him to within a few hundred yards of the rancho. Our other troops then made their appearance and commenced the attack, which lasted over an hour. The Indians were armed with bows and arrows, and fought remarkably bravely. It seemed that they must have supposed their assailants to be Mexicans, who they had been in the habit of putting to flight immediately, and therefore were unwilling to believe that they would not yet whip them. Their numbers were variously rated by our own men from 50 to 80. How many wounded

twenty of their warriors slain. These showed great muscular power and handsome forms—but the savage was apparent in every part. Our men received many arrows in their clothes, but were all uninjured, except the Captain, who had two slight arrow wounds on the chin. A Mexican distinguished himself here by his skilful use of the lasso, having, with it, dragged down and killed two of the Indians. This is a terrible weapon in an experienced hand; and I have since heard that among the forces sent out to meet us at Santa Fe, there were about one hundred thousand lassoers. I would much rather encounter a Mexican armed with a carbine, than one holding a lasso. We had a man very badly injured, a short time after the period I am referring to, while away from camp. He was caught by a mounted Mexican in this way, and dragged some distance, tearing his face very much; but, luckily, the lasso did not go down low enough to entirely secure his arms, and he succeeded in freeing himself."—*A Campaign in New Mexico with Colonel Doniphan*, 139–40.

made their escape, it was not know[n], but it was asserted that 13 dead were left on the field—6 that had been dragged up to the rancho by the Mexicans—2 that lay not far off—and 5, as was said, who were more distant. It was disgusting to [see] the dastardly conduct of the Mexicans toward these dead Indians, whom they were too cowardly to fight while living—kicking and abusing them. There were some 6 or 8 Mexican prisoners rescued from them—a woman or two, and the rest girls and boys. There were also captured about 250 head of horses & mules— among them an *atajo* or two with *aparejos* still on, which had been taken but a day or so before.—The Americans lost no one killed—nor wounded, except Capt. Reid, who, in his impetuous bravery, received two slight wounds—one in the chin, the other in the shoulder—by arrows. Ibarra was also said to have acted very bravely in the skirmish.

This is certainly a novel warfare:[48] fighting and defending the same people at the same time—and killing those who would be our allies, if we would permit them. True, although at war with the Mexican *nation*, we have never pretended to hostilize the unarmed citizens; and, under no circumstances, could we permit the savages to butcher them before our eyes. This display of a spirit to defend the people against their worst enemies, the Indians, will, I hope, be attended with a good effect.

Frid. 14—E. 10° to 20° S. 18 m. to top of ridge—thence, to Parras, E. 40° S.—& to San Lorenzo [MARGINAL NOTE: Lat. of San Lorenzo, as taken on night of April 11, 1847, is 25° 30′ 29″.] Hac. de Abajo, E. 15° S. 8 m. [MARGINAL NOTE: San Lorenzo to ridge S. 50° W. 1 m.—& S. 10° E. 4 m. to Parras.] Encamped—i.e. Col. Donophan's command, in the Alameda, in the immediate town of Parras. [MARGINAL NOTE: My comrades and myself took a room in town.] This, to say the least of it, was imprudent. Besides the facility it afforded to commit depreda-

[48] Edwards makes the same remark of surprise that the Americans should be fighting the Mexicans and at the same time, when the latter were victims of Indian forays, undertaking to attack the Indians.

tions, Parras being an exceedingly abundant place of wines and ardent spirits, the volunteers being immediately in town, would take advantage of their opportunities of drinking to excess. This was the occasion of at least one fracas,[49] which was very mortifying. A volunteer accused a servant of the house of Don

[49] The unfortunate episodes at Parras appear in the several chronicles of the march from Chihuahua to Saltillo. Hughes gives the victim's name—Lickenlighter of the artillery. Wislizenus indicates the uproar was so serious that as a precaution against more disturbances, the Missourians shortened their stay at Parras. Edwards presents a circumstantial account, which is worthy of quotation:

"On entering the pretty town of Parras, we encamped in the Alameda. Here, General Wool had encamped for some time. The Alcalde told us that we must be very careful, or the Mexicans would steal everything from us—that General Wool, who was a Catholic, had very wrongly allowed them to thieve and abuse his men without giving the soldiers any redress. Our officers assured him that they would have rather different folks to deal with now. We were not five minutes in camp, before a thief got so beaten and kicked as to be hardly able to drag himself away.

"The next day, a horrible occurrence took place. One of our cannon drivers, a young and remarkably inoffensive man, who had been on the sick list for a week previous, had started, with two or three companions, to take a look at the town; but, after proceeding some way, he had found himself too weak to go further, and had separated him from his companions to return to camp, when a thorn having entered his foot, he drew off his boot and sat down in the street. He was looking into his boot, when a stone struck him on the forehead, and knocked him down senseless. He supposed that the Mexicans then beat him on the face with stones, and left him for dead. On recovering his senses, he made his way down to camp; and I never saw a more horrible sight than his face presented; his forehead was broken through in two places, and the flesh all cut to pieces, and his lower jaw broken; besides a fracture just below the eye. His wounds were dressed, and he seemed to be rapidly recovering at the time we left him at Saltillo; but I afterwards heard that he died of lockjaw. The sight of our friend's bloody figure at once excited some of the soldiers; and they sallied into the town, and closed most of the shops. Vengeance was sworn, and each felt that, after what had happened, it would not require much provocation to produce an outbreak. Nor did it. A short time afterwards, a Mexican sat down on the pole of one of our wagons. The driver who was sitting near, and who, from having been a prisoner among them for some time, spoke Spanish, told him mildly, to get off, as the hounds were broken, and he was injuring the wagon by sitting on that part. The fellow insolently responded: 'I shall not—this ground is as much mine as yours.' Without another word, the teamster caught up his heavy iron-shod whip, and struck the Mexican on the left temple, fracturing the skull over four inches. He fell, but staggered off. However, he died the same night. This occurrence happened before the house of the constable of the alcalde, who came running out with his staff of office in one hand, and a drawn sabre in the other, crying out, 'Respect the law.' But an American, standing by, knocked the constable down with his fist, and seizing his sabre, bent it up and threw it into the sako. The constable moved off, and did not venture to interfere in that or any other matter during the day. In the night, a Mexican was found dead, with a horrible sabre wound in his breast, lying in the street."—*A Campaign in New Mexico with Colonel Doniphan*, 141–42.

Lorenzo Garto of stealing from him, and demanded the privilege of inflicting summary punishment: but, as Garto believed his servant innocent, he refused to deliver him up; upon which a mob of volunteers collected to take him by force, and endeavored to break down Garto's door; but fortunately, Capts. Weightman and Reid heard of it, and very promptly stopped it. Now, Garto had, on former occasions, treated the American soldiers with unusual kindness—particularly a number that were left there sick when Gen. Wool marched to Saltillo, in December last.—Some other outrages were committed, and others feared —especially from a desperado by name of Ben Leaton[50] and his clan; yet, by prompt measures they were checked.

Parras, from the arrival of Gen. Wool's division there, in December last, has been famous for its friendly deportment toward the Americans. In fact, I fancy it one of the best and most agreeable places in the interior of Mexico—not only with regard to the inhabitants, but the soil, climate, and country generally. It is famous for grapes and fruits generally—such as apples, peaches, pears, figs, pomegranates, etc. And what adds no little to the beauty of the gardens, orchards and vineyards, is that the hedges are nearly all of rose bushes, which, at this season were generally in bloom—were fully so in April, as we passed up.

The wines made at Parras resemble those of Paso del Norte, but of superior quality. The annual product of liquors (wines & *aguardientes*) is said to be from $50,000 to $60,000 worth—so ex-Gov. Viesca informed me—an agreeable and intelligent gentleman—who gave me also the following information:

Parras was founded in 1622—population of city proper about

[50] Ben Leaton is an uncertainty, so far as Mexican War times are concerned. Tradition has it that he was a member of the Doniphan forces, but Gregg's reference does not bear out that story. Very probably Leaton had detached himself from the army and embarked upon a career of lawlessness with certain companions. About a year later he and three others—Larkin Landrum, John Daley, and William Russell—established themselves on the American side of the Rio Grande a few miles below Presidio del Norte. They somehow got possession of an old mission, erected, so it is said, in 1684, and converted it into "Fort Leaton," an almost impregnable adobe stronghold. Leaton's treatment of Indians and Mexicans was ruthless and brutal. He died about 1852.

6,000—but including Haciendas de Arriba & Abajo 7 to 8,000. —This was anciently called "Pueblo de Santa María de las Parras,"—but now only "Parras." It was so called from its principal product—*Parras* meaning *vines*.—This valley has ever been famous for grapes, producing the best for wines, of any district of Mexico. Parras & Paso del Norte [are] the only good wine-producing regions in Northern Mexico. Grapes are produced at Cuatro Ciénegas, but make bad wine. The liquors of Parras are chiefly sold at Zacatecas, Durango and Parral. It is remarkable that though no wines are made about Monterey and Saltillo, little or nothing has been sold there: not a wine-drinking people.—Products of valley of Parras, besides fruits, etc. are corn and wheat—but no cotton and sugar is planted: it is probably too much elevated for the latter.—The valley of Nazas produces, without irrigation, superior corn, cotton, wheat, etc.— Lake Tahualilo was the original (anciently called *Cayman*) in the Bolson de Mapimí—that of San Salvador, Maigran, S. Nicolas, Muerto, or Avas, commenced farming about 1832.

Latitude of Parras, according to two observations, is 25° 26′ 30″—Barometer, at Parras, May

May 15/47—12½ o'clock—nearly clear—stood—

Barometer, height mercury	25.17 in.
Thermometer, in atmosphere	80°
" in mercury	82°

And, May 16/47—10 o'clock A.M.—clear—it stood—

Barometer, height mercury	25.24 in.
Thermometer in atmosphere	79°
" in mercury	82°

Mon. 17—Left Parras this morning—5 m. to San Lorenzo— thence, N. 7° E. 2½ m. to point of ridge—then N. 35° E. 1 m. —then E. 40° N. 4 m. to Puerto de S. Francisco—E. 15° N. ½ m. to hill—whence to Lake W. 30° N. (?)—course up and down valley about E. 20 S & W. 20° N. Tinaja, W. 10° N.—Cienega Grande, W. 10° S. (?) Thence, Parras W. 25° S.—Lake, W. 40° N. (?)—Tinaja, E. 30° N. 12 m.

Tues. 18—E. 20° S. 8 or 10 m.—Thence S. 40° E. 10 or 12 m. to Castañuela. Camp nearly 2 m. N.W. of Castañuela, & half mile east of Rancho Nuevo. The dispositions of Col. Donophan were in strange contrast, this evening, with those of yesterday evening. He then camped in the very border of the village, where there neither wood nor grass, though informed that there was a good camping site half to a mile below—fine grass and water, with sufficiency of wood. Consequence, horses fared badly, and fences, etc. torn down for fuel. But this evening he issued an order, with little apparent necessity—for all—volunteers or others—to leave the village at an early hour.

Wed. 19—8 m. to hill—whence back to Castañuela W. 25° N.—to Rancho Nuevo, W. 35° N.—To Patos, E. 5° S.—From hill to Macuyú branch, 3 m.—whence to ridge 1 m.—thence to Macuyú village, W. 40° S.—to ford of branch, W. 20° N. (forming equilateral triangle).—S. Antonio Cr. 7 m.—Vaquería de Patos, 3 m.—thence to Patos, N. 35° E. ¾ m.—To Muchachos and Aguanueva, about E. 30° S.—Gap in mts. of Patos Cr. S. 20? E.—Shower this evening.—Lat. of Vaquería, 25° 22' 20" —Do. of Patos, say, 25° 23'.

Thurs. 20—4 m. to hill—whence to Patos, N. 40° W.—to Agua Nueva E. 20° to 25° S.—Hill to Muchachos, 10 m.— Derramadero, 2 m.—& San Juan de la Vaquería 5 or 6 m.— Nooned.—Army remained encamped; but our mess concluded to continue on to Encantada.—5 m. to Dividing ridge, E. 10° N. —whence to Agua Nueva, S. 37° E. & to Encantada, E. 30° N. 6 m.—when I passed, in December, Encantada was a rancho of 40 or 50 souls, but was abandoned soon after, and torn down by our volunteers.

At Encantada, May 20—6 P.M.—windy—clear—

Barometer, height mercury	24.17 in.
Thermometer, in atm.	68°
" in merc.	70½°

Fri. 21—To Saltillo 12 m. [MARGINAL NOTE: From hill

above Saltillo to Buenavista, S. 26° W.—6 m. To Guerreadero, S. 23° W. 5 m.]—Before reaching Saltillo, we heard that an express (of Mexican officers) had arrived from San Luis, with communications, purporting to be from Mexico, which all hoped might savor of peace—a convention between Scott & Santa Anna, or something so: but it turned out but an impertinent communication from the commandant at San Luis inquiring of Gen. Taylor, how he contemplated prosecuting the war—if like savages or civilized nations, etc.! Certainly, the Mexicans are the last, that should make such allusions—as their warfare has been so completely savage. However, the principal object of these *emissaries,* was to see and learn what was the probability of Gen. Taylor's advancing upon San Luis. I am not sure but they should have been treated as spies.

The terms of the several regiments of volunteers being about to expire, they are returning home. The three regiments of Kentucky Volunteers, and two of Ohio, had already left; and the Missourians were ordered to leave on the 23ᵈ inst.—the Indianians (2 regiments, under Gen. Lane) on the 24th; Two regiments of Illinois on the 30th; and the Arkansas cavalry on 5th June.

[*Note Accompanying Manuscript No. 3*]

[NOTE 7, from page 100]—In an official communication from the commanding officer at Chihuahua, I find the following statement as to the Mexican force, some time prior to the battle:— Troops about 2,000:— Artillery, 2 eight-pounders, 1 six-pounder, 7 four-pounders, and six esmeriles. These were brass guns, calibre near an inch in diameter, 5 or 6 feet long, rigged with locks, etc. in form of muskets, intended to be mounted on mules; but, in this case, they were on wheels—2 to 4 on each.—These were all taken by the Americans. It is altogether probable that the number of their troops was increased before the battle.

PART III

Revisiting the States

Revisiting the States

MAY TO NOVEMBER, 1847

Diary, May, 1847[1]

SUN. 23—I had no idea of returning to the United States yet; but to-day, Saml. Magoffin[2] renewed an offer of co-partnership (mercantile—he to furnish the means), which he had made at Parras as well as here. After due reflection; and the necessity I was in to endeavor to better my pecuniary condition, I concluded to embrace his offer, and leave for the U.S. with the Missouri volunteers. The terms agreed on, were that, I proceed to Phil^a & N. York with about $20,000 which he would furnish, and buy perhaps near $40,000 worth of merchandise ($20,000 on credit), which I was to introduce via Matamoros, to Monterey and Saltillo: chiefly intended, however,

[1] Gregg's career shows more than once quick changes of program and intention. With almost no preannouncement, the diary shows him at this stage becoming ready to re-enter the ranks of American merchants in Mexico. While traveling with the Doniphan expedition from Chihuahua to Saltillo, he received a proposal from no less an outstanding proprietor than Samuel Magoffin, which offered an advantageous copartnership. Gregg accepted without delay, and immediately began preparations for a return to the States, where he was to fulfill his assignment, buying the stock. While he was in Philadelphia and New York, full of enthusiasm for a task in which his experience and ability might well serve, he learned that Magoffin had changed his mind through fear of the risks involved. Though disappointed, Gregg at once gathered together such equipment and impedimenta as might enable him on returning to Mexico to undertake what was closest to his heart—namely, exploration and collecting scientific information. Getting back to Mexico was a long-drawn-out experience, but Gregg used the weeks during which he was marooned at his brother John's, near Shreveport, to complete his gathering of topographic data of that region. During his stay at his brother's he found that he had filled the pages of Manuscript No. 3, and under date of November 15, 1847, opened Manuscript No. 4.

[2] Gregg evidently felt a pardonable glow of satisfaction at this partnership with one of the wealthiest of the American merchants in Mexico.

133

for the San Juan and Zacatecas market, provided either that peace should be made or the army advance. Of the former we now had strong hopes—after the success of our army at Cerro Gordo and Chihuahua, and the demonstration of the increase of the "peace party" in Mexico.—It was now noon, and I had all my arrangements and preparations to make for my departure before sleeping that night—as I had my baggage to dispatch at daylight. [MARGINAL NOTE: Made three observations with barometer today, resulting as follows:

Saltillo, May 23/47—12½ o'clock, noon—clear & nearly calm— Barometer stood 24.845 inches.

Thermometer in atmosphere 68° Do. in merc. 70½°		
Do. Do—3½ o'clock, P.M.—a little windy—half cloudy—		
Barometer, highest mercury	24.755	inches
Therm^r in atm^e 76°—in mercury	74°	
Do. Do—9 o'clock, P.M.—half cloudy—a little windy—		
Barometer, height mercury	24.8	inches
Therm^r in atm^e	70½°	
" mercury	74°	

[See Note (4) at end of this MS.][3]

On emptying my barometer (for I was provided with tubes to fill at pleasure) the last time, the top was burst off by the violent reaction of the atmosphere. Having no other serviceable tubes, I could make no more barometrical observations. Yet I have since been kindly furnished by Dr. Wislizenus,[4] (who travelled with Mo. regiment) with the result of his observations with Barom^r. In return I furnished him my latitudes, etc.]

[3] Gregg's brackets. Note 4 itself occurs on pages 73 to 75.
[4] Dr. Adolph Wislizenus gives the details in the following passage from the preface to his *Memoir:* "After having outfitted myself for the trip [into Mexico] by private means, and being already on the road, the war between the United States and Mexico broke out, very untimely for my purposes, and deranged my plans considerably. By the arbitrary government of the State of Chihuahua . . . I was detained for six months in a very passive situation; and after the arrival of the American troops in Chihuahua, seeing the impracticality of continuing my journey as far as intended, I accepted a situation in the medical department of the army, and returned with it, by way of Monterey, to the States."

I regretted to perceive that the Missourians completed the devastation of the Hacienda of (de la) Rinconada, by tearing roofs from many of the houses, tearing out window frames, doors, etc. This place (belonging to Don Mariano Ramos) had suffered exceedingly—being on the road from Monterey to Saltillo: many houses had been burned or torn down—fences, orchards, etc. greatly damaged—cattle killed, etc. etc. Even the son of the proprietor was waylaid and shot through the arm, by some cowardly wretch of the 2d Ohio regiment. Gen. Butler promised the proprietor to make him some remuneration for damages, but this I suppose he forgot before leaving for the U.S.

Passed Gen. Lane, this evening, with 1st & 2d regiment of Indiana vols. encamped some 12 m. from Saltillo. I felt desirous (and so proposed it to my comrades) to wait for Gen. Lane's brigade, as I felt sure that we would receive more accommodation from him than from Col. Donophan.

Tues. 25—Encamped a mile or two east of *el molino* (the mill) 3 or 4 m. west of Monterey. Had a shower of rain this evening.—Course from "Alto" to Ojo Caliente W. 20° S.—to Rinconada, W. 3° S.—Alto, E. 20° N. 3 m. thence to Monterey, W. 5° S.—From S. Rafael (a small rancho of but one family, I think—some 10 m. from Alto) to Pesquería Grande N. 30° W. —From 5 to 6 m. back to same, N. 15° W.—From Santa Catarina (near 4 m.) to Pesquería Grande, W. 35° W.—Molino, East— Monterey E. 5° S.—The mill above-mentioned is a water-mill of much better finish, and more extensive, than I have met with farther north in Mexico. But there is one nearly equal at Santa Maria, near Saltillo.

Wed. 26—Passed through Monterey to-day, and encamped at "Walnut Grove" tonight—where Gen. Taylor has had his camp ever since the taking of Monterey, in Sept. last—with the exception of the time he was absent in the direction of Victoria—and afterward at Saltillo, etc.—I doubt if he has slept in a house since he has been in Mexico.

135

Thurs. 27—The Missouri regiment continued its march to-day; but owing to detention in the providing of corn, etc. it was 11 o'clock before it got off. Before leaving, Gen. Lane came up with the Indianians.

I forgot to allude, in a more appropriate place, to the very injudicious measure of our government in having enlisted volunteers for 12 months, instead of for the war. The larger portion of those who are now going home are well trained—one regiment worth two of the new recruits: besides the leaving of the occupied posts without a sufficiency of troops, and crippling up the operations of our army by want of force—to say nothing of the additional expense of transporting the old ones home and the new ones to the seat of war. But, as this has to be done, it is again remarkable that no provision was made to allow a commutation to those in the field, for going home and returning, provided they re-enlisted, as a bonus to encourage their re-enlistment. It would thus have cost the government no more than to bring new recruits from the U.S.; and, as before remarked, the old ones were worth double as much as the new.—But, verily, it is difficult to conceive why the government did not enlist for the war at first; as it is well known that there was even competition for the privilege of volunteering; so that there could have been no difficulty in filling up in that way: & had the war lasted but 12 or even one or two months it would have been the same to our government.

On account of my occupations, I had not yet been able to call on Gen. Taylor: therefore, after saddling my horse (or rather *mule*) this morning, I concluded to ride by the General's camp, in company with Dr. East, as we started. Approaching Gen. T.'s tent, I was surprised to see him in uniform: that is, with blue cloth pants (and I think stripes), a blue cloth coat, with buttons and shoulder straps, and a somewhat new cap.—all in striking contrast with anything I had seen him wear before: for I had never seen nor heard of his wearing since he entered Mexico, anything but an old brown citizen coat, etc. with no indication of uniform. Really, I scarcely knew him; and while my attention was attracted by his *novel* appearance, I forgot to attend to the sentinel before his marquee, who, having two or three times called to us to halt! brought his musket to a present or aim at us, and cried out, in broken English—"Damn, you no stop, I shoot!" I was the less prepared for this, as I had often visited Gen. Taylor's camp, not only without being hailed by a sentinel but without having even perceived one. It was evident that he was beginning "to feel his keeping." Seeing the parade made in the U.S. about him, he had begun to conclude that he was really a much greater man than he had ever before dreamed of, and consequently must command more respect.—I may be permitted here to say a word about Gen. Taylor.[5] As a sober, honest and really clever old gentleman of sterling integrity, and of good sound judgment I have a high opinion of him: and as a general his judgment is, I believe, very good;—yet, wanting quickness of intellect and brilliancy of general talent, this detracts something from his ability as a general, and still more as a statesman, perhaps. Moreover, he has had too little to do with politics, to be well qualified to conduct affairs of state. Yet, there is still a more important reason, which causes me to regret seeing his name pushed forward as a candidate for the presidency (and I feel little or no doubt he will be elected)—and that is, the principle of bringing forward men for the highest office in the gift of the people, solely for their military exploits. I supposed Gen. Taylor's best friends (and I feel myself among this number, except as a presidential candidate) will not deny that he never would have been dreamed of for president, but for his military fame. Nevertheless, the *principle* of the thing, as before suggested, is my chief objection; for with all his want of talent, etc. he can scarcely be behind Mr. Polk: and unwavering integrity

[5] This opinion of General Taylor is an instance of the acuteness of Gregg's estimates. When not influenced by dislike, Gregg was decidedly canny in his judgments of men.

is at last the most important qualification: I would therefore support Gen. Taylor in preference to a man in whose honesty I had no faith.

Gen. Taylor's design, in "dressing up," seems to have been to make a favorable impression upon the Missourians, whom he was just preparing to go out and review. It will be remembered that a high prejudice had existed against him, in Missouri, ever since his unfavorable report of the conduct of the Missouri militia in Florida:[6] aspiring as he now evidently is, he deemed it expedient to strive to put down this prejudice as much as possible. On this account, I suppose also, the Missouri regiment has in every regard, been treated by him with unusual favor.

This point, known as the "Walnut Grove" and "Walnut Springs," is one of the handsomest places for a camp that I have seen in Mexico, and has been a very favorite spot of Gen. Taylor's. Though called by Americans, "Walnut Grove," there is not a real walnut tree in it (or in fact, anywhere in that region of country that I have heard of): it has been so named from an ignorant translation of Americans. Though *nuez* seems the legitimate name of *walnut*, Mexicans apply the same term to hickory-nuts, paccans, etc.: in this grove there is some of the finest, largest paccan timber that I have met with in Mexico—called by the natives *nogales*, and consequent[ly] the grove *nagalal*—literally, but not properly, in this case, "Walnut Grove." There are also fine large live-oaks in this grove, besides some other species of timber. In this grove there are several very fine springs of excellent water.

From "Walnut Grove," 2 or 3 m. to village of Santo Domingo —thence 5 or 6 m. to San Francisco—thence say 3 m. to Agua-

---

[6]In the Florida campaign in 1837, General Taylor had assigned the Missouri contingent of volunteers a difficult piece of swamp fighting which proved too much for them. When the Indians, from concealments, poured a galling fire into the Missourians at twenty yards, and killed their leader, Colonel Gentry, the volunteers stood ground long enough to return the fire once, and then broke into disorderly flight. General Taylor's report recited the facts about the panic-stricken Missourians, but that did not take the sting from the matter, so far as the Missourians were concerned.

fría village & creek (same that passes Rinconada)—village chiefly on N.E. side—though part on S.W.—thence 4 m. to branch (running briskly)—then 1 m. to another branch—3 m. to Salinas River—& 2 m. to Marin—course from Aguafría to Marin E. 30° N.

Marin, before the war, was a flourishing little town (rather recently founded) of nearly 2,000 inhabitants; but it is now much dilapidated, and not half—perhaps not over a fourth— of the original population remains in it.—I was at a Mexican house, this evening—and was a little annoyed by the rudeness of some volunteers, who were drawing water from a well in the yard. The family desiring to get a little water for use, solicited me to get permission for them to draw it; but instead of this I only received insults: so the poor family had, I suppose to do without drinking, or their suppers—although the volunteers might have procured water in abundance from a small creek, on the other side of the camp, nearer to them than this well.— Lat. of Marin, 25° 52′ 40″.

Frid. 28—Rained lightly this morning. To Aguanegra, E. 25° S. 3 m.—½ m. to another small branch. Near this, it was, that, on 26th Feb. last (I think was the date) a large train— upward of 100 wagons—were defeated. Most of the wagoners were killed, besides some others; and a small escort of about 25 volunteers taken prisoners. This was a most inhuman massacre, as the wagoners were butchered unarmed—and many, it was believed, burned alive! This cut-throat band was under command of Gen. Urrea—variously stated to be from 500 to 2000 in number.[7] The wagons were rifled and burned. Besides some public property and money, there was a considerable amount of

---

[7] General Urrea's destruction of a provision train is described by Edwards in the following passage:

"The next day, we passed the place where the large train of wagon's was burnt by Urrea's men, about the same time that the battle of Buena Vista was fought.

"It was, indeed, even then a horrible sight to behold; and disgrace must ever attach to those officers having charge of the wagon-part of the quarter-master's department, who allowed the poor drivers to go unarmed, and the wagons to proceed

sutler's goods. It was many days after, before the murdered wagoners were buried; which was so badly done that the wolves had scratched many of the bodies up again, and their skeletons still lay bleaching on the plain! It was very surprising to me that Gen. Taylor should have remained encamped for weeks and even months, within 25 or 35 miles of the uninterred bodies of Americans, and with idle troops, without sending a detachment to bury them! We could also see where many of the wagons had been burned.—From here, 3 or 4 m. to Ramos, which but recently was said to have been a beautiful little village, of 500 souls or more; but now reduced to ashes, without a soul remaining.[8] It is said to have been burned by one Capt. Gray, of the Texan Rangers, of whom the Mexicans on this route still speak with horror.—The principal reason assigned for having burned this town of Ramos, was, I believe the atrocities committed upon the train, in that vicinity, and the supposition that the citizens had been concerned in, or at least favored them. This, may not have been just, for the mere fact (which was all our people seemed to know about it) of the people having permitted these Mexican troops (or marauders) to stop among them was no proof against them, as this may have been matter of compulsion; and that a few rogues of the place may have joined them is more than probable; yet the punishment fell more upon the best and most innocent, as would seem most probable, not only because the evil persons generally place themselves in security, in anticipation, but because they seldom have property to lose.

---

with so exceedingly a slight escort. Every here and there were the burnt remains of wagons which the brutal Mexicans set fire to without unharnessing the mules from them, so that the frightened animals dashed off until they became wedged among the trees, where they were burnt with the wagons—and the bones of the slaughtered drivers were lying about in all directions. A spot was pointed out to me where one of the teamsters had been staked down, and then inhumanly butchered inch by inch;—others were burnt alive, and but few escaped."—*A Campaign in New Mexico with Colonel Doniphan*, 152.

[8] This ravaging of Ramos at the hands of Captain Gray of the Texas Rangers was another of those outrages committed by the Texas volunteers, who were addicted to cruel retaliations for Mexican barbarities during the revolution.

Equally unjust seems to me, the order promulgated after-ward by Gen. Taylor, in a circular, that the inhabitants of the three contiguous departments, Tamaulipas, Nuevo Leon & Coa-huila should pay for all the robberies and devastations com-mitted by Urrea's band. Verily, this places these poor people in a most wretched position: first, the seat of Gen. Taylor's oper-ations being almost exclusively within their boundaries, they have to suffer nearly all the burden and damages of the war: 2dly, being Mexican citizens, they are, according to the laws of nations, guilty of treason for showing us any favor,—giving us any aid; and are liable to be punished hereafter as traitors by their own government: 3dly, we seem nevertheless to hold them crim-inally responsible for not being our friends—for any aid afforded their countrymen, though it may have been compulsory. As to the mere fact of their furnishing provisions to our enemies, how could we expect anything else when threatened by their armies? And though a few may have joined in the depredations, as we well know there are numbers of *robbers* among their best com-munities, it has been to me a matter of surprise, that so few should have done so—that among a population that ought to have afforded 100,000 men able to bear arms, not 1000—perhaps not much over 100—should have joined Urrea's band: we feel con-vinced that there were more than an equal number of rascals who seek every opportunity to join in robberies. Then, as nearly always happens in indiscriminate punishment, the burden is most apt to fall on the innocent, as the guilty generally have not only least to lose, but are on the alert to keep out of reach.—This, is upon the supposition that rascals only joined Urrea; yet I do not understand why we hold good citizens criminally responsible for joining their armies, as we would not only do so ourselves, under similar circumstances, but we would consider as very crim-inal all such as failed to do so. True, we would not commit simi-lar atrocities; nor have we proof that the better class, even of their armies, were concerned there.—I do not understand that

141

the people of the country should be any more responsible for the deeds of Urrea's army, than for those of Santa Anna's & Miñon's.

From Ramos 6 or 7 m. to a hill (opposite point of Mountain to left—say, 14 m. from Marin),—whence course to Monterey, W. 22° S.—Bishop's Hill, W. 20° S.—Marin, W. 7° N.— Ramos, W. 20° N. (?)—1 m. to Papagallos. Whence N. 40° W. 18 or 20 m. to Rancho Viejo. Camped 1 m. back, at Carrizitos. Lat. of Carrizitos, 26° 0′ 20″—This & Papagallos small abandoned ranchos: Rancho Viejo, larger—abandoned & burned.

Sat. 29—N. 17° or 18° E. 7 or 8 m. whence course back to Papagallos S. 30° or 32° W.—Stopped to noon. We had not been here long when we learned that the Texan Rangers had caught a man who, it was said had belonged to Urrea's band.[9]

[9] This execution of a member of Urrea's band was a grim affair that drew the attention of all the chroniclers of the march. Gregg shows his fair-mindedness and judicial attitude by expressing doubt as to the justice of the sentence. So do many other writers of the time. Connelley quotes the following from a letter of June 14, 1906, by Odon Guitar, who was a member of the Doniphan expedition and at that time a private in Company H, First Regiment, Missouri Mounted Volunteers:

"The incident was one of the most outrageous events of the Mexican War, and came near resulting in a mutiny in our regiment. A majority of us were in favor of rescuing him [the guerrilla chief], and it would have been done but for the personal influence of Colonel Doniphan and our other officers had over us. I have always insisted that he was the *coolest and bravest* soldier that ever died for his country. A circumstantial recital of the facts attending the execution of the Mexican officer would bring tears to the eyes of every brave and generous-hearted man who might read it, as it did to my eyes, in after days, when I recalled them. I am still determined, if I can, to have the authorities of Mexico erect a monument to his memory at the City of Mexico. This incident alone, with appropriate comment, would furnish matter for a volume."—*Doniphan's Expedition*, 487n.

Frank S. Edwards' account follows:

"While we rested at Ceralvo, I witnessed the execution of a Mexican supposed to be one of Urrea's lawless band. The Texians pretended to consider him as such; but there was no doubt that this was only used as a cloak to cover their insatiable desire to destroy those they so bitterly hate. A furlough was found upon this Mexican from his army to visit his family, ending as our furloughs do, that should he overstay his leave of absence, he would be considered a deserter. This time he had considerably overstayed; and he himself stated that he had never intended to return, being in favor of the Americans. But the rangers tried him by court-martial; and adjudged him to be shot that very day. As the hour struck, he was led into the public plaza; and five rangers took their post a few feet off, as executioners. The condemned coolly pulled out his flint and steel, and little paper-cigarito; and, striking a light, commenced smoking as calmly as can possibly be imagined, and—in two minutes—fell a corpse, with the still smoking cigarito yet between his lips.

He was tried and convicted—some said upon very vague testimony,—from the best I could learn, that of a guide who was with the Texans: however, I believe he did not deny having been a soldier under Urrea, but protested that he was not connected in the massacre of the wagoners, etc. He was condemned to be shot this evening; and Col. Donophan delayed his regiment to witness the execution. For my own part I was disposed to doubt the propriety of the sentence. All the testimony that was arrayed against him may have been malicious and false: and even had it been proven that he was on the very expedition against the train, unless it had appeared that he was actually concerned in the inhuman massacres, I do not see that the Texans had any right to do more than treat him as prisoner of war, for Urrea was an authorized officer of the Mexican government,—and the prisoner it is presumable, had not the individual power, had he tried, to prevent the murders.

Cerralbo is said to have contained about 1500 souls before the war; but it is now much dilapidated and abandoned: I doubt if there are 500 souls in it.—Hence, N. 30° E. 15 m. to Puntiagudo: this village also abandoned and burned: looks like it may once have contained 2 or 300 souls.—Lat. 26° 14′ 13″ of Puntiagudo.

Camped at Puntiagudo—and soon after stopping, I fell in with Capts. Weightman and Reid. The desolate appearance of the place brought up the subject of the propriety of these devastations; and though I was gratified at the mild, gentlemanly and equitable expressions of Capt. Weightman, I was much surprised and equally grieved to find that Capt. Reid was disposed

---

I did not see a muscle of his face quiver, when the rifles were levelled at him, but he looked coolly at his executioners, pressing a small cross, which hung to his neck, firmly against his breast. I turned from the scene sickened at heart."—*A Campaign in New Mexico with Colonel Doniphan*, 156.

Wislizenus states that the man's name was Nicholas Garcia, and adds: "Some rumor was afterwards started that he was a brother of General Canales, but at Ceralbo I understood that he was well known there; that his mother lived there yet, and that he had no other connection with Canales than belonging to his bands."—*Memoir of a Tour to Northern Mexico*, 80.

to justify every act of the kind—burning, killing, the execution of to-day, etc.! but the Capt. was in a passion—the opinions expressed were scarcely those of Capt. Reid but of excitement and anger: I will not believe that he holds similar ideas when "properly at himself": for I had all along considered Capt. Reid (as well as Capt. Weightman) among the worthiest officers of this corps.

Sun. 30—E. 10° N. 3 or 4 m.—(thence course to Agualeguas, W. 40° N. 5 to 10 m.—) E. 10° N. 2 or 3 m.—thence say N.E. 6 or 7 m. to bend in creek—thence, 1st half E. 20° N. 2ᵈ half, E. 35° or 40° N.,—14 or 15 m. to Mier, on S.W. bank of Rio del Cántaro (less than a *legua* from Rio Grande), formed by junction of Agualeguas & Alamo rivers, 5 *leguas* above Mier. Branch 2 m. from bend of cr.

Mier is a town of 2 or 3,000 inhabitants (I suppose) and shows less signs of dilapidation, on account of the war than any place on this route. It has become famous on account of a party of Texans having been taken prisoners there in the year 18[—].[10] This was an irregular party of adventurers, who first entered Laredo; but the fame of their outrages and depredations having gone ahead of them, the people of Mier were prepared, beset, and took them prisoners. The adventurers may have merited this fate, had their conquerors treated them like civilized people afterward. But the atrocities subsequently perpetrated upon those prisoners got up a decided sympathy in their favor.—Lat. of Mier, 26° 26′ 10″. [MARGINAL NOTE: Subsequent for lat. by Polaris resulted in the same—or 26° 26′ 9″.]

Mon. 31—E. 25° S. 3 m. to creek—then E. 40° S. 2 or 3 m.

---

[10] The Mier expedition (1842) was an incident of the Texas Revolution. A party of Texans descended upon the town of Mier, on the Rio Grande, but were overcome by the Mexicans, who greatly outnumbered them. Once in the hands of the Mexicans, these two hundred or so Texans were subjected to harsh and vindictive treatment. At one time the Mexican officer in charge ordered decimation, those to be executed being selected by the drawing of black beans. Thomas J. Green, one of the prisoners, has given the classic account in his *Journal of the Texian Expedition against Mier* (New York, Harper & Brothers, 1845).

to another creek—then east, 6 m. (in all 10 or 12 m. to Mor-
terito (rancho of perhaps 20 souls)—river ¼ m. distant—
Thence 2 m. (last course)—to Refugio (rancho of perhaps 50
souls on river bank)—E. 5° S. 1½ m. to Guardado de Arriba
(rancho say 50 or 60 souls, on river bank—E. 10° S. 2 m. to
Guardado de Abajo (say 60 or 80 souls, on *estero* or *slue* of the
river)—thence E. 20° or 25° S. 2 m. to a creek—then east, ½
m. to river again—thence (1/3 E. 20° S.—1/3 E. 40 S.—&
1/3 S. 30° E.) 5 or 6 m. to Camargo, on east bank of Rio de San
Juan. Course down river from Camargo, N.W.—up do. S. 25°
W.—Mexicans call it a *legua* from Camargo to Rio Grande.—
Lat. of Camargo, 26° 18′ 21″.—Camargo has been made the
most important military depot on this line, on account of the Rio
Grande's being navigable (and the San Juan) this high, most
of the year. But, on account of the present very low state of the
water, boats had stopped coming up here: so we continued our
march next day to *el puerto* de San Francisco.

❄ DIARY, JUNE, 1847

Tues. 1—E. 35° S. 6 or 7 m. to Puertecitos (rancho of say 50
souls)—then E. 10° N. 1 m. to San Francisco. About a mile
above Puertecitos a very serious casualty occurred. A Missouri
volunteer was riding two or three hundred yards ahead, and
alone, in advance of the advance guard, when he was waylaid
and shot down by some Mexican bandits! The van guard soon
coming up, they found one Mexican, and showing suspicious
signs, he was shot. They found upon his person, as I understood,
a paper containing the *roll* of the party, he being in the character
of Sergeant. But the friends of the murdered volunteer were
not satisfied with this. I happened to come up just at this period;
and seeing Capt. Walton and his company set out, much excited,
toward the ranch of Puertecitos, a little to left of road, I followed on with them. I much feared some atrocities would be
committed at once, as the men were swearing vengeance, every

step—inquiring of each other if they had matches to fire the huts! and, on seeing Mexicans around the cabins, they exclaimed "Let's go to shooting at once," etc. but between Capt. Walton[11] and myself we prevailed on them to desist at least till they could find some sort of evidence of their guilt. I passed on, but learned afterward that some 4 or 5 of the rancheros were taken prisoners and carried to the camp at San Francisco. Here they were tried; and no evidence appearing to convict them of being concerned in the murder, they were set at liberty. The cause of suspicion was, the finding of a horse or two at the rancho, somewhat jaded and sweated, and a ranchero with a little blood on his shirt. Both these, however, might easily have occurred from innocent circumstances. Yet the friends of the deceased were not satisfied. They must have vengeance by "blood for blood," though the sacrified Mexicans be innocent. Seeing the danger of the prisoners, they were sent of[f] under guard; yet, I afterward learned that they were followed by some reckless fellows; and after the guard left them, at least three (and perhaps more) were killed! Indeed, I was told that the enraged volunteers continued on to the rancho, shot all the Mexicans they could find, and burned the cabins! I extremely regretted afterward to learn that there were officers among the Missourians, who justified the killing of the *rancheros!* Now, though it should have been just to have executed them, an officer should never justify an unauthorized proceeding.

Reynosa

There being no boat at S. Francisco, and very little prospect of any ascending higher than Reynosa, Col. Donophan concluded to proceed by land to that place: so the regiment marched this evening about 4 o'clock, P.M. intending to travel all night—or at least, till they reached Reynosa.[12]

To Pajarito Cr. about 15 m. 1st third, N. of E.—2d east— 3d

[11] William Parr Walton, captain, Company B, First Regiment, Missouri Mounted Volunteers.

146

S. of E. thence 4 m. to rancho on left—½ to do. on right—1 m. to do. on left—course S. of E.—then S.E. (nearly), 2 m. to another rancho on left— S. 30° E. 4 or 5 m. & E. 2 or 3 m. to another rancho—E.N.E. 2 m. to another rancho on left—1 or 2 m. same course—then E.S.E. 2 m. then E. 10° or 15° S. 2 or 3 m. to rancho on left—then 2 m. to San Antonio de Reynosa on western bank of Rio Grande—whole distance from Pajarito cr., say 15 to 18 m. therefore the above series of distances too long.—There were several other ranchos on route (and especially just below San Francisco—with population) which I did not here note. Most of those below Pajarito cr. are said to be depopulated.—Reynosa is a town of perhaps 2,000 inhabitants, when in a thrifty condition. Now our principal depot is there— or at least landing for troops and supplies, as boats cannot conveniently ascend higher up Rio Grande, at present stage of water. —I endeavored to get latitude of Reynosa by meridian altitude of moon, (as Polaris was obstructed by clouds), yet owing to the clouds, I did not get it accurately. Latitude resulting, 26° 13′ 40″—but think it probably 3′ to 5′ too great, as my altitude was too small.—Lat. since taken, 26° 6′

At Reynosa we found two or three small steam-boats, in which the Missouri regiment prepared to embark. Finally, however, after two or three days' delay, we concluded to proceed to Matamoros by land—as well on account of the difficulty in getting

[12] Gregg, too absorbed in his own affairs, failed to note some matters which a writer like Edwards, with more of an eye for the picturesque, tried to make something of, even though they were trivialities. Edwards reports:

"News had been brought to us that five steamboats were lying at Reinosa; and several regiments, which had been discharged by Taylor being also on the march for that place, we were obliged to push on as fast as possible, in order that we might get the first chance. This we did, and we managed to get ahead of all but one regiment, which was only a few hours' march before us; so it was resolved to push on all this night, as we were moving as rapidly as possible, we came upon the above regiment encamped; and they, perceiving our object, at once struck tents, and came after us; but we had got much the start of them, and they did not arrive at Reinosa until after our officers had secured the only two available boats; three others being hard aground on the bar below the town, and the water falling fast."—*A Campaign in New Mexico with Colonel Doniphan*, 160.

passage on steam boats, when there were so many troops waiting (and the vessels belonged to the government) as because we
could not here dispose of our wagon and team. But, as the route
was most probably infested by banditti we should not have ventured to make this land trip, but for Capt. Lee[13] (Missouri quartermaster) taking down a considerable number of wagons and
teams by land, to deliver them over at Matamoros to the Qr.Mr.
dept. Capt. Lee was much vexed at Col. Donophan (and it would
seem with some justice) about this affair. He had been ordered
at first to deliver all the Government [property] over at Camargo, but this the Col. would not permit him to do, as he
wanted the wagons to transport his regiment to Reynosa—although this might have been dispensed with, as the Qr. Mr. at
Camargo proffered to furnish other transportation to Reynosa,
if the Col. would wait 6 hours. But this his impatience would
not permit him to do; and after reaching Reynosa, he ordered
Lee to return to Camargo with the wagons, etc. But, Lee, feeling
urged by almost unavoidable business with his regiment, to be
with them in N. Orleans, he "assumed the responsibility["] of
proceeding to Matamoros, where he succeeded in delivering his
public property without difficulty.

Frid. 4—One inducement for us to continue on to Matamoros
by land was, that, the river was so very low, that the boats were
getting aground, every few miles, so that we fully contemplated
getting down sooner this way than by water; but this morning it
rained a very hard shower, which made the roads very bad, in
the flat country, through which they passed to Matamoros, and
raised the river to a good navigable state.—Started after the
rain—say about 8 o'clock, A.M.

General course about E. 10° S. 21 or 22 m. (a little over 8
leguas measured) to Charco Azul—a small rancho, now abandoned. Here we found the water so wretchedly bad that we not

[13] Gregg's spelling may be awry again; according to Hughes the name should
be James Lea.

only had to send to Rio Grande (3 m. distant) for drinking water, but found it necessary to drive our stock there also; for though there was an abundant pond of water, it was so filthy and the borders so miry that our animals could not be got to drink. The rain had been but light here; therefore the water but little improved. Really, I certainly never saw such an abundance of bones of cattle, etc. and decaying carcasses. There were perhaps 100 in a putrifying state—and the bones of, literally, "thousands" lay about the borders of the pond. During dry weather, I suppose there was no other water in the vicinity, so that all the cattle in the neighborhood resorted there to drink; and the borders of the water being miry, many stuck fast and died. Some contended that the water contained some deleterious [substance] which killed the animals—and really, it looked a little like it, as many carcasses lay many yards from the water. What gave rise to this idea among us, was that two or three mules belonging to the train sickened and died during the night, which were said to have drank some of the water.—There are several abandoned ranchos along the road from Reynosa to Charco Azul.

Sat. 5—Road forks at Charco Azul—left follow near river border—we took the right. Passed two or three small depopulated ranchos. 10 or 12 m. to Encinada, and 15 m. to Guadalupe —general course, E. 10° S.—thence, E. 35° S. 6 m. to Matamoros. Rained a light shower or two to-day—& very little last night.

The city of Matamoros is beginning to assume quite an American appearance—brick and framed housed, with shingle roofs. Population, I should suppose, between 3 & 5,000.—Latitude of Matamoros, by means of two nearly correspondent observations of Polaris, 25° 53′ 5″.

While delayed at Matamoros, I may indulge a remark or two about the country—from here to Monterey, and even thence to Chihuahua—as I have not had time to do it before. For agricultural purposes, I have seen few districts in Mexico equal to that

149

about Monterey—in valley of the river—and much of that between here and there: perhaps most of the way, were we to follow the course of Rio San Juan. Also the valley of Rio Grande
is generally of a fertile alluvial soil, well adapted to cultivation.
These large streams afford a rather greater abundance of water
than is usually found: true Rio Grande is virtually inexhaustible,
though for want of sufficient fall it will be somewhat difficult to
get out in ditches for purposes of irrigation. The upper portions
of Rio de San Juan, are rather scant of water in dry weather—
though otherwise well adapted to irrigating purposes. The soil
in all the valleys from here to Monterey is generally rich alluvial, which would produce corn, sugar, and I should think, cotton (though not cultivated) were the rains more abundant.

From here to Monterey, it is generally a plain country—occasionally a little undulating: we leave the last mountains (on
the left) a little on this side of Marin. On the route down the
river, via China, we would lose sight of the last on the right,
I suppose, about Cadercita, between 20 and 30 m. below Monterey.

In point of timber, it is rather better supplied in this region,
than in any other portion of Mexico I have been: Somewhat
similar to the country about Rio Grande, up at the Presidio. The
timber, however, is generally small and scrubby—though including large underbrush, there is the greatest abundance for fuel.
The most interesting growths, are the Mexican *ébano* (or ebony)
and Mexican *brazil*, both beautiful little trees, growing sometimes (in fact, frequently) 20 to 30 feet high, with trunks a
foot or more in diameter. We also find abundance of mezquite
and *una-de-gato*, both growing sometimes over 20 feet high—
sometimes 30 or more, especially the former. We find also in
greater or less degree of abundance *anacua*, *nacahuita*, cottonwood, etc, etc. The truth is the whole country is almost one continuous chaparral (or thicket) from Matamoros to Monterey.

From Monterey to Saltillo, the face of the country is shut

up with mountains—the plains and valleys with less timber and poorer soil.

From Saltillo to the Bolson de Mapimí, timber is still more scarce—mountains abundant—water scarce—and tillable rich soil scarce—though there are sections, as those of Patos, Parras, etc. of remarkable fertility.

The Bolson de Mapimí is an immense mountain cove, enclosed almost completely by mountains on every side, and out of which water seldom—some say never—escapes; although there are continually emptying into it, besides numerous smaller streams, the rivers of Nazas and Guarraval, or Buenavá as currently called by the people. These form the great lakes of Tahualilo, Muertos, Alamo, and small smaller collections of water I fancy that this valley was once much deeper than at present,—but has gradually been filling up—perhaps originally an enormous pit or crater—until it is now getting on a level with the lowest outlet—via Pastora, Alamo Mocho & through Anelo or Salinas river to Rio Grande. What seems to render this more probable is the comparative newness of the lower lake—Muerto or San Nicolas, having been formed, as more than one old resident of the country has told me, within the present century—in fact, they date it back only to within the last 15 or 20 years. Rio Nazas seems before to have discharged itself in Lake Tahualilo and Alamo.

This valley—the Bolson de Mapimí—extends from Latitude about 25° 40″ to between 26° & 27°—course about W.N.W. —length about 100 miles and width 20 to 40. A large portion of this valley is of fertile soil; though portions are too sandy. Water is, however, remarkably scarce, there being none, anywhere in the interior of the valley, except the lakes, which go nearly dry during summer droughts—and Rio de Nazas, the lower portions of which also go nearly dry during dry weather. And when it contains water, there is not fall enough to use it for irrigation. Therefore, there are but few parts—immediately around the borders—of this valley, that can be irrigated. Otherwise this would be one of the most beautiful and extensive tillable regions in the interior of Mexico. However, the imme[diate] valleys of the Nazas, are said to produce very well without watering; and the soil being of a deep alluvial vegetable mould, it produces fine corn—superior wheat & cotton,—and it seems to me it ou[gh]t to produce sugar—unless its great elevation—some 4000 feet above the ocean—renders it too cold. The timber in this valley—covering, I may say, "hundreds of thousands" of acres, is also better than common: abundance of mezquite, often growing 40 or 50 feet high, and of proportionate dimensions. There are some other kinds of trees, and a great exuberance of annual vegetation. The higher portions of the Bolson are more sparsely set (sometimes nearly naked prairies) with smaller mezquites and other scrubby growths.

From Mapimí to Rio Conchos waters, it is mostly a barren waste—but little water—as little timber, except shrubbery—dry plains interspersed with detached ridges of mountains. For 50 or 60 miles southeastward from Guapiquilla it is almost a perfect irreclaimable desert—there being little water, except in wet weather. The valley of Rio Florido, though scant of timber (& that chiefly mezquite and uña-de-gato) contains much fertile alluvial soil, but the river does not afford near water enough to irrigate it through the summer.

The valley of Rio Conchos is of a similar character.—still richer I believe, with also rather more timber, though of the same kinds: yet a similar scarcity of water for extensive cultivation prevails.

The country about Chihuahua, is an intermixture of mountains and high valleys. The "bottoms" of the streams are generally rich and produce good corn and wheat when there is sufficiency of water for irrigation, but this is also scarce. Timber is very scarce, except in the depths of the mountains, at a distance.

Mon. 7—The boats with the Missouri regiment had all passed

down—the first with Col. Donophan, the same day arrived here
—and the little steamer "Warren," arriving from above, to-day
with the advance of the Indianians, we got passage on her to the
mouth. I certainly feel under lasting obligations to Gen. Lane
(was on board) for his kindness and favor on this occasion, as
well as on several previous and subsequent ones.—We left Matamoros about 4 o'clock, P.M. Capt. Lee with the Missourians also
got passage on the same.—Stopped some ten miles above Palo
Alto for the night, and slept on shore.—Took latitude of this
point on the river and found it, 25° 50′ 22″. Rio Grande exceedingly crooked from Matamoros to the mouth.

Tues. 8—Arrived at village (government depot) on north
side of mouth, about 8 o'clock, A.M.—There is a little village
on south side of mouth, called Bagdad. These villages are within
less than a quarter of a mile of the Gulf. The Rio Grande is remarkably narrow near the mouth—some places (and generally)
even 10 m. from mouth, it is scarcely 100 yds. wide, and here,
between the two villages, it seems to me not 200 yards—at any
rate it can be very little over. From Matamoros (by the river)
to Palo Alto about 35 m.—thence to Burita, 10 m. and mouth
10 m. more.—Burita a point of some elevation, on the S.W. bank
of the Rio Grande: as far as I could see, a much prettier site for
a town than Matamoros. Unless there are disadvantages which
I could not perceive, I could not but wonder why it was not made
the principal town and port instead of Matamoros. Schooners
go up that high when they will not venture higher. In fact, any
schooner than can get into the mouth of the river, can go up as
high as Burita. This was the first Mexican village taken possession of in Mexico by our armies.[14] Its population is perhaps two
hundred.

Through the favor of Gen. Lane we got transportation from
the mouth across to Brazo de Santiago, about 10 m. by land.

[14] Burita (spelled Burrita), about 20 miles from Matamoras, was the first Mexican village occupied by the American armies. General Taylor placed troops there
in May, 1846.

Course from Brazo de Santiago to mouth S. 10° E.—to Point Isabel W. 30° S. 3 to 5 m. Brazo de Santiago is a very low sandy point, around which a very small arm of the sea (or rather a marshy *slue*) extends,—whence the name—and wherefore it is sometimes called by our people, "Brazos Island." It is the only port for even medium-sized vessels anywhere in this quarter. The harbor is between the point and the main land. There is about 9 feet water on the bar at the entrance, I believe. It has grown up into a small village, but the principal buildings belong to the quartermaster's department—being the principal U.S. depot.

Arrived at "Brazos," at 3 P.M.; and finding a steam ship (the "Telegraph," belonging to the U.S.) which had just arrived from Vera Cruz, and prepared to sail next day for New Orleans, I went on board at once and made an arrangement at once with the captain (Auld) to take my comrades and self, with our bullion, baggage, etc. He said, though a government vessel, he had the liberty of taking a few passengers: so I thought all was right. We therefore commenced at once getting our bullion and baggage on board; but as the vessel was moored behind two or three others, it occasioned us so much trouble and delay, that, before we got done, one of the vessels, a steam boat, was moved out, and we could not possibly get to the vessel. I inquired of the Capt. if his ship would not be so moved up as to enable us to finish taking our goods aboard: but being pretty "tipsy," he flew in a great passion,—and swore that we should not go at all—should take off what we had put on the vessel. Even afterward, in his soberer moments, I found, that, to take him all in all, Capt. Auld is one of the most disagreeable officers I had had ever to do with. We should perhaps have had much trouble on this occasion, had not Gen. Lane come up just at this time and "set things straight" again.

Wed. 9—Left "Brazos" to-day at half past 1 o'clock. Although not storming, it was windy enough to make a rough sea, and to make us generally pretty "sea-sick" by the time we had got fairly out on the gulf.

Sat. 12—On the evening of the 10th, it calmed; but we lost several hours, by the engine's getting out of order. The truth is, although the vessel bore a good character, I had understood before starting, we found she was quite old and "rickety." We learned that on the night of the 9th, she sprung a leak, and might have filled, had it not been discovered.

To-day in the forenoon (about 10 o'clock) the Capt. stopped to sound; and on letting steam on again rather too suddenly, they burst one of the cylinder heads, which it took 8 or 10 hours to repair, so as to run at all, and then with not over half-press of steam. Soon after this accident, it was made known that the water was nearly all out. This was anything but agreeable news; for had a "norther" sprung up, we would have been blown out to sea, and almost inevitably lost. It had been calm ever since the evening of the 10th—a beautiful time for running under steam; but though the sails were hoisted, he scarcely moved through the water at the rate of half mile an hour. About 6 P.M. we got under way again. By this time everybody was becoming thirsty, and some suffering considerably. What added to the general uneasiness, was that the Capt. appeared lost, as he had said, early in the morning that we were but about 30 m. from the mouth of the Mississippi—which we had discovered to be "wide of the mark." What added to the unpleasantness of our situation was that there were about 600 of 2d regiment of Ohio volunteers on board. These were commanded by Lieut. Col. M. Cook, a young man, who, though doubtless clever enough otherwise, was not only unfit for a commander, but, being elated by his elevation, he seemed an upstart, who put on airs very disagreeable to many on board. In the cabin and its appendages, there were, I suppose, some sixty passengers (officers, etc.); and as this was very small we were exceedingly crowded. Unless one took a start, it was difficult to find room even on the floor to spread one's length. One night I was a little too late going to bed; and I surveyed the deck twice over before finding a vacant place large enough to spread my blanket!—I had set up late to-night, until we should get into the mouth of the Mississippi, so as to get a drink of fresh water. This we entered about 11 o'clock, and I suppose water seldom had tasted better than it did then to any of us. Ever since it had become dark, we had been looking out for the light house at the mouth, with the greatest anxiety; and great was the joy when we caught the first glimpse of it.

Sun. 13—I had one of Colt's patent carbine's on board, which I had left sitting in the stern of the vessel, near where we all slept—and had seen it there the day before; but looking for it this morning to shoot alligators, it was no where to be found: some rascally volunteer or passenger had stolen it! When taken apart, it was short enough to put in a small trunk and therefore easily concealed. I had been unfortunate in this line: a small pistol (of same patent) which I had, I lost on the battlefield of Saltillo. Laying it down (on 21st May) I went off and forgot it; and when I returned next day to look for it, I could not find it— picked up, I suppose by one of the Missouri or Arkansas volunteers who had been strolling over the field: And though I had general inquiry inst[it]uted, I could not hear of it.—Arrived at N. Orleans this evening between 5 and 6 o'clock.

Mon. 14—As the N. Orleans mint had a bad reputation with most of my acquaintances of the Mexican traders, we concluded to take the bullion we had (about $36,000, belonging to S. Magoffin, Dr. East & Mr. Fristoe) to Philadelphia to get it coined. We embarked on Steamer "Belle of the West" for Cincinnati, and left this evening, about 8 o'clock.—Passage $15.—I had hoped henceforward to get rid of a crowd, but as between 50 and 100 Ohio volunteers took passage on this boat, we were greatly thronged again.—On the 17th, passed Vicksburg about 5 A.M. —18th, Napoleon at 1, P.M.—19th, Memphis at 8 P.M.—20th, New Madrid at 10, P.M.—21st Cairo at 7½, A.M.—Paducah at

1, P.M.—22ᵈ Evansville at 9, A.M. 23ᵈ Foot of Canal at 11, A.M.

Wed. 23—Took back from locks to Louisville.—owing to detention by other boats in canal above, the "Belle" did not get up to Louisville till about 10½, P.M.—Left again about midnight.

Thurs. 24—Arrived at Cincinnati this evening about 6 o'clock. Besides the little comfort, on account of crowd, the "Belle of the West" is a decidedly slow boat, as is demonstrated by our having been 10 days from New Orleans to Cincinnati.

Wed. 25—Left on Packet "Hibernia Nᵒ 2," for Pittsburgh. Passed Portsmouth at 11 P.M.—27th, passed Wheeling at 12 noon—and at Pittsburgh before day. The Hibernia is a decidedly fast and comfortable boat—though it too was a good deal crowded. The truth is, the packets I have found the best boats between Pittsburgh & Cincinnati.

Mon. 28—Arrived at Pittsburgh at 2 o'clock, A.M. Left this evening at 9 o'clock, via the Canal, as we could not otherwise conveniently convey our bullion.

❂ DIARY, JULY, 1847

Frid. 2—Arrived at Philadelphia, at 3 o'clock, P.M.

Mon. 5—Being anxious to obtain some more definite information regarding the introduction of goods into Mexico, I concluded to make a trip to Washington City. Left this evening at 4 o'clock, but went to Brandywine springs on a visit to my friend Peter L. Ferguson.

Wed. 7—Arrived at Washington yesterday evening—did my business this morning—left on 12 o'clock cars,—and arrived at Philadᵃ again the same night at 2 o'clock—via steam boats & Frenchtown & Newcastle Rail Road.

Mon. 12—From the information I obtained at Washington, prospects appeared better than I had contemplated, for our Mexican enterprise: so I left this evening for New York, in company with Mr. James Abbott[15] (firm of Woods, Abbott & Co.)

---

[15] James A. Abbott, a member of the Philadelphia wholesale firm which Gregg mentions.

157

to buy our assortment of merchandise—started, 4½ & arrived at 9½ P.M.

Wed. 14—Having looked through the New York market, and found assortments of English goods, subject to drawback, more abundant and cheap than I had expected, we were just prepared to close bargains for the entire stock (near $40,000), when we received to day, about 12 o'clock, a telegraphic dispatch from the firm of Wood, Abbott & Co. at Phila not to purchase any goods, as Mr. Magoffin had countermanded the order, by letter to them. Magoffin also wrote me (which I afterward received), stating that he had become frightened on account of the heavy duties imposed by our government, and so had concluded to give up the enterprise. His explanations were not at all satisfactory; for of course I knew much more about those circumstances than he: he should therefore have left it something to my option. He has thus done me great injustice, and caused me immense inconvenience; for I had left most of my baggage at Saltillo, upon the faith of the engagement to return. I suppose I shall have to go back, anyhow, were it for nothing but to get my baggage, books, instruments, etc. But, having nothing else in contemplation, I do not know that I can do better at present, anyway, than to return into Mexico, were it but to engage in the practice of medicine.[16]

Thurs. 15—Made a visit to day to the N.Y. state prison, at Sing Sing with my friends, Dr. East & Reuben Gentry, who had arrived at N.Y. on Wednesday night. They left again on Saturday morning following for the west, via Saratoga and the Lakes, etc.

Sun. 25—Having delayed at New York, on business—correcting the stereotype plates of my work,[17] etc., I did not leave till this evening. Left at 4½ & arrived at Phila 9½ P.M.

[16] Gregg had now found it necessary to recant his previous statements about not undertaking to practice medicine. See Part I, 180, 384.

[17] It is difficult to understand Gregg's constant "correcting plates" whenever he was in the East. The successive editions of *Commerce of the Prairies* show only the most minor corrections.

Wed. 28—Left Philad^a at 3½ P.M. for Washington City, via steam boat, etc.

Thurs. 29—Arrived at Baltimore after midnight—left this morning at 6½ & arrived at Washington at 8½ A.M.

☼ LETTER TO DR. GEORGE ENGELMANN

Washington City, July 29, 1847

MY DEAR SIR:

Your highly agreeable favor of the 13th inst. was received in Philadelphia, where it arrived while I was absent in New York. Thinking I would not delay long in that City, I carelessly neglected to reorder my letters forwarded; and when I returned, I found yours in the office, with many others.

I doubly regretted not having received your letter in New York (enclosing the very grateful favor of Dr. Wislizenus) on account of the instruments etc. which he ordered. For I could not find the "viometer" nor even the prismatic compass anywhere in Phila; and I did not remain long enough there, on my return, to order them from New York. The truth is, it is doubtful if the road-measure could be had anywhere, without having it made. The only man I could hear of in Phila. who had made them, lately died. And even if I could have got one made, it would have taken more time than I remained in the City.

Seeing no other chance to get a prismatic compass, I wrote to my friend Alexander Megarey of New York, dealer in nautical instruments, etc. to send you one and draw on you for the cost—provided this did not exceed $15. Should the price be greater, I directed him to write you information of the subject, and wait your orders. I put in the maximum of "some $15" because I have seen them priced as high as $20 or $25; and I was not sure if Dr. Wislizenus would like to pay so much, as he may not have anticipated the high cost of the instrument. Fifteen dollars is, I believe, the lowest I have seen them priced—except mine, which I bought for $9, said to be unusually low.

I procured the nautical almanac for 1848, which I will send you from Louisville with the plants; that is, provided I do not go to St. Louis myself, which, though it would be exceedingly agreeable to me, is not very probable.

As the principal object of this note is to inform you touching Dr. Wislizenus's instruments, etc. and of my having authorized Mr. Megarey to draw on you for the cost, if he sent the compass, I will not undertake here to answer your last letter. I will defer a full communication till I send the package of plants—which will be soon; as I will leave here in two or three days for Pittsburgh—and thence immediately down the Ohio.

Permit me to repeat my thanks for your kind notices and advice; and believe me, as I truly am,

Your friend, etc.

Josiah Gregg

Dr. George Engelman

P.S. Please present my regards, and sincere thanks, to Dr. Wislizenus. His barometrical memoranda are very full and interesting to me; more copious, indeed, than I could have asked him to draw for me.

I regret I am not prepared to send him a table of my latitudes, etc. for want of leisure to make the calculations; but I will not fail to profit by my leisure on the Ohio River and complete the calculations, when I will send them immediately.

❀ DIARY, JULY, 1847

Sat. 31—I had concluded to come by Washington with a remote idea that I might obtain some government employ in the direction of Mexico: but having become thoroughly disgusted with government affairs, I left this morning without having made my business known to the President or his officers. The truth is, having made a visit to the President, on Friday evening, I was so astonished at the evident weakness of Mr. Polk, that I then felt like I would not accept anything at his hands—and departed accordingly. It is remarkable that a man so short of intellect should have been placed in the executive chair! But, our surprise is diminished when we reflect that he was, virtually, not elected by the people, but by a caucus at Baltimore, who rather desire a "creature" than talents, to serve designing politicians as a tool. Really, it savours illy for the stability of our institutions that a set of demagogues should point out to the people, for their president, a man never dreamed of before, and that these should so implicitly obey the will of the caucus, as to elect without discussion, the man they were bid to vote for! Left Washington this morning at 6 o'clock, on cars for "Relay House," and thence by Do. to Cumberland; where arrived a little before 6 P.M.

❁ DIARY, AUGUST, 1847

Sun. 1—Reached Brownsville by stage, this morning before 11, and left on steamboat "Consul," for Pittsburgh, where arrived this evening about 6 o'clock.

❁ LETTER TO JOHN BIGELOW

Pittsburgh, Pa., Aug., 2d, 1847

DEAR BIGELOW:

I was almost ready to scold you—indeed I was—when I left New York, for your neither calling to see me nor being at home, never, when I called to see you—which was about half a dozen times.

I wished to chat with you about a "heap of things"—about the Langley affair[18]—about future prospects of my book, and about half a dozen other little *quelques-choses* "too tedious to men-

---

[18] For the full details of this unfortunate choice of publisher see the chapter in Vol. I, "Adventuring Authorship." While in New York and Philadelphia this time, Gregg may possibly have taken possession of the plates and transferred them to Philadelphia, perhaps placing them in the hands of Thomas J. Rockhill, his friend and adviser. At any rate, the reprintings of *Commerce of the Prairies* in the 1850's come from Philadelphia and bear the name of a firm of booksellers: J. W. Moore, 105 Chestnut Street.

tion." Did you receive the *debt?* I should be greatly grieved at your suffering on that score, were it not for the "consolation" that I have suffered so "exquisitely" myself; and, as you are aware, how I became "hooked" in with that house, I don't think you will complain of suffering a "gnat" while I am groaning under a "camel." Don't infer, however, that I at all blame you for recommending Langley to me, I know how you were deceived as well as myself.

You are aware that the plates, etc. of my book have been hypothecated to Craighead and Walker.[19] I take it that this proceeding forfeits his rights as publisher; and if he should attempt to reacquire and republish, I shall protest against it, as I have already informed him. I would rather another copy were never issued than under his auspices—or those of such a house. That you may the better understand his proceedings, I ought to inform you that he pledged—in effect, sold—the material of my work, without any reservation of my rights, though of course he knew I was half owner of everything. It was afterward that Craighead and Walker found that I had a half-interest—though they thought only in profits.

You have, I believe, my account current (which Langley had furnished me) and my copy of the articles of agreement[20] between him and me, which I suppose Rockhill sent you from Philadelphia. Please take good care, especially of the latter, and return it to T. C. Rockhill, Phila, when you have done with it.

I am now on my way direct—should nothing transpire to divert me from my course—to Saltillo, Mexico, again. I hope you will write me; do try to do a little better in that regard than you have done heretofore. Direct to Saltillo, via New Orleans, Matamoros, &c.

I remain, very truly,
Your Friend and Serv't,
Josiah Gregg

[19] Craighead and Walker were presumably creditors of Langley.

❋ DIARY, AUGUST, 1847

Thurs. 5—Left Pittsburgh about 2 P.M. on steamer "Swatara" (a boat of inferior order—regular packets being stopped on account of low water), and Sun. 8—Arrived at Cincinnati this morning, between 5 & 6 o'clock; and left about 2 P.M. on steamer Colorado—very poor boat.

Mon. 9—Arrived at Louisville to-day, near 11 A.M. having been delayed a little, last night, on account of fog.

❋ LETTER TO DR. GEORGE ENGELMANN

Louisville, Ky., Aug. 13, 1847

MY DEAR DOCTOR:

You must allow me to apologize again for my delay in sending the collections, etc. which I have so long promised you.[21] I regret more particularly not having forwarded the Nautical Almanac at an earlier day, even by mail, as it may not reach Dr. Wislizenus in time: yet I still thought, from day to day, I should have everything ready to dispatch them together. But other indispensable business prevented me from completing the arrangement of the plants until the present time; and I now dispatch a package with them and the Almanac, etc. on the steamer "Monona," leaving today for your port.

Dr. Wislizenus's opinion that the *piñones* I sent you may have been baked a little, is very probable, as that is the most usual

[20] In an earlier entry, Gregg described the agreement thus: ". . . I now closed a contract with Henry G. Langley to publish for me. I am to get half the profits. Besides I am to have 1000 copies at cost and to get 10 per cent on 1000 more (2000 constituting the first edition) and am to have whatever amount of copies I may want thereafter at thirty-five per cent discount on trade prices."—I, 141.

[21] In the "Botanical Appendix" which Dr. Engelmann prepared for the Wislizenus *Memoir* are several references to the specimens Gregg forwarded during his travels to Dr. Wislizenus. The esteem in which these contributions were held is summarized in the following paragraph:

"In examining the collections of Dr. Wislizenus, I have been materially aided by having it in my power to compare the plants which Dr. Josiah Gregg, the author of that interesting work, "the Commerce of the Prairies," has gathered between Chihuahua and the mouth of the Rio Grande, but particularly about Monterey and Saltillo, and a share of which, with great liberality, he has communicated to me. His and Dr. W's collections together, form a very fine herbarium for those regions. *Memoir of a Tour to Northern Mexico*, 87.

mode of preparing them for market. On this account I did not send them as seed to plant; but that you might see their appearance and character, and more particularly as a curiosity in the way of an edible, though I suppose you had received them already from Santa Fé. Although I observed no perceivable difference in the tree, you will have noted that those of Saltillo are both harder and larger than the New Mexican.

I feel really thankful to you, and shall profit by it hereafter, for your advice as to the preservation of plants, etc. and particularly with regard to numbering. As I before observed to you, I had no hope that my collections, up to the present time, would be of interest enough to keep a series of numbers, as I was but in my "schooling." I shall in future, however, though with still very little hope of their being useful—number the specimens I collect. But I repeat that your instructions in every regard, have been of infinite use to me, and I can only endeavor to give an earnest of my gratitude, by striving to furnish you with a series of the fruits of my labors—which, though they can have presented but little interest heretofore, I indulge a hope may prove of more in future.

As I believe I before mentioned, the few geological specimens I sent you, I could see no interest in except as samples to show the character of the prevailing rock of the country. I do not know whether Dr. Wislizenus found any interesting fossils, in the same regions—at least I did not.

I send you a few specimens (all I met with) of the yellow-vine, which, I believe, are those you took a special interest in. I will not fail to collect everything of the kind I may meet with hereafter. And you will perceive that I have followed out your instructions in another regard, and that is of collecting specimens of everything I saw, be they interesting, new, handsome or otherwise.

As usual, you will also find the same plants duplicated frequently, and even put up in several places. This has occurred as well from oversight and ignorance sometimes, as oftener, perhaps, purposely; for I frequently collected the same plants at different times and in different localities, not only to get better specimens, but to show their geographical extension. And though, in some cases, on readjusting them, I collected the species together, I had not time to do it in every case.

Though, as a general thing, I endeavored to keep the dates in regular succession, they became disordered, in some cases, in the drying, while travelling, and I neglected afterwards to regulate them; therefore you will sometimes find considerable confusion in the dates, etc.

I have, this time, adopted a set of semi-hieroglyphic characters to indicate, in a slight degree, the size and abundance of the plants—which you will find inserted on most of the labels. Thus, (—) signifies *scarce*; (+) in *medium abundance* only; (x) *abundant*; and a duplication of these characters indicates an increase in their signification: as (— —) *very scarce*; (xx) *very abundant*; etc. Two different characters joined together imply a degree between them; as (+ —) *rather scarce*; etc. The number prefixed to the character shows the usual height of the plant in feet. Thus (2 —) is read *two feet high, scarce*; (½ +) *½ foot high* and found in *medium abundance* only; (5 x) *five feet high* and *abundant*; (1 xx) *one foot high* and very *abundant*; etc. etc.

There are doubtless other explanations which should be made, but I cannot think of them. However, the explanations and remarks accompanying the previous packages are generally applicable to this.

The trifle I have expended for Dr. Wislizenus is of course not worth taking account of. Should opportunity present itself of my being any service to him or to you, I should take great pleasure in being occupied by you more frequently, and shall frankly occupy both of you in a similar manner, as I have done heretofore.

I believe I mentioned in my former letter that I am bound directly for Saltillo again, and thence, possibly, for the City of

Mexico. Any additional commands, I hope you will direct to me at Saltillo, via New Orleans and Matamoros. If you write early, please direct care of Moses Greenwood (Commission Merchants, etc.) in New Orleans, and it will find me there; if not, Mr. Greenwood will forward on.

I remain most sincerely, my Dear Sir,

Your friend and serv't,

JOSIAH GREGG

P.S. I have not yet been able to extend my calculations of latitude and longitude; but I think I can assert that I will be able to bring everything up, by the time I reach N. Orleans (health permitting), and will send them to you from thence.

❂ DIARY, AUGUST, 1847

Sat. 14—Delayed at Louisville, on business till to-day. Left about 12 o'clock on steamer "Martha Washington." The first day after leaving Louisville, we lost several hours by getting aground. At the bar just above Shawneetown, we lost nearly two days. Here two other boats (that had left Louisville a day before us) were also aground. This afforded some comfort! for though an extremely uncharitable sentiment, we cannot well help feeling comfort in having "companions in misfortune." And what is even worse, we are sometimes even chagrined at the better luck of others: for seeing other boats pass without sticking—and each of the other two which were aground (the "Taglioni" & "Duroc") get off before us, I saw evident marks of chagrin in the countenances of many of our passengers: although their success could not, of course, retard us in the least!

❂ LETTER TO DR. GEORGE ENGELMANN

Vicksburg, Mi., Aug. 24, 1847

MY DEAR DOCTOR,

I believe I have nothing at all of interest to communicate to you, except that the accompanying table of latitudes, etc., which

166

though it goes direct to Dr. Wislizenus, I hope will also serve your purposes, so far as you may incline to turn your attention in that way. I should also send the notes upon which the calculations were based, but I did not deem it of sufficient importance to trouble you with them; for the principal errors must be those of the instrument.

I should have made more observations for longitude during the Chihuahua tour, [FOOTNOTE: I was also prevented by clouds from observing for latitude at several important camps; as at San Pablo, Santa Rosalia, etc.] but, first, for want of time on account of the rapidity of marching; 2dly, Jupiter was not in position to observe his satellites to advantage; and 3rdly, the moon, in the most important stretch—from Parras to Mapimí—both going and coming—was too near the sun to be used with accuracy. Besides, I feared my sextant, roughly carried as it was, was not sufficiently reliable for lunar observations. My longitudes taken at other periods, are, I feel very certain, within five miles— which, as you are aware, is about as near as we can expect to get it, with our ordinary means. My latitudes, prior to this last tour, as they were taken by sun, moon, planets, and fixed stars—both north and south—I think I can generally warrant within a few seconds. But those on the Chihuahua route may often contain errors of full $\frac{1}{2}'$; yet even these are accurate enough for all practical purposes.

Owing to the reports of the very great virulence of the yellow fever in New Orleans (and possible at the Mouth Rio Grande, etc.) I have nearly concluded to turn my course up Red River and through Texas. In fact, after all, this route will suit me about as well as the other.

I remain, truly, Your friend and humble serv't,

JOSIAH GREGG

DR. GEORGE ENGELMAN
ST. LOUIS, MO.

P.S. If I go up Red River, I shall write to New Orleans to

have my correspondence forwarded accordingly; and though I may go through Texas, I shall steer to the same point, Saltillo; therefore, please direct as before, until I advise you.

☼ DIARY, AUGUST, 1847

Thurs. 26—I had embarked with the intention of proceeding directly to N. Orleans, and thence to mouth Rio Grande & Monterey, etc. Yet as we passed down the Mississippi, we were continually meeting such horrific accounts of the virulence of the yellow fever in New Orleans, that I finally concluded to turn up Red River to Shreveport, on a visit to my Brother John's;[22] and thence proceed through Texas by land; or return via N. Orleans, after the abatement of the fever.—Landed at mouth Red R. this morning about 9 o'clock.

While observing the boatsmen at work, getting off the bars, I could not but note the great self importance, and commanding tone of the "mate." Really, these petty steamboat officers exercise their authority with more "zest" than a general over thousands! But "mates" are not alone affected with the *"importance"* of their commands. Captains and clerks are unfortunately too often as crabbed and unaccommodating as though they commanded half the world—perfect despots within their little floating realm!—In the taking out and putting in freight on these occasions of getting aground and "lighting," I could not but remark what it is true I had before observed—the utter uselessness of marking "Glass," "This side up, with care," etc. on boxes; for they are nevertheless tumbled about as [if] they contained nothing at all damageable. In truth, from the rough treatment I have seen boat-hands give such packages, I am almost uncharitable enough to believe it were safer not to mark any indication of their being damageable, upon them: for, though I

[22] Gregg's brother, John, had settled on a farm about five miles from Shreveport. The date seems to have been 1844 or 1845, the latter being the time of Gregg's first visit to the place. See I, 159.

cannot believe all possessed of a similarly evil spirit, there are nevertheless many who enjoy particular pleasure in the idea of committing damage upon some one: their organs of "destructiveness" must be highly developed!

This was one of the longest trips ever made from Louisville. True, we were aground once or twice more in Ohio, and once in the Mississippi, losing in all about four days; yet even eight days was a remarkably long trip from Louisville. But, though I was at first favorably impressed with the "Martha Washington" she turned out decidedly slow—with unpleasant unaccommodating officers—especially the clerk, named Thorn.

Frid. 27—Got off this morning at 2 o'clock from mouth Red R. on small steamer, "Ellen," from N. Orleans for Alexandria. A wretchedly mean clerk again!

Sat. 28—Arrived at Alexandria this morning at 1 or 2 o'clock. But the boat running above the falls, not having sufficient freight deferred starting up until arrival of next boat from N. Orleans. —While delayed at Alexandria found latitude to be 31° 16′— barring a small error from want of adjustment of instrument.

Tues. 31—Left the landing above Alexandria falls this evening between 3 and 4 o'clock, in little stern-wheel steamer "Jim Gilmer." Another mean clerk! *Les Rapides* or Falls of Red River at Alexandria, are a very serious detriment to navigation; for during low-water, even the smallest boats cannot run over them. In fact, the "lower falls," a quarter of a mile above the town, is nearly 5 feet in a few yards. Then the "upper falls,["] are two or three feet in a rod or two. The whole amount of falls is about as follows: Lower falls 5 ft. Upper Do. 2 ft. middle rapids 1 ft.—in all about 8 feet. As the rock over which the falls are formed, is but a sort of soft "soap-stone," easily cut out, it is believed that, with little labor, a channel might be made for small boats: certain it is that a way might be cut through the rock, provided boats could pass through on account of rapidity of current.

⚙ DIARY, SEPTEMBER, 1847

Frid. 3—Arrived between 10 and 11 A.M. at Shreveport—
and at my Brother's (5 m. west of town) soon after: and was
gratified to find him & his family all well.

While at my Brother John's, I took the latitude of his place
(which he calls Rockwell) and found it (by several observations
of sun & Polaris) within a small fraction of 32° 28′ 30″ and
Shreveport, being full 3 *miles* further north, its latitude is consequently 32° 31′ and perhaps a few seconds. [MARGINAL NOTE:
According to a subsequent observation of Polaris, Nov. 15/47—
the lat. of Shreveport wharf (which compares with central portion of town) is 32° 31′ 13″.] The longitude of Rockwell, according to mean of 2 observations of eclipses of Jupiter's satellites, and 3 of lunal distances, is 93° 42′ 15″, [MARGINAL NOTE:
The following were the results of the several observations:
Lunar distances—Mars & ☽, Oct. 18—Long. in time, 6 h. 14′
20″—Do. Oct. 26,—6ʰ 14′ 33″—Jupiter & Moon, Oct. 26=
6 h. 14′ 10″: Eclipse of Jupiter's Satellite, Oct. 18—6 h. 15′ 49″
—Do. Do. Oct. 25—6 h. 15′ 15″—the mean of all which is
6 h. 14 m. 49 s. or 93° 42′ 15″.] and Shreveport being 4½ m.
east, its longitude is consequently 93° 38′, or thereabouts.

The temperature of two wells,—one 50, the other 30 feet
deep (atmosphere at about 70°) was 65° Fahrenheit—the shal-
lowest one perhaps ¼ to ½° warmest.

⚙ DIARY, NOVEMBER, 1847

Shreveport, La. Nov. 15, 1847

When I visited my Brother (five miles S.W. of this place),
but the continuance of the yellow-fever, in N. Orleans, in the
first place; and afterward, a desire to wait for Mr. G. C. Pickett[23]
& family, who were expected on a visit to my brother's (and

---

[23] George C. Pickett was a member of the firm of Pickett & Gregg, at Van Buren.
He and John Gregg were brothers-in-law, having married sisters.

who finally arrived on 7th inst.), added to very low water, detained me till the present time.

While there I paid some little attention to the geology of the country. The stratified rock, which are mostly deep—say 10 to 20 ft. above low water-mark of Red River—and nearly horizontal,—are all of a sandy character: In the vicinity of Shreveport, there are strata, several feet thick, of a sort of impure and very sandy carbonate of lime—of different grades, of perhaps half sand to nearly all sand. Many strata are also impregnated with iron. I found some isolated rocks which were even slightly magnetic. In the highlands about Shreveport—in fact in all the country for many miles westward and N.W. there abounds a sort of wood fossil, some very perfect: I have seldom seen petrified wood show the grain, knots and rotten spots more naturally than some of these specimens.

But one of the most interesting geological productions is a sort of coal, found in a stratum, about 3 feet thick, below Shreveport, a mile or two, along the bank of Red River—say 20 ft. above low-water. It is also found in other places—I was told, up in the vicinity of the lakes (Caddo or Cross lakes), and also east of Red River, in the vicinity of Lake Bistineau: but I do not know how it lies with respect to the strata of Sandy limestone—below, I should think; yet I in no place saw strata of the latter in connection with the coal—nothing at least here but a sandy "soap-stone," several feet thick (say at least 10 feet) both above and below. This coal has been tried in blacksmith's fires; and is found to burn with a pretty white blaze, but is too light for smithing. I tried it myself; and although slow to ignite, it burned on a hearth, very prettily, leaving white ashes, very much as from wood. But an unpleasant sulphurous stench which it emits would render it disagreeable for family use.

Another interesting feature in this region, is that of the great lakes (as they may be called here) of Caddo, including Cross & Clear lakes. Their outlet (about as large as the principal branch of Red River), is just above Shreveport. They extend 40 to 50 miles west (and in some places 5 to 10 m. wide) of Shreveport; and are fed from the west, by the Cypress Bayous and from the North by (besides Jim's bayou & others) Red Bayou, which comes out of Red R. above the Raft, and conveys near a third of the water of the river into the lakes. These lakes are said to be of recent formation—in fact, the great quantities of dead timber still standing in some places, prove many portions of them to be so. But there are men now living who assert that they can recollect when the beds of those lakes, were, as other river & creek bottoms, traversed by the hunters. In this case they could scarcely be 50 years old—some say but little over 30. Whether formed by the sinking of their beds, or the rising of the bed of the river at their mouth, occasioned by the raft, is a somewhat interesting question for the geologist: however, I am of opinion that it was the latter. There are also similar lakes on the east side of Red River—formed, doubtless, in a similar manner: Lake Bistineau, etc.

Shreveport is in the border (in fact, formerly at the upper end) of what was known, from time immemorial, as the "Great Raft" of Red River.[24] This raft perhaps once extended to, or commenced near the mouth of Red River; and, as it filled up above with the immense quantities of "drift-wood," brought down by the annual freshets from upper Red R. and its tributaries, it broke loose and washed out below, until, at the time it was opened by Capt. Shreve (some ——— or ——— years ago[25]) the lower end of it was between 10 and 30 miles above Natchitoches, and the upper end about at the present town of Shreveport: a distance of about two hundred miles by water.

[24] The Great Raft of the Red River, a famous natural curiosity, which had to be destroyed in the course of modern transportation. Collected driftage in the Red River had formed a sort of natural dam, almost a hundred miles long, which impeded navigation.

[25] Possibly Gregg's blanks may be filled by the words "nine" and "ten," since it was in the 1830's that Captain Shreve removed the impediment, using a drag boat of his own contriving which was nicknamed "tooth-puller."

True, it was not continuous—only in "patches": the main raft was said to be some 60 miles long. It is amusing to read some of the accounts of this raft—particularly one by Mr. Farnham,[26] who gives as the present state of the raft (though taken from an ancient exaggerated account of it), that the channel was not only completely filled up with logs, but so overgrown with timber for many miles, that the traveller might pass entirely across the river without knowing it![27] Nevertheless, I have never seen the person who has witnessed such a state of the river, although I suppose it must have been as dense up to the time of Capt. Shreve's commencing to open it, as it ever was.

True, the channel was, in many places, entirely filled up with logs, so that a man might walk across upon them with facility— and these frequently covered with annual vegetation; but when they became so densely filled up with dirt as to support trees, the water found its way around in new-formed channels. In this way, an immense valley, say 200 miles long, and 5 to 30 wide, was cut up with innumerable sluggish deep bayous—which, in their turn would become so choked up with timber and sand as to stop the water, and cause new ones again to be formed. It was in this condition when Capt. Shreve was sent to open it. After exploring the most important Bayous he selected the one which it appeared could be most easily made navigable. True, Bayou Pierre (which separates from the one opened by Shreve, but 4 or 5 miles below Shreveport, and does not join it again till some 5 m. above Natchitoches) is asserted by many to have been the

[26] Thomas Jefferson Farnham (1804–48) made important contributions to the geography of the Far West. The book Gregg refers to was *Travels in the Great Western Prairies, the Anahuac and Rocky Mountains and in the Oregon Territory* (Poughkeepsie, 1841).

[27] Mr. Farnham says: "Three hundred miles from its mouth commences what is called 'The Raft,' a covering formed by drift-wood which conceals the whole river for an extent of about 40 miles. And so deeply is this immense bridge covered with the sediment of the stream—, that all kinds of vegetable common in its neighborhood, even trees of a considerable size, are growing upon it." This exaggerated account is [also] found, I think, in Capt. Lewis's account of the western rivers.— GREGG.

173

largest and most favorable branch at that period; and they accuse him (the Captain) of having selected a western (or rather a middle) one, for the benefit of his town site, since Shreveport. There was thus a stretch in the navigable river of 200 miles, in which there could be no town located, especially on the western side (over a hundred miles that there could not have been one on the eastern), with any prospects of commanding the back-country trade, as there was nothing but low bottom sites, not only subject to inundation, etc. but without communication with the hills, except by crossing one or more bayous and marshes;—while Bayou Pierre touches the western bluff in several places.

The town of Shreveport was named for Capt. Shreve—indeed, I believe, founded by him about the close of his labors upon the raft. When I first knew it (in 1841) it was a very insignificant place; and, indeed, when I visited in 1844, it appeared to me, to contain scarcely 200 souls. But it has rapidly increased since; so that I suppose it must now contain 1000. The truth is, it appears to me to bid fair to become a city of some importance. Besides the advantages already ennumerated, it is at the highest point of Red R. below the present raft, whence a free outlet can be had westward. [MARGINAL NOTE: Since the Great Raft was cleared out by Capt. Shreve, one of several miles in length has since accumulated, some 20-odd miles above Shreveport.] It therefore commands a very considerable trade from Texas, not only from that portion directly west, to the distance of 200 miles, but very frequently from 200 miles above—even from counties bordering Red River, as the region about Clarksville, and still higher: sometimes, indeed, they bring down their wagons from the very upper settlements of Texas on Red R.

Having determined to leave by the first conveyance, after the arrival of Mr. Pickett, etc. I was again compelled to take passage on the dirty little stern-wheel steamer, "Jim Gilmer," which left the wharf tonight at 10 o'clock; but lay at a wood-yard but 2 or 3 miles below.

The nine notebooks containing Josiah Gregg's "Memoranda"

Tues. 16—We got aground occasionally, this morning, but did not remain long, and soon found ourselves below the outlet of Bayou Pierre, and some smaller bayous, and in the narrow portion of the river—seldom passing 100 feet, in width, and sometimes but little over fifty. A remarkable feature in this portion of the river is its very low banks—even at the present extreme low stage of the water, seldom over 10 feet high. A stranger would suppose that the numerous farms along this low bank, with such a contracted channel, would be inundated, even with but a moderate rise of the river. But here, as well "in narrowness and sluggishness," and in some other regards, it a good deal resembles a canal. The bed of the river being higher than that of Bayou Pierre, as well as than that of other adjacent bayous and lakes, and there being numerous outlets, into these, the water in a freshet, is let off, as from a canal, and thus kept at a pretty regular stage, the water seldom fluctuating more than from five to eight feet, while, in other places it rises and falls from 10 to 20.

Red River, from the Texas settlements to its mouth, is greatly infested by alligators; and passengers who may happen to be provided with guns, amuse themselves in shooting them. Did they stop at this we could see no objection in the "sport," as it serves to destroy a noxious reptile; but it is a painful testimony of depraved human nature to see men shooting at every animal, how innocent soever, that comes within reach of the boat, only, as would seem, for the pleasure of taking life!

As I have before observed, this river is now unusually low—lower than it has been known for many years before, as is said; and nevertheless, we get along pretty well, drawing 30 inches, and that with a very unwieldy, churny boat: a proof that with properly constructed boats, Red River is navigable at all seasons from Shreveport to the Falls of Alexandria.

Thurs. 18—The boat lay, last night, two or three miles above Compté, and though but 8 or 9 miles by land it was 20 or 30 by water, from Grande Ecore, the present landing for Natchitoches, during low-water. Having some business to transact at Natchitoches, I came over last night, to Grande Ecore, and visiting Natchitoches early this morning, I returned in due time to meet the boat, which did not arrive at Grande Ecore till 10 o'clock.

In the bluff bordering the river at Grande Ecore, there are three or 4 strata of coal, of a similar character to that near Shreveport—though perhaps a little more slaty, and consequently less combustible. The principal stratum, some two feet thick, is say 30 feet above low water. 5 or 6 feet below, there is a narrow stratum, nearly a foot thick; and higher up, there are two strata each nearly a foot, the first 15 or 20 feet above the thick stratum, and the other 12 or 15 feet above that—all apparently horizontal: and encompassed, above, below, and between, in strata of sandy "soap-stone." In this soap-stone, there are numerous "boulders," from a few hundred to several tons weight, with rounded corners and edges; and stratified, with the strata generally horizontal—of an impure sandy limestone, somewhat resembling that at Shreveport; though here I met with no distinct strata. From some of the bluffs below, however, I saw projecting a stratum, which appeared somewhat similar, at a distance. Among the soapstone at Grande Ecore, there were some singular thin strata, of a rather ferruginous character, with every dip or inclination, some times cutting up the soapstone into sections.

Sat. 20—Arrived last night at the head of the Falls (Les Rapides) of Alexandria. These falls completely interrupt navigation, during low water; though in high water they are not perceived; and even at but a medium stage of the river, boats pass them without difficult[y]. In the distance of little over a mile, the river here descends about eight feet, viz.: at the upper fall, say one foot—at the next, ¼ mile lower, one foot, with a descent of about a foot between them. Then the lower or principal fall, (nearly a mile below, and say ¼ mile above the town of Alexandria) is 4½ feet, with six inches descent between this and the next fall above. These falls are occasioned by a ledge of that soft friable "soapstone" found elsewhere, extending across the bottom of the river: and though the descent is great, persons acquainted think a passable channel might be made through them; and the base being so soft, it is singular that the general or State govt. has never undertaken it. But what seems most remarkable, is, that such a fragile and apparently soluble material [should] withstand the action of the waters. Although, some feet above low-water a stratum of firmer rock is seen, projecting in the eastern bluff, which, from what I could learn, is similar to the most sandy strata of impure limestone, about Shreveport, yet this is entirely above the bed of the river.

Our baggage had to be hauled nearly two miles to Alexandria, where we found the same little boat I came up on last, the "Ellen,"—which, were it not for her surly unaccomodating clerk, Boissat, she would do very well.

We left Alexandria at 1 o'clock, but delayed about six hours taking in cotton a little below.

Sunday, 21—Arrived to-day, about 2 o'clock at the outlet of Red River into "Old River," a former great bend of the Mississippi, which was cut across about the year 1835, I believe. We stopped till night, at a plantation on the island, immediately opposite the mouth, taking in cotton. Although Sunday, we found that the negroes were kept at work, as on other days. On one occasion, we heard, for some time, the popping of a whip (sounding like an ox-whip, and the corresponding "Ohs!" of a poor negro who was receiving the lash: and soon after I saw come out, exclaiming at the same time, "You are not to stop before nine o'clock!"—a dark fellow, which I took to be a negro. It is very common to use negro "drivers," or sub-overseers on the large plantations; and, it is said, they are the severest "masters" than can be employed.

Mon. 22—Arrived at New Orleans, to night, quite late.

Wed. 24—Owing to being very busy trying to get a vessel to take my luggage upon, at once, I did not go to a hotel till this evening, when I took quarters at "Hewlett's Exchange"— a house good enough, were the servants a little more attentive —& were a clerk named Fallon out of it—a most surly, unaccommodating, and I fear ill-faithed fellow—as he made a couple of blunders against me, in settlement, etc.

Last night the steamer "Alabama" arrived from Vera Cruz, bringing over a number of our gallant officers—among them, Gen. Shields, Col. Harney,[28] Maj. Bonneville[29] and Maj. Borland,[30] with whom I was well acquainted; and Gen. Quitman[31] and many others, with whom I had no acquaintance. A great stir was made today, and for the next day or two, on the occasion of their reception.

This is but proper and merited attention; but the astounding parade, which is in preparation for the reception of Gen. Taylor, is, I think, carrying it a little too far. Due respect and attention ought to be shown the old hero; but it is certainly not a propitious trait in the American character, to see them running crazy after men of military fame: it augurs, I fear, rather illy, for the stability of our republican institutions.

❂ LETTER TO DR. GEORGE ENGELMANN

New Orleans, Nov. 24, 1847

My Dear Doctor,

You will doubtless be astonished to find me here at present: I am a little so myself. But I made a rather uncontemplated stop

[28] William Selby Harney, for a time the chief cavalry officer of General Wool's column. Gregg had formed an admiration for the dashing, headstrong officer, but their association had terminated when Harney was detached from General Wool's division. Doubtless there was much pleasure on both sides at this meeting.

[29] Benjamin Louis Eulalie de Bonneville had also been associated with General Wool's division. He and Gregg had come into acquaintance, although there was none of the reciprocal warmth of feeling between them that existed between Gregg and Colonel Harney.

on Red R. with my Brother on account of the virulence of the
yellow fever here, in the fall; and I remained much later than I
had contemplated. But I am now on my way to Monterey & Saltillo—and I hope to the City of Mexico.

Your very kind favor of the 21st August was forwarded to me
at Shreveport; and, as I contemplated being on my journey sooner, I delayed answering until I should arrive here. But truly, I
have at present only leisure to acknowledge its receipt: I [shall]
look over it and answer it more at leisure. But one thing I cannot
omit to do: acknowledge—and th[a]nk again most heartily—
for the many useful and important suggestions you have (as
heretofore) been so kind as to make.

As Red River I supposed to be a rather unexplored region, as
well botanically as geologically, I have made several collections
in both branches. An occasional item may possibly be new to
you: at least they may serve to show the geographical extension
of objects already known to you. As to Geology, I picked up a
little of everything so as to fill a box until I got together a much
greater bulk than I had contemplated—they include about every
rocky formation to be found in the circle of my travels, except
pebbles. I have done nearly the same botanically: omitting only
such articles as I *knew* to be familiar further east and north. You
will not suppose, of course, that I send you all this "stuff" for
preservation: it is only for your inspection, expecting you to throw
away all except an occasional article which you might find interesting and new—if any.

As the specimens of coal from about Shreveport bear some resemblance, I think, to the "cannel" coal about St. Louis, I should
be much abliged to you if you would examine it a little, and,
should you deem it useful, write a brief statement of its character

[30] Solon Borland, lieutenant colonel, Arkansas Mounted Volunteers. As an earlier
entry in the diary shows, Gregg regarded him as "out of his element in a military
career, his taste being literary."

[31] John A. Quitman (1798–1858) was a brigadier general of volunteers (Mississippians). At this time he was governor of Monterrey by appointment of General Scott.

and value to my brother John Gregg, near Shreveport, La. Upon trial I found it burned with a very pretty blaze when fanned; but I had no grate to try it in.

You may perhaps be disposed to "scold" me for not numbering my plants. My present excuse is that I looked upon these as of too little importance: I assure you I shall commence a "regular series" as soon as I land on the borders of Mexico.

I send you a few sprigs of the long grey moss, with the seed pods. You are of course familiar with the moss, but I thought you might possibly not have had the opportunity to examine the seed. What say you as to the question of its being a true parasitical plant taking root in the tree?

I found no well-marked fossils, except the petrified wood I send you; nor vegetable remains, except recent ones, in the strata of "soapstone," etc.

It had long been my desire to request you to accept a copy of my "Commerce of the Prairies"—not as an article of any value or interest to *you*, but as a token of friendship and gratitude on my part. But when I have sent you packages before, I had not a copy of the second edition at command. But I have now procured one—though I regret that it is not better bound; yet it is the only binding of this edition that I have—which I trust you will do me the kindness to place in some unoccupied corner of your library.

I send the box by steamer, "Julia," and, as before, to care of Joseph Charless, Druggist.

You recollect specimens of the bean of the *Guizache* which I sent you. In connection I think I mentioned that the natives made writing ink of them. I boiled carelessly and very imperfectly a few of the *hulls*, and, adding a little sulphate of iron, the result was the ink with which I write this paragraph. I also boiled the seeds separately, but the result was a very imperfect color— which convinced me that the virtue (gallic acid, I suppose) resides chiefly in the pericarps.

There were many plants in the lot I sent you (from Louisville) last which interested *me* very much from their novelty, their beauty, their qualities, etc. concerning which I should like to hear your opinion, especially as to how many, if any, were entirely *new*. My particular favorite, I believe, was a willowlike shrub, called by the natives, *Mimbre*. Its flower when fresh was beautiful, and very odiferous—that of a rose, with the scent of honey, etc. in addition. If I can procure any of the seeds, I will send them: there were none when I left.

I shall expect to hear from you. Direct to Saltillo, Mexico, via New Orleans, Matamoros, etc. till further advice.

> In haste I remain, truly,
> Your Friend, etc.
> JOSIAH GREGG

P.S. Please excuse blunders, for I have been occupied until the hour of closing mail, and have not time even to read over what I have written.

☀ DIARY, NOVEMBER, 1847

Sun. 28—I had not intended to solicit transportation in a government vessel, and was therefore looking up a private conveyance; when my friend Col. Harney insisted on my taking a govt. vessel, going at once with me to the Quartermaster's office, and getting a promise from Maj. Tompkins (Qr. Mr.) that I should have a berth in the propeller, "Ashland," which, he said, would leave Saturday evening (yesterday). I was informed it was unnecessary to take any order, as my name would go on the list, which would be sufficient.

Accordingly, I came down to the government wharves (about 2 m. below the hotel) yesterday evening at the hour directed; and yet the Capt. of the "Ashland" would not admit me, for want of an order, as he said. I was thus kept on suspense till it was too late to have my property taken care of; so I had to camp with it till morning. The vessel not leaving, I went up this morning again, and got a full order for everything I had, and consequently was embarked. [MARGINAL NOTE: While Capt. Dubbs of the Ashland was making an immense ado about my luggage lumbering up the deck, etc. I learned from himself that he had several hundred dollars of "private stores" on board, for sale of course.] Yet I have had no little reason to regret not having taken a private vessel in preference: as well because this one is one of the meanest of her order, as because the master is one of the most surly, unaccommodating, crabbed, fellows, I have ever had to do with. I also fear Maj. Tompkins is equally unaccommodating. I am sure it would be a case of great necessity that would induce me to *accept* transportation from him again: I did not solicit it, nor never have I solicited free transportation. When coming from Brazos, I made arrangements with the Capt. of the steamer Telegraph, to pay passage, etc. though, circumstances afterward caused it to turn out free—or nearly so—except board bill.

We finally got under way to-day, near 2 o'clock. P.M.

Mon. 29—Anchored, in the middle of the current, last night, but 20 or 30 m. below N. Orleans; and a freshet in the river having brought down & lodged a large quantity of drift up the bow of the vessel, they were unable to get her clear and underway, this morning till 11 o'clock.—There could be no reason perceived, why we should not have continued running last night—at least till late, when a fog rose—for when we stopped, it was clear star-light.—Barometer, stood this morning, just before starting—say 10 o'clock 29.97 inches—Atme. & Mere. 78°—foggy morning, but now half clear.

Tues. 30—Arrived last night, at 10 o'clock. Anchored, and did not get underway this morning till 10 o'clock. The morning was spent in repairing engine, and preparations by our indolent tardy captain. [MARGINAL NOTE: Barometer at S.W. Pass, Nov. 30/47—9 A.M.—30.05 in.—Temperature of mercury, 73°—Atmosphere 75°—½ cloudy—wind E.N.E.]

PART IV

Practicing Medicine in Saltillo

✳✳✳✳✳✳✳✳✳✳✳✳✳✳✳✳✳✳✳✳✳✳✳✳✳✳✳✳✳✳✳✳✳

Practicing Medicine in Saltillo

DECEMBER, 1847, TO DECEMBER, 1848

Diary, December, 1847[1]

WED. 1—A strong gale commenced yesterday, from S.E. and continued all night, and until a late hour this morning—when it was found that, by the very culpable carelessness of the second engineer, George Judkins, the water had been permitted to become too scarce in the boiler; wherefore, it was so burned and damaged, that steam could not be raised: in fact, it was fortunate that the boat was not now blown up by it.

Being thus deprived of steam, and the vessel almost unmanageable by sail,—and having been blown off our course north-

---

[1] Upon reaching Mexico again after a trying seventeen-day voyage from New Orleans, Gregg undertook to get himself and impedimenta down to Saltillo, where he proposed to establish headquarters for the time being. To devote himself to exploration and scientific activities was his intention, but for these he needed to put money in his purse, and the readiest way was through the practice of medicine. Saltillo was now turbulent with withdrawing American soldiers, but Gregg found himself comfortably and congenially located there. "I have often thought that if I could make myself as easy in American society," he wrote in one of his letters, "I would be willing to live in the United States." This avowal, however, did not imply that Saltillo was to become a permanent dwelling place. To his friend Dr. Engelmann he wrote: "The last twelve months of my life have been chiefly dedicated to the public service, with considerable pecuniary loss to myself; and I am sure that the future will be still strictly of a public character." As a resident of Saltillo, Gregg developed a thriving practice in medicine. He formed a partnership with a former army surgeon, but the association proved not satisfactory. In explaining the rupture between the two, Gregg indicated that he and Dr. Prevost were not compatible. Prevost was young, handsome, agreeable, haughty, self-important, and lacking in system and order, while Gregg was the reverse in almost every particular. Thus did he limn himself.

185

ward, very considerably, the Capt. concluded to put [in], if possible at Galveston, for repairs; but in a short time, the wind veered to the N.W. (blowing up a very strong "northwester") which carried the vessel very rapidly to the southward: so that in less than 48 hours [we] were in latitude 27½° having, in the mean time made but very little headway to the west. During all this period, the Captain lay abed at least three-fourths of the time, apparently paying very little attention to what was going on; although we were evidently in considerable danger. I could see no other cause for this than "the bottle"; for although he of[ten] complained of a "very violent pain in the stomach," he gave indication of anything but disease at the table.

Frid. 3—Finding, by this time, that the Capt. was at least half his time so drunk as to render him unfit to take care of the vessel—which, in addition, we saw was almost wholly unmanageable, we came to conclusion (our party consisting of six passengers, viz. John Bellow, L. Stephenson, Oscar F. Shaw, Patrick Walsh, C. H. White, and myself) to offer the Capt. $100 to hail the first vessel that might appear in sight, and put us on board of her. It was not long till a schooner was espied to the northwestward; and a flag of distress being raised, she soon hove to. She turned out the schooner "Miranda" of New York, Parmele, Master. They were told our condition and asked to take us aboard, with the offer of the most satisfactory remuneration. But to our utmost surprise and mortification they refused to do it, under pretext of a "want of accommodations!" And so they moved off. In a few minutes, however, the schooner hove to again; for I suppose the Capt. began to have some compunctions of conscience for thus leaving us in distress. He therefore proposed to take us on board, provided our Capt. would lower his boat and take us to his vessel. This our surly unaccommodating Capt. angrily and peremptorily refused to do: and so both masters having considered, I suppose, that their consciences were satisfied by this *pretended* effort, the "Miranda" again moved off and left us in despair! Such an act, I cannot believe that any, except such mercenary Northern masters (as both ours and that of the "Miranda" are) would have been guilty of. True, the sea was at the time very rough; and it would therefore have been attended with some difficulty and danger to transfer us from one vessel to the other. But the storm was abating, and in a few hours, had the "Miranda" remained near us, we might have been transferred with facility.

Our Capt. took this occasion to get in quite a passion with us, saying that passengers who could not be satisfied on board of a vessel ought not to have embarked! etc. etc. But the fellow was again "in his cups." Just about as well have said that we ought to continue satisfied to remain on the wreck of a vessel!

Mon. 6—Yesterday morning I took a lunar distance (moon & Jupiter), and the resulting longitude being far more east than we supposed (scarcely 93°) we concluded there must have been some considerable error—and paid no attention to it. This morning I took another lunar distance—between the moon & Venus—and though this distance was not in the Nautical Almanac, I calculated out a longitude of about 94½°. But the Capt's. reckoning being near a degree higher, he got in a great passion—swearing there were too many "calculators" on board —that *he* knew *precisely* where the vessel was (not 100 m. from Brazos de Santiago²)—and that he was Capt. and would navigate the vessel to his own liking, etc. Now, I could conjecture no cause

² Whether to use singular or plural of *el brazo* in the designation of the island was a matter of confusion to the chroniclers of the Mexican War. To Gregg's matter-of-fact mind the singular made the greater appeal, perhaps for the reason implied in the passage from Edwards. "I believe the position of this place [Brazos Santiago] is not properly understood. It is simply an island formed by a shallow arm of the sea, which is nearly dry at low tide on the western side, where the water is narrow which separates it from the projection of land forming the mouth of the river [Rio Grande]. On the north-east, across the strip of water, which is here of considerable depth, is Point Isabel. . . . The island of Brazos is supposed to have been the site of one of the largest and richest of the ancient Mexican cities, but which was swallowed up by the sea."—*A Campaign in New Mexico with Colonel Doniphan*, 174–75.

for this passion, except the mere fact of my observations not agreeing with his reckoning; for, in the first place, I had reason to suppose my efforts to obtain the longitude met his entire approbation, not only on account of its need to us (he had no sextant wherewith to take it), but because he had on more than one occasion invited me to observe with him: and, in the second place, I had made no attempt, or even expressed opinions, to control the movements of the vessel. The sequel proved that my longitude (the last one) was rather above than below the truth—the first one scarcely having been too low.—We were now in latitude about 26° 5′.—

We were now in a rather critical position—south of Brazos—and another "Northwester" would have sent us off directly southward, into the middle of the gulf: but fortunately today, there sprung up an easterly breeze, which continued all night; and increasing next day to a clever gale, we moved westward for near 24 hours at the rate of 5 or 6 m. an hour.

Wed. 8—Believing, as the Capt. did that we were near Brazos, even on yesterday morning, the sails were mostly reefed last night; and we spent the night without making headway; but, in the morning found our latitude above 26° 30′. The breeze which had now a good deal abated, was from S.E. and notwithstanding the wind stood as much south as possible, at noon my observation was 26° 46′—that of the Capt. 26° 51′. This northing was as well owing to the vessel as to a very strong current, setting northward. [MARGINAL NOTE: This wretched vessel is short and round-bottomed, without keel or "cut-water, and therefore would slide over the water sidewise" before the wind.]

It was therefore very wisely determined (as would seem—the vessel being unable to make any southing) to put in at Corpus Christi, then nearly a degree north of us. We therefore steered northwestward, and early in the afternoon came in sight of Padre's Island. We had known for the last 24 hours, that we were approaching land—the light green tinge (instead of former deep blue) indicating shallower water. At dark, we anchored a mile from Padre Island Shore.

Thurs. *9*—This morning, the breeze continuing brisk, and toward the north, the course of the shore, we were in high spirits, thinking we would reach Corpus Christi by noon: but we were surprised to see the Capt. lie abed until late breakfast, and afterward make no attempt to weigh anchor until nearly 10 o'clock: He then made a sort of effort (pretended, I suppose), but finding some difficulty, stopped again, and seems determined to lie here until—I can't conjecture when: I suppose, until another storm blows us on shore or out to sea again.

What caused him to change his determination of putting in at Corpus Christi, I can't imagine—unless, as is indeed probable, that we expressed our satisfaction at the measure, as we could thus find other transportation to our place of destination; and he could not, after fully bethinking himself, bear the idea of accommodating us. The truth is, he is perfectly satisfied: he gets his salary; and makes, in addition, off of us, at least four dollars a day clear profit for our board—which, to a narrow minded soul, like his, is a little fortune, which he is not in haste to let out of his grasp.

Frid. *10*—It seems that,—to our great surprise, after their having denied that there was a bit of boiler-iron on board, in answer to our urgent solicitations that some attempt should have been made from the time of the accident, to mend the boiler,— that now an abundance of good boiler-iron has been produced, and they have gone to work to repair the damage. This can only be accounted for by supposing that the superlatively unaccommodating captain could not bear the idea of gratifying us so much as to land us at Corpus Christi, as he had promised (in time of semi-intoxication), and which might have been accomplished yesterday early: he would now rather undertake a labor which would occasion more delay; but which he was too negligent and reckless to undertake at the proper time.

True, he *"politely"* offered to set us ashore, yesterday, to walk 70 miles over a barren beach to Brazos; and, in company with a comrade or two, I had really determined to undertake it this morning, rather than suffer further annoyances[,] when we found the boiler was in rapid progress of repair.

The wind veering to the northward to-day, anchor was weighed, and we set sail south down the coast to-day at 12 o'clock. At dark, however, anchor was again cast, in latitude 26° 42', where we lay for the night, with a beautiful brisk breeze still continuing (which still continued nearly all night). The consequence was, that the wind had veered nearly due east next morning, blowing directly to the land, which rendered it impossible for us to move until a change of wind, or the steam got ready,— while there seems little doubt that, had we continued sail during to-night, we might have reached Brazos before the wind veered —perhaps by midnight.

Sun. 12—The boiler was ready to raise steam early yesterday evening; but having unshipped the propeller wheels, and taken the parts of the machinery to pieces (that the wheels might play round freely, and retard the sailing of the vessel, while without steam), it took them till late today to get the engine ready. The wind, meanwhile had veered more to the south (about S.E.) so that it was impossible to use sail; so that we did not get underway again, until to-day after 1 o'clock, P.M.—wholly by steam.

A breeze commenced from the northward this evening; and, about dark, it began blowing a brisk "norther," which compelled us to anchor about 15 m. north of the Brazo. It blew almost a hurricane during the night, yet we rode safely at anchor, shipping sea occasionally, however, but to no particular damage: the wind died away in the course of the following day—still remaining at anchor.

Tues. 14—This morning being calm, steam was again raised, and we proceeded southward; yet it was not long till one of the patches was burned off the boiler, and let out considerable water;

yet without injury to anyone. This stopped steam again; but the patch having been again fastened on, steam was once more got up by about 3 o'clock. The water being too shallow on the bar for the "Ashland" to pass, we came in to Brazo de Santiago in a tow-boat, late this afternoon: put up at "Greenwood Hotel," a tavern kept in the cabin of an old steamboat, which is up on the beach. We were in our 17th day from N. Orleans, a voyage that is sometimes made in three days, and generally in four to six!

The troubles of voyage, vessel and captain, are (at least some of them) set forth in the following representation, got up and signed by all the passengers, and given to Maj. Eastland, U.S. Qr. Mr. at this place:

Brazo de Santiago, Dec. 15, 1847

We, the undersigned passengers, on board the U.S. Propeller "Ashland["] during her late unpropitious voyage from New Orleans to this place,—while we deem it proper and laudable to give due credit and praise for the meritorious conduct of the masters of vessels,—hold it equally encumbent upon us, not only of right but *duty*, to reprobate the contrary qualities. Therefore, we feel called upon to express our entire conviction of the *incompetency* (in every important sense of the word) of Capt. Dubs, of the "Ashland," to control a vessel with safety and comfort:— without entering, however, into the question of his nautical experience and qualifications—of which we know little, and deem it unimportant to know; for what import acquirements when neutralized by countervailing qualities? The circumstances attendant upon a painful and perilous voyage of over a fortnight upon the Gulf, (we arrived on the 17th day from N. Orleans) has forced the conclusions upon us, that Capt. Dubs is

1.—*Intemperate,*—because he was in the habit of shutting himself up, several times a day, as well as night, in the pantry, where the position of some of our berths frequently enabled us to see that he was engaged in *drinking something*, and his *condition* showed very well *what it was*— he being in an evident state of inebriation a large portion of his time, so as to disqualify him from the safe management of the vessel. We challenge an examination of the subordinates and crew on this subject.

2.—*Indolent, negligent, inefficient* and unnecessarily *dilatory,*— because he lay abed nearly three-fourths of the time, particularly during the period of the greatest danger, without our being able to perceive any

191

just reason for it, except sluggishness and "the bottle"; for though he not unfrequently complained of a "very violent pain in the stomach," it doubtless had its origin in the same; for his "service at the table" afforded indications of anything else but disease. During these periods, the vessel would unquestionably have been safer without him; for his disagreeable, petulant and despotic deportment toward those under him, would deter them from taking even important measures, without his command, which, as before indicated, he was so frequently incapable of giving. Fortunately the subordinates were generally sober, industrious and attentive men. We would particularly recommend the meritorious conduct of Mr. Morand, the second mate. In view of every circumstance and incident, we feel justified in adding our belief that he was about as well satisfied to reach port at the expiration of a month as a week. Among other proofs, we might adduce the fact, that no attempt whatever was made to mend the damaged boiler of the boat for over a week after the accident which deprived us of steam (on the first inst.)—denying, in reply to our urgent instances that some attempt should be made, that there was no boiler-iron on board, and that it was otherwise utterly impracticable. What must have been our surprise, then, after his having proposed (and very properly we thought—being unable to make any southing, on account of the prevailing southern winds) to put in at Corpus Christi, to find that he remained at anchor, 30 miles south of that inlet, off Padre's Island, on the 9th inst.; and commencing to repair the boiler, had it ready to raise steam in a little over 48 hours, abundance of boiler-iron having been produced when necessary! His undertaking to mend the boiler at this particular juncture, also tended to confirm our opinion (which we had already had abundant reason to entertain) of his determination, not only not to accommodate us in anything, but to take every measure to annoy us; for we could scarcely conjecture a motive for his sudden change of resolution, except that we had expressed our great satisfaction at his determination to put in at Corpus Christi, where we proposed to leave the vessel and seek other conveyance: at least his not *deigning* to afford us the satisfaction of the slightest explanation, left us to form this conclusion.

3.—*Crabbed, captious* and *ungentlemanly,*—because his deportment was insupportably of this character: a civil answer to the most civil question having very rarely been received from him by anyone.

4.—*Unobliging* and *void* of *humanity,*—because we were not only unable to obtain any accommodations and comforts from him, but those under him not unfrequently appeared afraid to extend them, lest they should incur his displeasure: the steward, when asked to do something by a sick passenger, has been known to say, "Wait till the Captain is not looking"; and during rain as well as floods of spray upon the deck, with the sea rolling very heavy, so that even a well man could not stand, he has ordered a passenger suffering with the severest sea-sickness to the deck, instead of permitting a vessel to be brought to his berth!

With such qualities, we leave it for others to judge to what extent the accidents and delays of the "Ashland" should be attributable to the neglect and mismanagement of the master.

While we express our unqualified disapprobation, however, of the conduct of Capt. D. we should state our belief that the "Ashland," from the outset, was in a very ill condition; and we would therefore regret to believe that the Quarter-Master in New Orleans knew what Capt. Dubs asserts he did know or ought to have known, as he and other credible persons had so informed him, viz. that this vessel was altogether unseaworthy, as well on account of her disordered steam apparatus as her unmanageableness by sail: it would indicate an exposure of life and property, of which we are not prepared to believe that honorable functionary capable. [FOOTNOTE: After all, I am not sure but there is too much truth in this assertion: among other proofs, the fact that no mail was sent upon her, although it had been some time since one had been dispatched to the Brazos, would seem to indicate a want of confidence in her: and the freight was of the least valuable class—forage and the like.]

In conclusion, we may sum up our opinion of both Master and vessel in very few words, to wit: that nothing could induce us again to embark with the same Master in any vessel, nor with any master in the same vessel.

(Signed)   JNO. BELLOW OF NEW ORLEANS
        JOSIAH GREGG, OF MISSOURI
        LEMUEL STEPHENSON, OHIO
        OSCAR F. SHAW
        CHARLES H. WHITE, OF MISSOURI

(Mr. Walsh, the other passenger, was fully of accord with us, but is absent.)

While at Brazo de Santiago, I took latitude by 2 obs. of sun & 2 of Polaris—mean 26° 4' 2"—2' less than laid down on the charts. Longitude by lunar distance (Moon & Mars), 97°7'30".

[MARGINAL NOTE: In time, 6 h. 28' 30"—I have taken the

mean of obs. here and at the mouth Rio Grande: also adopted the same mean + 30″ for longitude of mouth.]

Barometer.—Dec. 15–47—20 feet above sea level—clear—brisk breeze from north—at 4 o'clock, P.M. Stood . . . 30.33 in.

With Mercury	68°
" Atmosphere	66°

Course from the Brazo to Point Isabel (say 3 or 4 m.) W. 22°. N.—From Brazo to Mouth Rio Grande (about 10 m. by road along beach) S. 5° W.

Thurs. 16—This evening (not being able to get my luggage from the "Ashland" till to-day) I got a Mexican to haul my outfit over to Mouth of Rio Grande.

Latitude village, east bank of Rio Grande by Polaris, tonight, 25° 57′ 48″—Longitude by Moon & Mars, 97° 8′ = In time, 6 h. 28′ 32″.

Measure[d] width of Rio Grande, by a trigonometrical calculations (but distance stepped on bank), and, to my surprise, found it only 115 yds. wide at a point about 400 yds. from the Gulf, and 135 yds. some 200 yards higher up!

Frid. 17—Finding a government steamer, the "Gen. Jesup," prepared to leave this morning at 9 o'clock, for Reynosa, I got passage upon her; but with great mortification and vexation, from want of accommodation and the ignorance of the Quartermaster at the Mouth, Maj. Anderson. After ungentlemanly and rude treatment—and I having explained to him what I had, to wit, my baggage, a few packages of outfit, and my dearborn carriage, he gave me the following order, which I copy *verbatim, literatim,* etc. as a fine specimen of official composition:

"Capt. Walworth of steamer "Genl. Jesup" is permitted to take Mr. Gregg up with his baggage on the boat, under your command.

NATHL. ANDERSON
QRM U S. ARMY"

At the same time Maj. Anderson asserted that the Capt. of

the steamers had a right to take passengers on their own account: and thus his order amounted to nothing—only granting what I could do any how—and making no mention of the essentials, my extra luggage and carriage.

Sat. 18—Arrived at Matamoros, last night, about 10 o'clock, having been delayed 3 or 4 hours on the way, by stopping, and by getting aground. The distances, by the river, according to my "guesses," this time, are about as follows: mouth to Bunta, 12 m.—Palo Alto, 18 m.—Matamoros, 35 m.—By land, it is estimated variously, from 25 to 40 m.: I should think it could hardly pass 30 m.—Latitude,—last night—mean of 3 obs. one of Polaris, a meridian alt. of Canopus and another of Sirius (all nearly corresponding)—of Upper Landing, 25° 53′ 26″—which being nearly half a mile N.W. of the Plaza, the latitude of this is about 25° 53′ 8″—corresponding very nearly with my observations in June last.—Longitude—mean of lunar distance (——), and eclipse of Jupiter's Satellite—97° 30′ 45″—[MARGINAL NOTE: As it was inclined to be a little foggy, the satellite disappeared rather soon—therefore I have not used the resulting longitude—this being that of the lunar distance above.]—In time, 6 h. 30′ 3″.

Width of Rio Grande here—from bank to bank—according to trigonometrical measurement—122 yards.

[MARGINAL NOTE: The population of Matamoros is said once to have amounted to 8 or 10,000; but it does not now contain half—perhaps not a fourth—of that number of Mexicans—with perhaps, 1000 foreigners. An intelligent native told me it was founded but 50 or 60 years ago. First known as the Rancho del Refugio (I believe is the name—see elsewhere) but called Matamoros for the revolutionary hero of this name.]

I was gratified to find here, as chief of the Quarter-master's department of Matamoros, my acquaintance and friend Capt. Chapman,[3] whose polite, kind and gentlemanly and obliging

[3] W. W. Chapman was quartermaster at Matamoras.

conduct toward me, I shall remember with gratitude—contrasting very remarkably with my treatment by Maj. Tompkins at N. Orleans, and Maj. Anderson at the Mouth.

As the very small and light draft steamer, "Oreline" arrived last night from the Mouth, and bound for Mier, (to which point I preferred going by water, I concluded to transfer my luggage to her—in obedience to the suggestion and kind offer of Capt. Chapman. The master of this little craft, is a son of the celebrated divine, Rev. Mr. Moffitt.

I also had the gratification to find here, my very worthy friends, Maj. Hunter[4] (Paymaster), and his amiable lady. Mrs. Hunter (as I have remarked somewhere else) has been the heroine of the entire campaign, from San Antonio de Bexar, to Parras —thence to Saltillo, Monterey; and finally with Gen. Taylor (but a short time ago) to this place. When she came down here with her husband, it was with intention of proceeding to the U.S. in company with Gen. Taylor; but loth, as on former occasions, to separate herself from her husband, she again resolved to remain—being now, as she remarked within "striking distance," so that she can go home when she may wish.

Left, to-day, at 3 o'clock, P.M.—On River, at this hour— nearly clear—light breeze from S.E.—Barometer stood 30.18 in.

Temperature of Mercury	70° Fahr.
" " Atmosphere	68° "

Sun. 19—Took latitude at Rancho de San Antonio, S.W. bank Rio Grande, and found it, 26° 2¼'—Ran till 10 o'clock, and tied up for the night—say 20 m. by water, though perhaps not 10 by land—at Rancho de la Palma (S.W. bank of river). Latitude by Polaris,—26° 2' 23"—Longitude by eclipse of Jupiter's Satellite, 97° 59' 15". In time 6 h. 31' 57". This point, from

[4] In an earlier diary entry Gregg had written of Mrs. Hunter, who had earned his admiration by the way she had accompanied her husband on the march from San Antonio to Saltillo with General Wool's column: "She is certainly a very amiable, meritorious, and remarkable lady, who is truly the heroine of Gen. Wool's campaign, having been the only respectable female in the army."—I, 331.

what I can learn, is about 5 to 8 m. east of a place on the road I passed last summer, called El Charco-azul. La Palma is said to be a little over half way to Reynosa from Matamoros—Pop. 2 or 300.

Mon. 20—On Rio Grande, 9½ o'clock, A.M.—clear & nearly calm—

Barometer stood	30.26 inches
Temperature of Mercury	71° Fahrenheit
" " Atmosphere	70°

Opposite Charco-Azul or a little above, made an imperfect observation for latitude, and found approximately, about 26° 12′ (Doubtful.)

Lay at Rancho de Santa Ana (S.W. bank) tonight—said to be about 25 m. below Reynosa by the river—hardly over 10 by land. Lat. by Polaris, 26° 3′.

Tues. 21—Arrived at Reynosa, to-day, at 10½ o'clock, A.M. —The steamer, "Gen. Jesup" had arrived by a short time before us; but could not cross the bar ½ m. below the landing. Precisely with us, arrived from above, the private small steamer "Lama"—also a few minutes after, the private steamer "Tom Kirkman"—so that there were four boats here at once—and a few minutes after the two last left (say 1 or 2 o'clock), the govt. steamer "Rough-&-Ready," arrived from above.

Width of Rio Grande at Reynosa landing, 170 yards.—To-day at 12 o'clock—¼ cloudy or hazy—brisk wind from north—

Barometer stood	30.44 in.
Temperature of Mercury	64° Fahr.
" " Atmosphere	58° "

Wed. 22—Latitude by Polaris, this morning, (of landing), 26° 6′ 19″—over ¼ mile north of Plaza—making centre of Reynosa about 26° 6′.

Reynosa, I was told, was founded about the year 1801 or 1802. The original town (now known as Reynosa viejo) some distance above, on the river (say 15 m. by land, though near 40 by water) was founded at a much earlier period; but a great overflow having inundated it, at the time above mentioned, the town was transferred to the present site, which is on a low point of high-land, approaching within 100 [or] 150 yds. of river—the first uplands I have seen since I entered the river. The town-site is based upon an almost bare bed of soft, porous limestone (said to make very good lime), with a hard crust of carbonate of lime on the surface.

The population of Reynosa is said once to have amounted to 2 or 3,000—whole jurisdiction, including surrounding ranchos, to 6 or 8,000—but it is now very much depopulated.

Left this morning at 6½ o'clock, the steamer "Rough & Ready," having also left for Camargo (with the freight of the "Gen. Jesup") a few minutes before.

By imperfect observation of sun to-day at 12 o'clock, with pocket sextant, made latitude in a north bend of river, 26° 20'—something too great, no doubt—below Reynosa viejo.

Barometer, today, 11½ o'clock, A.M.—¼ cloudy—breeze from N.W.—

	stood 30.235 in.
Mercury	65°
Atmosphere	68½°

Lat. tonight, at wood-yard, on N.E. bank of Rio Grande—about 5 m. by land, N.W. from Reynosa Viejo,—by Polaris—26° 13' 28": about half way, by land, from Reynosa to Camargo.

Thurs. 23—Arrived at Camargo, this evening about 2 o'clock. Some 10 or 12 miles below mouth of San Juan R. passed a tolerably large rancho, on west bank, which I was told was called China, but am not certain. Also came two miles below mouth, on east bank, passed "Clay Davis's Landing," an American settlement which seems to be growing into a village.[5]

[5] Clay Davis's Landing has not appeared on any of the early maps to which the editor has had access.

On arriving at Camargo, I learned that a large train of wagons had left that day for Monterey, and would encamp some 10 miles on the road. [MARGINAL NOTE: In Camargo I saw a joist with an inscription on it stating that it had been finished in the [year] 1796, or thereabouts, thus indicating a greater age of the place than I had supposed.] I, therefore, with much difficulty, got a Mexican to haul me up to the camp—leaving Camargo at 9 P.M. and arriving at the camp (at Guardado de Arriba) about 4 o'clock, A.M. and as the wagoners of the train were beginning to gear up. I prevailed upon the wagonmaster to haul my baggage, "luggage" and carriage to Mier, where I hoped to be able to get mules for my carriage, and private transportation for my extra outfit. [MARGINAL NOTE: Having been much annoyed heretofore, in travelling with the army, for want of something to haul my baggage, instruments, etc. I resolved this time to provide myself with a convenient Dearborn or "Jersey wagon."]

Frid. *24*—Arrived, today, at Mier, about 12 o'clock. [MARGINAL NOTE: This place is said to be somewhat older than Camargo. It was originally called Cántaro. Latitude of Mier, as by obs. of Polaris here, 26° 26′ 9″—being within one second of same that I had set down from my obs. in May.] I at once set about looking up mules, etc. and late in the evening, was able to buy a very good pair of little mules for my wagons, for 38 dollars. But after exhausting every effort, in vain, to get either pack mules or cart, I finally applied to the chief wagon-master, James W. Irvine, to haul 300 lbs. for me; but this he refused to do, though he had 190 lightly-laden wagons, and getting lighter every day, from consumption of provisions and forage. Had I had an item of merchandise, or had I not tried every means to get private conveyance first, I should not have thought hard of it; but as it was, I could not but consider it a most savage want of accommodation. The fact is, Quartermasters had always been in the habit of furnishing transportation to persons on scientific pursuits; and such were the chief objects of my enterprise.

Sat. 25—I was therefore left behind at Mier; and after having spent the forenoon of today in seeking transportation, even to the next town I resolved to repack my chemicals, medicines, etc. and thus reducing both bulk and weight, endeavor to haul my outfit in my carriage. In this laborious task, I occupied myself till night; and, after moonrise (about 11 o'clock) I set out, with only the company of my old Mexican servant, to overtake the train encamped 15 miles ahead. I had got everything into my carriage, very comfortably, and now got along with much more ease than I had expected—though slow. We arrived safely at the camp at daylight. Being compelled to stop a little while to feed and rest, the train again got off ahead of me, so that I did not overtake them till I reached their camp just above Puntiagudo.

Sun. 26—This morning, just after starting, we met a train of some 50 or 60 wagons and some pack-mules going down. We learned that they had been attacked by some guerrillas just above Cerralbo; and though these succeeded in driving off several nearly with their packs, all were recovered, except two or three.

This evening, just after arriving at Camp near Puntiagudo, I discovered I had lost all my keys. The prospect of recovering them seemed hopeless; for I not only knew it was 5 or 10 miles back when I last recollected having them, but the road being very dusty, they would be apt to bury themselves in it, on dropping in the road. I offered $5 to any one—to some Mexicans, particularly,—who would go back and find them. In fine, I bethought myself of a Mexican cart that came along just behind me, all day; and, on inquiry, found the keys in the hands of the driver of the cart, who said he had found them in the road nearly covered with dust. [MARGINAL NOTE: There are two villages of Puntiagudo, over a mile apart—one above our camp, the other and principal, below. Though lately entirely abandoned, some of the inhabitants have now returned. It was called so from a sharp-topped mound *(Cerro puntiagudo)* in the vicinity.]

Mon. 27—This morning, owing to some accident to my harness, etc. I fell a mile or so behind at the start; and afterward hurrying on, to overtake the train, I came up to the rear-guard stopped in the road, in a chaparral, so that I could not get by. With every possible courtesy, I asked the officer in command, Lieut. Gaines, to let me pass on, as it was with much difficulty I could keep pace with the train. He at first absolutely refused; but upon my expostulation, finally gave the road, yet all with so ill an air—so gruffly, abruptly, and unobligingly, that I could not help giving him a tart repartee. Truly, as I was constrained to remark to him, it seems that our armies think of any thing else more than affording protection to American citizens: many seem to suppose they have nothing to do but defend themselves and fight for glory. While, owing to the complete protection extended to them by their govt. and armies, the home of an English citizen is a safe passport in any country, American merchants and citizens are almost without protection! [MARGINAL NOTE: The annexed is an outline of the courses and outlets of the streams from Aguafria to Mier.[6]] Arrived to day early at Cerralbo—camped. [MARGINAL NOTE: Cerralbo (most usually written Cerralvo) is a compound of *Cerro* hill, and *albo*, white, and is said to have been so called from some chalky mounds in the vicinity. I was told by a respectable old native that Cerralbo is older than Monterey! (See preceeding margin.[7]) Latitude of Cerralbo by meridian alt. of Moon, 26° 5' 21"—yet this may be a little too small, as I might of taken the alt. a little before, for the meridian alt.]

Tues. 28—Owing to the train's having to lay in a supply of forage, etc. here, we did not leave Cerralbo till noon. Encamped at Rancho Viejo, 8 miles.

Wed. 29—Came a hard drive (some 18 m.) to the old aban-

---

[6] This is the legend beside a map in the original diary; it is impossible to reproduce the map itself here.

[7] This reference is to the aforementioned map.

doned Rancho of Papagallos. About midway of the drive we had
an alarm that the guerrillas were upon us; but it turned out, only,
that, a Texan Ranger on a Scout had discovered three Mexicans,
alighted from their horses, and firing upon them, they fled and
left their horses, and the Ranger brought them to the train. They
were supposed to have been guerrillas; but this is uncertain; they
may only have been travellers who had left the road, on account
of fear of us. A "Texan Ranger" would be apt to let no opportunity escape him of shooting at a Mexican, if he could have the
least excuse for doing so.—Road generally quite rough to day.
—On account of clouds I was unable to get an observation for
latitude, tonight.

Thurs. 20—Camped tonight at Salinas Cr. or river, some 2
miles westward from Marin. Lat. by Polaris of S.W. bank of
river. [MARGINAL NOTE: Lat. of camp at Salinas Cr. by obs. of
Polaris 25° 52' 31".]

Frid. 31—I encamped, tonight, near the Dragoon and artillery camp at "Walnut Springs"—the train camped a mile back:
the suttlers' and merchant wagons came into Monterey: of these
there were 30 or 40, I think. [MARGINAL NOTE: From Nogalal
(or "Walnut Grove or Spring) back to Santo Domingo 2 m.—
thence back to Mezquital say 2 m. (?) thence to S. Francisco,
say, 3 m.?]

❀ DIARY, JANUARY, 1848

Sat. 1—To day I rode into Monterey and called on Gen.
Wool, who was unusually kind and complaisant to me. Learning
that Capt[.] (Alias "Maj.") Howard, with two or three ambulances and wagons, was going up to Saltillo tomorrow, I went
out and drove my carriage into town this evening, so as to be
ready to start in the morning with the party. Took quarters with
my friend Dr. Madison[8] of the army. [MARGINAL NOTE: By
reliable information, I learn that from only half way to Guajuco

---

[8] Thomas C. Madison, an army surgeon.

do the waters run in the direction of Monterey: on the other half they run eastward and northeast, forming, with others, a stream sometimes called San Juan; but more properly, this joined to the Santa Catarina or Monterey river (considerable distance below Caderecita) constitute the Rio de San Juan.]

Sun. 2—Our party for [Saltillo], consisting of Maj. Partridge, Capt. Howard, Dr. Roane,[9] and some others, with two ambulances and a wagon, did not get off today till 12 o'clock. Having transferred half my loading to the empty vehicles above mentioned, I thought I should find no difficulty in keeping up with the party; but all hands of them, and especially the drivers, getting about "half-corned," they set off at such a mad career that I could not even keep in sight of them with my half-jaded *mulitas*. Consequently, I was left to travel alone to Rinconada, some 30 m. through a region considered as dangerous on account of guerrillas and robbers: but, though I frequently met with Mexicans, I felt very little fear, as I was well-armed; still this did not prevent me from philosophizing on the ungentlemanly conduct of my "travelling companions." I arrived, safely, at Rinconada, about 8 o'clock at night, with my mules nearly fagged, and a wheel or two of my dearborn about as near broken down. [MARGINAL NOTE: Lat. of Rinconada, by Merid. alt. of sun, taken on 3d Jan.—25° 41′ 10″.]

Mon. 3.—After my arrival last night, I took one of my rickety carriage wheels to the creek, to soak it till morning: and, in the dark, happening to find a deep pool (5 or 6 feet deep) at the foot of a fall, while letting the wheel down into the water, my Colt's repeating pistol slipped out of my belt, and plunged into the deepest part of the pool! It now seemed that I should stay late enough this morning to have it "fished" for, or give it up altogether, an alternative that I was loth to adopt, in this land of perils. I therefore resolved to remain to search for the pistol.

---

[9] Of this party, Dr. Edwin H. Roane had been the surgeon in the Arkansas Mounted Volunteers.

My party now left me for good—which, in fact, I expected, though they did not know I intended to remain.

As quick as it became light enough, I got a Mexican to go into the pool in search of the pistol; but both atmosphere and water were so very cold that he soon gave it up. My only alternative seemed now to wait till the day became a little warm, and about 10 o'clock two Mexican servants, with the promise of a couple of dollars, commenced diving for it, and fortunately found. Nevertheless, as I was now alone, I concluded to remain at the Rinconada till night, with two or three Americans that were keeping a sort of tavern there; and come through this somewhat dangerous stretch of 28 miles (in which it had not been long since a party of Americans had been attacked by a band of guerrillas); but near sun-down, a young Irish man, named Drum, rode up; and, at my suggestion, agreed to come through with me: so we set out at once, intending to come into the immediate vicinity of Saltillo before stopping; but finding a couple of merchant wagons encamped 10 miles from the city, we stopped with them, a little after midnight.

Tues. *4*—Last night about half a mile before reaching the camp, my feet having become very cold, I jumped out of the carriage to walk a while; but my feet and legs were so numb with cold that I fell; and my unfortunate pistol again slipped out of the case—which I did not perceive till I had proceeded several hundred yards. It being now too dark, I waited till this morning, when I returned and fortunately found it. About 9 o'clock, A.M. I reached Saltillo.

Thurs. *6*—I was unable to get a house till to-day, when I procured two rooms in the house of D. Mariano Ramos, in the Calle del Guizache, near the corner of the Parian or Market Square. Moved into it this evening. My *"friend"* Ramos,—for whom I had done an infinity of services—once rode to the Rinconada for him—another time sent my servant there to interpret for him—besides innumerable other services,—worth to him several hundred dollars, most probably—*only* charges me $10 pr. month rent: better rooms are often rented at from $3 to $6.

Frid. 7—Commenced boarding to-day, with the family who lives in the house—Viante Padilla.

Sun. 9—To day I took a lad named Francisco Próspero Cárdenas—a sprightly boy of honest parents, I think, though poor. I shall give him whatever I think he merits, as salary.

Mon. 10—It is not long since a private of Capt. Mears's Company of cavalry was executed (shot) for mutiny—an attempt to kill his captain; and to-day another of the same company was hung for wantonly killing a Mexican in the streets of this place.[10] He seems to have had not even an excuse for the horrid act, as he had had no difficulty with the Mexican: the latter was walking in the street, when the murderer called to him stop, and not obeying—not understanding, perhaps—he was shot down by the latter. I am glad to see Americans punished for such reckless deeds: cold-blood murder is murder, no matter upon whom committed: and it is no reason we should permit the like, because Mexican authorities would not, under similar circumstances, punish for similar deeds. The truth is, I have never heard of a Mexican having been executed by Mexican authority, for the murder of an American, though I have known of many such murders having been committed.

Mon. 17—This evening, at my instigation (and invitation) we had an appointment for the officers to meet at my room, preparatory to engaging in a course of regular parties for the study of the Spanish language—for mutual instruction. As for my own part I was willing to teach others all I could without any charge. I had three principal objects in view, in proposing these "castillian tertulias":[11] first, for the sake of having social collec-

[10] The Arkansas Volunteers continued a turbulent and undisciplined aggregation, possibly the more so that military discipline was relaxed under the expectation of the speedy coming of peace. Alexander Nucent is presumably the Arkansas volunteer who was hung at Saltillo, January 12, 1848, for murder. The name of the soldier shot for mutiny cannot be ascertained.

[11] Spanish assemblies.

tions: secondly, for mutual instruction in a language at present so desirable to the officers: thirdly, to endeavor thus to break up another species of "nocturnal" meeting, not only useless but decidedly deleterious; viz. card parties, at which many otherwise meritorious officers were losing their money as well as their rest: but I regret to say that the effort proved a decided failure. Only a few volunteer officers attended. I would not say by this that *all* the regular officers were occupied at these card parties; yet unfortunately too many of them, for their credit, health, or interest.

Wed. 19—A few days ago three discharged volunteers of Mississippi regiment, were massacred[12]—horribly butchered [and] cut up—by some villains, on the road between this and Monterey, some 15 miles from here. Five Mexicans charged with the atrocious deed, were apprehended a few days ago; and having been examined—and found, to the satisfaction of those concerned, guilty—in fact, many articles belonging to the unfortunate murdered men were found upon them—they were ordered by the Commanding officer, Col. Hamtramck,[13] to be executed, to day, at 11 o'clock; and they were accordingly hung in the public square. From best information, I can feel no doubt of the guilt of the culprits, and therefore only regret that they could not have been tried by a military court, as regulations have provided: but it is believed, and perhaps truly, that so many difficulties presented themselves in a regular course, as to render it almost impracticable—at least to have justice done. It certainly is to be lamented, if circumstances present themselves which render a violation of "law and order" necessary. [MARGINAL NOTE: See note (1) at end of this M.S.[14]]

❂ LETTER TO DR. GEORGE ENGELMANN

Saltillo, Mexico, Jan. 24, 1848

MY DEAR DOCTOR:

Your very gratifying favor of 17th Sept. (enclosing one from Dr. Wislizenus of 8th, which please permit me through you here to acknowledge), I found in the office upon my arrival here, nearly three weeks ago; and which I should have answered ere now, but for want of leisure as well as *material*. And even now I cannot enter fully into details as I should wish, though the fewer details the better perhaps of *dry matter*.

As to botany, I have done virtually nothing yet: the month of December was unusually cold, so that, from Matamoros here, vegetation was pretty much frost-bitten, except evergreen trees, of which I had already a tolerable assortment of specimens, which being generally in flower, rendered those to be had at the present season uninteresting—I shall therefore leave this subject—as well as other branches of natural history—to some future communication, for I have done little else as yet but endeavor to get myself to rights in my new domicile—barring a little attention to medical practice, into which I have been drawn by the Mexicans.

We get very little reliable news of interest here from the interior. Great anxiety prevails among all our troops upon this line, with regard to their future destiny. They are worried beyond endurance with the inactive life they have led for the last 11 months. If they are not ordered on, they want to go to Mexico via Vera Cruz, or to go home—anything but to lie here. As for my own part, I have not entirely lost hope of this column's being ordered forward as far as San Luis, whence a communication may be opened to the City of Mexico by Gen. Scott's army. I shall therefore not be in haste to leave here, with a view of proceeding to Mexico by another route. So, for the present, please still direct to this place.

My trip from the U.S. here was one of the most fatiguing as well as annoying, I ever experienced—more so, I am sure than

---

[12] Another indication of the lawlessness that had broken out.

[13] John Francis Hamtramck, colonel of the First Regiment of Virginia Volunteers, for a short time military governor of Saltillo.

[14] See below, page 232.

I ever had across the Great Western Prairies to Santa Fe. Though I had a dreadful voyage across the Gulf—17 days out from N. Orleans to Brazos—the height of my labors and vexations were from Camargo here. This was owing, chiefly, to two circumstances: first, a large "train" had just left Camargo, before I arrived, and therefore I deemed it expedient to use every exertion to overtake it, so as to travel under protection of the escort. I was therefore unable to prepare myself with the necessary outfit, etc. And secondly, not being personally acquainted with a single officer belonging to the train or escort, I could get no aid or accommodation; and therefore having a little more "luggage" than I could conveniently get along with, I was troubled without measure.

This has suggested to me the expediency of endeavoring to procure from the Department at Washington an order to have any necessary luggage and travelling equipments hauled in the government wagons, which are seldom or never heavily laden. I think if the object of my tour were made known to the proper department, I could not fail to be furnished with such an order. The last 12 months of my life have been chiefly dedicated to the public service, with considerable pecuniary loss to myself; and I am sure the future will be still more strictly of a public character.

As I feel greatly loath to ask directly for such an order, myself, I shall be greatly obliged to you, should you have a suitable acquaintance at Washington, if you would suggest the matter there. Should you think proper to make the representation, please direct that, should such an order be procured, it be forwarded to me, to care of Capt. W. W. Chapman, Quartermaster at Matamoros, who will forward to me wherever I may be.

If we could procure an order to this effect, I should thus be enabled to send out any collections I may make.—The order should include my necessary travelling equipage for such a tour as I am upon, instruments, chemicals, preparations, collections, etc.

Please pardon this annoyance. It is only a suggestion which you can act upon or not as you may deem expedient.

I remain, my dear Doctor,

Very truly, Your friend, etc.,

JOSIAH GREGG

DR. GEORGE ENGELMANN,
ST. LOUIS.

P.S. Although the ravages of war seem to be suspended here the cruel agents of death are still active among us—in the shape of murders and executions. Besides anterior casualties, a private in a volunteer corps of cavalry here, was shot some time ago for an attempt to kill his captain; and a couple of weeks ago, another was hung (of the same corps) for the murder of a Mexican, in the streets of this city. But a still more horrid affair has since occurred. Three volunteers, discharged on account of ill-health, having started home were most inhumanly butchered on the road to Monterey, some 15 miles from here. A portion of the perpetrators (five) were caught, and all hung last week in the Public Square. There seemed to be no doubt of their guilt, and it is only to be regretted that they could not have been condemned in accordance with the rules provided; yet I perceive that all those best acquainted with the affair deem that to have been [in]expedient if not impracticable, and that the course taken—a sort of official lynching—was necessary.

✺ DIARY, FEBRUARY, 1848

Wed. 16—To day I removed to the house of the late D. Juan de Arispe (occupied now by his daughter, Dª Cármel de Arispe), having been virtually forced out of my quarters by the occupation of the house for a court of inquiry—and for quarters of officers. [MARGINAL NOTE: This house was soon after occupied by one Capt. (alias Maj.) Howard, appointed Quartermaster by President Polk, perhaps because he was a Texan of some fame in the Santa Fe expedition. Howard brought into the house with

209

him a family of his prostitutes, to the exclusion of a very honest family that before occupied it! This Howard was known to have expended several hundred (more than $1000) dollars on women of this character, all of which he doubtless swindled from the government.]

Speaking of the court of inquiry, I might mention that it was being held for the examination of the conduct of Col. Payne (actual military governor of Saltillo) in certain difficulties which had occurred at the Camp of Buenavista, between said officers, and a portion of the Virginia Regiment. I was happy to learn afterward that the conduct of the Colonel was fully sustained by the court—as was doubtlessly very just it should be, in a meritorious effort to quell mutiny, and enforce order and discipline in the camp.

Tues. 22—To day I was a little annoyed on account of an application of my landlady, dᵃ Cármel, to get her husband, Cecilio Flores, released from prison, where he had been put, on account of having been caught drunk by the American patrol, drunk in the streets. On the one part, the punishment was certainly merited; yet, taking circumstances into consideration, I could not consider Col. Payne's conduct less than tyrannical in stubbornly retaining the fellow 48 hours in prison, distressing a poor innocent family, while American soldiers were to be seen continually staggering and swaggering about the streets in shameful intoxication: while, in fact, the vice was virtually encouraged by his own public acts, viz. the licensing of "dram-shops" by dozens in every part of town, for the sake of an insignificant revenue! This last, it is true I cannot attribute exclusively to Col. Payne, as I believe it was also practised by his predecessors, much to the discredit of the American army!

About this time, we were much gratified by the report of the signing of the treaty on 2ᵈ inst.[15]

[15] The treaty of peace was signed February 2, 1848, at the suburb of Guadalupe Hidalgo.

☼ LETTER TO JOHN BIGELOW

Saltillo, Mexico, March 13, 1848

MY DEAR BIGELOW:

I was a long time getting here. I did not arrive till in January. The reason was that the yellow fever was exceedingly bad in New Orleans, &c. and, having no particular desire to catch it, I concluded not to "run the gauntlet" and so went to visit my brother at Shreveport, Louisiana, where I remained until late in November. Add to this a passage of 17 days on the Gulf and you will have the causes of my delay.

On my arrival here, I received your very gratifying letter of Aug. 29, and have greatly desired a perfectly leisure while to say a word about our friend, Gen. Taylor. I think I told you, when I saw you, something of my opinion, that he was a very clever sort of old fellow, but as to his being a very *great* man— even as a warrior, and much less in every other regard—it is all nonsense to talk about it. Most of his best friends here are amused at the idea. I feel sure that no one who knows him would ever think of calling him a great man, except for interest's sake. But as the world is full of this class of people—"small potatoes"— who see no other means of enhancing their own fame but by lauding a public favorite, you will find many of his intimate acquaintances endeavoring to make a Washington of him. In saying what I have said I give you an idea of my *sentimental* opinion of Gen. Taylor—and that is enough. But I will repeat, as a real clever goodhearted man, I think him one of the best; and if the people would let him stand at what he merits, there is no man whom, in his way, I would esteem higher than Gen. Taylor.

As to news, we have none of interest that you will not have heard more direct through other sources—such as signing of a treaty of peace, etc. This is now all the talk among us; yet, though we think it probable this treaty will ratified by the U.S. Gov't, we think it more than doubtful in Mexico; there are too many of the interior states that have had nothing to do with the "enemy," and consequently remain "invincible"—at a distance —for them to sanction an unfavorable treaty. The fact is—and I suppose you know it—that they are one of the bravest people in the world—at a distance—or on paper—yet when the enemy approaches within "shooting distance" their nerves unfortunately fail them, and they are "taken with a running"—they can't "stand up to their fodder." Had an army marched through all the large cities from here to the City of Mexico, there would have been no trouble in ratifying the treaty. Should peace not now have been made, I hope our government will come to its senses, and order this line southward, to meet a division from the City of Mexico.

The little force, in this quarter, is now scattered about the country; besides occupying the line from here to Matamoros, there are detachments in Monclova, Parras, Mazapil, &c. If the enemy do not attack some of these outposts, they are certainly the most imbecile people, infinitely, in the world—especially Mazapil, which is 100 miles southward, and within striking distance of the "hot beds" of the enemy—Zacatecas, San Luis, Durango, &c. I fear for our troops at Mazapil.

I hope you will write me, still directed to this place—as I shall remain here till peace—or till the army moves southward, when I expect to "move" with it.

Truly, Your Friend, &c.,

JOSIAH GREGG

⚜ DIARY, MARCH, 1848

Frid. 31—About 18th inst. I was attacked with inflammation in my right frontal sinus—an affliction which I had suffered on different occasions, many years before—resulting at present from a severe catarrh with which I had been afflicted for two or three weeks previous. After having been confined to my bed for nearly two weeks, I gradually recovered—more from the use of quinine and morphine (with blisters, etc. to temples) than anything else, I think—and, about this time began to be able to attend a little to business again.

⚙ DIARY, APRIL, 1848

Frid. 14—Walking up Main street (or Calle Real) this evening after 9 o'clock, to see a patient, I was hailed by a sentinel at Col. Hamtramck's door (present Military governor), and was informed that he was ordered to permit no one to pass after 9 o'clock, except commissioned officers, without a written permit. As I had been in the habit of passing at all hours, previously, in all parts of town, without such interruption, I was not disposed to believe it; for I could not conceive, now that the armistice had been publicly proclaimed, why more rigid regulations should be performed than previously. I therefore stepped into the colonel's office to inquire into the truth of it, when I was informed by said officer himself that such was the case:— an old order which had been formerly neglected, (as he expressed it) but which he had lately deemed necessary to enforce—for no other purpose, of course, than to show that he commanded, and to have the pleasure of exercising his tyrannical temperament—now that his "important career" was coming to a close. In fact, it was difficult to imagine any other excuse for it, as all was now quiet and without suspicion—armistice existing, with which such an order would seem little to accord—and far from effecting the object which some pretended—of preventing vagabond soldiers and others from committing outrages about town: for there being scarce over half a dozen sentinels, on half the number of streets, vicious persons had only to avoid these, which was done without difficulty, while honest men, going about their lawful business, were prohibited from passing. The doughty colonel deigned, however, to order his adjutant to give me a "pass"—yet which *I* never "deigned["] to carry—preferring to avoid sentinels, or to leave even important business unattended to, to acquiescing in an annoying order for which I could not see even the shadow of a necessity.

Speaking of this "noble" colonel, I might add, for pomposity, vanity and parade, he was not even excelled by Gen. Wool. He was in almost the daily habit of riding about town, in full uniform, with a long tail of a guard in his wake, putting on airs which Gen. Taylor never thought of.

❀ DIARY, MAY, 1848

Mon. 1—For some time past the street (Calle del Cerrito) passing by my door is being put in repair by the prisoners of the public *Calabozo*. The style of paving streets here (like every thing else in this country) is decidedly ancient—with round smooth pebbles, forming an inclined plane on each side to a gutter in the middle; so that there is no level portion—often so much inclined, indeed, as to render it exceedingly disagreeable —to ride or run a carriage upon.

The culprits at work upon the streets are mostly chained together by the feet—in pairs—yet this does not seem in the least to deject them; for a more jovial, lively funny sett [*sic*] of fellows are seldom met with full of glee, song, mirth, and "jollification."

While our street was thus "enlivened" by day, by night we are amused by the *sereneros* or watchmen. These men, whose chief employment (apart from pretending to keep order during the night) is to attend to the lamps with which the streets are lighted, are a queer set of fellows. At every half hour, which the town clock strikes, they cry the hour, but in such a distorted voice and style that no one can possibly understand them. Their cry usually is (supposing it is to be 12 o'clock at night, for instance) "Ave Maria purisima!—*"Las doce, y sereno,"* or *"nublado,"* etc. "Twelve o'clock, and clear," or "cloudy," etc. as the case may be: but using every effort to distort their vocies, they are wholly unintelligible, as already remarked.

Frid. 11—Some days ago, (5th inst.) upon the faith of the armistice, Gov. Jose Mᵃ de Aguirre came into the city, for the purpose of establishing, as provided for, the civil government: but Col. Hamtramck, requiring the governor to present himself to the U.S. Military authority, and the latter refusing, he was arrested; [MARGINAL NOTE: See note (2) at the end of this M.S.[16]] and to day he made his escape. This arrest by order of Col. Hamtramck, was generally, I believe, if not universally disapproved of by the Americans generally, as being, not only tyrannical, but wholly in violation of the spirit of the armistice.

❂ LETTER TO JOHN GREGG

Saltillo, May 15th–48–

MY DEAR BROTHER:

Having received, a day or two ago, yours of April 8th it reminds me of scratching you another epistle though it should be short and [un]interesting. Three weeks having passed since writing you last as usual in these times, we have in general news that would interest you[.] "Peace stock" is rather "looking up" at present as, from latest information, it is generally believed that the treaty will be ratified by the Mexican Congress, but you will hear all about this matter direct from the city of Mexico before this can reach you.

I got a letter a few days ago from our old friend Dr. Connelly,[17] at Chihuahua. No particular news; except he was just starting for the U.S.

You mention that, "from some cause," only 8 bales of your cotton have been sold. Is it not the carelessness of your commission merchants? From my own little but less experience with Wright, Williams & Co.: I take it for granted that you must be "out with them." Is it possible there is not an honest merchant in N. Orleans? I wrote you that I had remitted them (Feb. 7) a

---

[16] See below, page 232.
[17] For Dr. Henry Connelly, see page 100n.

draft for $100—with a bill of articles to be sent me. I have not only not received the articles, but not even a syllable in answer, though I urged on them to write me immediately, that if the draft failed I might get a duplicate! They cannot but have received, as I wrote three or four letters, one by a very careful private conveyance. In fact, I have long since received answers from Beelen[18] at Pittsburgh to letters of same date, by same conveyance. Thinking me in a savage land, they perhaps intend to "cabbage the money." I should be glad you would have it inquired into.

I had as well, perhaps, fill up with medical gossip. My practice continues as brisk as usual or a little more so. In fact, I am worried beyond endurance. There is not a day, or come a meal that I get to eat in peace. In the morning before breakfast they are after me. When I come to dinner I rarely fail to find several waiting for me. At least half the nights I am kept from eating my supper till 9 o'clock, when I sup at 7. I often refuse to go, and send them to my night doctors, when I can. Though, it often happens, when I refuse to go, they will get some one of my friends to come after me, whom I can't refuse. So you see I have gained some sort of reputation. Though it is difficult to say how; except by my knowledge of the language, customs, etc., and my tact at making myself agreeable among "the natives." I have often thought that if I could make myself as easy in American society, I would be willing to live in the United States.

Your Brother

JOSIAH GREGG

P.S. I bought a little pony of Frank for $15—having cost him the same; but which is now worth about a thousand! In pacing, he is only second to Tabbaquenna.[19]—lively as a "cricket" and

---

[18] Anthony Beelen lived at Pittsburgh, Pennsylvania, from about 1812 until his death in 1850. He established an iron foundry and engaged in merchandising. Gregg had come into business relations with him during Santa Fé trading days, and Beelen had proposed a partnership, "selling iron and Pittsburgh goods," so Gregg puts it, in the Far West.

gentle as a lamb. He at once learned the houses of the patients, and paces at the rate of "nine knots an hour" from one to another, and I can ride him into the house and feel a patient's pulse, if I choose, without getting off.

Note: I made a rough estimate of my practice for the month of April. It amounted to between four and five hundred dollars. This month will doubtless be more. I charged from memory heretofore; but on first of May, I commenced keeping accounts, which at current prices amount to $30 to $40 per day. I will have to reduce on these, but the average net must be over $20 per day. My entire monthly practice has been about as follows: January less than $100 — February near $200 — March would have been full $300 — I was sick half the month — April over $400. If I could keep on raising the $100 per month, it would do pretty well. The truth is, if I could get up to the "high water mark" in charging, it would now amount to a thousand or more a month. However, in this case, I would doubtless not get so much custom. I know of one bill of a neighbor Doctor of over $200—and they finally settled on $175, which I could not have thought of charging over $30 or $40 for. At such rates my practice would be worth over $5000 per month. Note: One thing flattering is, that I have never been discarded for another that I know of: whereas I am frequently offered the patients of other.

[*The remainder of this letter is not preserved.*]

❀ DIARY, MAY, 1848

Mon. 22—This morning died D. Antonio del Bosque (whom I was treating) one of the wealthy men of the city. Sr. Bosque, like many others, suffered considerably from our army; and, I believe as unjustly as any, as his disposition always seemed

---

[19] Tabbequena ("Big Eagle") was a Comanche chieftain whom Gregg visited when he set out on his trip in 1839 from Van Buren, Arkansas, to Santa Fé, mainly along the Canadian River. Tabbequena furnished information of value about the route. Afterwards Gregg seems to have named a favorite horse for the Indian.

friendly towards us. In December, 1846, when Gen. Butler was looking for quarters, I spoke to him for his residence house, as he talked of leaving for his rancho; and he offered to give it up with much willingness. But as Gen. Butler finally did not want it, he afterward gave it up to Capt. Hughes,[20] (of Top. Engineers); and it was continued to be held by one and others of our officers till the close of the war, while his family had to reside in an inconvenient little house. A few days before Sr. Bosque's death, he sent a solicitation to have his house restored, that he might die in it; but this was denied him!

❀ DIARY, JUNE, 1848

Wed. 14—Official information of the ratification of the treaty having been received, two or three weeks ago, the troops departed from Saltillo to day, in obedience to previous order. On this occasion, Col. Hamtramck fully sustained that very unenviable character, which he had already establish[ed]. One is almost justifiable in believing (as he must have know[n] that such would be the result) that he placed the Mississippians and Texans in the rear, purposely to commit outrages;[21] for it was well known that these were the most desperate corps in the comman[d]—the "noble colonel" himself leaving in advance, leaving them without restraint. Here Col. Clarke, commanding the Mississippians, did anything but credit to himself, in dismissing the regiment in town, thus permitting them to do as they pleased; so that half of them were drunk in an hour. Such a scene I never witnessed—500 drunk men in the square—yelling, swearing, outraging every Mexican they could see (though the latter, frightened to death, mostly shut themselves up in their houses),

[20] In the earlier stages of the war, George Wurtz Hughes had been chief of the topographic staff of General Wool's division. Towards the end of the war, he was appointed governor of Jalapa.

[21] Gregg found it difficult to stomach the outrages and excesses that the withdrawing soldiers were committing upon the Mexicans. He was decidedly sympathetic towards the Mexican population and did what he could to see that they were treated with kindness and fairness.

and one Mexican at least was shot (killed) and it is said so are others wounded. On one occasion a mob of soldiers collect[ed] at the calabozo, and forced out an American, who had been imprisoned for some outrage.

I myself did not fail to feel the effect of their outrages. A Mississippian seeing my little servant boy with my favorite pony, dismounted him and galloped away with the horse; but I was so fortunate as to recover him again.

Frid. 16—Having concluded to go to Monterey with the troops, the first night I lay 12 miles from Saltillo with the artillery and Virginians—and next day, joined Maj. Webster of the Artillery. I should note that the Major is one of the most worthy, mild, agreeable and gentlemanly officers with whom I have had to [deal].—Night of the 15th we lay at Rinconada, and this evening I arrived at Monterey—the command camping at the Molinos (Mills) 5 m. back.

Meeting with my former acquaintance, D. José Rafael de la Garza (on my arrival in Monterey), I inquired where I could find a room to rent, when he virtually forced me to take quarters with his brother, the priest, D. José Antonio de la Garza. I must say that I could not well have been placed in a more comfortable situation, or treated with more kindness and attentions than by this worthy old priest.

The troops were dispatched from Monterey in detachments—some before my arrival—others while there,—but a considerable portion not till after I left. Gen. Wool left about the 26th.

Sun. 25—Left Monterey yesterday morning about 4 o'clock, and arrived at Capellania about 8 A.M. where I slept. Arrived to-day about 10 o'clock, A.M. in Saltillo. A few hours after my arrival, Gov. Aguirre and Gen. Mexía arrived from San Luis Potosí—though without any troops. It was not till in first of August that a few companies of Mexican troops arrived.

I should note here, that though many fears were entertained, on the leaving of the army that Americans remaining here would be in great danger of all sorts of outrages, if not of assassination; yet so far from this, I have to confess that for months that I remained in Saltillo—and called into all parts of the city by my business—I never received even an insult in word or action.

I might also note that I concluded to remain in this city for a while (and my chief object in doing so was) for the purpose of proceeding to the city of Mexico through the interior, in the fall: continuing, meanwhile, in the practice of medicine here, at which I am able to do a very good business.

☸ DIARY, JULY, 1848

Frid. 28—To-day Col. Washington's command passed through this city, bound for New Mexico and California. The command consisted of near 1000 men—5 companies of dragoons and four of artillery, I think.

This was a rather unfortunate affair—certainly very objectionable, if not in violation of the treaty. That clause declaring that the troops were to abandon the country at the soonest possible period—copy words from treaty[22]—could have no meaning if it permitted a portion of our army to march from Matamoros (on the line—nay even from east of Rio Grande, as a part did) via this place and Chihuahua, to get out of the country a month or two afterward.—It is but little excuse to say that the people generally did not object to it—were glad of it, indeed, as they thereby sold a great deal of corn, beef, etc.: every thing which could be construed into a violation of the treaty, should have been most strenuously avoided on the part of the U.S.: it is of course everything but noble, to take advantage of strength and power.

☸ DIARY, AUGUST, 1848

Wed. 2—Tonight my friend Dr. G. M. Prevost[23] (formerly assistant Surgeon of the army) arrived from U.S.—having resigned before leaving Monterey for U.S. in May last, I think.

Thurs. 3—To-day, an affair, rather amusing than otherwise, came off in the city. A Mr. Collingsworth having received the *nomination* of vice-consul of this place from Gen. Wool (of course the General had no authority to *appoint*) the former procured the American arms and stuck them up over his door, and assumed all the duties of consul. Gov. Aguirre being a violent passionate fellow, objected to this proceeding, as Mr. C. not only had no regular appointment, but had not been acknowledged by the Mexican Government; therefore had no right of course to act as such. But Collingsworth, determined to "stick up" for what he fancied his right, and the "dignity of his office," persisted in keeping his colors up, when the governor threatened to take them down *"vi et armis."* To prevent any disagreeable consequences, I went to Mr. C. and explained to him that he could not persist in forcing his colors to remain, as this could only be granted him by courtesy, he of course being no consul really as yet. But being yet unwilling to cede publicly, he adopted a *ruse,* taking down the "arms" at night, and declaring next morning, that "some d——d rascal had stolen them during the night!"

Sun. 6—To day is the feast of the *gran función del Santisimo Cristo,* much celebrated in this region of the country: but, as in all celebrated feasts, the principal *función,* is on the eve. Therefore, yesterday evening the main public square was filled with asses, dressed with fripperies, shawls, flags, etc. laden with pine wood to make bonfires. These were lighted after dark—besides illuminations on the houses—and a quantity of not very badly executed fireworks.

Sat. 12—Dr. Prevost having left for Monterey on 8th inst. he returned to day, with his baggage and medicines, etc.

---

[22] Gregg never found time to copy the clause about the date for the withdrawal of the American soldiers. It is to be found in Articles III and IV of the Treaty of Peace. In substance the provision was that soldiers were to be withdrawn inside of three months.

[23] For further details about Dr. Grayson M. Prevost, see Gregg's comments on pages 229–30.

In accordance with a previous proposition, I engaged in partnership with Dr. Prevost, in the practice of medicine, for the period he expected to remain here—until leaving for Zacatecas.

Mon. 14—Up to the present date, since my return from Monterey, I had lived in the house of Don Ignacio Ramos, on Calle Real, a little below principal *plaza*. But the house being required for the Tribunal de Justicia, we removed to day again into the house of Arispe, which I previously occupied, on Calle del Carrito—anything but an agreeable place, to be sure, on account of the filthiness of the family, and the noisy crowds which so frequently visited the house; but we could do no better.

Wed. 30—Started to San Antonio—etc.

☼ DIARY, SEPTEMBER, 1848

Sun. 3—Returned to Saltillo this evening again. My objects were, a *paseo* for recreation and health,—and to collect plants and other objects of natural history.

The village of San Antonio is in the mountains, southeastward from Saltillo—courses and distances as represented in the map of next margin[24]—distances say as follows: Palomas to Alamo 8 m.—thence to S. Antonio 18 m.—Thence to Guachichil 20 m. thence to Saltillo 25 m.—The place is rather a number of ranchos, scattered in a valley—farms all cultivated with irrigation, as there is but little water. There are many of the handsomest and richest valleys that I have seen in Mexico; and might be extensively cultivated (especially in wheat) but for want of water, even for the indispensable purposes of drinking, etc. The truth is, only along the immediate borders of the mountains, is [it] damp enough to produce with any degree of certainty. The mountains are timbered with pine, etc. and their borders and hill-sides with piñon, cedar, etc. One thing remarkable in the vegetation might be noted—that there are none of the numerous species of cacti which abound in lower regions, to be found in these hills or val-

[24] See opposite page 223 for the map referred to here.

Sept. 1846.

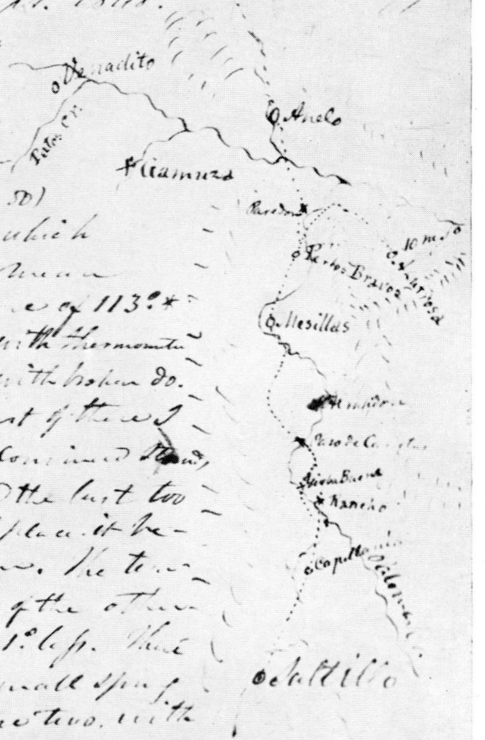

leys—nor, in fact, any others (that I recollect of) of the various species of *thorny* plants and shrubs, so abundant elsewhere in Mexico. [MARGINAL NOTE: No maguey, lechuguilla, junco, etc.]

During this excursion I collected a considerable number of quite interesting specimens of plants—some I think entirely new.

In these valleys (prairie) there are to be found considerable (immense) numbers of *tusas* or "prairie-dogs," so abundant on the plains betwixt the frontier of Missouri and New Mexico. I measured a large-sized one which I killed, which gave the following dimensions: From tip of nose to root of tail, 12 in.—tail bone 3½ in.—head 3 in.—ears very short—color grayish brown—tail covered with hair like body (say ½ in. or more long.)—tip of tail sometimes black.

This region is inhabited by a class of people, generally having bad character—mostly said to be robbers. I stayed two nights with one which I was afterward told was looked upon as a "captain of robbers." While on our way from Palomas to San Antonio, we met three men who had been tied and robbed by a very small party, but a day or two before; and between S. Antonio and Guachichil we passed near the place where this robbery had taken place. What was remarkable, and, in fact, one of the causes of so many robberies in this—three men permitted themselves to be robbed by but an equal number of rogues—who would not have ventured to rob one American.

This region of San Antonio is elevated, I doubt not, some 2000 feet even above Saltillo. While there, the nights were decidedly cool—sleeping under three or four blankets with comfort. The mountains—the highest of which hardly rise 2000 feet above the valleys,—are exceedingly picturesque; and with the clean, smooth, rich valleys which intervene,—and their borders picturesquely covered with timber, are decidedly romantic and beautiful.

The geology is not particularly interesting—nearly all lime:

the higher portions of the mountains solid blue lime stone—
their borders of a soft, friable, cretaceous lime.

Guachichil is but an insignificant hacienda or rancho—population scarcely 100 souls. The population of the valley of San
Antonio (including several ranchos) may be near 500.

❂ DIARY, SEPTEMBER, 1848

Sat. 16—This being the anniversary of Mexican independence,
it was celebrated here (at Saltillo) with some little pomp. This
celebration, however, did not consist of much that was interesting,
beyond the fire-works, which were about identical with those of
6th of Aug. And on the night of the 17th (Sunday) they had a
"national ball." As repugnant as the celebration of balls on Sun-
days appear to protestants, nothing is more common in this country; and, on this occasion, it was had a day after the regular
period, so as to have it on Sunday night! Another notable circumstance connected with this ball—characteristic of the celebra-
tions everywhere that I have visited the Republic, and of the
character of these people—is, that not a foreigner, except one
or two naturalized, was invited to the ball: partially owing to
prejudice, but more to a peculiar self-conceit, bigotry, and
jealousy.

Tues. 19—Left, this morning for a warm spring, called "Le
Azufrosa." etc.

Sat. 23—Returned to Saltillo, this evening late.—The objects
of this expedition were substantially those which took me to San
Antonio—& in addition, to examine the sulphur spring, etc.

This warm mineral spring is situated, down the creek from
Saltillo, at the aggregate distance of about 50 miles: The courses
and position is represented in the map of next margin,[25] to some
approximate degree of accuracy: the distances (intermediate) are
nearly as follows: Saltillo to Capellania, say 10 m.—thence to
rancho where leave creek, 6 or 7 m.—to Paso de Carritas, 6 m.

[25] See above, Note 24.

224

—To Mesillas 12 or 13 m.—Perros Bravos, 6 m. Azufroas, say 10 m.

There are two sulphur springs but a few yards from each other (say 50) the largest of which indicated a mean temperature of 113° [MARGINAL NOTE: It is asserted that during some seasons of the year this water is much warmer; yet the difference is perhaps but little.] (Fahr.) i.e. with thermometer No. 1–116° & with broken do. 110—the first of these I have been convinced stand too high, and the last too low: so I place it between them. The temperature of the other spring is 1° less. There is a very small spring between these two, with temperature (mean) 78° —Temperature of atmosphere about 80°. The largest of these sulphur springs may discharge 30 gals. water per minute—the other, about half as much.

I had neither the means nor time (nor, in fact, experience) sufficient to undertake to analize this water completely. The sulphur being chiefly precipitated on cooling (considerable quantities are to be found in the spring-branch) the taste of it is scarcely perceptible after standing a while. It also evidently contains considerable saline matter—soda and potash—also lime—and from the black color produced by nutgalls: the same indications are produced, however, to a greater or less degree, in the common water of Saltillo: the fact is, that the Saltillo water evidently contains a large portion of lime—besides some (minute quantities) of soda, potash and iron.

There are said to be many other mineral springs (generally warm) in the mountains in the direction of Monclova, and the Rio Grande.

Of plants, I collected during this excursion, several new and interesting species: the most interesting of which is one called *siempreviva* (life-everlasting) as it does not die in the winter. It is a herbaceous (and very succulent and mucillaginous) plant, with thick pulpy leaves, somewhat of size and figure of those of common plantain, and disposed in a similar manner. The seed-

225

stalk grows up in the centre to the height of about two feet, producing on its head a sort of whorl of very pretty flowers, between yellow and orange in color.

☀ DIARY, OCTOBER, 1848

Sun. 1—About this time commenced the famous *Feria del Saltillo.* It is the custom at various fixed points in Mexico, to have annual fairs (at regular determinate periods) where merchants from "the four winds" of the Republic resort to buy, sell and barter merchandise and all sorts of wares.

These *ferias* are pretty things, and, in many regards, useful affairs. They serve to call together extensive assortments of merchandise, in which every one expects to find all that he wants, and that at reduced prices, as goods can be sold cheaper on these occasions than in regular trade—not only on account of the quantity expended, but because all effects expended on these occasions are exempt from the burdensome *derecho del consumo.*[26] It is therefore, that people resort here not only from all the villages and ranchos of the neighborhood, but from the towns and cities at a considerable distance. I suppose the population of the city must be very nearly doubled, on these occasions: not only most of the entire families from the vicinity, but traders from Monterey and Matamoros—from Tampico and San Luis Potosí— from Zacatecas and Durango—from Chihuahua and even Texas, etc. etc.

The regular stores not being sufficient to accommodate all the merchandise accumulated here on these occasions, immense numbers of shanties (or as we would call them in Indian phrase, *wigwams*) are erected for the occasion. As I have often witnessed on the Plains, an Indian village spring up in a barren desert as if by magic in a few moments, at once filled life and bustle, so here the previous dry dirty public squares were filled with these shanties, at once teeming with wares, gewgaws and frip-

[26] Sales tax.   [27] Beggars.

peries—two squares nearly filled—as well as some short streets connecting commercial points, were completely lined with these temporary shops.

But there are many drawbacks to the utility and convenience of these *ferias*—I mean the frauds, rogueries and vices generally, practised at them. Besides the "more innocent" vices of Bull and Cockfights, puppet-shows, rope-dancing, fandangoes, etc. gaming of every description is carried on to an incredible extent. The *plaza principal* contained [dozens] of shanties dedicated to this vice alone—besides numbers of gaming houses in other parts of the city. On walking through the square, one's ears were stunned with the jingle of money, dice-boxes, etc. and the cries of the monte-dealers, etc. who were continually bawling out at the top of their voices—"Here's jack!,—there's the king!—No[w] comes the eagle!—upturns the may-flower!" etc.—for these *worthies* have a technical name for even all the "spatter" cards of the deck.

Besides the frauds and rascalities publicly carried on at these gaming establishments, all sorts of rogueries and robberies are practised with almost equal impunity. Few attempts have been made on foreigners, for the rogues are generally afraid of these. On one occasion, however, two thieves entered the store of some foreigners, while the owners were out, but these happening to return at this period, one robber was taken; and the other wounded with a pistol shot as he made his escape.

I have been told of an amusing robbery which occurred in the streets. A rogue sprang upon a horse hitched at a door, while the owner was occupied within—and galloped down the street. The owner immediately cried out "Catch the thief!—Stop him!—there he goes!"—when the robber at once joined in the cry, "Stop the thief!—look, seize at him!—yonder he goes! ["] etc. and thus made his escape, while the crowd were straining their eyes to see which of the dozens of *leperos*[27] seen in the distance was the robber sought after.

I have alluded to the bull-fights; (*Toros*) and though these have been described dozens of times, I may give an outline of those practised here, as differing perhaps in some respects from those elsewhere. It is more common to have a permanent bull-pen prepared; yet here a temporary scaffolding in form of an amphitheatre was erected for the purpose in one of the squares (*Plaza Nueva*). In the large pen or corral formed in the centre of this large amphitheatre (which is filled with spectators) a wild savage bull (with long keen horns) is turned loose, and at once beset with the *toreadores*—and after being rendered desperate and furious, by red flags, and tasselled darts stuck into his skin—the cry is "Kill him! Kill him!"—and he must be killed. The captain of the band then takes a straight sabre which he thrusts into the chest of the animal, while the latter is making frightful lunges at him. This seems the climax of delight for the idle crowd—to see the poor brute's life's blood gush out!—to see him tremble! totter—reel!—fall—expire!!—The air is now rent with joyful yells and huzzas!—As some intelligent Mexicans have remarked to me—these amusements are indicative of the barbarous temperament and character of the people: in fact, they serve to create them in the rising generations. Having been taught to delight in the flow of blood and torture of even brutes, they cannot but become cruel and inhuman themselves.

One interesting circumstance attending these public amusements, is that the *ilustre ayuntamiento* was in constant attendance, directing the order of the brutal operations.

[For a fuller account, see letter to Brother John, and to John Bigelow, N. Y.][28]

About this time we have been kept in continual alarm, from the report that a band of *aventureros* were organizing in the U.S. with the ostensible object of aiding the four frontier states of Tamaulipas, Nuevo Leon, Coahuila and Chihuahua to separate themselves from Mexico and form an independent Republic,

[28] Gregg's brackets. Apparently the letters have not been preserved.

with title of *República de la Sierra Madre:* but the true object was doubtless, *fame* with the leaders, and robbery, with most of the privates. Though we have been yet very well treated by the people and authorities generally—in fact, I have never suffered an outrage or insult in word or action—yet this enterprise would tend to place our lives and property in more or less jeopardy. It is to be hoped that so unjust an adventure will fail—if not for want of will in those concerned, at least for want of *means* to carry it into execution: to say nothing of the measures which it is to be hoped the government of the U.S. will adopt to check it. It is said there is no existing laws by which the adventurers can be stopped or punished! If this be true, it is a fault which certainly ought to be corrected by congressional enactment.—Were these people in a state of revolution, and inviting succor, as was the case in Texas, there would be some reason for the movement; yet there is nothing of this—nor do I believe that it is the desire of the people generally. I cannot see how any one can justify an invasion with no other evident object than conquest or robbery —it is falling back into the earlier ages of the "Old World." [See also the before mentioned letters on this subject.][29]

Monday, 23—To-day my former partner, Dr. G. M. Prevost left for Zacatecas. Much to my disappointment, this engagement turned out anything but agreeable to me. Though I expected to lose money by it, from the first, there were other desiderata which seemed of more interest to me. Having much confidence in the medical experience and talent of Dr. Prevost, I expected to obtain much practical information from him: but in this I was to a great degree disappointed, as, showing frequently a degree of reluctance, I could not consult with the freedom I had expected.—I also sought congenial company, as there were no foreigners here with whom I wished to associate: and I believed Prevost to be much of my own habits—sober, temperate, studious, etc. And, in fact, these seemed to have been his natural

[29] Gregg's brackets. Evidently the letters referred to in Note 28, above.

habits and temperament. But circumstances prevented them very much (in fact he showed not the least inclination to studiousness) while with me. He unfortunately became in love—desperately so—and what was more remarkable for a man of his intellect, with a little girl (13 years old) without any special beauty or merit—and still less talent and intelligence. This (with his high empassioned temperament) was perhaps the chief cause of his being too restless to remain at home, except the time indispensably occupied in sleep and business. In addition to this we might use the common-place expression, that he had been "petted until he had become spoiled." Besides the distinction shown him by myself, he was caressed by the Mexicans generally, and particularly courted by the "fair sex": for being a young man of 25 years of age—of rather unus[u]ally handsome person—agreeable manners,—and many worthy qualities, in fact—he was almost the "toast of the city." This, with the influence of the unpropitious school of the army (to which he had belonged) caused him very frequently to put on very disagreeable airs of haughtiness and self-importance.—An other object of the connection with him was to gain time to bring up my memoranda, and attend to other private business, etc. Yet in this I also failed:—owing in a great degree to Prevost['s] custom of having all his patients to come to the house either for medicines or treatment—causing much trouble and annoyance to me, as they so frequently came in his absence. I was also occasioned much loss of time by his utter want of system and order—leaving everything in the way of medicines topsy-turvy and in perfect confusion.

❀ DIARY, DECEMBER, 1848

Wed. 6—Gen. Miñon, with a few hundred troops, arrived ten or 12 days ago from the south, on his way to the frontier, whither, with his little force, he will leave in a few days. This evening I made a visit to the General, in company with my friend, the wealth[y] D. Jacobo Sanchez. We found Miñon engaged at a game of cards (something like the English game of *brag*, as it appeared) with some of the nabobs of the city—and clever heaps of money before him. The Gen. seemed so absorbed in his game (very *politely* inviting me to join them, which honor I as *politely* declined) that we had very little conversation with him—consequently not much opportunity to judge of his talent and acquirements. He appeared, however, separating him from his game, to be a rather clever, polite, social, gentlemanly—but rough—sort of a fellow: rather tall, lean and coarse featured—age perhaps 50. It is told of him that he commenced his career as a chief of bandits: though I can by no means assert it as a fact. Nevertheless, though it be, it is too common in this country to be a disgrace: Even the same is told of Gen. Santa Anna and other such.

Gen. Mexia passed on about a month ago, in the same direction. The ostensible object of these movements toward the eastern frontier, is to prepare against the "invasion of the *aventureros*" spoken of before. Gen. Mexia is rather a low, heavy set, well-looking & apparently a very clever, gentlemanly and rather polished sort of a fellow—but also addicted to that almost universal vice of this country—gaming, etc.

Gen. Juan José Sanchez (brother of the curate of Saltillo) remains here as comandante general of the State. But, having been suffering for more than 20 years with gravel—and now most of his time confined to bed—it is difficult to judge of him. He would seem however a decidedly clever kind hearted sort of a man—exceedingly bland in his manners—excessive talker, in fact, to an annoying degree, recounting continually the exploits of his youth, etc. Among other things, he frequently told me of an adventure at the battle of Buenavista, where he was. He says a general, superior in command to him, permitting his soldiers to massacre some American prisoners, he (Sanchez) remonstrated severely inquiring why he committed such dastardly and savage deeds: and that said general's answer was—"Because I wear pantaloons!![”] [MARGINAL NOTE: I regret since to have learned that he had a Texan prisoner, who had escaped from an execution ordered by the Mexican govt. (of the famous black beans)[30] shot in Saltillo, against the solicitations of the citizens generally.]

[Notes Accompanying Manuscript No. 4]

[NOTE 1, from page 206]—Expecting the army to move ahead toward San Luis, finding, generally, under such circumstances, difficult to procure transportation for my collections of plants, etc.—and as there were more for public than private benefit—I concluded to write to Hon. Chester Ashley of U.S. Senate, to procure an order to have them transported in the government wagons: but the Qr. Mr. General, Gen. Jesup refused it! I was only surprised that the *honorable* functionary did not ask (as ignorant Mexicans frequently do) "What are all those herbs, etc. good for? Will they serve for food or medicine?—So little idea have many of our public functionaries of utility to natural history, or to science, generally.

It is a notable fact, that the army officers, who are receiving salaries, attend to no objects of natural history: not even do the Topographical engineers make observations for latitude: I am sure I hazard nothing in asserting that I alone have done more in this line than all the engineers and other officers in the army put together—chiefly for public benefit, and at my own expense —yet I could not even get these *public* collections hauled by the government wagons, though these are generally lightly laden. —Jan. 31.

[NOTE 2, from page 215]—The communication of Col. Hamtramck (which is in English, and under his own signature) giv-

---

[30] Some of the Mier prisoners had made a break and gotten away, only to be retaken by the Mexicans. As a punitive measure, Colonel Huerta inflicted decimation. One hundred and fifty-nine white beans and seventeen black ones were placed in an earthen vessel, and the prisoners were required to draw. A few hours later the unlucky ones were executed.

ing his reasons for the arrest of Gov. Aguirre would doubtless all be worth preserving, as one of the most complete specimens of bombast, vanity, and presumption that I have met with. Verily, Hamtramck's elevation to the command of this branch of the army has very nearly if not quite turned his noddle. For want of time I only copy the following occa[sional] paragraphs from the original letter, sent me [by] Lieut. or vice-governor D. Eduardo Gonzales to whom it was directed:—"I could not but construe the mode in which he reported himself by a note sent by the hands of a common servant as an act of intentional disrespect to the high authority of the United States vested in me.

————"I feel myself compelled by a sense of violated dignity to adhere to my determination," etc.

————"He sends a note by a servant to inform the highest authority of the United States, in this state that he has arrived," etc.—

————"I have been invested with the command of a major general, a command corresponding with the rank of generals Scott and Taylor, the highest military grade in the U. S. Army."

"It is true that we cannot boast in the U.S. of such high grades of distinction as are granted to individuals in other countries, yet this does not in the least affect the equal consideration due to an officer holding the highest rank which the United States can bestow, when he meets a foreigner of a nominally higher grade. For example, the highest rank in our navy is that of commodore, while in England it is only a third grade; but when a commodore of the U.S. Navy meets a Lord High Admiral of England, he is recognized as an equal, and treated accordingly. A Senator of the United States has a rank equal to that of a member of the House of Lords in Great Britain, though one is but a commoner, in the English acceptation, and the other a Peer of the Realm. Assuredly then, an officer with the rank of Colonel in the U.S. Service, when invested with the command of a Maj. Gen[l] is at least equal

233

in rank to a governor of a conquered Department: yet Gov. Aguirre says that the dignity of his office forbids his reporting in person."

P.S. "—The enclosed communication from the General Com. S. by which your excellency will perceive that Mr. Aguirre's "office as governor has long since become defunct in the state of Coahuila."

It would seem a little singular how Col. Hamtramck could arrogate to himself the title of a Major General's command, when Brig. Gen. Wool was at Monterey, and Hamtramck only commanded a branch of Gen. Wool's Division.—How Gen. Wool was informed that Gov. Aguirre's office had "long since become defunct in the state of Coahuila," I know not: what I do know, is that the same Gov. Aguirre continued to be acknowledged as the legitimate executive, until he himself resigned, late the following fall.

PART V

Visit to Mexico City

****

Visit to Mexico City

December, 1848 to April, 1849

Diary, December, 1848[1]

THURS. 14—To-day being the day appointed to leave for Mexico our old Cura, D. José Ygnacio Sanchez Navarro (brother of Gen. Sanchez), the head of our party, set out quite early, for the purpose of avoiding the annoyance of visitors—persons, friends calling on him to take leave—to accompany, etc. The truth is Cura Sanchez is very decidedly popular—almost adored—in Saltillo; & in truth, to a degree at least, I think he merits it. My own experience has certainly about convinced me that he possesses a good deal of virtue, goodness and kindness of heart.

The rest of our company got off about 9 or 10 o'clock; yet I could not get ready till 2 P.M. Nevertheless, I arrived at Aguanueva about 7 P.M. near 20 m. where I found all our party. These

---

[1] While practicing medicine in Saltillo, Gregg had entertained hopes of continuing to Mexico City by the fall of 1848. It was not possible, however, for him to start until December. Then he became a member of a distinguished party of Saltillonses, and was once more in his element as a traveler. He was not a member by sufferance, as it were, as in the days of his army connection. It was more like traveling with a Santa Fé caravan, this company of some forty men and a few women. In addition, he had a position of distinction, although his penchant for stopping to make scientific observations and records was sometimes annoying to the others. The journey took Gregg into a section of interior Mexico entirely new to him, and he evidently enjoyed the experience. He took delight in the Indians and their ways. He frankly states that Mexico City was less impressive than he had expected, but made the most of opportunities for sightseeing. When the excursions out from Mexico City began, Gregg found it necessary to start a new notebook, and began what he designates as Manuscript No. 5 with the entry "Real del Monte, March, 1849."

237

consist of Cura Sanchez (as before mentioned), Dᵃ Teodoria, wife of D. Francisco Cepeda, and her niece, D. Merced Campa—with their respective servants and retinues & *agregados*—these last consist of D. Antonio Goríbar, who manages the affairs of our priest; and five or six young men coming to college, etc. Wherefore the number of men—principals & *agregados* (including myself) is about 8—of servants about 15 or 16—so that our entire number of men is from 23 to 25—with three ladies and three servant women.

Agua Nueva is an hacienda, watered by a large spring—pop. scarcely over 100 now. We had a windy disagreeable night.

Frid. 15—S. 4 m.—S.W. 8 m.—S. 6 m. to Tanque de la Vaca —an artificial pond, dry up in dry season,—with an abandoned hut or two—nooned.—A few miles back, my attention was called to what my comrades styled a *volcan* (volcano) in the side of a hill. It turned out to be only a cave or pit, some 40 to 50 feet deep—of no particular interest: no signs of its having been the crater of a volcano.—Afternoon, S. 5 to 10 W. 10 m. to Encarnacion, pop. some 2 or 300 souls. [MARGINAL NOTE: Lat. of Encarnacion 24° 49′ 26″ Polaris] Water tanque & noria—not abundant. Borland, Gaines, etc. taken here—particulars.

Sat. 16—S. 30° E. 16 to 18 m. to Ventura (Rancho of about 100 souls, half a mile east of road—Jesus Mᵃ & San Juan Nepᵒ to northward on other road which joins at Tanque de la Vaca: each perhaps of one to 200 souls.)—S. 20 E. 10 m. to S. Salvador —Nooned—Rancho of about 100 souls. This and other three before mentioned ranchos watered by tanques and small wells —therefore neither certain nor abundant.—S. 15 E. 7 or 8 m. to S. Miguelito—Rancho or Hacienda of say 50 souls, nearly new—Noria.—S. 10 E. 10 m. to Salado. Hacienda of possibly two or three hundred souls. Most miserable place: nothing to be had—not even wood—watered by a noria, etc. quite saltish. —water all brackish from Encarnacion here. Country almost a dead level; lined with low mountain ridges on each side. Natives say no water ever runs in valley even during great freshets: some say natural outlet ought to be northward; yet I think it most probably eastward, through the hills, opposite Salado. [MARGINAL NOTE: Lat. of Salado 24° 19′ 1″ Polaris]

This place has become somewhat famous, as being the point where the Mier prisoners (in 1843?) rose and liberated themselves from their guard. Mexican officers have told me they were on parole: if so, it was certainly a very reprehensible act: yet the story as told by themselves and friends was as follows: [See an account of the affair; seek an account in Kendall or elsewhere— and of their subsequent decimation!][2]

Sun. 17—S. 5 W. 5 m.—S. 25 W. 5 m.—S. 6 or 8 m. to Parida —neither people nor water—but formerly a rancho with a tanque.—S. 12 or 14 m. to Punta de Vanegas—village of perhaps 100 souls—two or three small springs of water, with tanques. (Course from here to S. Juan de Vanegas, near border of mountain, S. 10 E. 6 m.—also to Catorce, in middle of mountain, S. 10 m. (say) straight line.)—S. 15 or 20 W. 3 or 4 m. to Vanegas—Hacienda of say 100 souls. Water quite aboundant —brisk stream (sufficient for small mill) descends from direction of S. Juan de Vanegas. [MARGINAL NOTE: Lat. of Vanegas by Polaris, 23° 52′ 11″]

Mon. 18—S. 35 W. 10 m. to Ranchito (thence to Catorce S.E. 7 or 8 m.)—S. 30 W. 4 or 5 m. to San Cristobal, nooned—S. 20 m. to Guadalupe del Carnicero, Hacienda of perhaps two or 300 souls. Brisk little stream of water descends from mountain to East—through pipes—into a tanque. (S. Miguel, small rancho —4 m. from S. Cristobal, and Refugio also small rancho 8 m. back—both supplied with water by Norias. [MARGINAL NOTE: Lat. of Carniceros by Polaris 23° 26′ 4″ Lat. of S. Cristobal 46° by Mer. alt. sun 23° 43′ 46″]

---

[2] The brackets are Gregg's. His evident intention was to look up the incident in George Wilkins Kendall's *Narrative of the Texan Santa Fé Expedition* or some other source.

239

Tues. 19—S. 6 m. to Tanque de la Pulgas—water but no settlement. Here I saw a fence of a coarse granite—from a contiguous little mountain—the first granite of any kind I have seen since entering the republic by way of Matamoros: though it is *possible* that, in some of the higher mountains about Saltillo, it may come to the surface. Up to Carnicero, the road continued level, rising very little, but this morning we entered the hills, and soon after passed what appeared a divide between the Salado and Venado waters.—S. 15 E. 6 or 8 m. to Berrendo, nooned—tanque now nearly dry—no settlement.—S. 6 m. to Hac. de Laguna Seca, half mile or more to east of road—pop. 100 or more, I suppose.—S. 20 W. 8 or 10 m. to rancho of Guadalupito, say 50 souls.—Same course 5 or 6 m. to Hac. de los Charcos—say 200 souls. The town (or city) of Charcos is at the distance of a league or more, a little north of west in border of mountain. This (latter place) was once an important mining place; and is yet producing something. Nevertheless, Catorce is now the most important mining town in the state of San Luis (which we entered between San Salvador and Ventura). This Real, or mineral, produces from one to two barras[3] (1 to $3,000) daily, as I am told. [MARGINAL NOTE: Lat. of Hac. de Charcos, by Polaris 23° 5′ 45″]

Wed. 20—S. 15 E. 3m. S. 25 W. 2 m. to Creek and Rancho de Laborcillas—same course, say 12 m. to Venado. This is a town, or city as styled, of some little importance, being the head of a department or subdivision of the state. The prefect, who treated me with much politeness, furnished me with the following statistical data of that and the neighboring towns, though as he confessed, notwithstanding the populations are from actual census taken the present year, is not very reliable—can only be considered by approximates: viz. Population of the city of Venado, between 3 & 4,000—founded 1552:—Pop. of Hedionda 2 to 3,000—founded same year: Pop. of Mineral de Charcos,

[3] Ingots.

two to 3,000,—founded 1574: Pop. of Matchuala 6,000—
founded 1682:—Pop. of Real de Catorce, 9,000—founded
1768.—Though arrived at Venado 10 or 11 o'clock, remained till
next day. [MARGINAL NOTE: Lat. of Venado, by Mer. alt. sun,
22° 55′ 34″/Lat. of Vocas, by Polaris 22° 31′ 16″/Lat. of
Hedionda, by Mer. alt. of Sun, 22° 44′ 46″]

Thurs. 21—S. 15 m. to Hedionda, nooned—watered by small
creek—S. 10 W. 6 or 8 m. to rancho de San Francisco (pop. not
50)—S. 5 W. 12 or 14 m. to Vocas, watered by a brisk creek,
running N.E.—Hacienda of 2 or 3,00 souls. Great deal of the
highlands from Venado here, cultivated without irrigation—
being the first extensive highland cultivation that I have met
with. Here joins the road which comes by Matchuala.

Frid. 22—S. 10 E. 8 or 10 m. to alto or divide—S. 5 W. 5 m.
to Garapatilla (little rancho, where nooned)—thence S. 15 m. to
San Luis. This morning, ascending a dry ravine to divide, we
passed the roughest road we have had since leaving Saltillo;
though even this *pedazo*,[4] with a little repairing would be a good
wagon road. In fact, it is almost a perfect level from Tanque
de la Vaca to Guadalupe del Carnicero—thence frequently undulating, yet excellent road generally. [MARGINAL NOTE:
Whole dist. from Salt⁰ to S. Luis 284 m.?]

The city of San Luis Potosí is one of the ancient settlements
of the republic—founded (see 3 Siglos)[5] for mining purposes
—the mines in the mountain of San Pedro, north eastwardly
were among the richest of the republic; but these have long
since ceased to produce anything, and are now not worked.

The population of this city is said to be 25 to 30,000—is supported now chiefly by manufactures and agriculture. Some of
the principal streets present a good deal of elegance of architecture and beauty. About a mile from the main plaza, to the south-

[4] Stretch.
[5] *Los Tres Siglos de Mexico Durante el Gobierno Espanol*, by Andrés Cavo
(Carlos Maria Bustamante, Mexico City, 1836), was one of Gregg's stand-bys in
matters of history.

241

westward, is the Santuario de Guadalupe, around which Santa Anna commenced his famous fortifications *against* the American army: yet it is difficult to conceive any other object than to shut himself and army up—proposing only defend themselves, and leave the city at the mercy of the invaders: for it is on a level plain, commanding neither the city nor any of the main roads of entrance: the fact is, the city being in a perfectly level plain, there is no eminence sufficiently high to command the city, nearer than four or five miles distant.

I did not go into the mountains to examine the geology, but I find very good building granite used in the city, as also a sort of coarse sand-stone, easily worked, and substantial enough for ordinary purposes. In most of the valleys we find strata of a soft lime-stone, called here caliche, which makes good enough lime, but is not hard enough for building. This also abounds about Monterey, Saltillo, Quesétano, etc.

It is too much out of season to find much interest in the botany hereabouts. The Perú is the most interesting tree I see—resembling some species of the acacia, but bearing clusters or racimes of red berries, instead of legumes. This fruit is not edible; yet the seeds being near as large as pepper, have a pungent flavor, and are sometimes used as a spice: in fact, I am told by Goribar (who [seems] to have some intelligence on the subject, having been an apothecary in Mexico) that, when dried, the[y] blacken, and so much resemble pepper in appearance, that this spice is often adulterated with the Perú seeds.—The *organo* is a species of cactus found from Venado south in great abundance. It is so called because it grows up in straight stems, 10 to 30 feet high—which when planted in rows as is common for fencing, resembles the pipes of organs. It is particular valuable in this country for hedging, as nothing is required but to cut stems and plant them in rows, where they take root, requiring very little water, and soon form an impenetrable wall. The common cactus is often used for the same purpose, as still better adapted to the dry plains as requiring no water but the scanty allowance supplied by the heavens; yet this is much slower coming to the necessary height to form a fence; and is not as impenetrable. There is another species of the same plant growing on the plains about San Luis, and thence occasionally to Quesétano, but instead of a single straight stem, its "joints" are from two to three feet long; and branching out a foot or two from the ground, the top forms an immense clump, generally 10 or 12 feet high, and often near the same in diameter.

I was much gratified with a casual acquaintance I formed with some very worthy Englishmen in San Luis, especially Messrs. Carter & Mariner, Davis the consul, and some others. These are a jovial, social and obliging a set of fellows as it has often been my good fortune to have to do with. Mrs. Carter, the only Englishwoman I saw in San Luis (in fact, I believe really the only one there), is surely an unusually kind and worthy lady.

It is certainly very agreeable to meet with such "countrymen" (as we are wont to style nearly all Europeans in this country) in this land of bigotry and exclusion.

The latitude of San Luis Potosí, reduced to Main Square, by the mean of four observations of sun and polestar, (2 of each) resulted in 22° 9′ 0″ [MARGINAL NOTE: Or, at Meson de Guadalupe, which is 8″ or 10″ N. of Main Square, 22° 9′ 8½″, —From my observations for longitude, I have not been able to obtain satisfactory results.]—the longitude by two rather imperfect lunar distances, appears to be ——— west from Greenwich. Very unfortunately there was neither a favorable eclipse of Jupiter's satellites, nor opportunity to take a good lunar distance, while in San Luis, as it was during the change of the moon. The following is the mean of my meteorological table for five days in San Luis:[6]

. . . .

---

[6] This table has been omitted from this volume because of the difficulty of transcription. It seems to be of no importance.

243

We remained in San Luis 4 days and 5 nights for the purpose of having some repairs done to wagon, sho[e]ing mules, etc. Here we had an addition to our company of Lic. D. Miguel Ramos, Diputado from Saltillo to Congress, Lic. D. Eugenio Aguirre, candidate for Lic., D. Miguel Gomez Carcenas and his lady, with two very clever young men, Jose Mª Aguirre & Rafael Gonzales—and servants—in all 5 principals, and 8 or 10 servants—making our party in all between 35 and 40 men strong —and an addition of a lady and a servant girl.

Wed. 27—This morning being the time appointed, I could not get ready until near 9 o'clock; when I found that all our party had gone and left me; so that I did not overtake them till night. I was, of course, vexed at this, as not only showing me little or no respect in starting without even letting me know it (they stopped at the Meson de San Y[g]nacio and I in that of Guadalupe), but leaving me to travel a day alone, in a region acknowledged to be dangerous for robbers; for it is notorious in this country that the robbers are much worst in the immediate vicinity of the large towns. But my comrades seeming to be conscious of their error, made acknowledgments, and all was right. [MARGINAL NOTE: The *Mesones*[7] of this country afford little or no accommodations, being immense buildings with unfurnished rooms—without bed or board. This of San Ignacio I consider hardly superior to any. Unable to get even a dirty room here, I removed to that of Guadalupe.]

From San Luis, S.E. 8 m. to Hac. de los Pozos, watered by Noria, etc. (road passes half a mile to south of the plaza of Pozos) —S. 5 m. to Hac. de la Pila, watered by Noria, etc. Has been a mining requestoria—S. 15 W. 20 m. to Valle de S. Francisco— some small ranchos on the road between here and Pila.—San Franco is a town of some importance, said to contain 3 or 4,000 inhabitants. It is watered by a pretty little creek, descending from southward. There was a feria at S. Franco causing a considerable

[7] Inns.

collection of people and goods, wares, etc. yet by no means to be compared with that of Saltillo. On this account we could scarce get accommodations in the mesones. [MARGINAL NOTE: Lat. of S. Francisco by Polaris, 21° 48′ 30″ reduced to main plaza.]

Thurs. 28—S. 25 W. 6 m. to rancho de Tequisquite—from S. Francisco to Jaral (pop. over 1,000 perhaps), S. 40 W. 15 m. —then S. 25 W. 5 m. to San Bartolo, where nooned (village, pop. perhaps 2 or 300—nooned)—Thence to gap S. 35 W. 6 or 8 m.—Same course from San Fran^co to gap—and Jaral very little west of straight line.—This gap in mountain or alto, proves to be the *sierra Madre,* [MARGINAL NOTE: Nearly all the rock in and about this divide in igneous.] dividing Atlantic and Pacific waters, as those of San Felipe run into Rio Grande of Guadalajara.—Alto to San Felipe W. 35 S. 8 m.—San Felipe is a clever little town of two or 3,000 souls, I should think. [MARGINAL NOTE: Lat. of S. Felipe, by Polaris (Plaza) 21° 28′ 35″ approximate only.]

Frid. 29—S. 32 E. 5 m. to Rancho de la Huerta—6 m. further & back to S. Felipe N. 28 W.—4 m. further & back to S. Felipe N. 30 W. & to Alto or divide N. 5 W. (This is opposite the Hac. de la Palma, which is half a mile to S. W. of road.)— S. 25 E. 3 m. to Hac. de la Quemada—2 or 300 inhabitants— nooned.—S. 3 or 4 m. to high ridge (about as high as that of the main divide) and back to S. Felipe, N. 27 W.—E. 30 S. 8 m. to an hacienda—Same course 5 m. to S. Pedro, rancho of hundred or two souls—same 2 m. to Puerto del Gallinero (Hac. of same name just beyond). Battle here—see history.[8]—2 m. further to Pueblo de Dolores. [MARGINAL NOTE: Latitude of Dolores by Polaris, 21° 9′ 34″—Longitude by mean of 3 observations—one of moon & Jupiter— & 2 altitudes.] This is a very pretty village or town of some 4 or 5,000 souls (even near double this counting immediate suburbs), originally all Indian, but now

---

[8] The battle, September 18, 1832, in which Bustamante inflicted a decisive defeat upon Moctezuma. Losses on both sides were exceptionally heavy.

filled up a great degree (at least the improved portion of the town) by Hispano-Mexicans. Dolores is famous in history as the cradle of Mexican Independence. Here was the residence of the Cura Hidalgo[9] (whose home is still to be seen on south side of public square, with "Casas Municipales" marked over the door) —here was the first declaration of Independence (Grito de Dolóres) on 15th or 16 Sept. 1810) which, however, was only in concert with Allende[10] of S. Miguel el Grande. Hidalgo has often been compared with Washington; but with no degree of propriety; for his revolution was without any fixed plan—any general concert.—He only counted on the Indians of his district. These it is true, flocked to his standard by "thousands and tens of thousands"—in fact, almost to a man—yet without order, arms or discipline. They depended on the virgin Guadalupe for success, rushing into the very mouths of the cannon of the enemy, thinking that even their *petate*[11] hats would ward off the balls. Had it not been for the particularly unfortunate condition of Spain, added to the general discontent throughout the republic as well as in all South America, this revolution could never have succeeded. In fact, the declaration of Hidalgo only served as "yeast" for subsequent "fermentation" for this was in effect completely quelled in a short time; but broke out again from time to time (being as often smothered) until the "treason" of Iturbide[12] consummated the Independence from Spain. [MARGINAL NOTE: I have seen no point in Mexico where the

[9] Miguel Hidalgo y Costilla (1753–1811), the "Father of Mexican Independence," was a revolutionist priest who revolted in 1810. Highly influential with the Indians, he used them in a successful initial campaign, but was eventually defeated, captured, and executed in Chihuahua City.

[10] Don Ignacio Allende was an army officer who became an adherent of the insurgents under Hidalgo. He was imprisoned and executed with that leader at Chihuahua.

[11] Palm-leaf.

[12] Austín de Iturbide (1783–1824) was a revolutionary leader who entered the city of Mexico on September 27, 1821, and brought Spanish power to an end. He was made emperor in 1822, but the next year he was forced to abdicate. He attempted to recover his lost crown in 1824, but was arrested and shot at Padilla. Santa Anna had appeared upon the scene as his opponent and had declared a republic.

uplands are so generally and extensively cultivated (with irrigation) as about Dolores.]

Sat. 30—S. 30 E. 3 m. to opposite rancho del Llamito, which is nearly a mile from road to right—same 1 m. to Hac. de la Erre (perhaps 200 souls)—S. 40 E. 2 or 3 m. to top of ridge—thence back to Dolores N. 35 W.—& E. 40 S. 20 m. to rancho & S. 40 E. 4 m. to Pueblo de Atotonilco.—On the following Monday a sort of feast or fair was to commence at Llanito—during which a famous picture of a saint, El Señor del Llanito, was to be promenaded about. We met hundreds of Indians on their way from Atotonilco and bord[er]ing country, on their way to this feast—generally on foot,—some with fruits, etc. for sale, on their backs or on donkeys—but mostly (in fact, we may say all) with wax candles to burn to the honor and edification of the picture. This is an important link in the chain of life these poor devils lead—work hard a portion of their time, and, after living the most abstemious and miserable lives, attend feasts the balance and spend all their earnings on the churches and priests.— In this way the little church (a sanctuary) of Atotonilco has been most splendidly furnished. To see this famous chapel was our only object of coming this way, being two or three miles to east of main road. The exterior of this church is altogether unimposing; yet I must confess I was astounded when I entered. I could not have dreamed (though I had heard of its fame) of finding so much wealth—elegance and lustre shut up in this miserable Indian village, of scarcely over 1000 souls. More than a dozen apartments are literally filled with rich figures and costly paintings—many of which might well be displayed to their credit anywhere—particularly the Lord's Supper, and some other groups—the Ascension, etc. and a really handsome representation of Mt. Calvary and the Crucifixion in 3 groups of figures— 1. the nailing of Christ to the cross—2. the crucifixion—& 3. the taking of him down.

Just as we were about leaving we heard down the road southward a strange combination of music—violins, drums, chanting, etc. mixed with occasional yells: and directly appeared in view a fantastic group of men women and children—the latter (consisting of boys from five to 15 years old, most romantically and fantastically dressed, which, though of modern textures, was said to be in imitation of the costumes of the aborigines on these occasions)—performing the dance of Matachinos, known as their most celebrated aboriginal dance. This dance I had witnessed elsewhere, with some little variety. There is usually a King and a queen, whom with the dancers (which here consisted of lads and little boys) are dressed most fantastically, in fancy shawls or hkfs. fripperies, gewgaws (including looking-glasses, etc.) and ribands. They arrange themselves in rows, and dance most comically, various curious and intricate figures, to the music of the violin and a sort of aboriginal drum—accompanied occasionally (but not generally, as is the case with the U.S. frontier Indians) with a sort of monotonous song. But the most comical figure is a masked personage representing a sort of clown, who dances among the boys, making all sorts of ridiculous contortions and expressions; also appearing to perform the office of a sort of regulator.

But prior to the dance, the whole party entered the church; and moved by curiosity I followed in after them. The spectacle was at once appalling, amusing and ridiculous in the extreme. The whole company (consisting of 30 to 50), were in a kneeling posture, and engaged in saying their prayers, to all appearance most vehemently—accompanied with sobs, cries and even tears trickling down the cheeks of many—well we might add "weeping and wailing and gnashing of teeth"—crying with all the earnestness of a child. To add to the strange variety of the scene, there were many babes whose cries were mingled with those of the men & women, and reminded one of the mewing of cats.

Poor, miserable creatures! Nobody demonstrates more fidelity or rather fanaticism, in their religion than they! But what is it at last but idolatry? It is only a change of names for them: their religion is virtually the same as it was before the conquest merely omitting human sacrifices, and making a change in some of their rites. And it was at the expense of these poor devils that this costly edifice was so extravagantly furnished. They are taught to believe that nothing is so grateful in the eyes of the Creator, or rather of Guadalupe, as to make donations to the church— which they do with the greatest alacrity and pleasure, whenever they get together (by hard labor and privations) a few dollars, or *reales* or even *clacos*.[13] Then candles themselves afford a very clever income; for besides purchasing them of the church at exhorbitant prices, they leave whatever portion is not burned during their ceremonies, (which is generally the greater portion) and these again are worked up into new candles to be sold them at high prices. Besides there is an arrival feast, usually attended by several thousand of these poor aborigines, every one being not only obliged to bestow a certain tribute, but to live during the several days of ceremonies, at the expense of the church; thus affording an annual income of several thousand dollars in this way alone. But, notwithstanding that tens upon tens—nay upon hundreds of thousands of dollars have been expended in ornamenting this establishment, we are not to suppose that the whole income goes in that way: the priests and friars must not only "live fat," but have an abundance for their vices and luxuries.

From Atotonilco, S. 40 E. 3 m. & s. 20 E. 3 m. to San Miguel de Allende—or as formerly called, San Miguel el Grande. Bad hilly rocky road today, being the first really bad road, except the crossing of the ridge beyond S. Felipe, that we have met with. The direct road passing to west of Atotonilco is said to be better. [MARGINAL NOTE: Lat. of S. Miguel, by Polaris & sun (mer. alt.) mean 20° 54′ 53″ Longitude of San Miguel, by distance Moon & Venus, & alt. Moon—mean—]

[13] Coppers.

The population of San Miguel is allowed to be from 6 to 8,000. It contains many very good edifices, and especially churches, in one of which, known as *el Sagrario*, I saw a considerable collection of quite respectable paintings. This place is famous as having been the "co-cradle" of Mexican Independence; for it was by concert between D. Ignacio Allende and Cura Hidalgo that the first declaration was made: in fact, it is said that the declaration of Allende at S. Miguel was one day first—on 15th Sept. 1810. The dwelling of Allende was pointed out to me, at the S.W. corner of the market square, with the following inscription over the door—*"Hic natus ubique notus."* I rode out to see a warm spring about 5 m. N.W. of S. Miguel, but it is of little importance —temperature of water 94° to 98° but containing nothing of interest. Large spring supplying town 78°. [MARGINAL NOTE: From San Miguel to Gaunajuato, W. 8° N. 15 leguas.]

☼ DIARY, JANUARY, 1849

Mon. 1—Owing to the baggage wagon of the old curate having broken again, we delayed in San Miguel during Sunday to get it repaired. This morning we set out again. San Miguel is at the foot of a high ridge to the south, which we had to ascend, in coming out of the city; and being fully upon it, we may say we were again on the main dividing ridge of the Sierra Madre, at an elevation of about (over?) 7000 feet above the ocean. After rising this ridge I stopped my baggage wagon to set my barometer, suggesting to D. Antº Goribar to make a halt, as I would hardly delay 15 minutes: yet, though my stop was only about 12 minutes, the party continued on, and at so brisk (in fact accelerated) a pace that instead of overtaking them, they gained upon me, until they stopped at noon. There was but little (yet acknowledged some) danger of robbers, to be sure; still the movement was ungenerous, and showed me so little regard, as not to leave me in a very good humor again: still I paid no attention to it. One thing seemed evident, however, that though Gori-

bar's former pursuits were semi-scientific (that of an apothecary) he seemed now to have an utter repugnance for everything
in the shape of science.

From S. Miguel E. 10 S. 8 or 10 m. to rancho de la Puente,
say 50 souls (water tanque, etc.)—E. 4 m. to Los Cerritos—E.
55.5 m. say 50 souls (tanque, etc.) to Hac. de Santa Maria, say
50 souls (Tanque, etc.)—E. 15 S. 2 m. to Rancho de los Ricos,
say one to 200 souls (Tanque, etc.)—Nooned—This is the highest point at which I had yet set my barometer; though the ridge
a short distance back is still higher by near 100 feet. (or more?)
—E. 40 S. 6 m. to Buenavista (Hac.) (water Tanque, etc.)—S.
20 E. 5 or 6 m. to Santa Rosa—say 200 souls. Here we stopped
for the night, though somewhat early—water, tanque & noria.
[NOTE: Lat. of Santa Rosa by Polaris 20° 45′ 12″]

    Tues. 2—S. 20 E. 8 or 10 m. to Hac. de Alvarado—same, 4
m. to Querétaro. Not only a part of the road yesterday evening,
but for five or 6 m. this morning the road was most wretched
and scandalous. It is certainly shameful for any such city as
Querétaro to have so miserable a road in its immediate neighborhood—and that the main highway heading to the north. Besides much of this road might have been easily repaired, being
filled with loose stones, requiring scarcely more than to throw
them out of the way.

    When I came within about a mile of the city I was hailed at
the *garita*[14] (having had the misfortune to get a few hundred
yards behind the rest of the party), and required to exhibit my
passes. I supposed it would all end with this; but no! I must now
(after waiting near an hour for a conductor) proceed to the custom house in the city. Here, I felt sure I should be dispatched
at once, having not a single article of trade; but no annoyance
seemed to be too great for me! I must now unload, and have
my packages registered and examined, and then leave one of them
as security that I would take them out of the city. This last ar-

[14] Sentry box.

251

rangement was particularly annoying, as our party wished to start early next morning: I therefore expostulated against it, but to no effect. In these annoyances I spent near three hours; for but for them I should have got into the city a little after ten, A.M.: as it was, I did not get into the Meson till about 1, P.M. So I thus lost 3 hours of important time, which I intended occupying in examining the city, etc. I should note that as chief clerk and cause of my difficulties (and whose name I hope to be able to pass to posterity as a most consummate custom-house brigand —though the head of the department himself, one D. Francisco Bustamante, I believe no better) figured a miserable excuse for a man and an officer, named José Dolores Trejo. Querétaro is allowed to contain about ———— thousand inhabitants, and there is considerable elegance and cost in many of the edifices. One of the most important structures is an aqueduct of several miles, in a series of arches, sometimes near 50 feet high, supplying water to the city—constructed by a count (I believe) who resided there, and whose statue is still erect upon the column of the fountain in the *plaza de armas*.[15] [MARGINAL NOTE: Lat. of Querétaro, by 2 obs. of Polaris 20° 35′ 27″—Plaza de Armas. Long. by dist. Moon & sun—do. & venus—do. & Jupiter— and two altitudes of moon—mean—100° 36′ 30″.—From Querétaro to Salamanca 24 m. (says Mr. Best—& same says) where Querétaro Creek joins main stream.]

This evening late, I accompanied my old friend the curate, to visit Gen. Bustamante,[16] former president of Mexico. The old gentleman is now nearly 60 years of age—rather corpulent though not in very good health—heavy set and rather low— good countenance and sober deportment—in conversation, indicates sober sound judgment, but little brilliancy of talent. I

[15] Usually the principal square, so called from its use as a parade ground.

[16] Anastasio Bustamante (1780–1853) had in 1831 acted with Iturbide and revolted. He became acting president of Mexico in 1832, but was conquered by Santa Anna in 1833 and sent into exile. He was, however, recalled, and became president again in 1842. This time he ultimately retired and was succeeded by Santa Anna. He served in the Mexican army during the war with the United States.

would therefore take him to be a very good well-meaning man; and I think the arts of his life have thus indicated. He was bred a physician; and was in good practice in the city of San Luis, when the revolution broke out: he left all, and turned soldier, in which he has succeeded pretty well, I think.

Wed. 3—This morning on going out at the south-eastern *garita*, I was required to pay $1.50 for "seguridad pública," as they termed it—that is, for the protection pretended to be extended to travellers against the robbers. This is ridiculous in the extreme, when we are reminded that more robberies are committed (and that with more impunity) in the immediate vicinity of Querétaro—especially this day's journey,—than anywhere else in this region: and what rendered it the more ridiculous and rascally was that, the rest of our party coming through a short distance behind me, these official rogues told them that I left word for them to pay my *peage*[17] also, thus collecting what was in itself a villainous contribution twice from me. [MARGINAL NOTE: We also had to pay $1.50 per carriage at San Juan del Rio, which I was informed since was also an extortion, as it was only required at the one place.] All in all, I came to the conclusion that Querétaro, not only in a city but as a state (as will be seen this evening) is the most villainous region—certainly this the most rascally *city* I ever visited.

From Querétaro, E. 12 m. to el Colorado (Hac.) say 200 souls—S.E. 3 m. to Palo-Alto-rancho—say 50 souls—same, 5 m. to La Palma (Hac. say 200 souls) nooned—Soledad 2 m. back, off to northward (Passed dividing ridge again this morning.—E. 40 S. 6 or 8 m. to Hac. del Sauz (say 100 souls) same, 12 or 15 m. to San Juan del Rio. This is a town of some 3 or 4,000 souls, and perhaps more famous than any other for highway robbery—or rather I should say perhaps—a town *of* highwaymen. —It is not a year since some Saltillo merchants, D. Fernando Cárdenas and D. Ignacio Arizpe, with a large lot of mdse. were

[17] Toll.

attacked in the very suburbs of the town—the former was mortally wounded and the latter slightly, & all their mdse. taken.
The owners themselves—especially Arizpe, saw their own goods
publicly hawked about the streets of San Juan for sale; and were
fain even to buy back their own goods frequently. The most
respectable looking ladies (if such could so be called) were also
to be seen sitting in the windows, publicly sewing these stolen
goods. Although some pretended efforts were made by the state
authorities of Querétaro to detect and punish these robbers, but
they remained impune, although many of them were publicly
known. Also, *we* were here told that the robbers had been publicly waiting for our party for several days past—having heard
of our coming—possibly through a well known highwayman in
San Miguel—one of the most wealthy characters of the place,
who, as is said, keeps the authorities "bought up," and gives notice to his banditti in every direction, when a party of travellers
supposed to carry money is approaching. [NOTE: Lat. of S. Juan
del Rio, by Polaris 20° 22′ 50″]

❀ DIARY, JANUARY, 1849

Thurs. 4—S. 40 E. 5 m. to rancho del Palmillo (say 100 souls)
same, 12 or 14 to Venta de la Soledad. This last stretch was
across what is called *el Llano del Casadero*—a beautiful level
plain, hemmed in by ridges of low mountain, ten to 15 m. across
in every direction—where it is said the aborigines used to collect
together, before the conquest, on a certain day of every year, for
the purpose of hunting game. They were distributed around the
plain in the bordering mountains, whence they drove all sorts of
game—deer, bears, antelopes, rabbits, etc. etc. into the plain,
and closing in upon them, they killed them by hundreds and
thousands, with clubs, etc.

From Soledad, S. 40 E. 15 m. to Arroyo Zarco (Pretty brisk
little creek) (Hac. of say 50 to 100 souls)—This was said to
be one of the highest settlements in the republic; and it proved

to be the highest at which I had yet set my barometer. [MARGIN-
AL NOTE: Lat. of Arroyo Zarco, by Polaris, 20° 6′ 37″]

Frid. 5—E. 40 S. 3 or 4 m. to first ridge which I found some
200 feet higher than the village—thence E. 3 or 4 m. to Puerto
de Capulalpa where I set my barometer, and found it near 200
feet still higher—and the highest settlement we had passed, is
a rancho about a mile back, called *Los Dos Caminos.*—Passing
through this mountain gap, we got a good view of the valley of
Rio Tula, and the two snow-capt. peaks beyond Mexico—Popocatepetl to right (course S. 42 E) and *Sierra Nevada* to left
(course E. 44 S.) Just after descending into the plain we were
beset by some miserable Indian beggars, women and children
from some little neighboring villages.

From gap of Capulalpa, E. 12 m. to Hac. de la Goleta (say
100 souls) Creek in vicinity & water brought out in ditch, to a
large mill—Nooned—E. 30 N. 5 m. to San Antonio (say 200
souls—water also abundant)—E. 2 m.—E. 55.5 m. (whence to
Sierra Nevada S. 36° E. & to Popocatepetl S. 33 E.) & E. 35 S.
6 or 8 m. to Tula. This place—though of ancient date in history
scarcely contains over 1000 souls—and but notable edifice, the
ruins, as they may now be called, of a stupendous church and
convent—of itself a fortification. This is on a creek known as
Rio de Tula, into which the Rio de San Juan also enters, and
flow in direction of Tampico. [NOTE: Lat. of Tula by Polaris
20° 2′ 16″.]

Sat. 6—E. 55.5 m.—S.E. 2 or 3 m. S. 20 E. 5 m. to Vata (a
rancho and extensive *pulqueria*). It is calculated to prejudice one
against this famous beverage—pulque, to visit one of these
"breweries." The juice of the Maguey is thrown into large vats,
composed of beef skins swung on frames in a baggage position,
with the hair in, which is constantly slipping off into the liquor,
to say nothing of the mice & rats, and other insects, which must
be continually falling into it.—Nooned. Whence S. 25 E. 10 m.
to Puerto de Moreno—S. 5 or 6 m. to Huehuetoca—perhaps

over 1000 inhabitants—outlet from lake Tezcoco passes here.—
same course, 3 m. to pueblo de Coyotepec. I rode through the
center of this village: I suppose it a pretty good representation
of these pueblos. I saw nothing that could be called a regular
street—roads winding among their huts and gardens—the former being nearly concealed by trees, *organos*, etc. Pop. perhaps
1000 souls.—same course, 10 m. to Cuauhtitlan. Pon. about
2,000. [MARGINAL NOTE: Lat. of Cuauhtitlan by Polaris 19°
39′ 44″]

Sun. 7—S. 5 W. 5 m. to ridge—S. 5 E. 5 m. to Tlanepantla
(pop. say 1000) E. 30 S. 4 m.—S.E. 5 m. to the town of Guadalupe, where we stopped for the night. Here we experienced (or
at least one of our party) one of these wretched arrangements
for the pretended protection of the country against highway robbers. Sr. Gomez, was asked for a pass to carry arms, and upon
his not being able to produce one, he came nigh having his arms
taken from him—with pretext that the arrangement was established to prevent robbers from carrying arms—as though highwaymen have any necessity for bringing their arms into the cities,
but naturally keep them out in the ranchos, etc. ready to operate
upon travellers: so that the regulation only serves to disarm
honest men, and place them at the mercy of the robbers. I cannot
believe the authorities so ignorant as not to be aware of this; and
therefore it affords another proof of their being connected with
the robbers, and thus act in their favor. [NOTE: Lat. of Guadalupe, by Polaris, 19° 29′ 10″? Long. by Dist. Moon & Jupiter
& alt. moon—mean—]

Some two miles before reaching Guadalupe, my attention was
attracted to numerous large heaps of earth, with occasional adobe
huts upon them, most of which I perceived to be inhabited; which
I at once concluded to be the ruins of some ancient pueblo, the
huge adobe edifices had tumbled down and mouldered into loose
dirt again, thus producing the heaps already mentioned: but
upon inquiring of the first person I saw, I learned they were

Salinas, salt-works. The mode of manufacturing salt here is curious and unique, compared with anything I had witnessed before.[18] After the water dries up from the ponds and flats, there remains a coat (not of clean salt, as in other places) but of saline earth, which is scraped up—thrown into hoppers (somewhat like those used in the farms in the U.S. for making lye of ashes), and throwing water upon it, it filters through, carrying with it the saline water. But the water I tasted was not more than half as strong as that of most of the salt-springs of the U.S. This water is evaporated by boiling as at our salt-creeks, except upon a much smaller scale: Indians being the chief manufacturers, every family has a little furnace with an earthen kettle or two. The refuse dirt after filtrating, is thrown out, and forms the heaps before mentioned; for the works are continued upon the same spot for a long while, being elevated upon the heaps of earth, and new huts built upon the same whenever these become so high as to be molesting. To N.W. of road between Guadalupe and Mexico there [are] other salinas of the kind—as also in other places, as at the Peñon, etc. as I subsequently witnessed.

Having stopped early at Guadalupe (about 12 o'clock), I walked out in the evening with my friend the old curate to look at the famous temple of Ntra Sra.[19] de Guadalupe. We first entered the principal edifice at the foot of the hill. This is a quite magnificent and costly church. Over the altar is collected in a frame covered with glass, the famous picture of Guadalupe, said to be the original produced by Juan Diego—or as they say, stamped upon his ———[20] by Guadalupe herself. As to the origin of the original, I need hardly express an opinion: as to this being the original, I am disposed to doubt—or rather, I think there is no doubt that it is not. Its appearance by no means indi-

[18] Gregg had been much interested in the procuring of salt from the salt lakes and the salt deposits on the Great Plains and in New Mexico.

[19] Nuestra Señora (Our Lady).

[20] The word was probably to be *tilma,* coarse cloth out of which the mantle of Juan Diego was made. Sometimes the word *ayate* is used for this mantle.

cates 300 and upward years of age. Nevertheless it is in a dark position, so as to render it impossible to see it distinctly. It is not painted up [on] *guangoche*[21] as I was once informed, (and stated in Cosm. of Prs.[22]) but on a much lighter thinner goods (somewhat resembling that used for mosquito-bars) called ———— and made of a finer fibre (coarse jute) from a sort of maguey.

I was shocked to see a friar, with his holy gowns on, engaged, while divine worship was being performed in the church, at a table on one side in selling medals, ribands, *rosarios*, saints, etc. to poor Indians. As we were walking through the church, we saw in another apartment, a table covered with the same for sale, and among them a number of lottery tickets. "Do you see that?" said an intelligent youth of our party (Miguel Gonzales) shaking his head, but ventured to say no more! Back of the main church between it and the hill, we entered another building enclosing the famous "boiling spring," whose temperature I found to be $67\frac{1}{2}°$, Fahrenheit—with not a very disagreeable taste of soda and carbonic acid, which last is discharged in abundance, producing a continuous rapid bubbling. It seems that this spring was much resorted to before the conquest, for the cure of various diseases—as well by means of bathing as drinking the water.

We ascended the hill of Tepeyaca (?) which gives a handsome view of the valley of Mexico, to the chapel there, being at an elevation of about 300 feet above the plain. Here is where Juan Diego was directed to ascend and bring the fresh roses, which is evinced as another proof of the divinity of the apparition, but the truth is—roses are blooming at nearly (or quite, most years) at all seasons not only here, but in all the country from here to Saltillo: there I have seen them in all December; and here in the town of Guadalupe, I was handed *fresh roses*, to day.

[MARGINAL NOTE: Whole dist. from S. Luis to Mexico 351

---

[21] Sacking.
[22] I.e., *Commerce of the Prairies*.

m.? From Mexico to Chuptelpec 2 m.—Jacubaya 2 more/ Chapultepec to Mol. del Rey 1 m.—S. Juaquin 2 m.—Jacuba 1 m. Encapusalio 2 m.—Carriga 1 m.—Jacubato Popocle 1 m. —Mex. 3.]

Mon. 8.—Arrived to day at the city of Mexico, between 10 and 12 o'clock. I was much deceived in the appearance of the city—it was by no means as magnificent, elegant and beautiful as I contemplated seeing it. True, I had heard it "lauded to the skies" as one of the finest cities in the world; and the disappointment of its not meeting my anticipations was an important cause, no doubt of its unfavorable appearance to me; as it did not look as well as it really merits. And, in truth, I find it improving in my conceit, as I become better acquainted with it. The fact is, the miserable dirty filthy suburbs contributed doubtless, in no small degree to give me, as it must every traveller upon his first visit, an unfavorable impression. As a town site, it is certainly one of the worst—a flat plain, scarcely elevated above the level of the surrounding lakes and swamps; and consequently with scarcely an outlet for the filthy water of the street gutters, which are at all times filled with stagnant stinking mud and water. Were it in any low southern climate—or in a northern climate of the U.S. this filth would doubtless cause serious epidemics. [NOTE: "The base of the city is almost a quagmire. It is often necessary to drive down cedar stakes to a great depth, to form a foundation solid enough to commence an edifice upon; especially in the new portion of the town—that which was lake at the Conquest."]

None of the edifices even, came up to my expectations—the *catedral* and colegio de Minería are the best—the latter certainly quite an extensive and elegant structure; but the church, though a huge edifice is far inferior to what I expected to see.[23] Although

---

[23] Gregg is outspoken in regard to *la Catedral* and the weak impression made upon him architecturally. He seems to scorn the massiveness and *grandeza* of its giant, rectangular bulk. The corner-stone of the present edifice was laid in 1573; but the building was not completed and inaugurated until 1667. The towers were not fin-

259

greatly larger, I do not look upon the frontispiece or façade (principal) upon the square, and the tower as being equal in architecture to those of Chihuahua; nor do they seem to me near as high. These are said to be but 70 varas,[24] in fact, while those of Chihuahua, as I have been assured, are about 100: and really, to the eye, there would appear to be that much difference. The *palacio*[25] is also far behind what I anticipated. It is an immense structure, to-be-sure, the front occupying one entire side of the main plaza—say near 240 yards in length—and covering an entire block. But it is only two stories high, with very little display of architectural elegance. [NOTE: "The larger portion of the best buildings of Mexico are three stories high—though a very rare one four. But the lower story is of very little use, being damp and insalubrious so that the better families do not reside in them, but in the 2ᵈ and 3ᵈ stories."] It embraces not only barracks in each end, but the president's house and the two halls of congress. The *Cámara de Diputado*[26] is fitted out with some degree of elegance; yet certainly not to be compared with that of the capitol of the U.S. The Senate chamber is inferior: the president's house is of no great elegance.

Frid. 12—Walking out in the *Alameda*, the young man who accompanied me (Miguel Gonzales) proposed to take a ride to Tacubaya, as we saw the *diligencia* (stage) coming up behind us. Tacubaya is about 4 m. distant,—a town of perhaps 2,000 souls (or less). The only edifice of interest is the Obispado—since known as the famous "*palacio de Tacubaya*" of Santa Anna,

ished until 1791. Gregg's appreciative account of the cathedral at Chihuahua is to be found in *Commerce of the Prairies*, Vol. II, 114 and 115.

24 "Spanish yard of 33 inches" to use the description of Gregg himself in the glossary prepared for the second edition (1845) of *Commerce of the Prairies*. In the book itself Gregg gives the following explanation, "the vara being thirty-three inches (nearly)"—*Commerce of the Prairies*, Vol. II, 112.

25 The palacio, more lengthily *el Palacio Nacional*, occupies a large city block, with a frontage on the east side of the *Plaza Mayor*. The present structure is the outcome of many additions and restorations, commencing with the time of Cortes. The appearance lacks architectural grace or beauty, but does have impressiveness.

26 Chamber of Deputies.

whence the dictator, in 1844–5, used to issue his celebrated decrees. This edifice, however, presents no external architectural elegance: but an ordinary stone building; and quite antique at that.

Thurs. 18—Visited the famous *Molino del Rey*, passing Chapultepec. [MARGINAL NOTE: This is the West Point of Mexico —the Military School being there.[27]] This latter fortification presents a rather imposing aspect, upon an isolated hill of 2 or 300 feet high (about 2 m. from Mexico); yet I cannot now speak of it in detail, as I did not enter. Another interesting appendage is the cypress grove which surrounds it. I saw there cypresses, which, though low in proportion, were between 10 and 15 feet diameter as high as 4 or 5 feet from the ground. Passing through this grove we perceived a human cranium, which one of the party got down to pick up; and when he overtook us, he remarked that there were five craniums with many other bones near by. Being no phrenologist I did not undertake to determine whether these were American or Mexican skulls: if the latter it is strange they had not been buried by the natives.

Molino del Rey is directly beyond Chapultepec, about a mile distant. Its *fortifications* consist in the walls of the houses of the mill, and the aqueduct. In addition there were two small redoubts thrown up to the N.W. out side of the mill houses, but these were but temporary and badly constructed concerns. Nevertheless this was one of the most—if not decidedly the most— bloody actions fought during the war. The ruins of the magazine, which was blown up at the conclusion of the action, are seen a quarter of a mile to N.W. of the mill.

From the Molino I concluded to visit an hacienda called Cariaga, where I had a thought of sending my mules to graze. From Molino to San Joaquin 2 m.—Tacuba 1 m.—Atzcapozalco 2 m. —Cariaga 1 m.—Tacuba to Popocle 1 m.—Mexico 3 m.

[27] It may be recalled that Gregg had visited West Point when in New York City in 1844.

261

Sun. 28—Having hired a little flat boat for an excursion across the lake, a party of us set out this morning at 8 o'clock for the city of Tezcoco, where there is a *feria,* which could not fail to call together a large concourse of people. Our party consisted of Lic. D. Miguel Ramos and his niece Dª Concepcion Ibarra, Don Miguel Gomez Cárdenas and his wife, Dª Merced Campa, D. Miguelito Gonzales, D. Ignacio Sanchez, Mr. John O'Sullivan, and two other young men and myself. Our main object was (or mine at least) a ride upon the lake of Tezcoco—famous in ancient history, as being the sea, upon which Cortez's celebrated fleet was launched, to aid in the consummation of the conquest of the city of Mexico. It will be recollected that it was a continuous lake from the very border of the city to that of Tezcoco (Tezcuco or Texcuco and Texcoco as generally written by the ancient historians.) But now there is a canal with a brisk current (say 2 m. per hour) running from this city (passing through the S.E. border of it from the remains of the lake of Mexico) to the lake of Tezcoco, down which we had to navigate for about 8 m. and thence through the lake near ten miles to the Tezcoco landing, which is still about two miles from the town.

Our craft consisted of a shallow flat boat about 30 feet long and six wide, with a "cabin" covered with a linen sheet upon bows like those of an ordinary road-wagon, across which there were adjusted five boards for seats. It was propelled, while in the canal, chiefly by two ropes pulled by two men upon the bank (for they seem to have never thought of using horses)—and in the lake by pushing with poles; for though it had four oars prepared, these were so badly arranged and the rowmen (who were Indians) so awkward that they were of little or no service. Our crew consisted of but three men: there should have been five—two to tow on each side of the canal, or to push with the poles on each side of the boat in the lake. Thus on account of our force being too weak, we had the mortification of being passed by every boat that came in our way; and were near 7 hours making the trip, which we should have made in less than five. The lake seems every where shallow—I saw no place (as indicated by the setting-poles), more than about two feet deep—generally about half a yard. It has been reduced in size and depth by two principal causes—1st by filling up by rubbish from city, etc. and by washings from the surrounding mountains; and 2dly, by an outlet which has been opened from the northern extremity of lake Tezcoco, passing out via Huehuetoca (?) into Rio Tula.—There seem to be very few waterfowl about these lakes except ducks, which are in great abundance. But insects abound more than anything else: a sort of small black fly (smaller than the common house-fly, but longer in proportion to size) literally covers the lake in many places. These are caught in quantities by the Indians, and sold in the city as food for birds; and their eggs, which are laid in immense abundance upon reeds, grass, or anything of the kind, found in the water, are collected, and used for food by the Indians themselves.

It was half past two when we arrived at the Tezcoco landing; and having to delay to get a coach, we did not all get fairly into town till near four o'clock: and by time we had dinner, it was night. So we could only walk about the town a little, and observe the "ways and doings." There seemed to be but little for sale except fruits and other edibles & "drinkables." The chief object of the fair seemed in fact to be gaming. On passing through the principal streets, there seemed scarcely to be a house without a gaming table—where the jingle of money would call our attention. The latter part of the evening we spent at the "theatre"— if we could so call a rough scaffolding in one end of a huge large room, upon which a homespun company displayed their awkwardness. Nevertheless, their rude efforts served to amuse us more perhaps than those of good actors in the city.

Tezcoco contains, I should consider, some 4 or 5,000 souls; and being a good deal scattered, presents quite an extended appearance. It is more interesting, however, on account of its historical associations than for anything else. [See ancient histories.][28]

Mon. 27—This morning near ten o'clock, we again embarked, and arrived at Mexico near 5 o'clock, *sin novedad*.[29]

❀ LETTER TO DR. GEORGE ENGELMANN

Mexico [City], Feb. 1st, 1849

MY DEAR DOCTOR,

A good long while has elapsed, it is true, since I have written you, though it is still longer since I have received anything from you. The truth is, our mail arrangements, to pass letters from one part to another in a foreign land, must be very bad. For I have not received a letter from the U.S. since a short time after peace was made, when they were forwarded, not by regular chance from the American to the Mexican post-offices, but by a friend at fort Brown, opposite Matamoros. Now, not only my relatives, but many friends, I am sure, have since written me numerous letters, as well to Saltillo as to this place, and not a *single one* since I have received a line from the U.S. This is most annoying; and what makes it more so, is the reflection that it must be on account of carelessness in our own postmasters, in not passing the letters from the posts by proper conveyances, into the Mexican republic; for all my letters written me within the republic come regularly, and therefore, I feel sure if they were passed to the posts, those would come likewise.

Well, a word concerning myself and arrangements. I left Saltillo in December (as I wrote you I expected to do) and arrived here on the 8th Jan. I have been occupied since chiefly in looking at the city and surrounding country. I make very few botanical collections in this vicinity, as I presume there is nothing new; nor could, unfortunately, make many between Saltillo and this

[28] The brackets are Gregg's. Lake Tezcoco had venerable enough associations. On its shores had stood the Aztec metropolis conquered by Cortez.
[29] Safe and sound.

place, as it was too much out of season.—A few winter plants and shrubs only could I pick up. The fact is, most of those on the way (being high valleys, plains and mountains) were those found about Saltillo.

When I left Saltillo I had not my future route fully planned out; but as I believe I have written you, I have, ever since entering Mexico last time, contemplated a tour upon the Pacific Coast, as far north as California, and perhaps Oregon: and now that so much is said about the mines of California, I have added inducement to go that way. I have therefore *about* determined—if not positively determined—to leave here toward first of March for the Pacific Coast, via Morelia (formerly Valladolid), Guadalajara, etc. to Mazatlan. If I can find that I can still proceed with safety by land, I shall continue through the interior to Guaymas —thence across the Gulf of California and proceed to San Diego, Monterey, & San Francisco.[30] Yet it is possible, owing to the danger of travelling by land, in some places, that I may conclude to embark at one of the ports, before reaching San Francisco. Still I shall be loth to do this as all the sea route is of course time lost. This route you will see is almost wholly "untrod" by the botanist, geologist, or naturalist of any kind: and it being a fine season for botany, I hope to be able to make some interesting collections in that line, to which I am chiefly dedicated.

In your last letter you proposed to me to make botanical collections and send you for sale. A want of leisure and transportation prevents me from collecting (and more especially in Geology) as extensively as I should. Still, I now make it a point whenever I can get them, to put up a dozen or more botanical specimens of every species—all of which I shall send to *you,* for I find it too inconvenient to make distinct packages to send so far to different points. With these you will be at liberty to make whatever disposition you may choose—present—sell—and keep

[30] This is the fullest disclosure of the aim of Gregg's "tour in the direction of California."

—as you may think fit; but without requiring any pecuniary return to me. All I ask—I will not say in *return*, for this would be asking too much for so little—but as a favor—is that at your leisure, you examine them, and write me out a brief (but quite brief indeed) botanical sketch of all the country I have travelled over since entering Mexico last—or rather since I commenced collecting botanical specimens in 1847. This I should wish to use (with full acknowledgement to you, of course) within about a year—if nothing happens.

I shall send you (via Vera Cruz) before leaving this place, my entire botanical collections, etc. not very extensive, to be sure, as I was most of the time at Saltillo, whose vicinity I had examined pretty well before. Still—all in all—including duplicates of many sent you before—I suppose I must have nearly as many species as I sent you before. These all will go numbered, keeping a memorandum of them myself.

I can't tell you how or where to write me until I reach San Francisco: in fact, an answer started immediately, would perhaps not reach there much before I. Therefore please write to that place, at once, by mail—or by private conveyance.

I will write again, when I forward my collections: meanwhile remaining most sincerely,

Your Friend, etc.

JOSIAH GREGG

GEORGE ENGELMAN, M.D.
ST. LOUIS, MO.

❄ DIARY, FEBRUARY, 1849

Thurs. 15—This evening my friend, Senator D. Domingo Ibarra, accompanied me on a visit to see General Juan Nepomuceno Almonte.[31] I found him a very agreeable sociable fellow —friendly and gentlemanly in his deportment; but indicating

---

[31] Almonte, Mexican general and statesman, had been second in command to Santa Anna in the Texas campaign in 1836.

more sprightliness than depth of intellect. He speaks pretty fair English, having been educated in the U.S.—chiefly in N. Orleans. His age is not so great as I had supposed, being scarcely over 40 years—according to the indication of his features. He is famous on account of his connection [with] the Texas campaign in 1836—his having been Mexican Minister to the U.S.—and his having filled several important posts in the government here.

Tues. 20—Being informed that there was to be a famous *paseo*[32] (with masked personages, etc.) in the Alameda & Paseo de Bucaseli, I rode out to witness it. The most interesting part of the scene was the number of coaches and the immense concourse of people. The number of coaches was certainly over 500—of horsemen perhaps 1000—and of men, women & children, on foot, between 5,000 & 10,000—in all, I should suppose, largely over 10,000 souls.—Several masqued parties "appeared on the field," in comical masks and costume & with corresponding gestures, etc.—Some with instruments of music—but none presenting any particular interest.

At night I attended a masquerade ball (the second given this season—and the last) in the Teatro Nacional. I attended this for curiosity & not because I approve of similar collections.—Some supposed there to have been at least 10,000 people present: I should think not so many—yet largely over 5,000. In the Boxes were to be seen nearly all the wealth and beauty of the city. I was pointed out several young ladies said to be *millionaires,* or at least possessing fortunes of hundreds of thousands. Among the masked personages too, we could see indications of considerable wealth, from the costliness of their dresses. One of the principal objects for which persons masked themselves, was to be thus able to ridicule and abuse with impunity (by altering their voices) persons against whom they had some grudge—and were to be found (as immense numbers were) without masks in the hall. The secretary of the Treasury (Ministro de Hacienda) was

[32] Promenade, parade.

267

pounced upon by a member of congress, in this condition, and worried until he was virtually compelled "to abandon the field." Another more reprehensible purpose is, arrangements between lovers that they may know each other by their masks and dress, and thus be able to have secret correspondence which they could not have elsewhere.—But, the most common purpose is, mere amusement, yet nothing, could seem to me much more ridiculous —brutally absurd. Nevertheless, all Mexico seems to be set crazy by them. Even the artisan—the laborer—and the servant—will expend the wages of months to equip himself to appear a night at the masquerade. The more intelligent strive to excuse this masquerade mania by saying, "Well perhaps it is well enough for us to make ourselves fools and monkeys once a year, by way of relaxation["]: for I believe they do not have these masquerades here, except at this season. Last Sunday night was the first.

Wed. 21—My friend (Irishman) John O'Sullivan accompanied me this evening on a visit to Gen. ——— Alcorta's.[33] I found the general agreeable—and familiar to an extreme: inclined, in fact, to be decidedly loquacious. Like many others of his age, he took great pleasure in recounting his own deeds. One of the most important eras in his career was during a portion of the war with the United States, when he filled the post of Secretary of War (*Ministro de Guerra*) during the Administration of Gen. Santa Anna—and especially at the time of the seige and capture of the city. Alcorta is an older man than his appearance would seem to indicate; for though he told me he was 55 years of age, his looks would indicate scarcely 50.—My principal object in visiting both Almonte and Alcorta, was to procure information statistical, geographical, etc. through them.

☀ DIARY, MARCH, 1849

Mon. 5—The Arc[h]bishop of Cesaréa (of Mexico—Sr. Irizarri) died last Thursday night; and having been exposed to

[33] L. J. Alcorta, general in Mexican army and for a time Minister of War.

the view of all, in the Catedral until today, he was buried this evening with considerable ceremony; though not quite as much pomp and parade as I had expected to see.

Sat. 10—This afternoon, I rode out to see the famous bath of El Peñol—between two and three miles from the city, to the N. eastward. The spring, which broke out originally at the foot of a small round hill, known as El Peñol, is now covered, and the water conveyed in tubes over a hundred yards, into a large bath-house, and there distributed into rudely-constructed baths, in various apartments. There not being a towel or anything of the kind at the bath (though the price of a bath was one dollar) with which to dry ones self, I could not bathe; and, on account of the utter want of civility and accommodation in the superintendent, it was with great difficulty I could get them to open me the place where the water first emerges from the pipes—but finally suc-ceed[ed] by paying a charge of half a dollar: and I found the temperature there to be 110° Fahr. though it is doubtless a few degrees higher at the foot of the hill. I could perceive no sensible mineral (or foreign) substances in the water: And though much resorted to as a cure for diseases, I could see no reason why a bath of *warm* water at home should not be as useful: in fact more so, as the patient could take better care of himself in his own house.

While at Peñol, I also visited the "Saltworks," (close by the baths). The saline earth is collected and salt extracted from it in same manner as at the "Salinas" near Guadalupe, (mentioned in the diary of 7th January); yet the water I tasted here, I per-ceived much stronger than that I saw near Guadalupe. Upon examining their "kettles" here, I found them broad tin pans (oblong square—say two by three feet—and but a few inches deep) collocated in a sort of rude furnace—but one at a place. The fuel used there was dried horse or cow-dung.

Mon. 12—Having received a *convite* through my friend Gen. Almonte, it reminded me of my previously formed intention of visiting the *Sanctuario* of Guadalupe, today, to witness the *funcion*[35] which is celebrated on the 12th day of each month, in honor of the *aparicion de Nuestra Sra.* de Guadalupe on 12th Dec. alternately by the several states of the union. Today's celebration pertained to the state of Michoacan. [NOTE: The *convite* [invitation] reads as follows:—

"El dia 12 del corriente, á las nueva de la mañana ha de verificarse la solemne funcion, que la sagrada mitra de Michoacan dedica anualmente a Maria Santisima de Guadalupe, en su Santuario; en la que predicará el Sr. Dr. D. Juan B. Ormaechea.—El Illmo. St. Abad y Venerable Cabildo de la insigne Colegiata, y los que subscriben, comisionados por el Illmo. Sr. Obispo, y venerable Dean y Cabildo de la espresada Santa Iglesia, suplican á V. les dispense el favor de su asistencia; á que le quedaran muy agradecidos.

Juan Gomez de Navarrete, José Ignacio Anzorenz, José Mª Aguilar y Lopez, Francisco Iturbe y Auriola, Lucas, Juan N. Almonte, José Ramon Malo, Luis G. Novellan, Mariano Aguilar y Lopez, Miguel Garibaz, Teofilo Garcia Carrasquedo, Everisto Barandcaran.—Mexico, Marzo 10, 1849.][34]

I found nothing of any special interest in the *funcion*. The sermon preached by the Rev. Mr. Ormaechea was too much like many of our circuit preacher's sermons—a mere exhortation— to be of interest. He confined himself chiefly to a eulogy of Sta. Mª de Guadalupe; and attributed their success in resisting the innovations of toleration to her: and what was still more notable, he considered they had received immeasurable benefits from her in the late crisis (war with the U.S.!) and lauded her for having so signally promoted the glory of the Republic!! One would have thought that the Rev. Padre might have found more apt

[35] Festival.

[34] The twelfth instant, at nine in the morning, is to be celebrated the solemn festival which the holy bishop of Michoacan dedicates annually to most holy Mary of Guadalupe in her shrine; in which Dr. Don Juan B. Ormaechea will preach.— The most illustrious holy abbott and venerable chapter of the distinguished collegiate church and the undersigned, commissioned by the most illustrious bishop and venerable dean and chapter of the aforementioned holy church, beg of you to do them the honor of being present; for which presence they will be very grateful.

3

March, 1849.

Real del Monte

demonstrations of the beneficence of their patron saint.—The rest of the *funcion* was of but little more interest than an ordinary *Misa*.[36] What would have attracted the attention of the inexperienced protestant was their band of music; being a theatre orchestra (chiefly of violins), who kept up, during the worship a strain of their liveliest music.

Real del Monte, March, 1849

Wed. 21—Having concluded, some time ago, to visit this place, for the purpose of seeing the mines (which are among the important ones of the republic), I left Mexico this morning in a stage which runs to Pachuca (where we arrived between 2 & 3 o'clock, P.M.) and reached Real del Monte between 4 & 5 o'clock this evening.

The following may be set down as the approximate average courses and distances of this route: to Guadalupe ———— 3 m. —Pueblo de Zacualco E.N.E. 2 or 3 m.—Do. of Santa Clara N.E. 3 or 4.—Cerro-Gordo same course, 1 m. (Relay)—Tulteclaque (Pueblo) ½ to left, 1 m.—Chiconautla (Pueblo) N.E. 6 or 7 m.—Ozumbilla, N.N.E. 3 m. (Relay)—Pueblo de Tecama, nearly N. say 3 m.—Another Pueblo—1 m. E. of road, say 3 m.—Pueblo de S. Gregorio, ½ m. E.—same course, 1 m. —Pueblo de los Reyes, ½ m. to W. of road, 1 m.—Tisayuca (Pueblo) 5 m. same course. (Relay)—Rancho (Relay) 12 to 15 m. course nearly N.E.—Pachuca, about same course, 10 or 12 m.—Pachuca is a town of some 2 or 3,000 inhabitants—some mines in neighborhood. Country between Pachuca and Tisayuca, especially, is mostly beautiful level plains, bestrewed with little ranchos, and extensively cultivated. Soil dark and rich, but no water, except that of wells and *Tanques*—they cultivate without irrigation. Corn and barley chiefly produced. From Pachuca to Real del Monte (or Mineral del Monte, as now oftener *writ-*

[36] Mass.

ten) course nearly N.E. distance say 5 m. A road from Pachuca
has been cut up the Mountain side, at great expense, to Real del
Monte, which is but half a mile east of summit. Elevation of
the "Casa Grande" of the Real, is, according to Mr. Buchan,
about 9,600 feet: that of summit, where road passes is therefore
about 10,000 above sea-level. Lat. of Real del Monte, according to Capt. Vetch (Englishman) 20° 8′ 11″—Long. by same
98° 39′5″. This is on the road to Tampico.

The first mines of Real del Monte were discovered in 1826;
and were worked for many years under the auspices of the proprietor, el Conde de Regla, with great profit. They since fell
into the hands of an English Company: but they have fallen
off very much in point of profit: so much so that the company
has sunk several hundred thousand dollars upon them. But they
now seem to be doing a little better, under their present active
and worthy director, Mr. John H. Buchan.

The ores are of various classes, all producing only silver. The
best qualities are smelted in furnaces; the silver being thus melted
out by heat; but the inferior ores (and these are much the largest
portion) are worked by amalgamation with quicksilver. This
process is conducted in various ways—sometimes by bringing the
ores in direct contact with the quicksilver, by mixing well, and
letting it lie for some time in heaps—but more commonly by first
heating the ores with common salt, thus forming a chloride of
silver, and then bringing them in contact with quicksilver, by
revolving them together in barrels, kept in motion by water or
steam power; so that thus the amalgamation is soon completed.
This latter process is now being adopted altogether, I believe.
But for either process, as well as for smelting, the ores are first
finely powdered. This is effected here in two or three different
ways. The old fashion is that of the ——— which consists of sort
of circular cisterns, around which several huge stones, flattened
to fit the bottom, are dragged around, by mule or water power,
and thus the stones are ground wet, into mortar, somewhat after

the system of grinding paints. Another grinding machine, which I saw in operation, consisted of two round stones, like large millstones, which were kept *rolling* around the cistern, after the manner of an old fashioned "back-mill." But the better and more modern plan of *grinding* is that of "stamps," consisting of a number of small wooden beams, shod with iron, set upright in an iron trough; and kept *pounding*, by a cogged horizontal beam or cylinder turned by water power. In this also the ores were pounded wet into a mortar.

The English company here, as is the case in most places worked by them, have everything in excellent order—systematic as "clockwork."—They are prepared to do everything within themselves—make their own machinery—cast their own iron, brass, etc. Make their engines, wagons, etc. their own carpenter's and blacksmith's work.

There [are] some very deep shafts—near 300 *varas*, out of which the water is cleaned by huge pumps, move[d] by powerful steam engines: at least to a horizontal shaft or adit, some 2 or 300 feet from surface, which discharges into the ravine near a mile below, affording water enough to run their grinding machines or stamps.

I intended to have penetrated to the bottom of one of the deep ravines (which is effected by means of ladders), but I was unfortunately too weak to undertake so arduous a task. As usually happens to me, the ride out in the stage so disordered my stomach, that I was greatly debilitated for a day or two after.

Thurs. 22—To-day I rode down through the *haciendas* (that is the establishments for working the silver ores) as far as Regla —some 15 miles. Here are extensive smelting furnaces—as well as a considerable number of grinding machines. The best ores are all brought here to be smelted.

However, the most interesting item I saw here was the *falls*, of some 50 feet—over immense and beautiful basaltic columns of near 100 feet high. These appeared to stand upon a gravelly

273

base, as indicated by the underhanging at the waterfall—which is of but a small creek.

The geology of this region, being mostly of a granite character, presented no very special interest, except for the metals—and the beautiful basaltic columns, before mentioned. The botany of these mountains would perhaps have been more interesting, had it been a more verdant season: as it was I found but little worth preserving.

While at the mines, I stopped with the *Administrador*, or principal director, John H. Buchan, Eng., for whose hospitality and kindness, as well as of his amiable lady, I will ever feel grateful. In fact, out of the city of Mexico, the English I have met with have seemed to be the perfection of hospitality, liberality and kindness. I also have to acknowledge many obligations to Mr. Buchan, for much important information he furnished me, of the northern interior of Mexico, where he had journeyed a great deal—particularly geographical.

Sat. 24—Rode down to Pachuca early this morning, again, and took the stage for the city of Mexico, at 6 o'clock: and arrived at the city between 2 & 3 P.M.

There are some peculiarities in the staging of this country which attract the attention of a foreigner. The stages themselves, are excellent Troy-made Coaches; but, although they often hitch in 5 or six animals, three or four are placed abreast at the end of the tongue. In this open country, this is, I think preferable to gearing them in three pairs; because those ahead are thus nearer to—and more manageable—by the driver. The horses, (being of the common small Mexican breed) though commonly gentle enough, are taught to break of[f] like mustangs as soon as let loose at a post; so that the stranger is apt to be frightened as they seem to be "running away." The drivers, to "show off," also usually enter the towns on the way, at full speed.

But the most annoying peculiarity I experienced, was on entering the city of Mexico. Though the stage passed immediately by my door, I could not prevail on the driver to set me down: "I will be fined $5 if I do so," said he: and thus I was compelled to continue my very unpleasant ride over half a mile further. This most annoying regulation has been adopted by the proprietor, a Guchipin, named Anselma Zurutuza, with the idea that he could thus prevent the drivers from clandestinely carrying passengers, whose names were not on the way-bill—not seeming to reflect that the drivers can set down all his clandestine passengers, wherever he thinks proper, and the proprietor is "none the wiser for it:" while he tenaciously holds on to those who have paid and are on the way-bill: thus the annoyance falls on these, and nothing is gained to the owner.

⚙ DIARY, APRIL, 1849

Sun. 1—Domingo de Ramos (Palm Sunday). Thousands of palm leaves, platted in various forms (fishes, tassels, etc.) were taken into church this morning to receive the benediction of the priests (benedicion de las palmas), and were afterward sold about the streets, and placed in windows, etc. to ward off thunderbolts.

Tues. 3—Having received a letter of introduction from Gen. Acorta to Gen. Tornel (who is director of Colegio de Minería), I called on the latter today. I found him a very social jovial fellow—speaking English intelligibly. He showed me into the college; and having introduced me to D. Antonio del Castillo (*"Ingeniero de Minas,"*[37] by title), at present *Catedrático de Mineralogia*[38] in the ———— I remained under many obligations to Gen. Tornel as well as to Sor. Castillo, for their polite attentions on that and subsequent occasions. Sor. Castillo seemed decidedly well informed in his branch (as well as in many others); and the mineralogical collections are among the most interesting and extensive that I have met with. The truth is, Mexico is doubtless one of the best fields in the world for Mineralogy. The

[37] Mining engineer.
[38] Professor of Mineralogy.

branch of Mechanics (phisica) is also pretty well supplied with apparatus: I did not see much else of particular interest, not having time to pass through the whole establishment. It has an observatory, but as the instruments were mostly packed away, there was nothing attracting to be seen there. The library is not very extensive, and the larger portion of the works in French. Gen. Tornel himself has a more interesting library: in fact, I should suppose there is not another private library in Mexico that equals that of Gen. T.—Some time ago I visited the Colegio de San Carlos, which, in many regards is more interesting than that of Mineria: here are the only gas lights in the city, I believe.— Gen. Tornel informed me that the edifice of Minería was reared about 50 years ago, costing about $800,000: it is in truth, one of the finest (if not the very finest) specimens of architecture in the city.

Sat. 7—This is the conclusion here of the ceremonies of the *semana santa* (Passion or Easter week). Early in the week the church was literally surrounded with shanties, reared for the occasion (some but simple tents) and the same were to be seen at the corners of most of the principal squares. The object of these was for the sale of *aguas frescas* and fruits. One happy regulation is that no intoxicating liquors are allowed to be sold—not even the almost indispensable *pulque*—from Thursday about 10 o'clock till Saturday, near same hour.

The city from Thursday on, began to be thronged—overflowed—with visitors from surrounding towns and ranchos— thousands upon thousands. On Thursday evening—and more especially Friday evening the main plaza, and the principal streets were so thronged with people, that it was laborious to pass among them. Thursday night the churches were all illuminated, and visited I suppose by everybody. Though raining and unpleasant, we could see great numbers of respectable ladies "traipsing" the streets from church to church. Although the churches looked pretty, they could not but engender painful reflections in a reasoning imagination. It was easy to perceive here, one of the great causes of the little advancement of the Republic: besides the time lost in such frequent ceremonies, and the amount of labor and wealth bestowed here, lying dormant, the myriads of wax candles alone, burned on this occasion, amount to a clever tax upon the people. But the "holy fathers" are unwilling that these and other expenses of this occasion [come] out of their ordinary collections of tithes, fees, and contributions: they must institute a special collection for the occasion. Thus a friar or two is to be met with in every door, continually—"Una limosna por el Amor de Dios—una limosna p^a el gasto de velas (or for such a ceremony, etc.)—Por una limosna se sacan almas del purgatorio—se consigue indulgencia plenaria,["]^{39} etc. and the frequent jingle of money in the plates show plain that these potent appeals are not in vain. Poor deluded people! They have never read that passage of Scripture which tells us of the people's giving food to their heathen gods, and the priests' consuming it at night.

But it is not on these occasions alone that we meet with the sanctified beggars. Not only to be seen very frequently standing in the church doors with alms-boxes in their hands, making their appeals, but I have witnessed them run out across the street to meet some poor ranchero, whining out—"Una limosna por el Amor de Dios—p^a la misa de las doce,"^{40} etc.

Thus we are continually annoyed with two classes of beggars about the church doors: for hundreds of poor miserable wretches make the air vocal with their appeals on our charity—and doubtless with much more justice than these friars.

There is another encumbrance generally found at the church doors here, to me particularly repugnant: and this is a soldier with a musket and bayonet on his shoulder—with the pretense,

---

^{39} Alms for the love of God—alms to buy candles—by alms souls are released from purgatory—full pardon is obtained.

^{40} Alms for the love of God—for twelve o'clock mass.

it is true, of checking disorders: yet I fear these same soldiers commit more disorders than the people would in their absence. On Thursday a guard from a French Corps of troops here, was placed at the door of one of the important churches—La Profesa—and the report was afterward out, that these our gallant "tasty" young heroes would let no body enter the church, but pretty girls and well-dressed matrons and gentlemen—I hope not so!

From Thursday 10 or 11 o'clock A.M. no coaches, wagons, horses, donkeys, or anything of the kind, were allowed to pass the streets, until Saturday. Neither were any bells to be heard, except those of the clocks. This recess of silence would have been decidedly pleasant, had it not been made up—for noise of some kind. Therefore, every boy in the streets took care to provide himself with a *matraca* (rattle-trap) with which an awful clattering was constantly kept up. And, in one of the steeples of the church (Cathedral) was placed the "rattletrap general"—a huge affair, which was put in motion on such occasions as required bell ringing (as at 12 o'clock, etc. etc.) by which a frightful rattling was produced.

This order of affairs (with various processions in the evenings), was kept up until late this morning. About 9 o'clock, great numbers of rough figures of men of paper (called *Judas's* —but on other occasions they have represented also particular personages, as Americans, etc. which was prohibited on this occasion), with fire-works attached: and at the moment the principal clock struck 9½ o'clock, the bells were all let loose again, and fire set to the crackers, the popping of which (and bouncing of the figures) added to the roar of cannon, kept such an uproar that one must imagine the heavens in commotion. At the same time coaches and horsemen filled the streets,—mules and donkeys with their tinkling bells loaded with pulque came rushing into the city—beer-wagons and market-carts were again running about: and tippling shops were soon thronged to overflowing;

so that, in less than an hour, more drunkards, and drunken ones, I scarce ever saw tottering about the streets—men and women.

Soon after this everything became calm again, and the streets comparatively abandoned; so that before night the city was as quiet as before the feast: and next day—Easter Sunday—passed off as but little more than an ordinary Sabbath here—except that everybody seemed to have gone to church in the morning.

Monday, 9—Rode out this evening to Churubusco and Contreras. The first of these places, being in the open level valley of Mexico, presented no natural elements of defense, but was rendered somewhat formidable by breast-works thrown up on the south side. Contreras is interesting on account of the extensive cotton factory in operation there—which with the dwellings of the operators seem to constitute the village. The fortifications which were stormed by the Americans were half a mile to N. Eastward; but they have now mostly fallen down.

The following are the approximate courses and distances: Mexico to Churubusco S. 20 W. 5 m.—Pueblo de Coyoacan, W. ½ to 1 m.—Do. de Chimalistaca W. S. W. 1½ m. S. Angel, same, ½ m.—Contreras W. 43° S. 3 m.—From Contreras to Guadalupe, N. 33° E.—Mexico, N. 38 E.—Churubusco, E. 32° N.—Returned to Mexico which left other road at Chimalistaca, passing ½ m. to N.W. of Churubusco.

Tues. 10—In accordance with a previous engagement with the superintending friar at the Santuario de Guadalupe, I rode out to that famous church today, with the object, as per previous quasi promise, of seeing the celebrated picture of *Su Magestad*.[41] And I was much indebted to the politeness of my friend the friar for taking me up into the altar and thus giving me a near view of the painting. It is rather a time-worn affair, with the paint scaled off in several places, thus plainly showing the threads of the ayate upon which it was painted, which are about as coarse as those of common canvass—but much more openly woven—

[41] Her Majesty.

but not so much as mosquito bars. I did not find one of the traditional miracles verified, viz. that upon near approach the figure nearly disappeared (owing to the openness of the texture): on the contrary, the nearer the plainer; for the ayate had been prepared as common canvass for painting, and thus the interstices partially filled up, generally. But I am disposed to suspect that in the 318 years which have passed since it was first produced, it has been renewed perhaps more than once—perhaps *ayate* and all! The *ayate* being of two pieces, the seam is distinct a little to left of middle.—As compensation for the privilege I had enjoyed, I handed the friar a dollar as limosna, besides purchasing several dollars of medals, figures, rosarios, etc. etc. most of which was clear profit to the church.

Seeing "Toros" advertised (and there having been none since my arrival here that I knew of) I concluded to go and see how they figured in such things in Mexico: but I must confess it was a most wretched affair in every regard—as well in regard to the "pen" as to the performance—and the spectators—not beginning to be as interesting as what I had before seen in Saltillo and San Luis. [MARGINAL NOTE: Becoming disgusted, I went out half an hour after performance commenced. On passing the door, the keeper offered me a return ticket, but I told him it was unnecessary.]

Wed. 11—Having received permission from Gen. D. Pedro Garcia Conde, Chief of Topographical Bureau, to examine and copy what I could in one day, of a large M.S. map of the Mexican republic, prepared for publication; but without hope of its being published, at least at present—I spent to-day (and part of Thursday morning) in copying the most interesting and important parts of it. This liberality is certainly creditable to Sr. Garcia Conde; but it is to be regretted that he did not carry it out; for it seems evident the map will not be published by the government, and thus it lies dormant. Sr. Garcia Conde's excuse for restricting me to a day, was that as he was going to deliver over the office, he could not dispose of it after Thursday at 10 o'clock. Yet he might as easily have permitted me to commence as much sooner as he had chosen—Monday or Tuesday, for instance, instead of Wednesday: so that it seems evident that they only intended me to have the privilege of a day: nevertheless, having made pretty good use of this short time, I was able to copy the rivers, boundaries, and most important cities.

Thurs. 12—I called this evening, a few minutes, on a visit to Gen. Almonte. He treated me with a "lecture" on the state and management of the republic, and its relations with the United States. He acknowledged his government & country in a state of infancy; and that there were many and almost insurmountable drawbacks to its advancement. "We have numerous difficulties to contend with," said he; "not the least formidable of which are the parties and prejudices of the country. The army subjects us; the priests rule us; and we have no sprinkling of aristocracy: influential [men] openly avow their prediliction for a monarchical government. Then we have to contend with the prejudices, and above all the superstitions and fanaticism of the people. They admit no important innovation, either in affairs of govt and religion, or in arts and sciences. They cling closely to old laws, old faith, old customs—old arts and sciences: we find many utensils, for instance, in use here, which have been in vogue ever since the days of the Romans: of the modern improvements we scarcely see anything or know anything.

"Well, having entered the world in such a state of backward infancy, much, of course, was to be expected of our adopted prototype and godmother, the U.S. of America. We strove to follow her as a model, in everything, except, in toleration, which unfortunately the state of fanaticism and superstition which has existed, would not permit. We seemed to have been accepted as a foster-child; but unfortunately our *Madrina*[42] proved a rather captious and scolding one. Instead of having patience with our

---

[42] Foster mother.

faults and childishness, giving us good advice and mildly leading us into the path of duty, she soon began to frown upon every little deviation, and to chide us on all occasions, as a vixy old mother is too wont to treat the faults of a child. The consequence was, that we soon became stubborn; and although we might frequently have acknowledged the justness of the reprimands, had they been given in a more charitable tone, we were too proud to permit ourselves to be scolded and 'switched' for our peccadillos, before all the world.

"Again, in our relations with the U.S. we have been very unfortunate in regard to Ministers. Since the day of Mr. Poinsett,[43] there has not been an American minister in Mexico fully capable, in every regard, of performing the duties of his mission. One of the important errors committed by us, as well as by our neighbors, and elsewhere, I suppose, is the appointing of ministers who are ignorant of the language [of] the country to which they are sent. It will be answered that they have only to employ good interpreters, who can supply this defect. So we might say of appointments to almost any other office; so that by the same rule, even a commanding general may be ignorant of the *mode* of performing his duty: he can employ expert agents through whom to do it! But there is even more in this: A man to be a good minister must not expect to do everything by official communications and formal diplomacy: these are all that show before the world; yet more is really done by private colloquies and social intercourse. If I am minister, and wish to effect an object—to arrange some business—to settle an affair,—I prefer meeting and conversing personally with the minister with whom I have to do—or the president himself if necessary; and thus to settle a thousand little difficulties, and particularities which could never be done by writing. In such cases it is a great embarrassment to

[43] Joel Roberts Poinsett (1779–1851), United States Minister to Mexico 1825–29 (and later Van Buren's Secretary of War), who negotiated a commercial treaty and otherwise sought to strengthen the bonds between the two republics.

have to perform this through a third person—an interpreter. Besides the occasional want of good faith, as well as unintentional errors, in these, every body ought to be aware, that we much prefer conversing directly on confidential subjects, instead of through an interpreter: many important things are often left unsaid, rather than have them heard by a third person.

"Moreover, for a minister to exercise properly and advantageously his mission, he should know something of the manners and habits of the people with whom he has to treat, and be able to hold social intercourse with them. It not only enables him to direct his operations with more *tino*,[44] but it establishes a confidence among the people, which much aids him in his efforts: he is rather looked upon as one of the people than as a stranger."

Frid. 13—Having had my mules, etc. brought in to a *Meson*, for the purpose of recruiting them a little, preparatory to my tour in the direction of California (which I had now determined upon), I engaged a couple of young men—named William Riley from Oswego County, N.Y. and William Sampson, from Richmond, Va—not only to attend to my animals; but for the tour to California. These young men seemed unusually serviceable and useful—Riley as muleteer or hostler, and Sampson as cook: therefore, in addition to an original recommendation which they had brought me, their conduct had the effect to inspire me with confidence: the fact is, I liked the boys, and fancied I had acquired a treasure in them. But to-day, having occasion to be out for two or three hours—as well as my little Mexico boy, I was surprised, on my return, to find they were absent, and had taken away their baggage, etc. I at once suspected they had fled, and of course had taken mules—I feared at least two apiece. On going to the Meson, w[h]ere my animals were kept, I found my fears partially realized—they had taken two of my best mules, with two of my saddles and bridles. I used immediate efforts to get persons to follow them, offering a reward of $50 for their ap-

[44] Skill.

283

prehension, with the stolen property. But I failed to get anyone to undertake it. Meanwhile, I strove myself to find out in which direction they had started. I was told that they had been seen in the direction of Guadalupe: I supposed of course they were making in the direction of California, as a party of Americans had left but two or three days ago, by way of Querétaro.

In this, however, I was also mistaken: and I did not "get on their track" till near 11 o'clock at night, and they had started about 11 A.M. It occuring to me that the stage from Puebla might have met them, I went to see the driver, near the hour alluded to, and he gave me so plausible an account of them—and that they would doubtlessly stay that night at Ayotla, but about 7 leguas distant—that I concluded to set out at once, in person, in their pursuit, accompanied by one Benjamin Richardson, from New York.

Mr. Richardson being also on his way to California, had concluded to join my party; and to relieve him from the expense of a room, I told him he could occupy one, free of charge, in the house I had rented. To-day he had ridden out to see some of the battlegrounds, being absent until 8 or 9 o'clock at night. Unknown to me, he had, as he since said, about $100 in cash, in his trunk, which he had left in an open room. It seems that my two young men, having come in, and found the house alone, could not withstand the temptation to break open Mr. Richardson's trunk (where Richardson had most probably imprudently intimated to them he had money), and having rifled it, it became indispensable that they should leave. This seems to have been the cause of their taking my mules as a means of making their escape.

Having spent some time in hiring a pair of strong horses—for self and Richardson—we got under way a little after midnight, and arrived at Ayotla, at break of day. But here we only learned that they had passed the evening before, and had probably slept at the Venta de Córdova, 10 m. distant, on the road toward

Puebla. We galloped thither, as soon as possible; but had the mortification to learn that they had also passed on, saying they intended to sleep at Rio Frio, near 15 m. further. Being much fatigued, with loss of sleep, etc. I determined to go no further: but hired a fresh horse for Mr. Richardson, and a Sergeant and a soldier or two to accompany him, with the hope that they would overtake the rogues in time to return that night to Córdoba. But as they did not get back, I came in, very early to Mexico on the morning of the 15th—as my business absolutely required. [NOTE: It was on account of Mr. Richardson's loss, more than my own, that I concluded to follow the robbers myself; for I had already become convinced that the trouble and cost of pursuit would be more than the worth of all they had taken from me. True, I felt a strong desire to bring the offenders to justice, even at a sacrifice to myself; yet the necessity for my presence in Mexico, on account of business, and preparations for starting to California, would most probably have forced me to forego this. —It was then very painful to me, after the favors I had done him —first in giving him a room in my house, and secondly in making sacrifices to aid him in recovering his money—that he should impliedly wish to hold me responsible for his losses! as it occurred in my house!! His conduct was so decidedly ungenerous, with a display of such a disagreeable disposition, that I soon afterwards found myself compelled to exclude him from my party.]

❀ LETTER TO DR. GEORGE ENGELMANN

Mexico, April 14, 1849

MY DEAR SIR:

I have various letters of yours before me, the latest of which are of Aug. 4 and 28—1848—and Feb. 18, 1849. The two first I have already answered, which I hope you have received; yet I will repeat some things here, to provide against accidents to the other.

In your letter of Aug. 4, you speak of a "dry berry" which I sent you as seed of the *junco* (green-thorn-shrub). I *aimed* at least to send you as well as Dr. Short, large branches of these berries. You say you had supposed it of some other plant; yet if you received the right ones, I don't know how you could mistake them, as they had twigs with thorns connected with them.

In yours of Aug. 18, you make a proposition to collect plants for sale. Circumstances and means of transportation will not permit to collect as extensively as would be requisite for that; nevertheless I make it a point to collect considerable number of specimens of every plant—where I can get good ones—all of which I will send you; yet not for sale on my account, but for you to make whatever disposition of them you may think proper. All I shall solicit of you (as I said in my last) is that, provided your occupations permit, you write me out a brief (though quite brief —suited to a short appendix) account of the botany of the regions through which I have travelled since commencing to forward you specimens; yet this I ask as a favor, and not as recompense for anything I have done or may do; for the trouble has doubtless been more on your side than on mine.

I hope to be able to publish within a twelvemonth, as I shall probably make my way home pretty direct from California.

I have now put up to send you from here some 700 specimens, including all my collections since I last entered Mexico. Among these I purposedly embraced a great number of those I had already sent—many others have doubtless been introduced without my knowing it; nevertheless I think more than half are distinct; and a few, I hope, new and interesting. I have now followed the system of numbering as you directed; but I find it impossible at present to copy my notes; yet I will do it as soon as possible and send you.*

I wrote you before of my contemplated tour to California— through the states of Mexico, Michoacan, Malisco, Sinaloa, and Sonora—the most interesting botanical route that I can now well imagine. I hope to forward you something of interest at the conclusion of this tour.

I believe your last letter contains nothing requiring special answers. I perceive by it that some of my letters had not reached you. This last of yours was forwarded to me from Saltillo to this city.

You will doubtless be surprised to find me here so late: I am myself, indeed, but numbers of interesting things have been daily presenting themselves to detain me among them several MS. maps of parts and whole of the Republic, which I have got the privilege of copying. In this line I feel sure I can produce something much more accurate than has ever been published.

My botanical collections about here amounted to but few, as I not only supposed the country well explored, but the season has been particularly bad—the country burned up by drought. I had not seen a drop of rain since sometime before leaving Saltillo, till 10 or 12 days ago; and though you speak of hard winter —ice—snow—sleet, etc.—I have scarcely witnessed a *frost:* the only time I have seen the thermometer *as low* as the freezing point, was two or three mornings on the plains this side of Saltillo. In this city I have scarcely seen it below 40°.

Very truly,
Your friend, etc.
JOSIAH GREGG

* Since writing this I have engaged a young man to copy off my plant notes, which I will place in Portfolio No. 1—between the board and the plants. I doubt not the copy will contain many errors; but I hope it may serve till I can send you a better copy, or the original.—I mark the box to care of Moses Greenwood, Commission Merchant, New Orleans.

You speak of "troubling" me; nothing that you can impose upon me do I consider trouble. On the contrary, I preserve your letters with care, and copy most of your "lectures" in my notebook—so interesting [and] useful are they to me.

P.S. Monday, April 23.—Since writing this letter I have suffered considerable detention on account of a robber. Two Americans who brought me a letter of recommendation, and [whom] I engaged for the trip to California, broke open the trunk of a friend in the house with me, and, stealing my two best mules, made off toward Vera Cruz. They were caught, however, and are now in jail; yet having made away with the mules, and most of the money, the amount recovered hardly paid expenses.

☼ DIARY, APRIL, 1849

Mon. 16—Having long contemplated, but as yet neglected, to visit the famous Castle of Chapultepec, I rode out this evening, not only for the purpose of seeing it, but of getting a view of surrounding country. The following communication to Mr. Clifford will give an account of my adventure on this occasion:

Mexico, April 20, 1849

To the Honble Nathan Clifford, Minister of the U.S. of America, near the Republic of Mexico. ·

The undersigned, citizen of the United States of America, having, a few days ago, suffered gross insults, and what he cannot qualify as less than outrages, from Mexican officers; and all his efforts for redress through the proper department of this government having proven ineffectual, his sense of duty as well to his government as to himself, impels the undersigned to solicit permission to lay before the American Minister, with due respect and courtesy, the following relation of the circumstances of the case above referred to; for the strict truth of which he solemnly vouches:

Desirous to see the Castle of Chapultepec, as well as to obtain a view of the surrounding country from it, I inquired of several intelligent and distinguished personages here, if it were necessary to obtain permission for that purpose: they all told me they thought not, as every body who desired to do so, passed in and out of said premises without interruption. Indeed, this was corroborated by my own experience, as well as that of others, as I had not long before ridden through the principal gate of the enclosure, in company with a Mexican citizen, without molestation; and others informed me, they had done the same.

Therefore, on the evening of the 16th inst., I rode out to the premises of Chapultepec; and, coming to the main gate-way, I inquired of the sentinel if I could enter: he very abruptly and grossly that I should not. He then called the sergeant of the guard, who answered in the same manner & tone. I rejoined that I had understood there was no embarrassment; but that if I could not enter I would go back and inquire further into it. Upon this the sergeant requested me to alight and pass in—which served to confirm me in my presupposition, that it was only their prejudice against Americans, which had induced them to stop me: indeed, even on this occasion I saw numbers of Mexicans passing without disturbance.

I was then accompanied by a soldier; and while on the roof of the edifice, looking at the surrounding country, a Capt. Galloso came up; and without deigning to notice me, he commenced chiding the soldier who was with me, very severely, ordering him to tell the sergeant, that if he again permitted the entrance of such a person, he would have him exemplarily punished, and he concluded by commanding the soldier to take me to the commanding general, that he might dispose of me as he should think fit. Ignorant of any particular cause of offence, and anxious to take the course of Tacubaya, I put my prismatic compass to my eye for that purpose, when said captain struck it with his hand, and insultingly ordered me to the general.

Having been kindly received and dispatched by Gen Saldaña, I was quietly passing down the hill from the castle, when I was met by one Lieut. Andelo, who reacted the scene of Capt. Galloso with the soldier, indulging in offensive expressions and gesticulations. I confess I was by that time very angry (as any body else must have been with similar treatment), and could not refrain from meeting his insults with a sharp repartee; and, after a few harsh expressions on either side (and, as I shall ever believe, very just on mine), said lieutenant ordered the soldiers to have me imprisoned. Having been conducted to Sergeant (calling himself) Murga, he very insultingly and cruelly executed the order; violently driving me into a sort of dungeon (*gariton*) near the gateway. I was then compelled to climb the hill again, to see the general, who received and dispatched me as before.

Now, though I have nothing to complain of, with regard to Gen. Saldaña, except, as I suppose, a remissness of duty, in not restraining his subordinates, I respectfully solicit, and believe it my right and duty to demand, that appropriate punishment be inflicted on Capt. Galloso for most wantonly insulting me, without my having given the slightest intentional provocation:—on Lieut. Andelo, not only for having done the same, but for imprisoning me for no other cause, than in revenge for a private altercation:—on Sergeant Murga for having executed the order of imprisonment in a barbarous manner, thereby adding cruelty to insult and outrage:

As already indicated, I represented this affair to the sub-secretary of war, and obtained his promise that the matter should receive attention; but I have been informed, that, having spoken to the president on the subject, his excellency replied that, as he supposed the officers alluded to had done nothing but their duty, they could not be punished. Yet, this is so far from according with my preconceived opinions of the high and honorable character of his Excellency, President Herrera that I am induced to fear he has never been rightly informed on the subject. It is therefore, that I venture to molest the Hon. Mr. Clifford with this Communication, trusting he may instigate such action upon it, as his better judgment may suggest as necessary and proper: thus conferring an important obligation on,

His obt. humble serv't.

JOSIAH GREGG.

I know not what will be the result of my representation: Mr. Clifford promised to represent the matter to the Mexican government at once; and he afterward assured me that he had done so; yet no answer was received up to the time of my leaving: so I presume it will be forgotten. One thing is certain, that I do not recollect ever having been treated more rudely and outrageously: and I shall hardly forget it, or any of these who had to do with it.—*Nous verrons.*

Wed. 18—To-day my two American robbers were brought into the city, by two or three soldiers from Córdova; they having been caught by a sergeant and soldier or two sent on with Mr. Richardson from this place, some miles beyond Puebla. They had swapped away my two mules for two ponies, and one of these, again, with a soldier for a horse of a Capt. who, having been informed of this by the soldier himself, sent after them, and had the horse taken away from them. What was amusingly knavish in the criminal alcalde or judge of Puebla, was, that though the soldier confessed the fact, and offered to give up the horse and $7 which he had received to boot from my men, said judicial functionary refused to permit the soldier to deliver the property, but took the same into his own possession until the matter should be adjudicated in Mexico; thus remaining with them altogether, I suppose, as I had no opportunity of sending for either horse or money.

I delivered my robbers over to the authorities of Mexico; and was afterward told that he [*sic*] had been sentenced to a few months' imprisonment! Poor fellows! it was truly unfortunate, as well for them as for me, that the temptation presented itself to them. To the last I was unable to believe [them] really so wicked: and the expense—the loss of time—and the loss of their service to me, were all severely felt—were worth hundreds of dollars to me!

Wed. 25—It was my intention to leave the city of Mexico, to day; but having many things yet to do, I found it nearly night before I could get my wagon loaded, and mules geared in. It is only those who travel much, and with a great deal of luggage, who are aware of the trouble of making a start. For me it is a most arduous undertaking.

Among other things which caused detention to day, was the necessity of procuring a passport for myself and party to carry arms. After having been urging the matter ever since yesterday —and the necessity of giving security for their good use—the passport was obtained to-day. But when it came it was simply for myself. It now seemed to become necessary that I should get new security and passports for each of my men; and only got rid of this through the influence of a friend. Thus every embarrassment is thrown in the way of those who ought to carry arms to defend themselves against the highway robbers, with the pretence of embarrassing the robbers themselves. Yet it is scarcely credible that the authorities should be so simple as not to see that these measures only serve to aid the robbers: thus serving to corroborate to current reports, that the former are leagued with the latter. As it costs 62½ cts. to procure each passport or permit to carry arms, many poor people are unable to bear the tax: others neglect it rather than submit to the mortification and molestation of procuring it. As to the robbers—even supposing the law rigidly executed with regards to them (which it rarely is, I trow)—they have no use for permits. As they operate on the public highways, and keep their arms and even themselves concealed until an opportunity presents itself to make an attack (not so much, it should be borne in mind, for fear of the authorities, as to be able to pounce upon their prey with greater facility), they have no occasion to expose their arms in public.

This I fear, is one of the sources of the backsets of Mexico. In despotic governments it behooves the sovereigns to keep their subjects in ignorance, and unarmed: but in a republic, it is just the reverse. For the preservation of this, the people should be armed—that this may be effective they must of course be taught the use of arms—and to effect this, their use must be encouraged.

Well, when I got "all set," it was near sun down: nevertheless, I resolved to make a start—to drive out, with the hope of reaching Tacubaya; yet my awkward wagoner got on so very badly, that I found it expedient to pass the night in a Meson, in the western part of the city.

Before getting out of the city, altogether, I ought to say a word or two about this famous capital. I have said elsewhere, that I was much disappointed, on my arrival here, as the place did not realize my anticipations. The suburbs, in fact, are so exceedingly uncouth and filthy, that the traveller is sure to receive a mal-impression, upon his first entrance.

Everybody who visits Mexico cannot but be struck with the error of the Conquerors in not having fixed their capital upon some of the neighboring hills, as those of Tacubaya, San Angel, Tezcoco, etc., all of which present beautiful undulating sites, with abundance of fine spring water at hand. As it is, the capital is located in a low valley, [not] only subject to inundations, but virtually in a quagmire, at all seasons, only kept dry by draining. The ground is so boggy that to make secure foundations for houses, it becomes necessary, generally, to drive down cedar stakes to a considerable depth, upon which to lay their stone ground-work.

The streets are generally badly paved, and in the ancient style —inclined from each side-walk to the centre. There are many fine massive costly stone edifices; yet but comparatively few which present much external elegance. The roofs are all flat terraces, and no dwellings, I believe over three stories high. The Cathedral church (which has obtained much fame) is not as fine a building as I had expected to see. The bell-towers are not even as high, I feel sure, as those of Chihuahua. They are said to be but 75 varas from the ground. Although there is much wealth in the interior, even this is not as great as I had expected to see.

. As yet there are no gas lights in the city of Mexico (except in the College of San Carlos) and therefore the city is lighted by lamps. I do not believe as dangerous, however, to pass the streets, either day or night, as I had heard it reputed. Although I was in all parts of the city, in the day, and in much of the central portion, occasionally at night, I never saw an indication of an attack by robbers.

The most annoying "customers" I met with, in the streets, were the beggars, hundreds [or] thousands of whom infest the city, begging under all sorts of pretexts. But the vendors of lottery tickets (that very rascally species of gambling—though licensed even in more advanced societies!) whose cries are truly annoying; and you cannot turn a corner without having tickets poked in your face, by men, women, children, and even beggars —under all sorts of imposing titles—as the "lot[t]ery of the little babes"—the lot[t]ery of the widows—and the lot[t]ery of almost every Saint in the Calender! Saints and angels and other holy personages are favorite names for everything intended to impose upon the ignorant and gull them of their money. It is customary to give these and other attractive titles to mercantile retailing establishments: thus the shop-keepers advertisement rarely directs you to a particular number of a street, but to the "Store of the Angel,"—to "the Gold mine"—to "The city of London"—to "The Port of Cadiz," etc. etc. where you will find the sign thus figured over the door.

The mode of naming and reckoning the streets, is peculiarly annoying in the City of Mexico. The space between every two squares or blocks constitutes a distinct street; so that the names are multiplied almost without number,—which renders it very difficult for a stranger to search them out.

Among the things which attracted attention in the *portales* was the variety of toys—and among others the toy-wagons, made to imitate the baggage wagons of the U.S. Army: we thus could see them with their miniature linen sheets, and "U.S. [the "S" reversed in stamping] N⁰ 134," etc. marked upon them. Now, one would have naturally supposed that they held these badges of their for[ced] subjection in too much abhorrence to make playthings of them for their children.

The city of Mexico used to be celebrated as the very hot-bed of religious fanaticism and superstition. Yet it has doubtless very much improved since the American occupation: for now a foreigner can walk the streets without being compelled to take off his hat in the broiling sun at the sound of the 12 o'clock bell— or to kneel at the appearance of the Beático—the Host: many Mexicans themselves have ceased to do it! I was much surprised to see in an almanac (the most popular of all publications) an article from the "American Star" published in Mexico, during the occupation—in which the priests and the army were denounced as the ruin of Mexico. True, the editor said he only gave it for what it was worth, without pretending to father it: Yet, no almanac-maker, if he valued his ears, or even his existence, would have ventured to give place to such an article, ten years ago!

One thing seems very certain—that at least two great benefits has Mexico reaped from the war—the destruction of the army, which ruled her destinies with a despotic sway—and the lowering of the priests: nevertheless, these last, as will be seen elsewhere, still bear down upon the ignorant and fanatical with a remorseless hand.

Before leaving the city of Mexico, I was very anxious to become acquainted with the President: [MARGINAL NOTE: or at least to see him—not for any exalted opinion that I had formed of his talents, but merely to satisfy curiosity.] Yet, my endeavors all proved fruitless! He has no general reception days, like the President of the U.S.—there is so much monarchichal ceremony required, that we have no means of being introduced into the presence of the President, except through the medium of some particular friend of his: and none of my friends or even particular acquaintances, happened to be his.

[Note Accompanying Manuscript No. 5]

[NOTE I, from page 291]—Before leaving the city of Mexico, on the 24th April, I visited two hospitals—the most famous, I believe, in the city—those of the "Sisters of Charity," and "San Lázaro." I found them both in a cleaner and better condition than I had expected to find them. The first contained perhaps near 100 patients (between 50 & 100), of both sexes, and of various diseases—fevers of a typhoid character, dropsies, rheumatism, ulcers, etc.—seemed the most common. San Lázaro contained a fewer number of patients, which were generally composed of such as the attending physicians of the other hospitals had given up as incurable. They were called Lázaros or lepers—their diseases being mostly ranked under the general title of leprosy; though, in fact, from a glance I had of them, I believed them mostly of a tertiary syphilitic character.

Part VI

Tour to California

Tour to California

APRIL TO AUGUST, 1849

Diary, April, 1849[1]

THURS. 26—Having nothing to embarrass us this morning, we got under way pretty early, we soon got out of the city, but did not so soon lose sight of it: for from a hill near where we lay tonight, we still had a fine view of the "valley of Mexico."

Our party consisted of seven foreigners and a Mexican servant: viz. Thos. Addicks and myself, Americans, Francis Okenfusz and Victor Runckel, Germans, and Robt. Callender, Thos. Keary and Bartholemew Pikens, Irishmen—or rather the first of these three a Scotchman.[2] All of these except Mr. Addicks were in my

---

[1] The Gregg party, on geographical and scientific exploration bent, left Mexico City on April 26, 1849. The six other men and the Mexican servant were, as Gregg says, "none very useful men for travelling purposes." They were to journey through a section of Mexico that had no beaten pathways for travelers, and their adventures and misadventures bore out the impression of being in the hinterland. Doubtless Gregg enjoyed this return to something like his experiences going back and forth over the Santa Fé Trail. At any rate he seems to have enjoyed the return to the self-reliance and self-sufficiency of the frontier. He also reverts to amassing geographical data, although botanical and even faunal information is beginning to crowd out latitudes, longitudes, temperatures, and the like. Unfortunately there was a drought, which thwarted the collection of plants. The hot weather eventually took its toll of Gregg's vitality, and it seemed wise to give over the attempt to take the party by land up to California. Gregg halted at Mazatlan until he could obtain boat passage Californiawards.

[2] No identifications can now be made of the members of Gregg's party, financed by his private means, except in the case of Thomas Addicks. He is the same person that Gregg railed at in an earlier passage of the diaries because General Wool had preferred him to Gregg as a civilian aide. Gregg omits all mention of how he and Addicks were thrown together again, or how he may have changed his opinion of Addicks. Addicks, he notes later on, left the party at Guadalajara. Robert Cullender

employ,—all very good responsible fellows; yet none very useful men for traveling purposes.

The course and distances of today's journey were about as follows: To Tacubaya (course, see elsewhere[3]) 4 m.—thence 235° (prismatic compass—counting around from North to east), 4 or 5 m. to Santa Fé—say 200 pop., same, 8 m. to Cuajimalpa —San Pedro de Cuaxamalpa, one mile back a little to north of road.

As we travelled out today, my attention was continually attracted by the Indian Cargadores[4]—some with charcoal, baled up in grass, generally—men, women, and little boys, each with a bale in proportion to his strength. Occasionally you would meet one driving a loaded donkey before him; yet the Indian also carried his load behind:—Others were laden with lumber: occasionally we would meet with one who displayed more ingenuity than his comrades, by mounting his load up a pair of truckle wheels; and tying a rope to the point of it, he trotted down the great inclined plain (for it is a continuous descent from the mountains to the vicinity of the city) with much [less] labor certainly, than if he carried it upon his back. But this is the gait even of the packers: they will trot for hours, with an immense burden upon their backs. Those who pack bales of coal, carry a long staff in their hands which they use to prop their bale (which is six or 8 feet long) in an erect posture, when they stop to rest, so that they may take it upon their backs with more ease again. Poor miserable aborigines! They are the virtual and abject slaves of the country. I know not how the Hispano-Mexican race could live without them: they are the only really laborious class of people we meet with. And yet they are most wretchedly paid.

---

died suddenly at Guadalajara (see page 315). Young Runckel is spoken of in a letter to Dr. Engelmann as "a pretty fair practical naturalist, who has been of a great deal of service to me, particularly in the preparation of fowls." (See page 333).
    [3] This information seems nowhere recorded in the diary.
    [4] Porters.

These abject beings will spend near a day in hewing out a joist or beam of pine, with their miserable axes; and then carry it 20 miles upon their backs, to sell it for half a dollar!

Having heard much said of a place known as "el Desierto," near three miles, in a S.S.westerly direction from Cuaximalpa, I resolved to visit it this evening, in company with three of our party, and a little Mexican guide: and, as the route was represented as rather declivitous (though it did not prove so much so), we set out on foot. It proved to be the ruins of an extensive ancient convent, in a romantic spot of the mountains, reared to promote the subjection of these mountain Indians, I dare say more than two centuries ago; and abandoned for the last half century —that is, ever since the expulsion of the Jesuits. But there were yet to be seen the remains of a vast convent, with its cells, and vaults, and chapels, and turrets. As in most other similar places, there was a traditionary report, that the Jesuits had left immense sums of their treasure concealed here. This had induced several of our countrymen to visit the place during the occupation of Mexico, and to dig up the floor, and into the walls, in many places, but all without success.

Frid. 27—Course 240° 6 m. to main dividing ridge of Cordillera or Sierra Madre (and ½ m. further to Fabrica de Aguardiente)—thence 260° 3 or 4 m. to a hill, whence to Toluca, 260° —to Lerma 255°, 8 or 10 m.—nooned.—This morning on leaving Cuaximalpa, we were called upon for toll (peage), and I had to pay four dollars for my little wagon, and other things in proportion! The road being kept in pretty good repair, however, the paying of this excessive toll was not so unpleasant, as to experience the ill-breeding & rascality of the agents. The road is a government affair; and was first opened through this mountain by the Spanish Government at a great expense.—Lerma is a village of some consideration—say one to 2000 souls—handsomely situated on what is virtually an elevated island, in a marsh (during the rainy season, a lake) of this valley of Toluca.

The valley of Toluca bears no small resemblance to that of Mexico: extensive—surrounded by mountains (even a snow-capt one to southward of Toluca—filled up with *pueblos*, villages, *haciendas, & ranchos*—very fertile, even more so apparently than that of Mexico—it presents a most beautiful appearance, as we descend from the heights to the eastward.—From Lerma, 283°—10 m. to Toluca—straight road, as it is level plain: that through the mountains back, is very serpentine, of course.

Toluca is the capital of the state of Mexico; and though presenting no great elegance of architecture, it is a pleasant-looking city, and of interest as being the emporium of this fertile valley. Population, I suppose, some 15,000. We stopped at the *Meson de San Rafael, ó el Pósito.*

Sat. 28—360° 1 m.—310° 6 m.—325° 8 m. to Rio de Lerma. —Nooned—crossed.—This is the head branch of the Rio Grande de Guadalajara—which we first crossed at Lerma.—5° 3 m. 232° 5 m. to Ixtlahuaca.—Pop. say 2,000.—Stopped at Meson de San Francisco.

Sun. 29—275° 5 m. (having crossed Lerma river again (on a bridge as at the other two points) a mile after leaving town.)— 283° 6 m. to Venta de S. José. Thence 330° 6 or 8 m. to opposite the Hac. de Mazapuí.—Here we stopped to noon. While engaged at dinner, our animals passed over upon a corn-field; but were soon driven off again. The damage was virtually nothing, as the young corn, scarcely 3 inches high would soon recover from the simple clipping of its blades. Notwithstanding, a young upstart of a fellow, named Manuel Mª Carmona, and calling himself proprietor of the hacienda, came galloping up; and, with insupportable insolence, accused us of being barbarians—ignorant of the *derechos de gentes*[5]—demanding payment, in conclusion, for what he called damages. However well I might have been disposed to gratify him, had he saluted us in a gentlemanly

[5] Civilized customs, laws of nations.

manner, I now of course was unwilling to be bullied into an injustice: I therefore told him, that as there was virtually no damage done, and I was not disposed to reward his ill-breeding, he could go as he came. Upon this he galloped away in a great flurry, swearing he would have me in the hands of the Alcalde in less than a twinkling: and truly, the demonstrations soon became very formidable: in ten minutes, a dozen rancheros, armed with lances came galloping up—soon another dozen—and so on—till we had quite a troop around us, ordering me to present myself, without delay, before the alcalde of S. Felipe, a village two or three miles distant. I told them that it was necessary that the alcalde or his agent (with sufficient evidence that he was such) should first present himself before *me*, and I would then respect him; but without this, I was not disposed to go so much out of my way upon the mere word of a band of what seemed to me to be very much like robbers. After much capering about upon their ponies and flourishing their lances (for they seemed to be aware that I was not so desperate as to be willing to imbue my hands in their blood), a personage came riding up, who was pointed out to me as the said alcalde—called Lino Ponce de Leon. I rode out to meet and salute him; and found this functionary altogether polite and civil. He said there was no need for all this hubbub, and requested that I should go with him to examine the damage. I did so, accompanied by his "secretary"—when the latter—upon looking over the field—exclaimed, "And is this all that 'scape goat has called us here for? We are pretty tools to be dragged about in this style!" And the Alcalde, turning to me said, "You will please excuse us for giving you so much molestation for nothing: we will accompany you back to your party; and you can go your way, with my best wishes." He fulfilled his word, and we parted after the exchange of an infinity of civilities. I was unable to determine whether the judge was really in good earnest,—or it were only a *ruse* to get out of what he considered a bad scrape; for it was natural to suppose that he thought it no child's play to force us into any measures of injustice. Nevertheless, I felt charitable enough to believe the former.

Thence, 330° 2 m.—305° 8 m. to Venta de la Jordana—a mere Meson, without other buildings.

Mon. 30—275° 3 or 4 m. to Venta del Aire.—305° 10 m. to Tepetongo (hacienda of 50 souls perhaps.)—Nooned.—P.M. 300° 5 or 6 m.—265° 8 m.—south, ½ m. to Venta Colorada.— 270° 1 m. 260° 8 or 9 m. to Maravatío. Stopped at Meson de Santa Teresa. This is a town of some consideration, containing some 3,000 or 4,000 inhabitants. It being the first place of any importance in the state of Michoacan (having crossed the boundary between this and the state of Mexico in a little ridge of mountains, a few miles east of Tepetongo) I was now obliged to get out *pases*[6] for my equipage, etc., and of course to suffer hereafter, all the annoyance of presenting to the *Garita,* and to the *aduanas*[7] of the internal customs or consumption duties. These have been abolished in the State of Mexico, and the Federal District; and it is to be hoped that the good example will be followed soon by the other states. Nothing is surely more annoying to commerce,—and very especially to the traveller—to be subject to have his baggage examined and detained at every town he enters: for though they profess that it is not necessary that be examined or even presented at the C.H. yet, with the excuse of there being a little more than they suppose a man ought to carry of baggage, etc. there is never wanting an excuse to give his trunks an overhauling, as occurred to me in Querétaro: and, afterward,[8] I had, even in Morelia, a good deal of molestation, by being stopped at the *garita*—taken to the C.H. and though they dispensed with an examination, my *pase* was detained till my de-

6 Permits.

7 Customhouses.

8 This reference evidences the fact that Gregg's diary entries were not impromptu; he evidently views these experiences in retrospect. When he had some leisure, he would write from memory, or possibly from rough jottings, which he destroyed, and make his account a flowing one with a reasonable degree of finish.

parture, which subsequently occasioned some detention. But I ought to add that no where else—not even in Guadalajara,— did I suffer any further moles[ta]tion, in this regard, except the mere presentation at the *garitas:* the officers of these, always told me politely that I could at once go my way.

❀ DIARY, MAY, 1849

Tues. 1—314° 3 m:—300° 2 m.—350° 2 m. to Pueblo de Tarandacuán.—260° 5 m. to Luna (nooned)—265° 8 m. to Acámbaro. This is a town of no inconsiderable importance, in the state of Guanajuato.—Pop. would seem to be 6 to 8,000 souls. Here I obtained an observation for latitude, which I had failed to do, owing to cloudy weather, since I left Toluca.

Here there was what is termed a "Topardo de Gallos,"[9] and a collection of a considerable concourse of people. This is a mode of bringing about a sort of semi-*feria*—by advertising that there will be bull and cock fights, dances, etc. for three or four days, which brings together all the idlers and curious, of the neighboring villages—some with their goods, wares, fruits, knickknacks, etc. for sale; but the larger portion for the object of gambling— and a large number for even more dishonest purposes. Gambling houses and tables are exposed in every corner and square, and a large number are always occupied in gaming and stealing—the latter with very little restraint—the former none at all.

Wed. 2—250° 3 m.—220° 2 m. & back to Acambaro 33°— 185° 2 m.—[MARGINAL NOTE: Acámbaro is but a short distance from Rio Lerma—Maravatio said to be 3 or 4 m.] 180° 1 m. to Rancho de Santa Clara. In this vicinity (and hence to Zinapé-cuaro) saw abundance of very pretty obsidian (in small pieces), and it is said that hereabouts, great numbers of Indian arrow-points, knives, hatchets, etc. of same had been picked up.—180° 1 m.—208° 5 m. to Zinapécuaro—Nooned.—Pop. 4 or 5,000.

[9] A place for cock fights.

Here we were called on again for *peage* or toll. This was a much less amount, but it was the more ridiculous as there was scarcely any visible improvement made upon the road.

From the heights, two or three miles before reaching Zinapécuaro, we had a view of the lake of Cuitzéo, off to the northwestward. This inconsiderable "pond" of water, being said to extend from east to west from 10 to 20 l. from Arason to Chucándaro, with a width of one to 5 leagues. Rio de Lerma passes beyond, instead of through it, as I had supposed.—P.M. 215° 6 or 8 m. to Hac. de Querendaro—230° to Pueblo de San Lucas (off to left)—same, 3 m. to Indaparapéo—Pop. say 2,000. Stopped at Meson de la Purísima.—This evening's travel was through a most delightful green, grassy, and cultivated valley. —Waters running toward Lag. de Cuitzeo.

Thurs. 3—225° 8 m. to Charo, which, though said to have been incorporated a city contains little over 1000 souls, and but a village in appearance.—255° 4 m.—220° 7 or 8 m. to Morelia. Stopped at Meson de Santa Teresa (?) about on parallel with Square—& near 200 yds. to west of Catedral.

Morelia presented a most beautifully verdant appearance, on approaching it from the heights to the eastward. A glimpse of the houses and streets were only to be seen here and there, through the foliage of the trees which adorned the backyards, and the gardens. The fact is, the situation is decidedly beautiful, as being a sort of flat knoll, with a gradual descent in every direction, even in that of the heights to the east, with which it is immediately connected. The elevation of the main *plaza* is 50 to 100 feet above the level of the creek which passes to westward. The city is abundantly watered by an aqueduct from a spring a few miles to S. eastward.

This city was founded about 1540 (See notes elsewhere for exact date—and other data),[10] by a vice-roy from Valladolid, whence the city bore this latter name, till after the Mexican In-

[10]This "date—and other data" is found nowhere in the diaries.

dependence, when it was christened Morelia, in honor of the partizan of independence, Morelos.[11]

I brought a letter of recommendation from D. Mariano Otero[12] (late or first Secretario de Relaciones [under] President Herrera), to Gov[r] D. Juan Bautista Cevallos; and I must not only feel under lasting obligations to the governor for his attentions—for statistical data, etc. he furnished me—for a MS. map of the state he loaned me, to copy—but for an order he gave me, addressed to the authorities on the way, and which might, had occasion presented, have been of infinite benefit to me; as it commanded that I should be supplied and aided with everything I need—that no embarrassment whatever should be thrown in my way, and that, if necessary, I should be furnished with an escort, at any point required.

Mon. 7—We arrived at Morelia, at midday on the 3[d] and I intended leaving on 5th; but on the evening of the 4th, I was attacked with a severe chill and fever, by which I was confined to my bed for two days, so that we did not get under way again till this morning: and even now I was barely able to ride: but though I had to endure excessive fatigues I continued to regain my strength rapidly.

Courses, etc. $255°$ 5 m.—$272°$ 6 m.—$245°$ 2 m. to rancho de Cuto—nooned—. P.M. $300°$ 2 m. $320°$ 3 m. to rancho de Tiristiran.

I shall not soon forget this place, for the misfortunes and adventures which fell to my lot hereabouts. In the afternoon, descending a steep rocky bank, with much carelessness on the part of the wagoner, the wagon was completely upset; though

[11] José María Morelos was the successor of Hidalgo in the War for Independence. He was a priest who was an intrepid fighter and a commander of ability, well deserving his title, "the hero of a hundred battles." He was, however, ultimately captured and shot at San Cristóbal Ecatepec in December, 1815.

[12] Don Mariano Otero was an able editor and statesman whom Gregg doubtless would have termed "an honest patriot." As senator from the state of Jalisco he was a strong influence in the *Moderados*, the party of moderation in the adjustments following the war. Gregg, however, may be mistaken about the cabinet position (Minister of [Foreign] Affairs).

contrary to my fears, with but little other apparent damage than the breaking of some of the bows, and the like. We soon had it upright again, and the loading replaced, but as we had advanced only a mile or two further over a terribly rocky road, when the hind axle-tree suddenly broke, and the wagon was again upon the ground. This was a much more serious accident than the first; for to reach the rancho of Tiristiran, near a mile ahead, was a very difficult matter; and then to make a rear axle, without either workmen or tools, was still more so. Obtaining a strong pole, however, we placed it under the broken axletree, the hind end upon the ground, and the fore end raised and tied to the wagon-body, in such a manner as to sustain that side of the wagon, and serve as a sled-runner. In this condition the wagon was pulled to the rancho.

Early next morning, I turned out in search of a stick of timber, which would serve to make a new axle; yet this was a much more difficult matter than I had at first imagined; for, the surrounding hills being covered with oaks, I expected to find a suitable tree directly; yet the oaks were all so scrubby, crooked and knotty, that, in reality I could find nothing which seemed to answer the purpose: and though I had a stick cut, I afterward found that the very pole which we had used to convey the wagon to the rancho was still better: so I set two Mexicans to work—called carpenters; that is, they know how to make Mexican ploughs. Their instruments consisted of a wedge-shapen axe, which, with the blade turned lengthwise, in the mortise of one handle, served for a chopping axe—and crosswise in another handle, for an adze. They had no auger; but were able to make the necessary holes in the timbers with a narrow chisel.

But never having seen the axle-tree of a wagon before, it would have been impossible for them to construct anything that would have served the purpose, had I not understood myself pretty well how it should be done: in fact, was able even to execute similar work, had I been possessed of suitable tools: but I confess

I could do nothing with the hermaphrodite axe and adze of the Mexican "carpenters."

My father having been a farmer, as well as skilled in several branches of mechanism, he taught his sons the "use of tools," how to do any little "jobs" which presented themselves about the farm, such as repairing ploughs, wagons, etc. telling us that it might sometime "come in play," and prove useful to us. And verily, I have since often found this to be the case; for, in my travels upon the Great Prairies, I hardly know how I should have got along had I not been able to repair a wagon, a gun, and any utensil of the road, when it became necessary. On the present occasion, I had not a single man in my company who could even use a chopping axe, much less do any other sort of wood-work. I had therefore to superintend the whole operations. My "carpenters" could only venture to act where I showed them.

By the night of the 8th we had the axle-tree very well fitted, however, and ought to have had it fixed in its place early next morning; yet the blacksmith's work, now presented about as great difficulties. A Mexican smith was sent for, to repair the broken irons of the axle, which he executed so wretchedly [that] they broke over and over again, before we could get them fastened in. Nevertheless, the poor fellow seemed to do his utmost; and I was even surprised that he was able to do as good work as he did, as his bellows consisted of two little patched-up, cylindrical "blow-flaps," with wooden pipes, and his anvil a block of granite! With all these drawbacks, however, we should have got under way again, after dinner, had not a severe rain and hail-storm come up in the afternoon.

Thurs. *10*—Having everything ready and the wagon reloaded the previous evening, we moved out this morning very early; and were gratified to see that our new axle-tree performed much better than the old one had done.

We experienced no little fright late yesterday evening. Our animals having been turned out to water, after having been chilled by the cold rain, they seemed to fancy they needed a little active exercise: so commencing to caper about, until their spirits were up, they scampered away, in a perfect *stampede:* yet when they got their play out, they were brought back by those who followed them.

From Tiristiran 305° 8 or 9 m.—260° 3 m. to Hac. de Tecacho (2 or 300 inhabitants.)—280° 7 or 8 m. to Punto de Juripitiro, a rancho, where we slept, having nooned two miles west of Tecacho.

Frid. 11—295° 15 m. to Zipeméo—Haciendas, say 300 souls —nooned—same course, 8 m. to Caurio—rancho of say 300 souls. This being looked upon as rather a rascally place, I sent for the *alcalde,* and showed him my order from the governor, telling him I should hold him responsible for any thefts, etc. committed upon me. This seemed to frighten him, and he at once collected some *pelados*[13] as a guard for us; but not only because it rained very severely, but because I considered them of no sort of utility, I sent them away again.

Sat. 12—250° 5 m.—300° 8 or 9 m. to Mula (pop. say 300) —Perépero, a considerable town, three or four miles southward —nooned a little west of Mula.—260° 2 m. 300° 3 m. to Tlasasalca—a town of a thousand inhabitants, or more. In this, the houses are all covered with burned clay tile roofs, which, being the first roofs of the kind we had seen, to any amount, gave the town a singular appearance, as we descended from the hills.— Thence, 275° 6 m. to a ridge.—& 270° 5 or 6 m. to Hac. de Santiaguillo—pop. scarce 100.

Sun. 13—280° 1 m.—247° 3 m. to Zamora. This is the second city in the state of Michoacan; and, in fact, Gov. Cevallos told me, it was the first, in population. This, however I am disposed to doubt, very much, for I believe the population to be considerably less than that of Morelia (say 12,000, at most—in fact,

[13] *Pelado* is a term of oppobrium used to indicate low class Mexicans—the equivalent of the Americanism, *greaser.*

some intelligent citizens told us 8 or 10,000), while that of
Morelia must approach 20,000—at any rate cannot descend below 15,000. And then the general appearance of the place is altogether inferior. Two-story houses are very rare, and even those
of one, display no elegance of architecture; while in Morelia we
see many very good edifices. In Zamora the houses are nearly all,
if not quite, covered with red tiles, like those of Tlasasalca, which
imparts to it the same unique appearance. [MARGINAL NOTE: I
was informed in Zamora that the appearance of an American
there was very rare—only one California party had passed that
way; and previously, scarce half a dozen Americans, or indeed
foreigners of any kind had ever visited the place.]

Not intending to remain here but a few hours, I was anxious
to get an observation for longitude, by altitude of moon, as well
as distances between this and sun; and as the former was getting
very low, it was necessary to be in very much of a hurry. Therefore, as soon as we entered the "Meson de la Parisiana," I got
out my instruments, but the operation excited so much curiosity
among the idlers, and elicited such a crowd, that it was almost
impossible to do anything. Therefore, owing to the trembling of
the artificial horizon, which they occasioned, all I could do was
to take a few imperfect lunar distances.

We did not get off from Zamora till two o'clock,—thence 320°
3 m. to a creek from north-eastward—same 1 m.—330° 4 m. to
hill (Sauceda one mile back, more north)—320° 1 m. to opposite San Simon (hac.) on the other side of river—30° 1 m. 310°
4 m. to Ixtlan—Pop. say, 500.

At Zamora, I had been told there were hot springs at Ixtlan,
but, I had supposed them of no importance. As we approached
the town (a mile back) after dark, my attention was attracted
by some vapor, and a roaring of water, which I at first thought, a
fall of the river, not far distant. I turned off to the point, and
was surprised to find the smoke and noise both to issue from a
blubbering spring. I got down, and was still more surprised to

find the water insupportably hot to the hand. I saw several of same kind, before reaching the village; but, as it was dark, I deferred any further examination till next morning.

Mon. 14—I visited the *Boiling* Springs (as I now found they truly were, early this morning, with my thermometer; and, if I was before surprised, I was now astounded to observe their temperature. I counted near 30 in all, though but 5 or 6 bold-running springs—the most distant N. east of Ixtlan about a mile —and scattered thence, in the valley on both sides of the road to within half a mile. I was told there exists many others in the neighborhood which I did not see. Their temperature was generally from 201° to 204° (Fahrenheit) and in one the thermometer rose half a degree higher, 204½°! evidently two or three degrees hotter than boiling water at this elevation, which is about ———— feet above the sea—the Barometer standing at 25.16, where water will boil at about 202°? These springs (the water) contain some foreign matter, as soda, especially in the form of common salt; also the sulphate, with some free sulphur, and perhaps potash.

From Ixtlan, 305° 6 m. to rancho to northward,—same course, on straight line, 6 or 7 m. to La Barca; but by road, 333° 4 m. to Buenavista—270° 5 m. to La Barca, on N.W. bank of Rio Grande, here known as Rio de la Barca—above as Rio de Lerma.

Here it was necessary to ferry this river, as, though fordable for those who were well acquainted, it was too deep, for us to pass it with the wagon. There being nothing but some large clumsy canoes, we had to unload, and carry the wagon over in a pair of canoes, placed side by side. The rascally ferrymen then imposed a charge of six dollars for the wagon and its loading, which is, I suppose, at least three times as much as any regulations would allow them: the animals were driven over. Width about 50 yds. La Barca appears to contain from 2 to 4,000 inhabitants.

P.M. 316° 5 m. to Hac. de S. José—300° 3 m. to Rancho de

la Esperanza. We slept here; but should have gone further—in fact, we should have stayed at Jamay, near the border of the lake (of Chapala, had we not missed our road in the evening, and finally took that by Esperanza; whereby we did not come upon the immediate border of this famous lake, thus losing a good view of it.—From Esperanza back to la Barca, 126°.

Tues. 15—280° 3 m.—240° 8 or 10 m. to Ferry near Ocotlan. Here we had to react the scenes at La Barca: but, in about 2 hours were all safely across the river and ready to travel again. This is the outlet of the lake of Chapala, or continuation of Rio de Lerma —known from here to the ocean, I believe generally as Rio Grande de Santiago.

After crossing the river, I rode upon a hill near by, and thus had a pretty good view of the middle portion of *la Laguna de Chapala*.

Our route now led down the southern valley of the river, till we passed Atiquiza. From ferry, 310° 3 m.—275° 3 or 4 m. to Village of Santa Cruz.—Same course 5 m. to Pueblo de Poncitlan —a town of 1000 or more inhabitants. Here there is a series of falls, of a ledge of rocks, in all of about 15 feet perpendicular, in the distance of less than 50 yards. This is an absolute barrier to navigation, without locks: but there are others of less importance, above Atiquiza; and still another of much greater, at Juanacatlan, 10 m. below the latter place. Had I known of this, I should certainly have passed that way. I have since been assured that the fall of Juanacatlan, is not only perpendicular of about 50 feet; but over a ledge of shelving rocks, so that a person may pass dry entirely under the *chute* of water. The volume of water passing down this river, at this dry season is not considerable: we might compare it perhaps to that of the Potomac, at lowest stage.

Wed. 16—280° 4 or 5 m. to San Miguel (small hac.) 260° 5 or 6 m. to S. Jacinto (Do.)—256° 6 m. to Atiquiza, large hacienda, which, including the pueblo on east side, may contain a pop. of near 1000 souls.—Nooned.—290° 5 m. to Hac. de San Antonio—Pop. say 200.

Frid. *17*—315° 12 m. to ridge,—then 350° 4 m. to Guadalajara. [MARGINAL NOTE: With regard to the route I came from Mexico to Guadalajara, I have to remark that, as far as Morelia, the road is pretty fair, and when the repairs which are now under way are finished, it will be a decidedly good wagon road: but from Morelia to Zamora, it is equally bad. For the first 20 miles west of Morelia the route is generally very rocky—and so it is in several other places, for miles together. Just east of Tecacho we had a very bad rocky hill to descend, and the descent into the valley of Zamora—6 or 8 m. from the city is still worse, as it is longer. From Zamora to Guadalajara the [way] was again pretty good. Nevertheless, the bad portions might be remedied with no very great labor, and the whole way made a good wagon road. As it is, the regular rout[e] via Querétaro is doubtless far preferable for wheeled vehicles.] This city is situated in a handsome valley, though of rather low appearance, and contains a population, says Gov. Angúlo, of about 70,000 souls, being the second city in size, and perhaps first in manufactures, in the republic. There are several extensive cotton factories in its vicinity; and it is famous for the manufacture of several kinds of earthen ware, as well as other branches of industry. It was founded says the Governor, in 1531.—Pop. of whole state (upon authority of same) 700,000. The same informed me that there were many rich silver mines in the state, though but few of gold, at present.

I brought a letter of introduction also from D. Mariano Otero (to whom I remain under lasting obligations, for I had no personal acquaintance with Sor. Otero—they were obtained by my friend Don Domingo Ybarra, senator from Puebla, to whom I am also under heavy debt of gratitude)—I say I also brought a letter from Otero to Gov. Angúlo, of this state. The governor treated me with great courtesy, though his kind offices were not of as substantial a character as those of Gov. Cevallos: for though

I intimated to him that a similar document would be more valuable and acceptable than an escort he offered me, and he promised to give it to me, in a pass-port; yet when this came, I found it but a printed form, which he extended to every body: therefore, I could feel under no special obligations to him on this score.

Sun. 20—Today, one of my party, Robert Callender, suddenly rose from the table, while eating dinner, exclaiming that he was very warm; and, before he could reach the door, fell in the floor. He was immediately carried out, and I was notified of it. I found him senseless, with symptoms a good deal resembling an epileptic fit; but I soon found it was something more serious even; and he expired in less than 5 minutes. There was most probably the rupture of a blood vessel about the heart: I afterward learned that he had complained of some disease about this organ. I had him buried as decently, on the following day, as circumstances would admit,—in Catholic Campo Santo of Belen—he being a Catholic. By this misfortune we were detained a day or two longer in Guadalajara than I had contemplated.

To-day, we had the celebration of the anniversary of one of those *pronunciamientos*, with which the Mexican Calendar is so overflooded. This one is for the revolution which re-established the Federal form of government, in 1846. At night we had a grand illumination in the principal square, with several bands of music.—I stopped in the *Meson de* S. Jose, but one square to S. eastward of principal plaza. This is a most wretched inn, and kept by a still more rascally *administrador*. But what is remarkable, is that the Mesones in the city of Mexico, as well as here and in other principal cities, are not as good as we frequently find them in the smaller towns and even villages on the main highways.

The first very hot weather I have experienced, was but two or three days before our arrival at Guadalajara, and it has continued pretty constantly since. It has been remarked by travellers —and it seems with some truth, though without my being able to account for it, that people perspire much less freely in these high plains, than in low-lands—which makes the heat more oppressive.

Wed. 23—315° 5 m. to Zapópan (creeks one & 2 m. back)—300° 1 m. to forks road—265° 10 m. to Venta del Astillero (nooned)—275° 5 m.—295° 10 m. to rancho del Arenal.— The Governor of the state of Jalisco, Sr. Angúlo, having urged upon me to take an escort of Mexican soldiers, five dragoons or rather of the state cavalry, made their appearance this morning, under command of a sergeant, and placed themselves at my orders. They seemed to me so useless, however—ridiculous the idea of 5 Mexican soldiers to be guarding 6 foreigners, I should not have taken them at all, except not to *desairar*[14] the governor; so they continued with me to day, and I sent them back next morning. [MARGINAL NOTE: Mr. Addicks separated from us at Guadalajara, but an additional German having joined me, we were still 6 foreigners in number. Add to these our diputado[15] and servant and 2 arrieros, which made 10 in all.] We may very fairly judge of the service these troops are as a guard, when we are informed that but the very evening before, a command of a dozen or more were chased into the rancho of Astilleros by a party of robbers. Nevertheless, our doughty guard made many indications of their bravery, secure of their own protection at least, as long as they were with us. Late in the evening, a few miles east of Arenal, they pointed ahead, and very exultingly exclaimed, "Do you see what is hanging yonder? They are *tifes* (corrupted from Eng. *thief*): that is the way we serve them["]: and in fact, I perceived three Carcasses dang[l]ing by the neck in the air, to a gallows erected for the purpose, by the road-side! "And are those some of those fellows who chased your comrades yesterday evening?" I inquired. "O, no," they replied, "those have been hanging there near a twelve-month! They are of a party of some 300 robbers, who collected together from various

14 Slight, disregard.   15 Deputy.

parts of the republic, and made an inroad here: those three ring-leaders were caught, shot and hanged; and they have been swinging there ever since!"—When we approached, I found they had dried into perfect mummies. Over their heads was painted, in large letters, the following inscription: *"Así castiga la ley á los ladrones y los asesinos."*[16] This very forcibly reminded one of the "scare-crows"—or dead crows—so frequently hung up in corn fields, as a protection against these mischievous animals: but this expedient against the robbers is not near as efficient; as will appear when we are informed that it was scarce at gun-shot distance from this very spot that a command of troops were chased into their quarters, yesterday evening, by a party of these light-foot gentry.

Thurs. 24—320° 6 or 8 m. to Amatitlan (village of near 1000 souls)—290° 10 m. to Tequila—nooned—Pop. say 3,000.— This place is famous for the manufacture of a sort of *mezcal* (distilled liquor) from a species of the *maguey* (agava Americana) known by the name of the *mezcal*—and seeming to differ from the common maguey, only in the blade's being narrower—and it is said not to produce *pulque.* [MARGINAL NOTE: It is very remarkable, that since passing the *Sierra Madre,* near Mexico, we have met with comparatively little pulque: & scarcely any at all from the time we descended into the valley of Rio Grande.] The entire plains and valleys, for several miles before reaching Tequila, are planted with *Mezcal:* virtually nothing else is cultivated, save in some gardens, and an occasional field or two of Indian corn, in the borders of the town. So celebrated has this place become, for the manufacture of superior *mezcal,* that that taken from here is known by the name of *Tequila.* It is manufactured from the onionlike bulb over the root of the plant, by roasting it in a kiln—"mashing" it or macerating it in skin vats, until it ferments, when the liquor is distilled in a sort of Alambique, as in the manufacture of ordinary whiskey.

[16] Thus the law punishes thieves and assassins.

P.M.—5° 1½ m. 300° 2½ m. 250° 5 m. to Obsidian ridge—
275° 3 m. to Magdalena—Pop. say 1,500.—On a high ridge
from 3 to 5 m. back from Magdalena, there were immense quantities of—in fact, in most places, nothing else but—obsidian, of
fair quality. Magdalena is situated at the border of a small lake
(four or five miles long), which presents a very pretty view, from
the elevation on descending to the town.

Frid. 25—305° 6 or 8 m. to Quemada (ranchito)—300° 10
or 12 m. to Venta de Mochitiltic (only a Meson.)—nooned—
P.M. West one mile to border of *Barrancas*—N.W. 3 m.—S.W.
2 m. to rancho of Barrancas.

I should have mentioned before, that, from the very bad accounts given of the road from Guadalajara on, I sold my wagon
in that city, and employed one Santiago Cepeda, with half a
dozen mules to carry on my luggage. Though the road was represented as being generally out of repair and bad (which I found
to be true) this was the point—Las Barrancas—which was chiefly
dreaded—as being utterly impassable with a laden wagon. And
although I did not find this place quite as bad as I had expected,
it is nevertheless a wretched pass to take wheeled vehicles
through. The descent from the east is the worst, and some narrow ragged passes down the ravine, afterward. To get down the
mountain hill, a sort of road is dug down the precipitous descent,
so narrow, tortuous and steep, in many places, that no road
wagon could be taken down it, without imminent risk occasionally of being tumbled over a precipice of 100 feet. Nevertheless,
I perceived that, with some care, I might have brought my light
wagon over the pass, by unloading it; and even was led to regret
a little that I had sold it; as there are to me so many inconveniences (or want of conveniences) in travelling with pack-mules.
—The lowest part of this immense gorge is about 2,000 feet
below the bordering hills from whence we descended. The little
creeks below afforded abundance of water, and the narrow valleys through which they wound, are fertile, and planted chiefly

in *plátanos*[17]—where they were sold at the rate of from three to five cents per dozen.

One Sor. Gomez, diputado in the general Congress from Lower California, with a small coach, had joined my party from Guadalajara for security. He had occasioned me a great deal of trouble heretofore, as it was necessary for my pack-mules to take circuitous rout[e]s, frequently, much out of the way, to accompany him on the coach road. But here, having made no provision for assistance (which is universal[ly] done by those who attempt to take carriages over this place) our trouble was redoubled. Being unable to stop my mules for him, I left two men to aid him, and I continued on to the stopping-place. In a short time these came up with the fearful account that Sor. Gomez's carriage had tumbled topsy-turvey over a steep *barranca*, and made a perfect smash of everything! "And we did not remain to aid him longer," they added, "because, instead of seeming thankful, he showed himself angry with us, after our having done our utmost for him." I at once went back with another of my party, it being now after dark. I found Sor. Gomez sitting, very composedly smoking his cigar, looking on at some awkward Mexicans, who were endeavoring to extricate the coach from the tops of a copse of underbrush upon which it had lodged below. I with my comrade, at once went to work, and having some experience in wagon difficulties, we soon hauled out the coach, piece by piece, and set it up again in the road—astonished to find that it had suffered no perceptible damage except the breaking of the glasses of the windows—thanks to the elasticity of the brush upon which it had fallen. "All set" again, I had a rope fastened to the body, and two men placed to hold it at every declivity to avoid a repe-[ti]tion of the accident. So that, about midnight, we reached the rancho of Barrancas in safety.—I could not but note, in Sor. Gomez, the same that my men had complained of—an ill-humored manner; and when we stopped at our "camp," he prepared

[17] Bananas.

319

himself a cup of chocolate, and very composedly despatched it in my presence—although I had incidentally mentioned to him before, that, in my hurry to come to his relief, I had left before supper.—Next morning his countenance continued to indicate the same ill-humor: yet, notwithstanding his signs of ingratitude, I continued to aid him out of every difficulty; for he and his servant were both perfect cyphers in this business; until (I might as well here add, not to be troubled with his name again) we descended into the valley of Tepic; when,—there being no more bad road—he made an excuse to slip ahead, and I never saw him afterward—although he resided in Tepic with his family!

Sat. 26—245° 3 or 4 m.—270° 10 or 12 m. to Ixtlan (pop. 2 or 3,000)—nooned.—It has been very notable on this road to see the number of bottles of *mezcal* by the road-side—at almost every *jacal*,[18]—for sale to travellers,—which I look upon as anything but creditable to the sobriety of the American character: for they have doubtless sprung up chiefly, since the "gold-fever" has brought so many foreigners along this route.—P.M. 270° 3 m. to Mizpa—same 5 m. to Aguacatlan—Pop. would seem to be 4 or 5,000.

Sun. 27—270° 5 m.—285° 5 m. to a malpais—300° 2 m. 330° 3 or 4 m. to rancho de Tititlan—nooned.—P.M. 330° 1 m. —310° 2 m. to Santa Isabel—320° 6 or 8 m. to Ocotillo.

Mon. 28—345° 8 m.—355° 7 m. to San Leonel—Nooned. —307° 20 m. to Tepic. This place is situated in a handsome valley among several little mountains, and on the south side of a pretty little river running off to north westwardly to Rio Grande. It has become of importance chiefly as the residence of some of the most wealthy merchants of San Blas, (the latter place being very unhealthy) and as a sort of emporium of the San Blas trade. The population of Tepic is 10 to 12,000. It is about 50 miles distant from San Blas.

Thurs. 31—Being a little detained in Tepic—as well to make observations etc. as to prepare all my heavy luggage to be sent

[18] Hut.

to San Blas for shipment, we did not get under way from Tepic
till 4 o'clock this P.M.—Having re-engaged my man, Arriero
Santiago to carry my baggage on to Mazatlan.

From Tepic, 310° 18 or 20 m. to Hac. de Ingenio (say 100
souls). Our descent has been very rapid this P.M. and road bad
for wheeled vehicles, on account of the asperities. My last available Barometer tube having broken in Tepic, I was now unable
to determine our change of elevation. When in New York last,
I had cast at the factory of ———— in Jersey City, half a dozen
barometer tubes; but owing doubtless to the carelessness and ill-
faith of the workmen, they broke, without the least violence (by
the mere effect of the atmosphere—the first in Pittsburgh, and
the last in Tepic) until I am now left without means of making
barometrical observations!

☼ DIARY, JUNE, 1849

Frid. 1—260° 8 or 9 m.—300° 8 or 9 m.— & nooned at Ranchito in valley of Rio Grande, though some distance from river.

P.M. about N.W. 6 m. to Santiago. Here we deemed it most
prudent to ferry the Rio Grande again (half a mile above the
town); though the animals forded it without any difficulty, being
scarcely over 3 feet deep at any place. Width say 100 yards—
with a gentle current.

Sat. 2—360° 12 to 15 m. to San Pedro—nooned.—The Rio
de San Pedro, passing on the northern side of this rancho (say of
scarcely over 100 souls) is no inconsiderable stream in time of
high water, as its bed is about 100 yards wide—though its current is now reduced to that of an insignificant creek. Such is the
case with all the rivers of this country. Many that are now virtually dry, become large impassable streams during freshets.
This renders travelling very troublesome, in the rainy season, as
we find no boats, and rarely even a canoe to aid us in crossing
those temporary rivers.—P.M. North, say, 15 m. to Rosa Morada
—rancho of perhaps 200 souls.

Sun 3—350° 12 m. to Buenavista (a miserable little rancho destitute of every accommodation)—nooned.—P.M. 350° 5 m. —330° 10 m. to S. Francisco, another wretched little rancho, of I believe, but one or two families.

Mon. 4—310° 8 m. to Acaponeta, a town of some 2,000 souls —295° 7 m. to La Bayona—nooned—285° 4 m. to Los Cedazos. —We are unfortunate in our stopping-places; for we are to night again, at a most wretched little rancho (say 100 souls), and rascally at that—and equally destitute.

Tues. 5—As all hands were busy, endeavoring to get an early start this morning, they neglected to guard the mules as they were turned loose with the packs on; and when the packs were all on, we found that two mules were missing, and one of these carrying my two principal and most valuable baggage trunks. We at once galloped all around, but could find nothing. This was so remarkable—for two mules to wander off from their company, that I at once came to the conclusion that they had been stolen—which was easy enough, as the rancho was surrounded by thick underbrush, penetrated in every direction by innumerable path-ways. The matter seemed so evident, that I resolved upon a little bravadoing—even a little lynching seemed admissable, as there was no possible mode of attaining justice through any regular course of law. I therefore inquired for the alcalde, when a semi-naked Comanche-looking fellow was pointed out to me. I told him the circumstances, and added, "It is evident these mules have been driven away by some of your people. I hold you and the village responsible for them! You may expect to find your town converted into ashes in less than three hours, if my mules and baggage do not appear!" By those who are unacquainted with the character of these *rancheros,* this would seem a rather bold measure, when we consider that some 20 or 30 men inhabited the village; and we were only six! I now directed several of my company (who had already made extensive search) to go in different directions, and I galloped in another myself.

I had been out about half an hour; long enough, however, to leave most of my coat and pants, hanging in tags to the numerous thorny underbrush through which I had to tear my way,—when I heard the report of a gun—and then another, and another,—in pretty quick succession. Instead of considering this as the indication of a hostile encounter, as some would perhaps, under such circumstances, I took it as a sign that the lost property had been found. I therefore returned to the rancho, as soon as possible, and had the gratification to see the two mules with their loading all apparently safe. The story of their discovery was about this: The alcalde, frightened to no small degree, by my threats, set out at once, with two or three of his "subjects," and taking a small pathway through the brush, followed without any deviation (as those of my party who were watching assured), for a mile or two, until they came up with the mules. This was too remarkable to suppose the discovery accidental, and therefore served to confirm me in the opinion, that they knew exactly where to find them. Now, whether they intended stealing the mules and cargoes, or merely to hide them out, for the purpose of getting a reward for finding them, I cannot assert: the latter is very frequently practised in this country; yet the former was far the most probable intention. As to my menaces, I must confess that I never thought of executing that of burning the rancho: I only employed the threat as a substitute for more unpleasant measures, which I feared were indispensable to the recovery of my property: for, I repeat, that here, a resort to legal means would have been absolute nonsense: and I doubt not I owe the recovery of my clothing, etc. instruments, memoranda, and what available funds I had, to the measures I adopted.

From Cedazos, 295° 15 m. and nooned at a little rancho near the border of the sea-marsh, though the ocean itself represented as being yet more than 20 miles distant. Thence 300° 22 to 24 m. to Escuinapa, a town containing about 2,000 inhabitants.

Wed. 6—290° 3 or 4 m.—320° 5 or 6 m. 335° 5 m. to Rosario

—nooned.—P. M. 290° 10 m. to rancho—same 5 m.—325° 15 m. to Aguacaliente (a large hacienda or village— near 500 inhabitants) chiefly dedicated to manufacture of *mezcal:* similar to that of Tequila.

Thurs. 7—270° 8 m.—260° 7 m. to Presidio de Mazatlan—nooned.—P.M. 275° 20 to 25 m. to Puerto de Mazatlan—say 15 to 18 m. straight from Presidio. On leaving the Presidio (pop. say 2,000) I rode out ahead of the party to take a view of the town; and then inquired for the road to Mazatlan. I was showed one, I followed it for a short distance; but finding the packs did not come on, I went back into the town, and inquired which way they had gone. I was told they had gone one route— then another— & another—and even a fourth; until I became satisfied that the wicked fellows were only aiming to annoy me, and put me out of my way: so thought it most expedient to return to the *Meson* and "track" them, in accordance with Indian custom. By this means I discovered they had started out on neither of the routes that had been pointed out to me: and I was soon able to overtake them.—I was rather agreeably disappointed, in riding into Mazatlan, to find it a more considerable, better improved, and more pleasant looking place than I had expected to see. The most of the site is rather low; nevertheless I consider it decidedly handsome and romantic—surrounded or among several small hills—with half a dozen pretty little mountain islands, on the sea side to enliven the ocean view. The place, too, seems decidedly healthy—which is not the case with its competitor, San Blas: and though the harbor is not first rate, by any means, it is represented as being perhaps the best any where on this part of the Pacific Coast. I am therefore of impression that it is yet destined to become an important city: not, perhaps, under the present government; but under the more favorable auspices which I look upon as awaiting it.

I have long been of opinion that the Anglo-Saxon race is destined to govern the entire American continent, at no very distant period—especially North America.[19] And now do I believe, that this California "gold fever" will serve greatly to accelerate the matter. *Placeres*[20] have never been desirable; and when the precious metal gold begins to fail, the "thousand and tens of thousands" of adventurous spirits who have flocked there, will begin to look about for something else to do, commensurate with their inclinations. Enough there will be, inclined to till the soil, but this will not suit the characters alluded to. They must then commence scattering out among their neighbors—whether in a friendly or hostile manner—whether in search of gold or other fortune. In this way do I believe that all the Pacific coast will soon be occupied as far South as this place, and ultimately further. Thus with the California adventurers on the one side, and the invading spirit of Texas on the other, I see no chance for the existence of the present Mexican government. And the intelligent classes of citizens in all parts, seem sensible of the near approach of their political dissolution. But what can they do? They are without means to prevent it. They can only fold their arms and rest upon that very philosophic conclusion that "What is to be *will* be."

There is yet another circumstance which cannot fail to hasten this event: the passing of so large a portion of the California adventurers, across through the interior of Mexico, at so many points: not so much on account of the information they obtained of the character and resources of the country, as because of the insults, injustices and outrages they have so frequently suffered from the natives. It is inseparable from the character of a spirited and adventurous people, to retain the memory of injuries received, and to desire and seek an opportunity to show the oppressors that there is a day of retribution. I have heard of the perpetration of many such insults and outrages, and I am the

[19] Gregg outspokenly subscribes to the doctrine of "manifest destiny," which was much under discussion at the time of the Mexican War.

[20] Placer mines; from the Spanish *placer*, a sand or gravel bar bearing gold.

more disposed to credit them, from the fact of my not being able always to steer clear of them myself—notwithstanding the important advantages I possessed, not only of a knowledge of the language, character and customs of the people, but of the favor of many influential personages.

Mazatlan has become famous, if not notorious, at a distance, and especially in the capital of Mexico, on account of some *pronunciamentos* and the like, which had their origin here. One of these came off but a short time before my arrival. The authorities of Mexico, having taken it into their heads to send a new collector of customs, to take charge of that department here, it did not agree with the tastes of the merchants and people generally, I believe; so when the new functionary was approaching the town, a sort of mob was raised, and the unwelcome visitor chased away again by menaces, and even by stones: and he has not since ventured another attempt to take possession of his office; but has kept at a "respectful distance" from Mazatlan. I know not how far justice was on the side of the *Mazatlecos:* but as I have never been willing to admit the propriety [of] exercising "Lynch Law," except in very extreme cases, where there is no possibility of obtaining justice by other means (such as my affair at Cedazos, for example?),[21] I am constrained to condemn the procedure—else I must suppose that a similar condition of affairs existed, and that they were reduced to this dernier resort to do themselves justice. If I were to judge from my little acquaintance with the people—the very agreeable and reputable society to be found here—the just and order-loving character of the many with whom I became acquainted, I should be inclined to the latter conclusion: *quien sabe?*

At any rate, I must say for Mazatlan, that for the time I was in it, it seemed to me one of the most pleasant places I had visited

---

[21] The incident at Cedazos was the theft of the two mules with their valuable baggage trunks (see page 322f.). Gregg effected their return by dire threats. He presumably was gifted with a vocabulary strong invectively and minatorially.

in the republic. The fact, is, it is a good deal under foreign, and especially English control, wherefore the habits of the people seem to incline in that way.

To me the place has been still rendered the more agreeable, on account of finding here, my ancient and well-tried friend, (formerly of Chihuahua) Mr. John Kelly,[22] an Englishman, and one of the most extensive wholesale foreign merchants of the city. It is very pleasant to meet with a friend, under any circumstances—an old and worthy one, more especially, and very emphatically, in a foreign land, and yet still more so, in a land like Mexico! Though a "bachelor" when I last before saw him, Mr. Kelly had married in England, some 4 or 5 years ago; and now lived with his family, in very comfortable style. And the very great kindness and agreeableness of his amiable consort, will long be remembered by me, with sentiments of constant gratitude.

Mon. 25—As is my frequent custom, I rode out this morning in search of divers plants, fowls, etc. and rode an animal that I had never ridden before; and was therefore unacquainted with its habits. Seeing some fowls in a pond, I alighted and shot at them, without (as had been my custom) taking the precaution to tie my horse, which at the crack of the gun, broke away at full speed, leaving me not even "with the bag to hold"; for my saddlebags, in which I carried all my shooting tackle, though thrown but loosely across the saddle, and which I expected to tumble off every moment, still remained hanging upon the saddle as far as I could see the animal. I followed on, and, in about half a mile, met a Mexican leading my horse; but without the saddlebags. He professed to know nothing about them; and as I did not know but that they had fallen off, I could not accuse him of them. I galloped in different directions, but could hear nothing of them. I followed another road until I came up with a ranchero who had passed that way, and who assured me he had

[22] Nothing further has been obtained about Mr. Kelly.

seen them picked [up] at a certain hut, occupied by fruit-vendors, which he described to me. I returned, but the proprietor professed utter ignorance; yet as he was possessed of an exceedingly rougish countenance, I, in my anger, foolishly applied to the authorities; but of course I obtained nothing, and the rogue was left to grin at my simplicity. I was excessive annoyed at the loss, as the wallets contained the loading implements, etc. belonging to my Colt's gun and pistol, and which could not be replaced here. To the last I felt sure that the fruiterer, had taken them; and could I but have felt at liberty to take the measures I did at Cedazos, I feel very sure I should have obtained them. Yet now only another resource seemed to remain to me: this was to offer a greater reward than the whole affair could be sold for. This I did at once; yet my old rogue, whether from fear that I would suspect him—or from contrariness and revenge for my having accused him—or, what may be more probable, a hope that my anxiety about the articles would make me offer a still higher reward, they are still held back, and I fear I will have to leave without them.

While looking for my saddlebags, I shot a very pretty, and rather singular species of iguana, about a yard long—with a crest on its head, and of light variegated color. I fastened it to my saddle; and some time after, as I returned toward the city, I got down to shoot a sort of large snipe, in a pond. When I went to mount again, I discovered my iguana was missing. I immediately returned upon the road to a point where I knew I had it; but found nothing. This was very remarkable. This was an animal not eaten by the people; and, therefore, no one seemed to have any motive in picking it up. Therefore, I was left to speculate upon the only two "horns of the dilemma," which appeared to account for it; first, that it had been taken by some Mexican, merely for the pleasure of stealing (there were no boys, etc. to carry it away); or it had resuscitated and run off itself! The latter seemed utterly inadmissable, as I had shot it an hour before, and left it lying half an hour where I killed it, during which it had never moved. I regretted the loss; as it was the only one I saw of the kind, and I intended preserving it.

Thurs. 28—I came here with an almost fixed intention of proceeding through Sonora, etc. by land to California; but the very great fatigue, which I had suffered before reaching here owing to the excessive heat, when fully considered, deterred me from prosecuting my undertaking. In addition, the season was most unpropitious for such a tour, in other regards. From Guadalajara (& even from Zamora) here, the country was so parched up by the protracted drought (since last fall) that there was very little of interest to be found in the way of botany, to collections in which I have now much dedicated myself. The truth is, vegetation is now in its "mid-winter" here—never perhaps in a less verdant state than at the present season. And though the rainy season is now about setting in, this will be more annoying than beneficial—will only serve to wet us—to make the roads bad— to raise the waters—while it would scarcely improve vegetation in time to benefit me. So I now resolved to embark, and consequently sold my animals: and am holding myself on the *qui vive*, for a steamer, which is being expected daily, for San Francisco.

This morning I was thrown in quite a flurry by hearing a cannon at day-break, in the direction of the harbor. I rose at once, and found that a steamer was really approaching: but without knowing which way she was bound. I soon learned however that it was the "Panamá," bound for Panamá—Capt. Baily. The[y] sent a boat ashore to receive passengers, but with orders to remain only ten minutes! The consequence was, that passengers who wished to embark, being all abed at that hour, it only served to arouse them and give them a great deal of molestation for nothing; for I presume nobody was able to reach the vessel. I knew one who started in a few minutes after the call—hired a little yawl to carry him to the steamer; but when even within hailing distance, she raised steam and moved off; leaving the

329

poor passenger to return again! Capt. Baily certainly merits a leathern medal for such demonstrations of his spirit of accommodation!

[NOTE: I had omitted any general remarks upon the face and character of the country over which I travelled, with intention of summing all up together, upon my arrival at Mazatlan; but this I forgot in its proper place.—From the time we began to enter the mountains, some 15 miles from the city of Mexico, I saw more timber than upon any other route of equal length, on which I had travelled in the republic. In this main dividing ridge there is abundance of pine, and scrubby oak, both black and white—and some cedar, etc. Entering the valley of Toluca, it was mostly prairie until some distance west of Ixtlahnaca, after which the open prairies were seldom large; but interspersed with groves or scattering trees and underbrush. In the mountainous ridges we meet with pines and oaks (as few as Tepic)—in the lower undulating lands and valleys of the streams we find mezquite, guizache, and other species of acacia—*palo bobo* and other species peculiar to the country. We scarcely find anything, in fact, in the vegetable kingdom, which is common to the U.S. nor to Europe, I believe. The *palo bobo* I don't remember seeing after descending to Zamora—nor am I sure of having met with it after passing Morelia—or at least, much afterward. I did not recollect seeing any Mezquite after passing Guadalajara, until I descended upon the sea coast near Mazatlan. I was surprized to find it occasionally in this last situation, as it seemed almost peculiar to the elevated country: true, upon reflection, it is quite abundant on the low valleys and plains about Matamoros.

The face of the country is generally uneven—mountains and valleys interspersed: The intervening uplands or high valleys, not generally so extensive nor so level, as in the elevated interior. As in most other parts of the republic, the roads wind along the valleys, and through occasional gaps in the mountains—with mountains always in view, on every side.

The road from Mexico to Morelia is generally very fair—will be a very good wagon-road when the repairs now being made are completed. From Morelia to Zamora it is exceedingly rugged and rocky; nevertheless, with some labor, bestowed in judicious repairs it might be made a fair wagon road. From Zamora to Guadalajara the road is altogether good enough for wheeled vehicles, being mostly through valleys. From Guadalajara to Tepic, the only important difficulty is the pass of the Barrancas; but this is by no means insurmountable: in fact, the western portion is now pretty well repaired, and the eastern might be done with very little more labor. From Tepic to Mazatlan, the only difficulty is in the descent to the valley of the Rio Grande, hardly 30 miles, which is quite uneven and rugged, yet a fair wagon road might be made with no excessive labor. Thence to Mazatlan it is nearly a continuous level—the few hills through which the road passes presenting no important obstacles. I should remark, by the way, however, that even in the condition the roads are now in, they are frequently passed by wagons, carts, and coaches.

The soil of the country over which I passed is better than I generally found it elsewhere. The valley of Toluca is one of the most beautiful and fertile I have seen in the republic—only lacking timber—superior to the famous valley of Mexico itself. The small valleys in the mountains, as well as those of the streams in the low lands, were generally of a dark rich loam: in fact, many of the rolling uplands presented very good rich-looking soils, only wanting water to make it produce well. This is in fact, the great defect on the whole route; yet this is partially obviated by planting crops at the commencement of the rainy season,—which in this latitude ripen before frost. The rainy season from Toluca to Zamora commences in the first of May generally (about the time we passed) and are apt to continue, I believe, all the month of August. Still, I doubt if more water falls (though with greater frequency) during this season, than

331

during an ordinary spring in the U.S.—The valley of the Rio
Grande, as well east of Guadalajara, as after descending to it
west of Tepic, is generally of very rich alluvial soil: but the
lower portions cannot be generally irrigated for want of sufficient descent to get the water out into *acequias*. The semi-uplands
in the immediate vicinity of Mazatlan are often very fertile-
looking; yet very little cultivated, as yet: in fact, they can only
be cultivated without irrigation, as there is a lack of water. Yet
it should be remarked that well water seems to be procured without difficulty.

The productions are confined mostly to Indian corn—some
wheat and barley in the elevated country:—with some fruits in
the various regions, in accordance with the respective climates;
but not to the extent and variety that they might well be cultivated.]

✿ LETTER TO DR. GEORGE ENGELMANN

Mazatlan (on Pacific Coast) June 30, 1849

MY DEAR DOCTOR:

I wrote both from Mexico and Guadalajara; yet lest those letters might fail to reach you, I will repeat here that I left in the
City of Mexico with Messrs. M. Calmont, Geaves & Co. to be
forwarded immediately to Vera Cruz, all my collections of
plants, etc. in one box, marked to your address, and to care of
Moses Greenwood, New Orleans.

I arrived here on the 7th instant; and have since been occupied
in preparing my collections to be sent to you. As I believe I before informed you, I now send all to you, as it is too troublesome
to make divisions. On the present occasion, it is true, I have
separated a small herbarium, putting a specimen or two of everything which would bear division, though it is not as complete
as the other. This I have done, principally with the object of
guarding against the loss of the first, which I will have shipped
to you by the first vessel for the U.S. The second I will after-

ward (in another vessel) have shipped either to you or to Professor Short. So, should you receive neither, you can inquire if he has received the one alluded to, which, under such circumstances, I hope he will place at your disposition. Should you both receive, please furnish Professor Short[23] with such notes as he may require, from the Botanical Memoranda which I send you (as before, packed on top of one of the bundles of plants), for I have not had time to get two copies taken. Nor even have I found leisure to examine closely the copy I send you; yet from a glance, I think it approximately correct. The numbers of the two herbariums of course correspond. They now ascend to 1,250 odd, there being nearly 600 in the herbarium I now send you.

It has not rained since some distance beyond Guadalajara, to this place since September last, until a few days past, when we had some light showers, indicative that the rainy season is about commencing. Owing to the protracted drought, I have collected but very little on this side of Guadalajara, except of trees and shrubs; and even of these I have had to pass many, to me new and interesting, for want of either flower or fruit, and often even for want of leaves; for it was "mid-winter" in the vegetable kingdom, on this route.

You will doubtless find all the defects in this that you have met with in my former collections; yet I hope you will meet with more that is interesting.—On this tour, I have had a young German with me, by the name of Runckel, a pretty fair practical naturalist, who has been of a good deal of service to me particularly in the preparation of fowls. Of these I send you some 15 or 16 specimens—but some of them are nearly spoiled. They were prepared by Mr. Runckel. These I rather send for deposit with you, as it may turn out that I may want at least some of them hereafter, and therefore would not ask you to take the trouble to have them prepared and set up.

I also send you a few shells, as well as some vials of insects,

[23] Professor C. W. Short, of Louisville. See Vol. I, 377n.

etc. from about here—none, however, which seem to me to be of any special interest. Also a few specimens of rocks and woods. I have not followed your instructions in either of these, as it seemed to me that the size you gave would have occasioned too much bulk and weight; especially in my land tours. I also send a good many seed—sometimes wrapped in separate papers, but oftener put up in the herbarium with the plants to which they pertain.

I had fully intended—as I wrote you from Mexico—to continue my tour, by land, to California; but, since my arrival here, I have concluded to abandon it—much, indeed, to my own regret. Yet, I am not very strong in health, and the heat and fatigue are so great, I have begun to fear that I may not very well be able to endure two or three months more of arduous travel in such an unpropitious season: and, withal, with so little of interest before me, particularly in the vegetable kingdom; for although the rainy season is about commencing, it will serve only to annoy —to wet—to make bad roads, raise the waters—without much improving the vegetation in time for me.

Thinking of nothing else, just now, to tell you, I close by assuring you of my constant endeavors, to keep you informed and supplied with everything of interest which comes in the way of

Your friend and serv't,
JOSIAH GREGG

DR. GEORGE ENGELMANN,
St. Louis, Mo.

P.S. Our news from California is not now very flattering to the gold-seekers. The placers are said to be failing very much; yet I think it is chiefly owing to the overflowing of the Sacramento river. When the water subsides again, I am in hopes that the mines will resume their flourishing condition—at least to a degree. It should be borne in mind, however, that the former bonanzas equally with the present unfavorable condition, have doubtless been greatly exaggerated.

TOUR TO CALIFORNIA

⚙ LETTER TO DR. GEORGE BAYLESS[24]

Mazatlan, June 30th, 1849

[MY DEAR DOCTOR]

I left Saltillo last winter for the city of Mexico where I remained until the close of April when "like all the world" I set
out toward California. I arrived here on the 7th; and have since
been occupied, first, in collecting plants, birds, & c in the vicinity;
and secondly in preparing my previous collections for the United
States. I had at first contemplated continuing my journey by
land, through Sonora, and California, via Monterey to San Francisco. But I have got so much worried out with the heat and
fatigue, that I have about come to the conclusion to embark here
directly for San Francisco. The fact is, the present season is one
of the most unfavorable for a land tour—and especially for
botanical collections. Vegetation is now parched up, as it has
hardly rained since last fall. True, the rainy season is just about
setting in; yet this will only serve to annoy—wet—make bad
roads—raise the rivers—while it will scarcely improve vegetation in time to benefit me.

[*The remainder of this letter is not preserved.*]

⚙ DIARY, JULY, 1849

Wed. 4—It is unpleasant to be compelled to let our glorious
day of national independence pass over without any demonstration [of] joy on the occasion. But this was unfortunately indispensable to day, unless I had been willing to join some of
our California adventurers or others, who met together with the
sole object of "spreeing."

Sat. 7—In a corner of one of the squares (fronting my windows) I observed this evening, a collection chiefly of the rabble;
and soon I saw two men mounted on horse-back, capering about
(while others were shaking handfuls of money at the bystand-

---

[24] Dr. George Bayless, one of the group of friends Gregg had gained during
his months in Louisville, Kentucky, as a medical student. See Vol. I, 389n.

ers) with all the indications of a pending race. And so it turned out. In a few moments, the two mounted men disappeared at the further end [of] a street which has its outlet where the crowd was collected; and directly they appeared again, at full speed—while the crowd made the air resound with their rejoicing yells—that is, the winning portion; for the losers were equally sober. This I am told, is common enough here—converting a street into a race-course! This but illy accords with the ideas of order & sobriety which I was otherwise disposed to form of the place: but I take it to be the fault of the authorities.

Sun. 8—My attention was attracted about midday (as it had also been on several previous occasions) by a band of music parading the streets, accompanied by several horsemen, fantastically dressed, in ridiculous representations of Indian costume— and ahead of the calvalcade, a still more ridiculous "clown," who exerted his lungs in making speeches to a rabble of boys and vagabonds, who crowded the wake. This is the usual style, as well in the interior towns of the republic generally, as here, of publishing a circus or bullfight (or in fact, any other public representation), to come off in the evening. This is the *convite*. Sometimes we see a party with but a guitar and violin, and a couple of songstresses parading the streets. This is the *convite* to one of those disorderly fandangoes which infest some parts of the town, especially on Sunday evenings: for this is the day here, as well as everywhere else in the republic, for all sorts of public amusements.

Mon. 9—This evening I was again thrown in a flurry by the arrival of the steamer "Oregon," Capt. Pearson, bound for Panamá. I seem ill-fated; two steamers having touched here, since I have been waiting; but both going the wrong direction. This, like the "Panamá" made a very short stop here; and what was worse, Capt. Pearson left a very unfavorable impression as to his want of accommodation and good-breeding—not only refusing to accede to a reasonable solicitation; but putting on insupportably insolent and haughty airs. Verily, these steamboat masters must think themselves very important characters when they get upon the Pacific, so completely out of reach of the owners!

Fri. 13—To day we came near having a general fracas between a mob of the rabble of the city, and the foreigners here. A quarrel was commenced between two and three Americans and some *léperos*, near the market, which extended to blows: and the police being called, they proceeded to arrest the Americans without, as would seem, taking any notice of the Mexicans who were doubtless at least equally guilty. The former, being ignorant of the laws, customs, and people of the country, and fearing they would not be protected, even if they delivered themselves over to the guard (rather it would seem than an absolute inclination to resist the authorities) resolved to defend themselves, refusing to be taken by them.

The police, accompanied by a considerable number of *pelados*, were pushing hard upon the Americans (three in number) when these were able to gain the door of the house occupied by the acting American Consular agent, Mr. Bolton. One of the Americans only (known as Capt. Ferguson) was armed: he had obtained from a friend, after the fracas commenced, a revolving pistol, which he carried in his hand. The police pushed so closely upon him that though his comrades were able to make their escape into the house, Ferguson was hemmed in a corner before he could get completely into the house: here he fired two shots at the soldiers who strove to take him, the last of which took effect in the head of one of the latter, killing him instantly—and, it is said a shot was fired by one of the police.

My room was not a hundred yards distant: and the report of fire-arms called my attention to the window. By this time a considerable mob had collected—over a hundred; and finally two or three hundred, perhaps; and now infuriated, vociferously demanded the criminal, threatening to break open the house; the doors having by this time been closed. Had they got hold of the

337

poor fellow, they would doubtless have torn him instantly into pieces; yet Mr. Bolton was able to protect the house—though with no little risk as well to himself as to the premises, from the exasperated mob, until a sufficient recruit of the police was obtained to protect the prisoner,—when he was delivered over and safely lodged in the *Calabozo.*

Directly I saw the mob break off, like a pack of hounds: they were pursuing a poor fellow, a comrade of the criminal (who had not been able to enter the house of the consul), who was endeavoring to escape in the direction of the *Mole:*[25] he was soon caught and conveyed to prison. Another comrade who had escaped to his quarters, very imprudently sallied forth again, with a revolving pistol, resolved to "show the dastards," that he could walk the streets, and "no odds to 'em." But he too was again attacked, and soon pretty well "used up," and "taken into safe keeping." Another again who had taken refuge in the consulate with the criminal, was also given up at the same time: so that four Americans were now lodged in the *Calabozo;* yet not perfectly "innocent and ignorant" of the affair, as I at first understood most of them were; but all had in some way or other been concerned in (or at least belonged to the party of the original affray.) Nevertheless, several "perfectly" innocent and ignorant persons were chased, and some received bruises from stones, etc. (which were the principal weapons of the rabble), but all were able to escape. Even the supercargo of an English brig was chased, and narrowly escaped.

The fact is, a general "war was declared" now against every foreigner seen in the streets! and soon after the mob was seen rushing toward the *Meson* or public inn, where the transient Americans were chiefly lodged: an attack on this was now contemplated. This was certainly a very bold and dangerous measure on their part; for in this establishment there were some 20 or 30 well-armed Americans. The police, however, was able to

[25] A landing place for boats.

check the rabble—who by the way had become convinced perhaps of the temerity of the attempt—and nothing more grew
out of this demonstration.

Mon. 16—All of the four Americans who were lodged in jail,
were detained there until this evening, when three of them (all
except Ferguson) were released in time to embark on the "Olga,"
the barque on which I was taking passage to San Francisco.

An effort was set on foot on Saturday night to get up a party
of Americans (chiefly from an English brig which was also just
sailing with a load of American passengers—to take the prisoners
by force out of the *Calabozo*. But this failed, partially for want
of combination and resolution, and partially for want of sufficient
boats to bring them to shore; and I was certainly rejoiced at it.
For whatever there might have been of injustice in the incarcera-
tion of the American[s], their violent liberation, besides the
abuse of "law and order," would have been attended with many
serious consequences: for though even a fourth of the Americans
in port might have succeeded, as there were largely over 200
Americans on board the two California vessels,—it would doubtless have been attended with considerable bloodshed (especially
on the part of the Mexicans), and worse still would they have
been to the Americans who remained here, and to such as might
arrive afterward, upon whom the exasperated Mexicans would
doubtless have [w]recked their vengeance!

The foregoing is as nearly as I could make it out from the
various stories I heard up to the present date. In such a country
as this, where we have no security for our protection, even in
the hands of the constituted authorities, I will not pretend to
determine how far Capt. Ferguson may have been justified in
resisting, and killing one of the police, I find the opinion of
Americans generally in his favor: yet one thing is certain, that
in a well-regulated community, such an attempt should not be
countenanced for a moment; and a similar perpetration would
be punished with the utmost rigor.

At the time of my embarking, I learned that, Ferguson came very near being shot, as was said, by mistake to-day! The circumstances were, that a Mexican having attempted to kill the Capt. of the Port (I believe) he was condemned to be summarily executed (shot) by order of Gen. Inclan, the Military Commandant. The Alcaide (jailor) *pretended* to mistake the order, and took out the American to be executed in the Mexicans place! And it was only discovered by a foreigner in time to stop it, a few minutes before the contemplated execution! In some such way as this the prisoner may be put to death, nevertheless, I am of impression that the authorities will otherwise not venture the execution. This circumstance goes to show how little justice Americans can expect at the hands of the Mexican government.

To-day at noon, I embarked on the barque "Olga," though she did not sail until about half past seven in the evening. She has a hundred and twenty or thirty passengers on board (chiefly steerage)—crew and all about 150 souls.

Thurs. 19—This morning at daylight, the mountains of lower California were plainly in view; and we hoped to double the cape of San Lucas this evening: yet, the wind turning near S.E. it was found impossible to make sufficient southing, without tacking to the south: and by 6 P.M. we had approached the land within about 10 miles, so that it became indispensable to tack to south —which was continued till about 4 next morning: longer, I believe than was expedient. We then ran till 6 P.M. on the larboard tack, which brought us in view of the cape again (say 20 m. to N.N.eastward); yet the wind now being still more to the north, it became necessary to tack again to westward. For some days more we had a stiff breeze most of the time from about a point north of N.W.; so that, as the ship was not able to sail within nearer than 6 points of the wind, our general course was about one point south of west—that is, as sailors express it, W. by S. This course was continued until the 24th, when we found ourselves over ten degrees west, and about three south of Mazatlan

—virtually no nearer San Francisco than the day we sailed! The captain's motive in keeping this course so long was, as the prevailing winds were said to be from the N.W. he wished to make his "westing" at once, so as to be able to take a direct course to San Francisco. Also some advantage was expected to be obtained from what were called the "trade winds" far out in the Pacific. Although I am disposed to doubt if these "trade winds" are at all constant. Under this impression I was very much disposed to question (in my own mind) the expediency of continuing a western direction so long: it seemed evidently not advisable, in fact, unless we could have felt perfectly assured that the direction of the wind would continue the same to the close of the voyage— which of course we could not. I say it seemed evidently inexpedient; because, on the larboard (instead of the starboard) we would have been at least a little nearer on the direct course toward our destination: and any subsequent change in the direction of the wind would have been favorable:—had it veered more to the west, we could have taken a more northerly westerly direction on either tack.

Sat. 21—This morning our attention was attracted by a "school" of perhaps 20 large "black-fish" (a species of whale), the largest of which was perhaps 30 feet long. They seemed to be making S.W. but coming upon the ship, they followed for an hour, awhile along the north side and then dropping in the wake—rising very frequently to the surface, to discharge their breath (which was with a loud puff) and take in a new supply.

Sun. 22—To day we were entertained for an hour by an agreeable sermon, from a Quaker Universalist preacher on board, the Rev. Mr. Bull.

It should have [been] said that the name of the Master of the ship is John C. Bull—though not a relative I believe of the Minister: the supercargo is named Hamersley.

Thurs. 26—For the last 48 hours we have had almost a dead calm—with the rare intermission of an occasional light breeze:

341

all therefore waiting with anxiety for the wind to spring up.—
In the P.M. we had a light breeze from the N.W. again—which
continued the following day from same course: and I regretted
to find our vessel turned on the starboard tack again, and consequently sailing a little south of west! Should the wind veer to the
east of north we might find as much trouble in making to the east
again, as we have had to the west.

Pacific Ocean $\begin{cases} \text{Lat. } 20° \ 47' \text{ N.} \\ \text{Long. } 117° \ 30' \text{ N.} \end{cases}$

Frid. 27—Yesterday evening at 6 o'clock, a young man named
Bostick died on board. He had for several months labored under
repeated attacks of diarrhea, which had now become chronic—
or perhaps chronic dysentery; and he was in a very low and precarious condition when he came on board—i.e. when we sailed
from Mazatlan. This morning at half past 8 the funeral ceremonies were performed. The corps[e] was closely sewed up in
canvass, with a bag to the feet filled with sufficient weight of
stones to sink it. Then after an appropriate prayer and service by
the Rev. Mr. Bull, the body was consigned to the deep—followed by firing a cannon. Such bereavements are painful enough
under any circumstances, yet certainly more so where we are
compelled to cast the body into an endless ocean. The deceased
had a brother along, whose attentions served to sooth his dying
moments. He also had, I believe, every necessary medical attention.

⚙ DIARY, AUGUST, 1849

Frid. 3—This morning there appeared in view to the south-
westward, a brig which all those who knew the English brig
"Louisa," (which sailed from Mazatlan for San Francisco, with
passengers the day before us) seemed confident it was the same.
If it was really the "Louisa," it is a remark[able] circumstance,
that two vessels should meet on so broad and uncertain a track,
after 18 or 20 days' sail: and it goes to justify the Captain of our

ship for having continued a westerly course so long: nevertheless, I cannot yet see why it would not have been better to have made northing on the larboard, instead of southing on the starboard tack. In fact, it always seemed most reasonable to me, to run on whichever tack took us the nearest upon our course: at least after getting a few degrees west of Cape San Lucas. Though I acknowledge that those who are acquainted with the peculiar winds, etc. of the Pacific, ought to know best.—The brig remained in view all day, but was not seen the following morning.

Sat. *4*—This morning we have a very fair breeze from the northwestward; but which will not permit us to run but between one and two points north of west. As we could hardly make over two points north of east upon the other tack, it is perhaps preferable to keep as we are. For the last week or more, have had an almost continuous succession of calms—with rare intermissions of light breezes.

Last night a little after twelve, I heard an uproar upon the deck, which indicated a violent quarrel: and as I supposed it to be between members of the crew, I came near calling the captain to quell it: yet I learned this morning that it was between the Captain, John C. Bull, himself, and Hamersley, the supercargo of the "Olga." Whatever faults we may attribute to Capt. Bull, he is certainly a very clever gentlemanly man, and I doubt not very well qualified for the station he fills: and, withal, he is, in my conception, a very superior personage to Hamersley. This opinion I have formed from experience, against preconceived ideas, as Hamersley was well recommended to me by some of my friends in Mazatlan. In fact, so many circumstances have thoroughly disgusted me with him, since my first acquaintance with him, in Mazatlan, that I have long since resolved to have as little as possible to do with him. Hamersley formerly belonged to the U.S. Navy; and whether he withdrew from choice, or was discharged on account of unworthy qualities, I know not.

Sun. *5*—A brig in view to southward, again to day, believed to be the same we saw on the third. If so, this is again a remarkable coincidence—that we should accidentally keep so near each other, after having run, under a pretty brisk breeze, for near 48 hours.

Wed. 8—Perceived a brig far astern, yesterday morning, first supposed to be that seen before; but on nearer approach found to be different, as it had a white stripe above water, whereas the other appeared all black. This morning we were able to speak her, as she had passed to our windward, and then lay to until we neared within speaking distance. Found to be the brig "Lady Adams" of Baltimore—*said* to be out 32 days from Callao, with 130 passengers (chiefly natives for San Francisco).

Sun. 12—For a week past we have had a constant and generally heavy breeze from north—generally northeastward—so that we have been able to make nearly northwestward: whereby we now find ourselves in lat. nearly 30° north, and long. about (near) 131° west, the course to Monterey where we have to touch, being due N.E. It is therefore wholly incomprehensible to me why the capt. prefers sailing W.N.W. to E. by N. or even due east, which might with the present wind be made with facility. But so it is: we are running further away from our port of destination, instead of approaching nearer!

Mon. 20—Since Tuesday last, we have been able to run on the other tack, with a course north of east—sometimes north east —and for near 24 hours past nearly N.N.E. with pretty good breezes (except the intervention of about two days calm); so that we now find ourselves about Latitude 24° and longitude 123° 40'.—This evening spoke brig "Zealous" 160 days from Liverpool and 54 from Callao—with 35 (?) passengers.

Wed. 22—Somewhat becalmed again, since day before yesterday; yet able, most of the time to make two or three knots per hour on our course—one to two points E. of N.—This morning much excitement (as usual on such occasions) prevailed, on account of seeing a whale occasionally—the large "hump-back."

This afternoon, early, we suddenly found ourselves (upon the partial clearing away of a fog which had much obscured the horizon for a few days past) within some ten miles of land—a ridge of mountains some two thousand feet high, at least, as would seem, immediately bordering the coast, which appeared to be recognized as the point of San Antonio, some 30 miles below Monterey. This would have been seen a day or two before had it not been for the fog. Nevertheless, we have believed ourselves about 30 miles from land; for the ship's chronometer was either some 20 miles wrong, else this coast is set that distance too far west on our charts.

Sun. 26—After having battled about in fog and calm, for over four days since we first saw land (scarcely over 30 miles below Monterey) we entered the bay this evening about 6 o'clock, and anchored before the port of Monterey, at 8 P.M. A cause—and the principal cause, perhaps—of our being unable to get into this bay, was a continual brisk current down the coast southward; owing, (I take it for granted) to the almost constantly prevailing N.W. winds.

I now became very well convinced that it would have been fortunate for us, had we continued further westward, when we were in long. 131° (see page 341); and Capt. Bull was justifiable in his perseverance in that direction: although, it is true, under a little more favorable circumstances—with such winds as we had afterward— from Monterey to San Francisco, it would even have been better to have turned eastward sooner than we did.

Tues. 28—Having landed at Monterey to leave a Mexican Family (Senor D. Manuel Mallen—who was voluntarily expatriating himself—from disgust, as he said, for their wretched laws and institutions—and who, together with wife and family, appeared to possess [no] small degree of merit); and being a little further delayed in taking in water, wood, etc. we did not get off from Monterey till this afternoon about 5 o'clock.

Monterey is on a very pleasant site—the uneven slope of a

hill—backed by handsome groves of pitch pine and some scrubby live oak: but it now seems in a delapidated condition—at least but little improvement going on,—although the seat of government is located here. Population hardly over 2000. Lat. by mean of sun and polestar—reduced to the mole—36° 36′ 20″.

Here, near 30 of our passengers—disheartened with the protracted voyage, and the dull prospects of getting to San Francisco speedily—left the ship and started to San Francisco on foot. I fear they may have reason to rue it. [Note: At Monterey I met with Maj. Rich, U.S. Paymaster, who was on his way home with a considerable amount of collections in natural history— such as botanical specimens,—birds—minerals, etc. It is very agreeable to meet with one in the thousands who will not permit their ample opportunities to escape, for improving our knowledge of Natural history.]

Having a fair wind—of three to five knots an hour—we were able to shape our course direct, the most of tonight.

Thurs. 30—By 10 o'clock, last night, were according to reckoning, scarcely 10 miles from the entrance to the bay of San Francisco; wherefore it became necessary to lay to, and wait till morning. At day light, we were under way again; and by 8 o'clock, we were in plain view of the entrance. This is decidedly romantic—being hardly two miles wide—with a bluff point, of low mountain ridge making in on either side—on the south side, it forms a very pretty projecting cliff, upon which a rough fort or redoubt was built during the war. This place might be made a second Gibraltar in impregnability, completely commanding the entrance to the bay.

This was a very lucky, and rather random hit; for while lying to, it was impossible to tell how much the current might have carried us away. We anchored in the harbor about 10 o'clock A.M. This harbor is capacious enough for all the navies in the world, being virtually the whole bay—the only objection therefore is its size, wherefore it is a good deal affected by severe north-easterly winds.

Now safe in port again, we will take an imperfect retrospect of this protracted voyage—45 days, including the delay at Monterey. The severe cold experienced since getting fairly out upon the ocean (the thermometer—Fahrenheit—being generally about 60° and often below). This has been owing chiefly to the constantly prevailing northern and northwestern winds. Another notable circumstance has been the dense fogs which have constantly obscured the horizon ever since we approached within 30 miles of the coast.

In all we had nearly 130 passengers—all except about half a dozen in the steerage. Of these many were genteel and well-bred persons; but whose want of means would not permit them to take a more agreeable berth. Others more rude and unprincipled, gave Capt. Bull no little annoyance, with their fault finding, & complaints. But, although the captain was a little rough and abrupt in his manners he always endeavored to do what was right with his passengers; and I doubt very much if a similar number had been better furnished on the Pacific for many a day: and of this I believe they all became convinced at the end.

Then, we had some odd characters on board: among these a French speculator, named J. J. Chauviteau. With some clever qualities he possessed many oddities and simplicities. He must examine the bay and found a new town to take the business from San Francisco: he must in short remodel everything. To counterpoise the self-conceit and presumption of this Frenchman, we had a plain Quaker Universalist preacher, the Rev. Mr. Bull—a man of sterling honesty, no doubt, and the best intentions, but of no brilliancy of talent. This caused the sermons which he preached for us every Sabbath, to be agreeable and interesting. Then we had a company of German minstrels—three lone females, who had wandered from their native land; first to England—then to the U.S.—afterward into Mexico—and now finally on their way to the "land of golden promise." They seemed not wholly destitute, as they sustained a character of virtue and unceasing industry.

Approaching the harbor of San Francisco, it resembled those of the large cities of the world, on account of the immense forest of masts which loomed up before us. The number of shipping now anchored in this port, from schooners up, is probably not less than ———.

I had the misfortune to be seasick nearly the whole (if not altogether) voyage. What most annoyed me perhaps of any other one thing, was the incessant *smoking* of some of the passengers, and especially of the supercargo. What a pity that the wholesome regulation of "No smoking in the cabin," is not established on the Pacific. Yet by the favor and kindness of Capt. Bull, but little smoking was allowed in the cabin.

Dr. Franklin has given us a list of knicknacks, etc. which he advises voyagers to take to sea; yet, in the present improved state of our packets, etc. on the Atlantic this precaution has become nearly unnecessary: nevertheless, upon the Pacific, they are doubtless full as necessary as they were there in the days of the celebrated philosopher. To *our* comfort, however, Capt. Bull had his vessel much better supplied than usual. Among other provisions, I here had an opportunity, for the first time to experience the delicious preserved meats—beef, veal, mutton—boiled and put up in N. York, in air-tight sealed cans—as also soups— which, being heated, are nearly as good as when first cooked.

Part VII

One Enterprise More

TRINIDAD BAY DISCOVERED!

RETURN OF A SUCCESSFUL EXPEDITION.

ARRIVAL OF SCH. CALIFORNIA.—There cannot live any further doubt of the existence of a harbor to which this name has been applied on this coast, for we last evening conversed with Mr W. C. R. Smith, a gentleman directly from the Bay in the schr California. He is one of a party which sailed in the brig Cameo from this port on the 9th Dec. last to discover Trinidad. After several days of ineffectual cruising, he made one of a boat's crew who left the brig on 16th March to land and examine the shore at a point which made out into the sea. The Cameo was lost sight of nor has she been seen since. They proceeded to survey the indentations of the coast, and, on doubling this point, there was the long hidden entrance to Trinidad Bay before them. They represent the bay as being perfectly accessible from the north, care being exercised to avoid a ledge of rocks making out in continuation of the point aforesaid. The country in the vicinity of the bay is a finely timbered table land. The bay is about ten miles in length, and affording good anchorage and security. About twenty miles from its head they discovered what they believed to be Trinity river, emptying into the sea. The Indians were disposed to be troublesome, and they kept them at a safe distance.

Near the head of the bay they found a large tree upon which had been cut the following information :

Lat. 41° 3' 32"
Barometer 29° 86'
Ther. Fah. 48° at 12 M.
Dec. 7, 1849, J. GREGG.

This bore silent but satisfactory testimony of the identity of the place. It was the work of the unfortunate adventurer whose death in returning from Trinity river overland we mentioned a few weeks since. Here on the lonely strand was a lasting evidence of the adventurer's usefulness. We gave a brief account of his journey in recording his death, and stated, at the same time the success of his party. Mr. Smith and party were on this shore eight days *without food;* when nearly starved they discovered the California in the offing and immediately went out and piloted her in. The Laura Virginia shortly after hove in sight and followed the C. in. She lay at anchor when the California left, last Thursday evening. We are promised additional particulars for our next. This hasty sketch is given to lay before the public the intelligence that Trinidad is discovered.

****

One Enterprise More

March 7, 1850[1]

DEATH OF CAPT. JOSIAH GREGG.

We learn from a member[2] of the Trinidad expedition recently returned, that Capt. Josiah Gregg of Mo., author of "Commerce of the Prairies," etc., died in the vicinity of Clear Lake on the 25th. He joined the company of Trinidad adventurers in November last, and encountered with them the hardships and perils

[1] Arrival at San Francisco brings to an end what is available of Gregg's own records. This epilogue-like section, therefore, contains what others have written about the California sojourn, including the last expedition of all. It is but a patch-work of obituary notices and reports, the items of which are given enough sequence to disclose the gradual resolution of the mystery surrounding the place and manner of Gregg's death in bleak and rugged northern California. As soon as the survivors of "Dr. Gregg's party" reached San Francisco, they gave out their tidings of success in discovery, but joined with that the sad news of the untoward fate of their leader himself. The report of his death, lacking particulars, reached Missouri and other sections where Gregg was known; but the full quality of his exploits did not become generally recognized until L. K. Wood, a member of the party, published his story in 1856 in one of the California newspapers. From known fact and from hearsay he told the story of the conclusion to Gregg's career, one of significance and dauntless courage.

By means of the account that John Gregg prepared for Dr. George Engelmann based on the communications he received from his brother Josiah, it appears that soon after his arrival in California Gregg found a challenge to his master-bias, adventure curiously mingling commerce and science, in the quest for the almost mythical bay the Spaniards had called *Trinidad*. The pity of it is that his last "memoranda," as he termed his records, seem gone beyond recall. Undoubtedly he perseveringly made his entries, undeterred by inclement weather, unsympathetic companions, or physical exhaustion.

[2] Probably Charles C. Southard, one of the trio remaining with Gregg after the party of eight Trinidad adventurers split into two factions because of divided opinion regarding the route of the return trip.

351

of their fatiguing travel. So incessant and severe were the trials of the journey that his physical powers sunk under them, and an absence of medical attendance, added to general debility, caused his death as above. Capt. Gregg was intimately known to a great number of our citizens, and his writings have given his name popularity abroad.

☼ ITEM IN THE *ALTA CALIFORNIAN*[3]

April 1, 1850

TRINIDAD BAY DISCOVERED: RETURN OF A SUCCESSFUL EXPEDITION—ARRIVAL OF SCHOONER CALIFORNIA.

There cannot live any further doubt of the existence of a harbor to which this name has been applied on this coast, for we last evening conversed with Mr. W. C. R. Smith, a gentleman directly from the bay in the schooner *California*. He is one of a party which sailed on the brig *Cameo* from this port on the 9th of December last to discover Trinidad.[4] After several days of ineffectual cruising, he made one of a boat's crew who left the brig on the 16th of March to land and examine the shore at a point

[3] John Gregg seems to have known this account of his brother's success from its republication in the *Washington Union*, May 9, 1850 (see page 358).

[4] In the winter of 1849–50 a furor developed over finding the more or less mythical bay then known as Trinidad Bay. The object was to establish coastwise communication with the Trinity River mines, an isolated region. The supposition was that Trinity River emptied into the ocean, and if its mouth could be found there would be an easy access up the river to the mines. Among the various expeditions setting out to explore the coast in search of some opening into the inland, there was considerable rivalry, not to say jealousy, because of townsite developments that would certainly ensue. The expedition carrying off the palm was that of the Laura Virginia Association. Lieutenant Douglas Ottinger (on leave from the Bureau of Internal Revenue) was in command of the expedition; the second officer was H. H. Buhne, an experienced navigator and explorer originally from Denmark. Although this expedition started much later than that of the *Cameo* and others, and possibly even after news of the Gregg party's success had filtered into San Francisco through the return of the survivors, the *Laura Virginia* entered the bay on April 14 and established a settlement that seemed enduring. Buhne named the bay Humboldt, in honor of the Prussian naturalist, von Humboldt, and called the embryonic town Humboldt City. Nowhere in the accounts of the *Laura Virginia* expedition is credit given to the Gregg party. In decidedly better spirit, Mr. W. C. R. Smith, a member of the less successful *Cameo* expedition, records the priority of the exploring party that sought the bay overland.

which made out into the sea. The *Cameo* was lost sight of, nor has she been seen since.

They proceeded to survey the indentations of the coast, and on doubling this point, there was the long-hidden entrance to Trinidad bay before them. They represent the bay as being perfectly accessible from the north, care being exercised to avoid a ledge of rocks making out in continuation of the point aforesaid. The country in the vicinity of the bay is a finely timbered tableland. The bay is about ten miles in length, and affording good anchorage and security. About twenty miles from its head they discovered what they believed to be Trinity river, emptying into the sea. The Indians were disposed to be troublesome, and they kept them at a safe distance.

Near the head of the bay they found a large tree upon which had been cut the following information:[5]

LAT. 41° 3' 32"
BAROMETER 29° 86
THER. FAH. 48° AT 12 N
DEC. 7, 1849   J. GREGG

This bore silent but satisfactory testimony of the identity of the place. It was the work of the unfortunate adventurer, whose death, in returning from the Trinity river overland, we mentioned a few weeks since. Here, on the lonely strand, was a lasting evidence of the adventurer's usefulness. We gave a brief account of his journey in recording his death, and stated at the time the success of his party.

Mr. Smith and party were on this shore eight days *without food;* when nearly starved they discovered the *California* in the offing, and immediately went out and piloted her in. The *Laura Virginia* soon after hove in sight and followed the *C* in. She lay at anchor when the *California* left, last Thursday evening. We are promised additional particulars in our next. This hasty sketch

[5] The mistake in latitude that John Gregg indicates (see page 358) seems to be that 6' should be substituted for 3'.

is given to lay before the public the intelligence that Trinidad is discovered.

❁ LETTER: JOHN GREGG TO PHILIP HARDWICK[6]

Shreveport, La. May 16, 1850

DEAR HARDWICK:

I have melancholy news to convey to you of the death of Brother Josiah.[7]

This news comes from a commercial house (Messrs. Probst, Smith & Co.,[8] unknown to me). They write simply that they had delivered to Jesse Sutton[9] a manuscript work entitled "Rovings Abroad"[10] by a request contained in a "letter to that Gentle-

[6] This letter is one furnished W. E. Connelley by Mrs. Andrew Loughrey, daughter of Mrs. Margaret Gregg Hardwick. It appears in *Doniphan's Expedition*, 174. (See Vol. I, 392n. for Philip Allan Hardwick.)

[7] Philip A. Hardwick planned a trip to California. He seems to have been prevented from going in 1849, and did not start until about May 1, 1850. When John Gregg wrote to him concerning the letter from Probst, Smith & Co., with its distressing news, he doubtless wished Hardwick to be informed prior to his trip of what had happened. The letter arrived too late to serve this purpose.

[8] Probst, Smith & Co. was a commission house in San Francisco.

[9] Jesse Sutton was an old Santa Fé trader, whom Gregg had known for a long while. After Gregg reached Santa Fé in the 1830's, he had become bookkeeper for Sutton, and later his partner. That there was this association is shown by the Aull Letters and Papers. Among these is a letter from James Aull, dated Lexington, Missouri, June 20, 1835, to the commission house of E. & A. Tracey, mentioning a shipment of wool partly owned by Gregg. The letter reads, "Shipped from Independence wool, $3,000, to be forwarded from Independence to Pittsburgh with privilege of reshipment to St. Louis to be insured in the name of Sutton & Gregg." Sutton is mentioned in Gregg's letter to Dr. David Waldo (see Vol. I, 119–20), in a short reference. And in *Commerce of the Prairies* appears a brief reference showing that Sutton was a resident of Chihuahua in 1839. Gregg was in trouble with the officials of Chihuahua, and was influenced to return and undergo some adjustment of the matter, at least in large measure by a letter "from a Mr. Sutton, with whom I had formerly been connected in business." What inclined him to adopt the course recommended by Sutton was that gentleman's character. "The manly and upright deportment of this gentleman had inspired me with the greatest confidence, and therefor caused me to respect his opinions."—*Commerce of the Prairies*, II, 128. Ten years later the two met in California. The old directories of San Francisco show Jesse Sutton as resident in 1850; he continued in the directories at least as far down as 1858.

[10] Gregg seems to have taken care to safeguard his nearly completed manuscript for a second book. Possibly he had consigned it to Probst, Smith & Co., using them as advisers in publication as he had the Philadelphia firm, Rockhill, Smith & Co. when he had *Commerce of the Prairies* on the stocks in 1843 and 1844.

man from your (my) brother, now deceased." There is not a word as to when, where or how he came to his death.

I am writing to Jesse Sutton and others in California to try and ascertain the particulars of his death.

The last letter I had from him was dated Trinity River, some 400 miles north of San Francisco. This river, I believe, empties into the ocean north of the Sacramento River.

We are well. Yet I am looking for sickness, as the spring is exceptionally wet and cold. Such weather has never been known here before.

Remember us kindly to Sister Peggy and the family.

Yours truly,
JOHN GREGG

❁ ITEM IN THE *ARKANSAS GAZETTE AND DEMOCRAT*[11]

May 17, 1850

We regret to learn by the last accounts from California of the decease of Capt. Josiah Gregg formerly a resident of Arkansas and well known as the author of "Commerce on the Prairies." Capt. Gregg died on the 25th of February at Clear Lake, California. He joined the company of Trinidad adventurers in November last and encountered with them the hardships and perils of their fatiguing travel. So incessant and severe were the trials of the journey that his physical powers sunk under them, and an absence of medical attendance, added to general debility, caused his death.

❁ ITEM IN THE *LIBERTY TRIBUNE*

May 31, 1850

Capt. Josiah Gregg of Missouri, author of *Commerce of the Prairies,* died on Feb. 25, at Clear Lake, California. He joined a company of Trinidad adventurers in November last and sunk under the physical efforts necessary to perform the journey.

---

[11] This item in the *Arkansas Gazette and Democrat* must have had as its source the mention of Gregg's death in the *Alta Californian* of March 7, 1850.

✼ LETTER: PHILIP A. HARDWICK TO MRS. HARDWICK[12]

Smith's Trading House, California
Sept. 21, 1850

DEAR WIFE AND CHILDREN:

I have deferred writing to you for a short time after I arrived in Cal. that I might be better able to give you some information about Josiah and the prospect of the country.

I have heard nothing different from him, so think he must be dead—others say he is not.

I saw one man who said that he saw him on the Trinity river two or three hundred miles north of this, last winter, and that he was doing some business for the government. I think that most likely. I shall continue to inquire till I learn something certain about him.

We had a long—very long and tedious trip. We got to Hang-Town[13] on the 2nd day of September—four months and two days on the road.[14]

[*The remainder of this letter has not been preserved*]

✼ LETTER: JOHN GREGG TO DR. GEORGE ENGELMANN[15]

Shreveport, La. Dcr. 24/50

DEAR SIR:

Your kind letter of 28th ult has just come to hand,—making inquiry of me in regard to the death and early history of my

[12] Philip A. Hardwick, like many others from Missouri, seems to have gone to California under the prevailing impulse of gaining riches. A secondary motive may have been to gather information about his relative. Having no news since November, the family had come to disquieting conclusions about Josiah Gregg's fate. Such uneasiness led Hardwick to undertake to find out definitely what had befallen this member of the family who, they all felt, was adding renown to the name of Gregg.

[13] Hangtown was an earlier but suggestive name for the mining settlement later known as Placerville. At that time it was considered the third largest town in the state, ranking after San Francisco and Sacramento.

[14] This length of journey would make the date of Hardwick's start May 1. In that case, he certainly failed to receive John Gregg's letter of May 16, which conveyed definite news of Josiah Gregg's death. How long Hardwick was in California is not known, but on his return trip he died on shipboard and was buried ashore at some port in Mexico.

356

lamented brother, Dr. Josiah Gregg. I am truly sorry to inform you, that up to this time, I have been whol[l]y unable, after the most diligent exertions, to obtain any information in respect to the particulars of his untimely death or even as to satisfy me as to the date—except what little I have been able to glean from the newspapers—which is doubtless the same you mentioned having seen. Immediately upon hearing of his death, I wrote numerous letters to acquaintances and friends in California; but none that have answered have been able to give any satisfactory information—except in one instance a friend wrote me that he had been unable, after much inquiry, to obtain any information in regard to his death, farther than that he was engaged in marking a road from Trinity Bay to Sacramento City,[16] and had reached Clear Lake, 60 miles from the latter place, at the time of his death.

[15] Only the first four paragraphs of John Gregg's biographical letter are here reproduced. The letter was printed in full in Volume I, 377ff., inasmuch as it contains important information on Josiah Gregg's early life. These opening four paragraphs show that by the close of 1850 John Gregg was able to piece together for Dr. George Engelmann what was available about Josiah Gregg's movements after reaching California. Jesse Sutton had procured from Probst, Smith & Co. the "memoranda," only salvage from Gregg's unquestionably extensive records and collections. Nothing, however, had been forwarded of his "effects," nor of the "geological and botanical collections" made in Mexico, although this material must have been deposited with someone before Gregg went into the Trinity River country. The "memoranda," or diary, thus preserved have formed the bulk of these two volumes.

[16] The family tradition has it that when Josiah Gregg went into northern California, he was under government commission. The probabilities are in favor of this. Gregg was certainly no ordinary gold-seeker; he knew well enough that physically he was incapable of such a role. His zest for observations, however, might naturally bring him into the Trinity River region. Nothing would have been more congenial than to mark out a suitable road into that isolated section, which could only be reached by a two-hundred-mile journey from Sacramento, the latter part of which, from the mining town of Shasta, was by mountain trails impassable to wagons. Gregg would readily perceive that the problem of getting supplies into that area might be greatly simplified if a port could be found on the coast, less than a hundred miles to the west. How much imbued he was with the idea of founding a town on the coast it is difficult to say; but he was always in some degree the commercialist. That his resources were at low ebb upon his arrival in California is evidenced by his borrowing from old friends he found established in San Francisco (see John Gregg's letter, page 360—It is therefore likely that he readily became a party to the scheme described by L. K. Wood in the latter's narrative (page 361 ff.).

At the time of his reaching San Francisco, about the 1st of Sept. '49, gold had recently been discovered in great abundance on the Trinity River some three or four hundred miles north of that place and much anxiety manifested to discover a bay and good harbor, at the mouth of the above river, which was understood (by tradition as I understand) to exist there.

[MARGINAL NOTE: He was naturally of rather feeble constitution, and sank from over taxing his physical powers and excessive exposure in a rigorous northern climate, I presume; yet his health was generally much better when travelling than at other times.]

He was detained a short time at San Francisco—having found it necessary to have a surgical operation performed for the purpose of removing a tumor from his shoulder, which had formed and become troublesome from the "rubbing of his clothes." So soon as he had recovered from this—which was in a short time—as was his wont—he set out in search of the aforenamed bay; with a desire and a hope to be the first to make the discovery: And in which, it appears, from an article in the Alta California of 1st of April last, he was successful. This you will find copied in the "Union" of Washin[g]ton City of the 11th May—except, that in the "Union," there is an error in the figures of Lat. & c.

The last letter I had from him was dated "Trinity River below 3d Cañon Nov. 1st 1849." In which he says "I leave this place today for the mouth of this river in search of the bay." On the same day he wrote his old friend, Jesse Sutton, of San Francisco to the same effect. In this letter he seemed to indicate some foreboding of evil to himself, (a thing entirely unusual with him) as he says to him "I will mention (though I believe I told you the same before) that should I chance to be lost, place my effects and memoranda (which are in the hands of Probst & Smith) at the disposition of my brother John." Mr. Sutton wrote me, when sending the memoranda referred to, that he had been unable to recover my brother's notes and diaries and the "Trinity

358

Country," as also his geological and botanical collections: And says, from all he "can learn, they are either lost or destroyed,"— I presume the latter, as my brother had it in view to make a location for a town—should he discover an eligible site—hence the loss of his papers amounted to an obliteration of whatever he had done....

⚙ LETTER: JOHN GREGG TO MRS. PHILIP A. HARDWICK[17]

Shreveport, La., January 6 [18]51

MY DEAR SISTER:

Your letter of the 25th of Nov. has just been received. We are much gratified to hear from you, as also from mother.[18] I had just written her and directed to Liberty to your care—having learned by letter from sister Susan that she expected to spend the winter at your house. This letter I will direct to Randolph, as I see yours was mailed there.

I have just received a letter from cousin Jacob Gregg,[19] who gave me the first information I had of our good old Uncle Ayer's death. He says he did not see Mr. Hardwick as they went on, but heard of him in the mines near HangTown. They were at Riley's, who lives at Napa City, near and north of the bay of San Francisco. His mother he said was in good health.

Just having written mother, I have but little to write you about ourselves, more than that we are in the enjoyment of reasonable health.

I have written many letters to California, trying to get some

[17] This letter is among those used by Connelley in his *Doniphan's Expedition*. It was placed in his hands by the Gregg family.

[18] This letter of John Gregg's gives the family in Missouri confirmation of their worst fears. "Mother" Gregg had gone to live with her daughter, Mrs. Margaret Gregg Hardwick, in 1850, possibly soon after Philip A. Hardwick left for California, and continued an inmate of her daughter's home until her decease in 1857. News of Hardwick's death at sea on his return trip had not yet been received.

[19] Others of the Gregg family and its acquaintances had gone to California. The "cousin Jacob" was probably one of the sons of Jacob Gregg, brother of Josiah. Nothing has been ascertained in regard to "Uncle Ayer" or "Riley."

information in regard to Brother Josiah's death, as well as his effects, but have been able to learn nothing. I lately wrote to Mr. Hardwick. Cousin Jacob wrote me that Riley had been able to learn nothing; but supposed his effects, if any, were in the hands of Jesse Sutton. Sutton enclosed me Brother Josiah's last letter to him, directing him to take charge of his effects and turn them over to me, in case he should be lost or never get back to San Francisco. He sent me his memoranda or Journal, and enclosed the letter I speak of above, but says nothing of anything else, but says he had written me before in regard to his death, &c. That letter I never got. Brother Josiah borrowed money from him on leaving San Francisco, and in the letter named above had directed him to pay himself out of his effects. It may be that it took everything to pay him. It may be that everything he had with him when he died, was lost, as Sutton says his papers were lost.

I have not heard whether John McClellan has got back from El Paso, nor have I heard from sister Susan since she got home. I wrote her a few days since.

We live on the most thronged highway in the Western Country; and the throng is now much increased by the extra-ordinary immigration to Texas. Shreveport is the receiving and shipping point for a large tract of country—extending far back into Texas. Its streets and sidewalks show the busy bustle of a large city.

I am in hopes you will write me often and I am very anxious indeed to receive a letter with Mother's name appended. To whom please remember me and Eliza kindly, as also to your children and the kin and friends generally.

And receive for yourself the kindest
wishes of Your Brother,
JOHN

ONE ENTERPRISE MORE

❖ FROM L. K. WOOD'S NARRATIVE[20]

The month of October, 1849, found me[21] on the Trinity river, at a point now called Rich Bar.[22] How I came there and from whence, over what route, by what conveyance, or for what object, it matters not; suffice it to say that I was there, and that, too without provisions, poorly clad, and worse than all, in this condition at the commencement of a California winter. The company at this place numbered some forty persons, the most of whom were in much the same situation and condition as myself. Near the bar was an Indian ranch, from which, during the prevalence of the rain that was now pouring down as if in contemplation of a second flood, we received frequent visits. From them we learned that the ocean was distant from this place not more than

[20] In this series of excerpts from the L. K. Wood narrative, the only available first-hand account of the Gregg party's attempt to find Humboldt Bay by a direct route overland from the Trinity River settlements, only those portions that show the experiences of the party have been uesd. The omitted portions largely relate to Wood personally and shed no light on Gregg's part in the expedition.

[21] Lewis Keysor Wood went from Kentucky to California in 1849. Soon after his arrival, he and his partner, Thomas Seabring, headed for the Trinity River country. Both joined the Gregg party, and both aligned themselves against Gregg's decision about the route of the return trip. After Wood, Seabring, Wilson, and Buck struck out down Eel River for San Francisco, Wood almost lost his life in an epic encounter with grizzlies. As soon as he had recovered from the arduous trip, he went back to the Humboldt Bay region as a leading spirit in the Union Land Company, composed of settlers recruited by himself and others.

His account of the ill-fated trip was published first in the *Humboldt Times* in the spring of 1856, under the title, "The Discovery of Humboldt Bay." It was republished in the same paper in 1863; in 1873, a pamphlet reprint was brought out by Wood's sons. In 1885 it was included in paraphrase as Chapter I in Bledsoe's *Indian Wars in the Northwest* (San Francisco, 1885). In recent years the narrative has kept its popularity. A facsimile reprint appeared in the *Quarterly of the Society of California Pioneers*, Vol. IX, No. 1 (March, 1892). It has received prominence in more recent times through articles and reprints by Professor Owen Cochran Coy who is familiar with the region.

Despite all this circulation, it is doubtful whether the Gregg family in Missouri ever had access to its disclosures of the circumstances attending Josiah Gregg's final trip.

[22] "Rich Bar" was a commonly used name among the mining camps, a fact that makes it almost impossible to locate definitely the one Wood mentions. Gregg gave its location in letter to John Gregg as "Trinity River below 3rd Cañon." Apparently it was on the main Trinity River, probably in the vicinity of Big Bar, which appears on present-day maps. The distance to the coast, as the crow flies, was about eighty miles.

eight days' travel, and that there was a large and beautiful bay, surrounded by fine and extensive prairie lands.

The rainy season, having now, to all appearances set in, alternate rain and snow continually falling[23]—a scanty supply of provisions for the number of persons now here, and scarcely a probability of the stock being replenished before the rains should cease, the idea was conceived of undertaking an expedition with the view to ascertaining whether the bay, of which the Indians had given a description, in reality existed. Among the first and most active in getting up and organizing the expedition, was a gentleman by the name of Josiah Gregg, a physician by profession, formerly of Missouri. He had with him all the implements necessary to guide us through the uninhabited, trackless region of country that lay between us and the point to be sought. No one seemed better qualified to guide and direct an expedition of this kind than he. Upon him, therefore, the choice fell to take command. The number of persons that had expressed a desire to join the company up to this time, was twenty-four. The day fixed upon by the Captain for setting out was the 5th day of November. In the meantime, whatever preparations were necessary and in our power, were made. The Captain had negotiated with the chief of the rancheria for two of his men to act as guides. Nothing more remaining to be done, all were anxiously awaiting the arrival of the day fixed upon, and a cessation of the rain, which was still falling in torrents.

The day of departure arrived, but with it came no change in the weather, save an occasional change from rain to snow. Many of the party now began to exhibit marked symptoms of a desire to withdraw and abandon the expedition. The two Indian guides refused to go, assigning as a reason, that the great storm we had experienced on the river had been a continuous snow storm in the mountains, and that the depth of the snow would present an

[23] The winter of 1849–50 was unusually wet, even for that section of California, which sometimes has annual precipitation amounting to forty inches.

insuperable barrier to our progress, and endanger the safety of the whole party, at attempt the passage [*sic*]. This was sufficient for those who had manifested a desire to withdraw; and the number was speedily reduced to eight men, including the Captain whose determination was only the more fixed, because too large a number had abandoned the expedition.

The company now consisted of the following persons:[24] Dr. Josiah Gregg, Captain; Thomas Seabring, of Ottawa, Illinois; David A. Buck, of New York; J. B. Truesdell, of Oregon; ———— Van Duzen; Charles C. Southard, of Boston; Isaac Wilson, of Missouri, and your humble servant, of Mason County, Kentucky.

Owing to this great diminution in the number of the party, it became necessary before setting out, to examine the condition of our commissary department—from which it was ascertained that the stock of provisions had suffered even greater diminution than had the company in point of numbers. The articles found were flour, pork, and beans, and of these scarcely sufficient for ten days' rations. Notwithstanding this, an advance was determined upon, and, accordingly we broke up camp. Here commenced an expedition, the marked and prominent features of which were constant and unmitigated toil, hardship, privation and suffering. Before us, stretching as far as the eye could reach, lay mountains, high and rugged, deep valleys and difficult canyons, now filled with water by the recent heavy rains. . . .

Toward the evening of the next day [i.e. the sixth from the start, the intervening ones having been spent in crossing the Coast Range on a westerly course], while passing over a sterile, rugged country, we heard what appeared to be the rolling and

[24] There is no need to add biographical details, especially since Wood has given the localities whence came the seven men composing the "Dr. Gregg party." All save Gregg himself, it seems, were primarily interested in making money, either through mining or "town-siting." All seem to have capitalized, eventually, upon their hazardous trip by becoming settlers in the region they had been, probably, the first Americans to visit.

breaking of the surf upon the distant sea shore, or the roaring of some waterfall. A halt was therefore determined upon, and we resolved to ascertain the cause of this before proceeding further, and here pitched our camp.

Early the next morning Mr. Buck left camp alone, for the purpose above expressed, and before night returned, bringing with him a quantity of sand, which from its appearance, as well as that of the place where it was gathered, he thought indicated the presence of gold; but not being on a gold hunting expedition, we thought it better discretion to use all possible dispatch in reaching the coast. The result of his search was that he found a stream at the foot of a rugged descent, whose now swollen waters rushed with terrific speed and violence. This, then, was what we heard. The gleam of hope that for a moment animated us was soon dispelled. This stream is the South Fork of Trinity.[25]

Having ascertained that it was impossible to effect a crossing at or near this place, we continued on down, keeping as near it as was possible, until we came to its junction with the Trinity River.

Here we succeeded in crossing. Upon gaining the opposite shore, we had a steep bank to ascend. As we reached the top of this bank, we came suddenly upon an Indian rancheria. . . .

It had been our intention to follow the river down, although its course, being from this point northwest, was not in the direction we desired to take. Against this, however, the Indians cautioned us, asserting that there were numerous tribes scattered along the river to its mouth, who would certainly oppose our passing through their country, besides, on being made to understand the object we had in view, they informed us that our best route, both in point of distance and on account of the Indians, was to leave the river and strike westward.

This advice we, upon the whole, thought the most prudent

[25] The South Fork joins the main Trinity River on the border between Trinity and Humboldt counties.

to follow, and accordingly commenced the ascent of the mountain that now lay in our path.

The night of the second day after leaving the river, having pitched our camp, we set about preparing a supper. I would not consume the time in detailing so minutely these unimportant items, but a portion of the material of that night's meal, although a morsel delicate and palatable in comparison with some of which we partook later in our journey, and it being the first time within my experience where necessity had reduced me to a like extremity, it made an impression on my mind which to-day is as fresh as if it occurred but yesterday. Our stock of flour was exhausted; the almost continual rain, however, had so saturated our entire camp equipage—the flour among the rest—and therefore had formed on the inner surface of the sacks in which it had been carried, a kind of paste which the dampness had soured and molded.

This paste was carefully peeled off, softened with water, and equally divided among the party—when each one, after the same had been submitted to a process of hardening before the fire, devoured his portion with an avidity that would have astonished and shocked mortals with appetites more delicate than ours. Nothing now remained of the stock of provisions that constituted our outfit—flour, pork, beans—all were gone. The night of the 13th of November we were compelled to retire to our blankets supperless. Our animals, however, had been without feed for the previous two days, but now were luxuriating in fine grass, which fact tended to render our situation the more supportable, for the preservation of our animals, next to food for ourselves, was of the highest importance, because upon them we depended for the packing of our blankets and provisions, when fortunate to find any of the latter.

During the succeeding day a halt was several times called to consider the proposition submitted by some to return; but as often as it was made it was overruled, upon the belief that the coast could certainly be reached in much less time than it would require to return to the river. After picking our way the whole of this day through an almost impenetrable forest, we came to a small prairie. This we reached about sunset, worn down with fatigue, and feeling most too acutely the painful sensations occasioned by a long abstinence from food. Here we determined to remain awhile, to hunt for something upon which to subsist.

On leaving the South Fork of the Trinity, we had hoped by this time to have gained the seashore, but in this expectation we were doomed to disappointment. The dim outline of distant mountains still marked the horizon, the same as when our first glance was cast in the direction of our route, upon reaching the summit of the first mountain.

In the morning all the party, save a guard for the camp, started out in search of food, and after a short hunt succeeded in killing several deer. A quantity of venison broiled or cooked in the ashes, soon appeased the extreme hunger from which we were suffering. Here we remained several days for the purpose of recovering our nearly exhausted strength.[26] During our stay at this place, we cured a quantity of venison with which, upon resuming our journey, we packed the animals and proceeded on foot ourselves, thinking that by so doing we could certainly take sufficient to last, if not until we could get through, at least until more could be obtained. But no; on we toiled, faithfully and constantly, until the last of the venison was consumed, and the first, and second, and third day of fasting came and passed.

During all this time our animals suffered intensely from want of food. The only kind that could be obtained for them was leaves, and in places even these could be procured only by cutting

26 That many days were consumed by pauses like the one described here is not surprising. Both men and horses needed recruiting; the larder had to be filled. Even after these replenishings only a limited amount of food could be carried. The horses were already loaded to the utmost with baggage and equipment, and their number was becoming diminished as they succumbed to conditions of weather and travel.

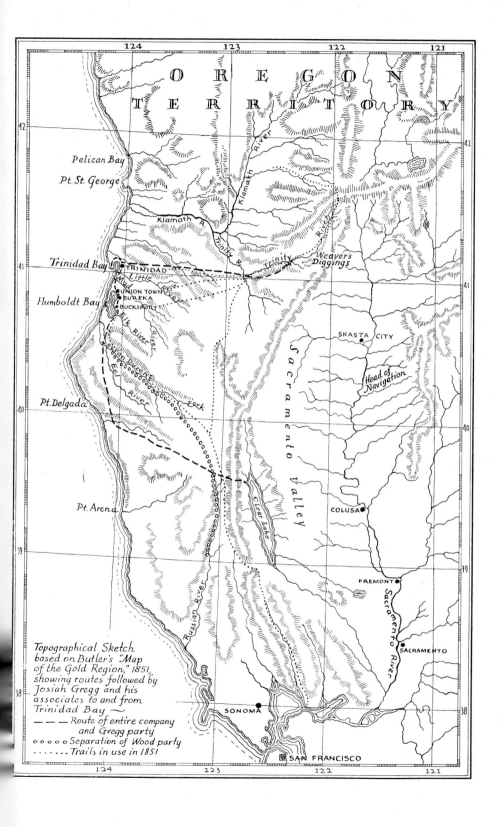

OREGON TERRITORY

Pelican Bay
Pt. St. George

Klamath R.
Trinity R.
Klamath River

Trinidad Bay   TRINIDAD
Little
Mad R.
UNION TOWN
EUREKA
BUCKSPORT

Humboldt Bay

Elk River

Van Dusen's
Eel River

Pt. Delgada

Trinity
Weaver's
Diggings

SHASTA CITY

Head of
Navigation

Sacramento Valley

Fork

Clear Lake

Pt. Arena

Russian River

COLUSA

FREMONT

Sacramento River

SACRAMENTO

Topographical Sketch
based on Butler's "Map
of the Gold Region," 1851,
showing routes followed by
Josiah Gregg and his
associates to and from
Trinidad Bay —
— — — Route of entire company
       and Gregg party
○○○○○ Separation of Wood party
. . . . . . Trails in use in 1851

SONOMA

SAN FRANCISCO

124   123   122   121

42   41   40   39   38

down trees. Two of them, however, were too far reduced to go further, and we were compelled to leave them behind.

Again we had the good fortune to reach a piece of mountain prairie where we found an abundance of game for ourselves, and plenty of grass for the animals. At this place we remained three days, collecting and preparing meat for use while traveling. We had now two animals less in number, and consequently were obliged to increase the loads of those remaining in order to pack sufficient to keep soul and body together for a reasonable length of time, for as when we left one camping place, when or where another would be found was of course uncertain, and to pack our provisions ourselves was a thing out of the question, in our present condition. . . .

Our progress up to this time had been very slow. The distance traveled per day did not exceed an average of seven miles. The appearance of the country now seemed to change—the mountain ridges were less high and abrupt than those over which we had passed, but much more densely covered with timber. Our belief now was that twelve miles further travel would bring us, if not to the coast, at least to a more level country, when our advance would be more rapid and attended with less difficulty and suffering. We therefore resumed our journey with lighter hearts and more buoyant hopes.

Our calculation of the distance to the coast or valley, subsequently proved to be not far from correct. The redwood forests,[27] however, through which we had to pass, were more dense and difficult to penetrate than any before; consequently our progress was in proportion retarded. Dr. Gregg frequently expressed a desire to measure the circumference of some of these giants of the forest, and occasionally called upon some one of us to assist him. Not being in the most amiable state of mind and feeling at this time, and having neither ambition to gratify nor desire to enlighten the curious world, we not unfrequently answered his calls with shameful abuse. His obstinate perseverance, however, in one or two instances, resulted in success. One redwood tree was measured whose diameter was found to be twenty-two feet, and it was no unusual thing to find these trees reaching the enormous height of three hundred feet. This may excite incredulity abroad, but trees have since been found in this redwood forest of much greater dimensions.

Through this forest we could not travel to exceed two miles a day. The reason of this was the immense quantity of fallen timber that lay upon the ground in every conceivable shape and direction, and in very many instances one piled upon another so that the only alternative left us was literally to cut our way through. To go around them was often as impossible as to go over them. We were obliged, therefore, constantly to keep two men ahead with axes, who, as occasion required, would chop into and slab off sufficient to construct a sort of platform by means of which the animals were driven upon the log and forced to jump off on the opposite side. There was not the least sign indicative of the presence of any of the animal creation; indeed, it was almost as impenetrable for them as for us, and doubtless was never resorted to save for purpose of shelter.

On the evening of the third day from our bear camp, as we called it, our ears were greeted with the welcome sound of the surf rolling and beating upon the sea shore. There was no doubt or mistake about it this time. The lofty tops caught the sound, which the deep stillness of a night in a forest rendered the more plainly audible and echoed it back to our attentive ears.

The following morning Messrs. Wilson and Van Duzen proposed to go to the coast in advance of the company, and at the same time to mark out the best route for the animals; to which proposition all agreed, and accordingly they left the camp. In the evening of the same day they returned, bringing the glad tidings that they had reached the sea shore, and it was not more than six miles distant.

At an early hour in the morning we resumed our journey with renewed spirits and courage. For three long days did we toil in these redwoods. Exhaustion and almost starvation, had reduced the animals to the last extremity. Three had just died, and the remainder were so much weakened and reduced, that it constituted no small part of our labor and annoyance in assisting them to get up when they had fallen, which happened every time they were unfortunate enough to stumble against the smallest obstacle that lay in their path, and not a single effort would they make to recover their feet, until that assistance came. At length we issued from this dismal forest prison, in which we had so long been shut up, into the open country, and at the same instant in full view of that vast world of water—the Pacific ocean. . . .

Our appetites, having again been sharpened by more than two days of fasting, soon awakened us from our pleasing reveries, and reminded us of the necessity of immediately going in search of food. Not long after we had separated for that purpose, Van Duzen shot a bald eagle, and Southard, a raven which was devouring a dead fish thrown upon the beach by the surf. These they brought into camp, and all, eagle, raven and half-devoured fish, were stewed together for our supper, after partaking of which we retired to our blankets [and] enjoyed a good night's rest.

Our prospects for a meal the next day were anything but flattering. Dr. Gregg therefore requested me to return to my mule which had fallen down the day before and been left to die, and take out his heart and liver and bring them to camp. I accordingly went, but judge of my surprise, when approaching the spot where I had left him, to find him quietly feeding. I determined at once not to obey my orders, and, therefore, drove him into camp.

The point at which we struck the coast was at the mouth of a

[27] The party had now encountered the Redwood Belt, a strip of almost impenetrable forests extending along the coast. In the vicinity of Humboldt Bay, it is from four to sixteen miles wide. Wood's expression, "prisoners of the forest," is indeed apt.

small stream now known by the name of Little River.[28] From this point we pushed on northward, following the coast line about eleven miles, when a small lake or lagoon[29] arrested our progress. Finding it impossible to proceed further without encountering the redwood forest which we were not in the least inclined to do, it was determined that we should retrace our steps and proceed south, following the coast to San Francisco, if such a course was possible. Traveling south about eight miles, we made a halt at a point or headland, which we had passed on our way up from where we first struck the coast. This we called "Gregg's Point," and is now known as Trinidad.[30]

During our journey over the mountains the old Doctor took several observations in order to prevent, as much as possible a departure from the general course given us by the Indians. As we advanced, and our toil and sufferings accumulated, we gradually cultivated a distaste for such matters; and at an early day regarded his scientific experiments with indifference, while later in our journey they were looked upon with contempt. It was not unusual, therefore, for us to condemn him in most unmeasured terms, for wasting his time and energies about that which would neither benefit him nor us in the least, or be of any service to others.

From an observation taken on this plateau, where the town of Trinidad is now situated, this point was found to be in latitude 40 deg. 6 min. N. This the old gentleman took the trouble to

[28] Little River, so called because of its shortness, enters the Pacific Ocean three or four miles south of Trinidad Head.
[29] What is now known as Big Lagoon.
[30] The time of arrival at "Gregg's Point" may be construed—from the *Alta Californian* report given by a member of the *Cameo* expedition—as December 7. Wood's chronology is, in fact, sketchy. If the date of starting was November 5, he has included in his narrative, by mention or implication, about forty days up to the reaching of this headland. His next definite date, December 20 (when the bay itself was discovered by Buck), would make an interval of thirteen days consumed in exploring the vicinity of the bay. As this is not plausible, it may not be amiss to suggest that the date inscribed on the tree trunk was December 17 instead of December 7. Such a mistake might easily occur through a slip of memory or a trick of type.

engrave upon the trunk of a tree standing near by, for the benefit, as he said, of those who might hereafter visit the spot, if perchance such an occurrence should ever happen. Here we remained two days, living on mussels and dried salmon, which we obtained from the Indians, of whom we found many.

Again we resumed our journey. In crossing a deep gulch, a short distance from the point, the Doctor had the misfortune to have two of his animals mire down. He called lustily for assistance, but no one of the company would aid him to rescue them. We had been annoyed so much, and detained so long, in lifting fallen mules—some remembered the treatment they received when in a similar predicament—that one and all declared they would no longer lend assistance to man or beast, and that from this forward each would constitute a company by himself, under obligations to no one, and free to act as best suited his notions. In obedience to this resolve, I immediately set about making arrangements in regard to myself.[31] Having for some time noticed the rapid strides the company were making toward disruption, and anticipating a result similar to that which had just transpired, I visited the chief of a tribe of Indians who lived close at hand, and explained to him, as best I could, what I wanted and intended to do, provided we could agree. I gave him to understand that I desired to remain with him awhile, and that if he would protect me and take care of my mule, and give me a place in his wigwam, I would furnish him with all the elk meat he wanted. To this he readily acquiesced, and in addition returned many assurances that nothing should harm either me or mine.

When the company were again about starting—for they all seemed bound in the same direction, whether in conformity to an agreed plan, or involuntarily, I did not know—they discovered that I was not prepared to accompany them, and demanded to know the reason why I did not get ready. I then

---

[31] Wood appears prone to get at variance with the rest of the party; at any rate, he did not practice or encourage harmony among the expedition.

informed them of my determination, and the agreement I had made with the Indian chief. All were violently opposed to the agreement, and urged as a reason why I should not persist in such a determination, that when all together we were not sufficiently strong to pass through this Indian country in safety, should they see fit to oppose us, and that to remain with them would be to abandon myself to certain destruction, while at the same time it would lessen the probability of any of them reaching the settlements in safety. I told them I had no horse that could travel, and I was not able to walk, and that I would as soon be killed by the Indians as again to incur the risk of starvation, or, perhaps, that which was worse, fall the victim of cannibalism.

Truesdell, who had two animals left, offered to sell me one of them for one hundred dollars, if I would continue with them. I finally accepted the offer, and proceeded with them.

Little River was soon recrossed, after which nothing occurred to interrupt our progress until we reached another stream, which was then a large river, being swollen by the heavy rains. Its banks ran full, and its waters, near the mouth, appeared deep and moved so slowly and gently that we concluded it must be a navigable stream. Our next difficulty was to cross this river. Here the harmony that had existed for so short a time was again disturbed.

The Doctor wished to ascertain the latitude of the mouth of the river, in order hereafter to know where it was. This was of course opposed by the rest of the company. Regardless of this opposition, he proceeded to take his observation. We were, however, equally obstinate in adhering to the determination of proceeding without delay. Thus decided, our animals were speedily crossed over, and our blankets and ourselves placed in canoes— which we had procured from the Indians for this purpose—ready to cross. As the canoes were about pushing off, the Doctor, as if convinced that we would carry our determination into effect, and he be left behind, hastily caught up his instruments and ran for the canoe, to reach which, however, he was compelled to wade several steps in the water. His cup of wrath was now filled to the brim; but he remained silent until the opposite shore was gained, when he opened upon us a perfect battery of the most withering and violent abuse. Several times during the ebullition of the Old Man's passion he indulged in such insulting language and comparisons, that some of the party, at best not any too amiable in their disposition, came near inflicting upon him summary punishment by consigning him, instruments and all, to this beautiful river. Fortunately for the old gentleman, pacific councils prevailed and we were soon ready and off again. This stream, in commemoration of the difficulty I have just related, we called Mad River.[32]

We continued on down the beach a short time, when night overtaking us, we camped. So long a time had elapsed since our departure from the Trinity river, and the constant suffering, toil and danger to which we had been exposed, that the main object of the expedition had been quite forgotten; and our only thought and sole aim seemed to be, how we should extricate ourselves from the situation we were in, and when we might exchange it for one of more comfort and less exposure and danger.

Immediately after halting, Buck and myself went in search of water. It had been our custom, whenever night happened to overtake us, there to camp—the most ceaseless falling of the rain affording us a continual supply of water. This night, however, we camped in some sand hills, about a mile back from the beach, without giving a thought how we should get water. A short distance from camp we separated. Buck going in one direction and I in another. I soon found slough water, which, although not altogether agreeable and pleasant to the taste, I concluded would answer our purpose, and returned with some of it to camp. Not long after, Buck came in and placed his kettle of water before

---

[32] Mad River rises near the South Fork of Trinity River, and takes a course almost parallel to it.

us without anything being said. The Doctor, not relishing the water I had brought, and being somewhat thirsty, was the first to taste the other. The suddenness with which the water was spit out, after it had passed his lips, was a sufficient warning to the rest of us. The Doctor asked Mr. Buck where he got that water. Buck replied, "about half a mile from here." The Doctor remarked: "You certainly did not get it out of the ocean, and we would like to know where you did get it." Buck answered, "I dipped it out of a bay of smooth water." This excited our curiosity and Buck seemed, at the time, to be rather dogged and not much disposed to gratify us by explanations. It was dusk, and he could not tell the extent of the bay. This was the night of the 20th of December, 1849, and was undoubtedly the first discovery of this bay by Americans notwithstanding a Captain Douglass Ottinger claims to have first discovered it.[33] We gave it the name of "Trinity Bay," but before we could return to it, Capt. Ottinger, with a party by water, discovered it and gave it the name of "Humboldt Bay."

The next morning, by daylight, we were up and moved our camp over to the bay, and stopped over there during the day. This was opposite the point where Bucksport now stands. We encamped, the night previous, under a group of small trees in the sand hills lying between the bay and the ocean, on a strip of land now known as the "Peninsula," or "North Beach." The reason we had not discovered the bay the day previous, in traveling down from the mouth of Mad River, was because we followed the beach—it being hard sand and easy traveling—and the low hills and timber on the strip of land, lying between the ocean and the bay, shut out the latter entirely from our view.

During the day we remained here, the Indians came to our camp, and we learned from them that we could not follow down the beach on account of the entrance to the bay, which was just below us. Mr. Buck, however, to satisfy us, took an Indian with

[33] Douglass Ottinger was in command of the *Laura Virginia* party (page 352n).

374

him and started down to the entrance. When he returned, he reported quite a large and apparently deep stream connecting the bay and the ocean, and considerable swell setting in, which he thought would make it dangerous to attempt to cross. The Indians also represented that it was deeper than the trees growing on the peninsula were tall; so we abandoned the idea of attempting to cross it.

Where we camped was the narrowest part of the bay, being the channel abreast of Bucksport,[34] and the Indians assured us that we could swim our animals across there, and offered to take us over in their canoes. Most of the party, including Dr. Gregg, were of the same opinion; but some of the party opposing the project, we packed up next morning and started northward, keeping as near the bay as the small sloughs would permit, for the purpose of heading it. After making our way through brush and swamp, swimming sloughs and nearly drowning ourselves and animals, we arrived toward night on the second day, after leaving our camp opposite Bucksport, on a beautiful plateau near the highland and redwoods, at the northeast end of the bay. At this point, which commands a fine view of the bay, stretching out to the southwest, we made a halt, and it being nearly night, pitched our camp. This plateau is the present site of the town of Union (now Arcata).[35]

Our camp was near the little spring, about two hundred yards from the east side of the Plaza, toward the woods. I have seen some of the old tent pins, still remaining there, within the last year (1872).

As soon as we had unpacked, some of the party started in search of game, and soon came across a fine band of elk, a little north of our camp, about where the cemetery now is, and fired several

[34] Founded in 1850. It was named for David A. Buck, who, so far as Gregg's party was concerned, was the discoverer of the bay.

[35] The town was established in 1850 as a rival to Humboldt City, started by the Laura Virginia Company a short time previously. At first it was called Union (sometimes Uniontown), but in 1860 its name was changed to Arcata.

shots, wounding two or three but they succeeded in reaching the thicket in the edge of the redwoods, and dark setting in they could not be found. We therefore did not get any supper that night. The next morning, early, some went in search of the elk and found one of them in the brush, dead, and brought it to camp.

The next morning, December 25th, we roasted the elk's head in the ashes and this constituted our Christmas feast. This was my first Christmas in California, and, having been reduced so often to the point of starvation, we enjoyed this simple fare, yet, you may rest assured, it was not that "Merry Christmas" I had been accustomed to in Kentucky with the "old folks at home." This day we moved down to the point of high prairie, near the mouth of Freshwater slough at the east side of the bay, and there camped.

The next day we made our way through the woods, following an indistinct Indian trail, back of where the town (now city) of Eureka[36] is situated, and came out at the open space in the rear of where Bucksport now stands, which place derives its name from one of our party, David A. Buck. We pitched our camp near the bluff, on the top of which is at present Fort Humboldt.[37]

The next day we followed down the bay, crossing Elk river, to Humboldt Point. . . .

It had been our intention at the outset, if we succeeded in discovering the bay, and providing the surrounding country was adapted to agricultural purposes, and was sufficiently extensive, to locate claims for ourselves, and lay out a town; but the deplorable condition in which we now found ourselves, reduced in strength, health impaired, our ammunition nearly exhausted— upon which we were entirely dependent, as well for the little food we could obtain as for our defense and protection—and des-

[36] Founded in 1850. It became the county seat in 1858.

[37] Fort Humboldt was established in 1852 to protect the settlers from Indians. It was abandoned in 1870.

titute of either farming or mechanical implements, induced us to abandon such intention, at least for the present, and use all possible dispatch in making our way to the settlements.

Accordingly, having remained at this camping place one day, we turned our faces toward the south. Our progress was extremely slow, as the rain was falling almost incessantly, rendering traveling difficult and fatiguing.

The third day after leaving the bay we reached another river, which arrested our advance in that direction. Upon approaching this river, we came suddenly upon two very old Indians, who at seeing us fell to the ground as if they had been shot. We dismounted and made them get up, giving them to understand that we were their friends; but it was with much difficulty that we succeeded in quieting their fears. They were loaded with eels, which they informed us they obtained from this river. Our appetites being in just such a condition that anything, not absolutely poisonous, upon which a meal could be made, was palatable, without asking many questions, we helped ourselves to nearly the whole of their load. Near where we met these Indians, we got them, with their canoes, to set us across the river, which was at this time a large stream, the water being high. We swam our animals as usual. The point where we crossed was just below the junction of Van Duzen's Fork, which latter stream takes its name from one of our party. Here we remained for two days, during which time we lived upon eels obtained from the Indians. In exchange for these we gave them some beads and some pieces of iron. They seemed to value these pieces of iron more highly than anything else we had to dispose of. I took an old frying pan, that had been rendered comparatively useless, having lost its handle and being otherwise considerably damaged and broke it into small strips. With these I kept the company supplied with eels during our stay, often obtaining as many as three dozen for one piece. We gave to this stream the name of Eel river.

At this camp a controversy arose among us in relation to the course now to be pursued.[38] Some contended that we should follow the coast down to San Francisco. Others again, urged as the shortest and most advantageous route to proceed up this river as far as its course seemed to suit, and then leave it and strike southerly for the nearest settlement.

Neither party seemed inclined to yield to the other. Not all the arguments that the most peaceably disposed members of the company could adduce, could quell the storm that was gathering. Harsh words passed, and threats were interchanged. As all prospects of a reconciliation had been abandoned, Seabring, Buck, Wilson and myself resolved to continue our journey together, over the route we had advocated. Accordingly we separated, and although the rain was falling in torrents, we left the camp. . . .[39]

I must now tell you something of the other four, Messrs. Gregg, Van Duzen, Southard and Truesdell, whom we left at Eel river, and within twenty miles of the bay or coast.[40]

They attempted to follow along the mountains near the coast, but were very slow in their progress on account of the snow on the high ridges. Finding the country much broken along the

[38] Such quarrels and break-ups as now overtook the Gregg party were not uncommon among pioneers and explorers. Several instances are on record in which parties crossing the plains or exploring the country underwent disruption when life seemed to depend upon the choice of a route or adopting a certain course of action. In this instance, what is surprising is that the members of the party did not perceive the wisdom of relying upon the experience and judgment of the person chosen captain.

[39] Wood and his three associates followed Eel River towards its source for three days; then they took to the mountain ridges, only to encounter snow deep enough to prevent progress. They made their way back to the river, and continued in its vicinity. In a tremendous fight with several grizzlies, Wood was severely injured. His companions, however, managed to take him along with them by strapping him to a horse. Eventually they came to the Russian River and followed it, reaching the Mark West Ranch, near Sonoma, on February 17, 1850. Six weeks later Wood got down to San Francisco.

[40] The three men who were staunch to Gregg returned to Humboldt Bay as soon as possible and became among its earliest settlers. The split into two factions at Eel River, however, still rankled to such an extent that these three never joined the other survivors in townsite activities. Southard became one of the founders of Trinidad, which had its period of prosperity as the terminus of a much-used route to the mines on Trinity River.

coast, making it continually necessary to cross abrupt points, and deep gulches and canyons, after struggling along for several days, they concluded to abandon that route and strike easterly toward the Sacramento valley.

Having very little ammunition, they all came nigh perishing from starvation, and, as Mr. Southard related to me, Dr. Gregg continued to grow weaker, from the time of our separation, until one day he fell from his horse and died in a few hours without speaking—died of starvation—he had had no meat for several days, had been living entirely upon acorns and herbs. They dug a hole with sticks and put him under ground, then carried rock and piled upon his grave to keep animals from digging him up.[41] They got through to the Sacramento valley a few days later than we reached Sonoma Valley.[42] Thus ended our expedition.

[41] In *Commerce of the Prairies*, Vol. I, Chap. I, Gregg forecast his burial. Referring in a footnote to the last rites for two traders, McNees and Monroe, killed by Indians, he indicated what it was to be buried "according to the custom of the Prairies." "These funerals are usually performed in a summary manner. A grave is dug in a convenient spot, and the corpse, with no other shroud than its own clothes and only a blanket for a coffin, is consigned to the earth. The grave is then usually filled up with stones or poles, as a safeguard against the voracious wolves of the prairies."

[43] Wood gives the date of his reaching the Mark West Ranch near Sonoma as February 17; the *Alta Californian* put the date of Gregg's death at February 25 in the vicinity of Clear Lake. Assuming that the split at Eel River occurred in early January, we may venture the surmise that the Gregg party in journeying some two hundred miles encountered added difficulties and delays sufficient to make, if we but had the details, a moving and compelling contribution to the annals of vanguard exploration in the early Far West. Doubly to be regretted is the disappearance of Gregg's notebooks. He must have kept at "memoranda"-making under all the adverse conditions that beset the party. Whatever else had to be cast aside in effecting escape from the imprisoning region, Gregg would have clung to his records and instruments to the very last. It is hard to understand the neglect of his companions to make a cache or similar storage of the materials. The group seems to have been infected with self-seeking jealousy. So there may be something to John Gregg's surmise about certain ones being glad to obliterate Gregg, records and all.

✳✳✳✳✳✳✳✳✳✳✳✳✳✳✳✳✳✳✳✳✳✳✳✳✳✳✳✳✳✳✳✳✳✳

Sources & Obligations

FOREMOST among persons conspicuously helpful in bringing into publication these Gregg volumes have been the late Mr. Claude Hardwicke
of Liberty, Missouri, and his widow, Mrs. Antoinette Hardwicke, now
of Tucson, Arizona. Some ten years ago I happened to call upon Mr.
Hardwicke, then in the complete invalidism of his last months, in my
ambition to verify a rumor that the Gregg diary was in his possession.
In particular, I wanted to know whether the diary gave a clue that might
help me to prosecute my search for Gregg letters published in newspapers
of the time. That was the special field I had selected as offering a chance
to add a few stones to the cairn of Gregg material Mr. John Thomas Lee
and others were erecting by their researches. I did not seek to conflict
with Mr. Hardwicke's plans for the publication of his great-uncle's records,
but rather sought merely to settle the question of Gregg's competency for
authorship, a matter being more and more called in question. In historical
and bibliographical circles much was being made of the fact that, in writing *Commerce of the Prairies,* Gregg had secured editorial assistance from
John Bigelow of New York City. Mr. Hardwicke answered my inquiry
by saying that if any Gregg letters appeared in the papers, they most likely
were printed in the *Louisville Journal.*

When I next visited the Hardwicke home, in hope that I might enjoy
with Mr. Hardwicke the sheaf of Gregg letters I had found by making
the search he had suggested, I learned of his demise some six months previously. Mrs. Hardwicke had naturally succeeded to the custodianship of
the diary and its companion material. My association with her, however,
did not become notable until after her removal to Tucson, a circumstance

I am happy to present, since it brought the Gregg materials into the Spanish Southwest, the locale of Gregg's travels and activities.

Close in importance to Mr. and Mrs. Hardwicke, I must place Mr. John Thomas Lee of Chicago, Illinois. His series of three articles—"New-found Letters of Josiah Gregg, Santa Fé Trader and Historian," "The Authorship of Gregg's *Commerce of the Prairies*," and "Josiah Gregg and Dr. George Engelmann," published in the early 1930's in various learned periodicals, gave me the impulse to make some further contribution to rounding out the account of Gregg. If Mr. Lee could find new material in the Bigelow journals and letters, as well as in the Engelmann archives, why might I not find those letters to newspapers, about which there was a persistent tradition? At the time I had no idea of doing more than adding a wing to the building that was becoming slowly and belatedly erected. When the idea developed of an edifice that might compete with *Commerce of the Prairies* as a memorial of the last decades of Gregg's life, I found Mr. Lee graciously cordial to my making whatever use I saw fit of these articles. His articles, especially the one embodying the Gregg-Engelmann correspondence, opened my eyes as nothing else had to the fact that the one-time Santa Fé trader had evolved into the traveler and explorer.

As the manuscript of a book began to take shape, I felt the need of bridging some gaps. There seemed no means of doing so unless I visited Mrs. Hardwicke and obtained access to the diary and letters. Always shall I remember as a landmark date the August afternoon on which she and I went over the contents of the comparatively small box in which she kept this historical treasure. Mrs. Hardwicke paid me the compliment of assuming that I had the ability to put the material into its true pattern, and willingly granted the use of a small number of passages and of summaries of other parts that might be serviceable. The manuscript that I finally forwarded to the University of Oklahoma Press proved so savory that at the request of that organization I went another time to Tucson and negotiated with Mrs. Hardwicke for the publication of virtually all of the material she was so carefully preserving.

By the side of the Hardwickes and Mr. Lee should be Paul Horgan. On most generous terms he was willing to assume the role of biographical essayist, although doing so meant the putting aside for a time of his more personal plans as a writer. For him, as for all of us who were joined together in bringing forth these two volumes, the moving force was admiration for Josiah Gregg, together with a realization that, with *Commerce of the Prairies* approaching its centenary, the time was ripe for publication of Gregg's other writings. Paul Horgan's absence on army duties during the past two years has been felt greatly, for both editor and publishers considered him a general adviser. To be candid, this second volume might have been better at some points had he been at hand, as he was during the preparations for the first.

I must thank several libraries and historical societies for their co-operation. Where there seems to be a certain member of the organization whose help has been more than of routine character, I have included that person's name in a parenthesis. The Library of Congress; the New York Public Library (K. D. Metcalf, chief reference librarian); the Louisville Free Public Library (Edna J. Grauman, librarian); William Jewell College Library, Liberty, Missouri; the Library of Kansas City University; the Kansas City Public Library (Martha Murphy, acting as a reference librarian for me, although she belonged to the order department); the Missouri Historical Society Library in St. Louis (Miss Stella M. Drumm, director); the State Historical Society of Missouri at Columbia (Roy T. King, director); the New Mexico Historical Society; the Bancroft Library (Edna Martin Parratt in particular); the California State Library at Sacramento (Mabel R. Gillis); and the University of Texas Library (both E. W. Winkler, bibliographer, and Winnie Allen, archivist); the Filson Club Library in Louisville (Ludie J. Kinkead, curator); the Missouri Botanical Gardens of St. Louis (Nell C. Horner, librarian and editor of publications). I have received helpful answers to inquiries from the following, some of them friends, others strangers who appreciated the cause generating the inquiry: Henry W. Harrison of Philadelphia; R. A. Prentice of Tucumcari, New Mexico; Hiram Park of Canadian, Texas; Sarah A. Vandegear of Many, Louisiana; Ruth Hosmer Kellogg of Van Buren, Arkansas; Captain Charles F. Ward of the New Mexico Military Institute; and Dr. W. A. Evans of Aberdeen, Mississippi. Perchance the best close to this inadequate paragraph of gratitude is the bookkeeper's phrase, "Errors and Omissions Excepted," added with the hope that oversights will be taken in charity as unintentional.

Now to become less personal and more bibliographical. I pause, however, in the doorway to avow again that my purpose has been decidedly more biographical than historical in the stricter sense. These two volumes are Gregg's autobiography for the last ten years of his activities. Hence there can be no point in overloading the material itself with elaborate lists of sources. In the long run of years since his death a great deal has been written about Gregg; but most of it is negligible in value, since it is partial or incomplete or otherwise faulty. Even Reuben Gold Thwaites, who edited *Commerce of the Prairies* in 1905 for the noted series *Early Western Travels, 1748–1846* (Cleveland, Arthur H. Clark Company, 1904–1907), made no energetic attempt to obtain personal data. Had Thwaites utilized the editorial tribute in *Garden and Forest*, issue of January 10, 1894, he would have derived from the article (said to be by C. S. Sargent) much that might have enriched his presentation of *Commerce of the Prairies*. About two years later, that is, in 1907, William E. Connelley made a beginning that was a significant steppingstone towards a Gregg biography by embedding in his edition of Hughes's *Doniphan's Expedition* (Topeka, the author, 1907) liberal notes regarding the Gregg family background and kindred matters. At last a would-be biographer had gone to the fountainhead while some of the Josiah Gregg generation were alive and able to furnish information. The next steppingstone was laid by Ralph Emerson Twitchell in a pamphlet appearing as No. 26 (*c.* 1924) in the publications of the Historical Society of New Mexico, entitled *Dr. Josiah Gregg, Historian of the Santa Fé Trail*. In this compilation Twitchell availed himself of the Connelley contribution for the earlier period, and of Bledsoe's *Indian Wars of the Northwest* (San Francisco, Bacon & Company, 1885) for its chapter I, a paraphrase of the L. K. Wood account of the ill-fated last enterprise of Gregg in Northern California. Twitchell's pamphlet, however, did add important biographical material when it furnished forth the Gregg–to–Bigelow letters in the New Mexico historical collections. In 1907, L. Bradford Prince, former governor of New Mexico, had procured from John Bigelow a statement concerning the latter's part in helping Gregg with the preparation and publication of *Commerce of the Prairies*. To this explanation were appended in somewhat abridged form several of Gregg's letters scattered through succeeding years. That Gregg had secured aid from Bigelow was a morsel of literary gossip that had been rolled under the tongues of some bibliographers until it had become almost canonized by getting into the authoritative Henry R. Wagner's *The Plains and the Rockies: A Bibliography of Original Narratives of Travel and Adventure, 1800–1865* (San Francisco, J. Howell, 1921). On the whole, however, Twitchell's sketch constituted the nearest to a full biography that had been produced, but he would be the first, I am sure, to smile at the way Gregg's own version refuted certain conjectures made by Twitchell. He would also admit the value of Gregg's records of trips into Texas and adjacent parts of the United States, and into the deep and less visited parts of Old Mexico.

Even though Gregg's diary and letters have not called for any considerable technical historical editing, I have, I trust, devoted the required amount of attention to this aspect of their publication. I have tried to avoid encroaching upon Gregg's own chronicle, except for two degrees of footnotes. In preparing those that concern parallel or collateral material from contemporary, and preferably eyewitness sources, I have dug into the files of old newspapers such as the *Louisville Journal,* the *Arkansas Intelligencer,* the *Liberty* (Mo.) *Tribune,* the *Glasgow* (Mo.) *News,* and others in the Missouri sector. More in this field I might have done, but unfortunately the old newspaper files are either incomplete at critical dates or entirely nonexistent. In the case of books, the situation is different. Certainly there is a superabundance of material about the Mexican War and its contiguous events, so much so that I feel that it would be an imposition to indulge in an extended bibliography. Adequate bibliographies exist, or can be easily assembled. Narrowed to what pertains to Josiah Gregg or to his times, I submit a few titles which I regard highly. The *Memoir* of Captain George W. Hughes, embracing Gregg's own account of the march of the Arkansas Regiment to San Antonio; Adolph Wislizenus's *Memoir of a Tour to Northern New Mexico, connected with Col. Doniphan's Expedition* (Washington, Tippin & Streeper, 1848); John T. Hughes's *Doniphan's Expedition* (Cincinnati, J. A. & U. P. James, 1848); Frank S. Edwards's *A Campaign in New Mexico with Colonel Doniphan* (Philadelphia, Carey & Hart, 1847); and Jacob S. Robinson's *A Journal of the Santa Fé Expedition under Colonel Doniphan* (Portsmouth [N. H.], Portsmouth Journal Press, 1848). I have found a few Gregg items in unpublished material, such as the Sappington papers, the Aull papers, the Ehinger diary, and the Albert Pike auto-biographic dictation. For Gregg's last ninety days or so of heroic exploration in California, nothing surpasses the account of L. K. Wood, entitled *The Discovery of Humboldt Bay.*

The second type of footnote offers certain explanatory material about persons and places and other kindred matters, even language. As in the case of the first type, I have tried to avoid such overplus as might mar the readability of the text itself. What is served forth is frankly derivative. In general I have relied on reference sources like the *Dictionary of American Biography;* Professor Ralph P. Bieber's proficient annotations in the volumes of the *Southwest Historical Series* (Glendale [Cal.], Arthur H. Clark Company, 1931–43); the briefer but useful annotations in Miss Stella M. Drumm's edition of Susan Magoffin's journal under the title, *Down the Santa Fé Trail and into Mexico* (New Haven, Yale University Press; London, H. Milford, Oxford University Press, 1926). Very useful, too, have been Justin Smith's *The War with Mexico* (New York, The Macmillan Company, 1919) and Carleton's *Battle of Buena Vista* (New York, Harper and Brothers, 1848). Valuable likewise was a pamphlet issued by the Arkansas Historical Commission under title of *Roster of Arkansas Regiment of Mounted Volunteers.* For the notes upon the California episode I have leaned heavily upon Professor Owen C. Coy's *The Humboldt Bay Region, 1850–1875* (Los Angeles, The California State Historical Association, 1929). I have also used the notes of C. P. Cutten that accompany a facsimile reprinting of the L. K. Wood account in the *Quarterly of the Society of California Pioneers,* March, 1932.

As the two volumes leave my hands for those of readers, I feel they are competent for their biographical purpose. I am conscious, however, of two omissions. One is not being able to locate an adequate and authentic portrait of Gregg. Daguerreotypes were just coming into vogue, and undoubtedly Gregg's curiosity for matters of that kind would lead him to "sit for a picture." Several pictures exist that are termed Josiah Gregg's, but I am compelled to be a doubting Thomas still, even with reference to the one which appears opposite page 14 in this volume. The Greggs looked alike; they used and reused the name Josiah, especially after "Uncle Josiah" wrote his book and became otherwise notable. In lieu of a portrait above suspicion, I venture to offer the following by John Bigelow to the editor of *Farm and Garden:* "I found Mr. Gregg to be at that time [1844] a man about forty years of age and about five feet ten inches in height, though from the meagerness of his figure looking somewhat taller; he had a fine head and an intellectual cast of countenance and temperament, though his mouth and the lower part of his face showed that he had enjoyed to but a limited extent the refining influence of civilization. He had fine blue eyes and an honest, although not a cheerful, expression, due, as I afterwards learned, to chronic dyspepsia. He was withal very shy and as modest as a schoolgirl."

My other omission concerns John Gregg, "Brother John," as Josiah usually wrote it. I had hoped to accumulate enough for an appendix which might do justice to the devotion between these two and the part the older (John) had played in the preservation of these Josiah memorials. I have, however, at the last to confess my inability to perfect the sketch. Once I examined in Missouri a thin packet of letters by John Gregg, written in the early 1850's when their writer, always, it seems, beset by the frontiersman's urge to move on into new regions, had gone into the heart of Texas. These letters, together with the admirable obituary letter to Dr. Engelmann about Josiah, convince me that John Gregg was in himself a remarkable man and worthy compeer or examplar to his younger brother Josiah. I have not been able to follow John Gregg very definitely in the 1860's and 1870's except to find in the older cemetery at Paris, Texas, the graves of his wife, who perished in one of the notable packet disasters on the Mississippi, and two daughters, who died in early womanhood. By the side of these graves is that of John Gregg himself, but he died in Aberdeen, Mississippi.

Behind this rather surprising fact lies a story, not altogether clear, but worthy of being given in its outline. The solitary figure of John Gregg, his wife and children having all become *avant-coureurs* into the halls of death, seems to have found surcease for his loneliness by becoming devoted to one of the other branches of the Gregg clan, namely that to which belonged General John Gregg, of Texas and the C.S.A., who was killed in the fighting around Petersburg, Virginia. After the Civil War, the General's widow, Mrs. Mary Garth Gregg, lived in Aberdeen, Mississippi, where her family, the Garths, had large plantations. Being a lady of great kindness of heart and wealthy enough to give bountiful expression to her feeling, she delighted to have her home—spacious and hospitable, indeed, even among those of that section—filled with a coterie of more or less permanent inmates—elderly relatives and others—who, from infirmities or misfortunes, were in need of friendliness. In such a cordial and gracious haven John Gregg's taper of life flickered to its end. He seems to have suffered a stroke in his seventies, and in consequence was not much abroad in the town of Aberdeen. Such a condition seems to explain the paucity of information that can be gathered from the older residents of that section of Mississippi about John Gregg.

I do not know the date of John Gregg's consigning the valuable "memoranda" and letters to Samuel Hardwicke, as that one of the Missouri Greggs most likely through wealth and ability to undertake the erection of a memorial to Josiah Gregg. Nor do I know the time when this obligation passed to Samuel Hardwicke's son Claude, but I do know that when I saw Mr. Claude Hardwicke in the one and only interview I had with him, he was working at editing his great-uncle's manuscripts. Even with the hand of death upon him, he worked a limited period each day. This particular day he was working on something pertaining to the account of the battle of Buena Vista, and his eyes glowed as he told me his impressions of that vivid piece of reporting. Mrs. Hardwicke inherited the commission, and modestly and assiduously worked towards having the diary and letters competently put before the world. She had made a beginning of having the manuscripts copied, but was glad to relinquish that to others. She would not consent to being named co-editor, but her co-operation has been unstinted. Always to the fore with her, and of greater import than pecuniary returns or personal renown, was the safeguarding of the integrity of what that unassuming kinsman wrote a hundred years ago in the way of his experience and observations, and of insuring a presentation of his achievements with commensurate dignity. We, that is the several who have been her agents, deem it an honor to have been allowed to place Josiah Gregg before the later generation as a great and useful Westerner, a man of scholarly inclinations, appreciative of the need of observing and recording, in the spirit of science, his "whereabouts and whatabouts," to repeat his vernacular phrase in one of the letters to

John Bigelow. He who began as Santa Fé trader closed his career as explorer. With only *Commerce of the Prairies* as a basis, an English journal dubbed Gregg "a practical traveler" and went on to say, "His very descriptions have an eye to business." With a larger basis from the materials comprised in the two stout volumes of Gregg journals and letters, we may bestow an extra title, "exploratory traveler," and add: His keen observation of human societies and the surroundings in which they carry on their activities award to him the maxim of Shakespeare's John of Gaunt:

> *All places that the eye of Heaven visits*
> *Are to a wise man ports and happy havens.*

Index

INDEX

cess at Sacramento, 103; removal of the regiment to Saltillo, 104; Col. Doniphan's treatment of the Mexicans, 111; inaccuracy in topographic information, 114; Maj. Gilpin's defense of misbehavior of volunteers, 116; Indian fight at San José del Poso, 123; inadvisability of twelve months' enlistments, 136; ravaging of Ramos, 140; Gen. Taylor's demands upon Mexicans for robberies and devastations, 141; justice of executing a supposed member of Urrea's band, 143; attitude of Missouri officers toward devastations, 144; indifference of army officers about protection of civilians, 201; the treaty of peace, 212, 215; success in practice of medicine in Saltillo, 216; disregard for treaty by Col. Washington, 220; value of *ferias*, 227; rumors of filibustering expeditions, 228; Col. Hamtramk's pompous letter, 234; costliness of religion and ceremonials, 249, 277; policy regarding carrying of arms and permits therefor, 256, 291; painting of Our Lady of Guadalupe, 279–80; benefits from Mexican War, 294; "Anglo-Saxoning" of the American continent, 324

—, scientific interests: geographic date, 34, 73 f., 84 ff., 133 ff., 169, 187 ff., 222, 236 ff., 271, 279, 280, 300 ff., 342 ff., 353, 358, 370, 372; weather and climate, 35, 83, 95, 106, 112; barometer readings from Dr. Wislizenus, 73, 160; botany, 85, 87, 88, 96 n., 127, 139, 150, 163, 179, 181, 223, 225, 242, 265, 286, 330, 332 f., 346, 367; geology and mining, 87, 117, 164, 171, 176, 179, 223, 224, 265, 272, 312, 330; animal life, 333, 341, 346

—, trips and sojourns: from Monterrey to Saltillo, 33; goes to scene of battle, 46; leaves Saltillo for Chihuahua with Collins party, 78, 89; returns to Saltillo with Doniphan's regiment, 106; returns to U. S., 133; from New Orleans to Philadelphia, etc., 156; starts back to New Orleans *via* Washington, 159; sojourn at John Gregg's near Shreveport, 168; from Shreve-

port to New Orleans, 174; journey from New Orleans to Reynosa (Mex.), 182; from Reynosa to Saltillo, 194; practicing medicine in Saltillo, 203; excursion to village of San Antonio, 222; leaves Saltillo for Mexico City, 237; arrival and first impressions of Mexico City, 259; excursions about Mexico City, 261 ff.; departure from Mexico en route for California, 299; sojourn at Mazatlan (Mex.), 324; from Mazatlan to San Francisco (Cal.), 342; arrival at San Francisco, 342; journey into the mining section on the Trinity River, 357 n.; route-seeking trip from Rich Bar on the Trinity to the Pacific (L. K. Wood's narrative), 361

—, verdicts about people: Gen. Butler, 34; Maj. Thomas, 34; Col. Yell, 50; Gen. Wool, 37, 62; Capt. Albert Pike, 94, 99; Gen. Taylor, 137, 211; President Polk, 161; Capt. Dubs (of the *Ashland*), 191; Gen. Miñon, 230; Gen. Mexia, 231; Gen. J. J. Sanchez, 246; Hidalgo, 246; Sr. Gomez, 319; Hammersley (supercargo of *Olga*), 343

Guadalajara (Mex.): 314

Guadalupe (Mex.): 256; church at, 257; painting of Our Lady of Guadalupe, 257 f., 279–80

Guajuquilla (Mex.): 99

Hacienda de la Rinconada (Mex.): 34, 203; devastation by Missourians, 135

Hamtramck, J. F.: 206, 213 f., 234

Hangtown (Cal.): 356

Hardin, J. J.: 50, 52, 83

Hardwick, Margaret Gregg (Mrs. P. A.): 359

Hardwick, P. A.: 354 n., 356, 359; letter from, 356

Harney, W. S.: 178, 181

Harris, Dr.: 59

Hitchcock, C. M.: 63

Howard, Capt.: 202, 203, 210

Hudson, T. B.: 103

Hughes, G. W.: 218

Humboldt Bay (Cal.): *see* Trinity Bay

Hunter, Edward: 36

Hunter, Maj. David: 196

Hunter, Mrs. David: 196

393

DIARY & LETTERS OF JOSIAH GREGG

EDITED BY

MAURICE GARLAND FULTON

HAS BEEN COMPOSED ON THE LINOTYPE

IN TWELVE-POINT CASLON OLD FACE

THE PAPER IS ANTIQUE WOVE

UNIVERSITY OF OKLAHOMA PRESS

NORMAN, OKLAHOMA